MONTHLY LETTERS

PUBLISHED FOR THE "WERKCOMMISSIE VAN HOOGLERAREN EN LECTOREN IN DE NEDERLANDISTIEK AAN BUITENLANDSE UNIVERSITEITEN" (WORKING COMMITTEE OF PROFESSORS AND LECTURERS OF DUTCH LANGUAGE AND LITERATURE AT UNIVERSITIES OUTSIDE THE NETHERLANDS AND BELGIUM)

DR. ADRIAAN J. BARNOUW

former Queen Wilhelmina Professor at Columbia University, New York

MONTHLY LETTERS

ON THE CULTURE AND HISTORY
OF THE NETHERLANDS

ASSEN, 1969

VAN GORCUM & COMP. N.V. - DR. H. J. PRAKKE & H. M. G. PRAKKE

Printed in The Netherlands by Royal VanGorcum Ltd., Assen

TABLE OF CONTENTS

INTRODUCTION

by DR. E. N. VAN KLEFFENS[1]

The era of Adriaan Barnouw's maturity consisted of two parts: that of his life as a high-school and university teacher in his native country, and the much longer period of his stay in New York, first at Columbia, and during the final years, in fruitful retirement.

It was my privilege to know him in both these periods, of which the longest was also the happiest. Barnouw was a great intellectual and artist combined, for whom it must often have seemed a hopeless and thankless task to try and get a group of boisterous teenagers at the Hague 'gymnasium' interested in medieval mystic poetry, or in the esoteric dalliance of shepherds and shepherdesses of a later age. What saved him from frustration during that era were his extra-curricular pursuits: work in the field of prose and of poetry; anglo-saxon and historical studies; drawing and etching.

Even in those early years at The Hague, there was a link with Manhattan: Barnouw was then a correspondent of the New York 'Nation'. During his period at Columbia, this tenuous tie with the great American metropolis became a solid bond. Barnouw felt happy there, and his sympathy found a ready response, witness his election, in 1924, as a member of the prestigious Century Association, which became for him a source of lasting happiness and inspiration.

Small wonder that Barnouw's literary productivity reached its apex in so stimulating an environment, as Dr. Jalink's 'Sketch' shows. The present Anthology, a choice made by Barnouw himself from the Monthly Letters written in the course of thirty-one years for the Netherland-America Foundation, bears eloquent testimony to the fertility of his mind during that long period.

The war brought us together again on American soil. Barnouw, who had become an American citizen, was indefatigable in his zeal for the cause of the country of his origin. The Netherlands owe him a debt of enduring gratitude for all he did in the land of his adoption to further their legitimate interests. He published books, he helped

[1] From 1939 to 1946 Minister of Foreign Affairs, 1946-1947 Netherlands Representative in the United Nations Security Council and Economic and Social Council, 1947-1950 Ambassador to the U.S.A.

the Knickerbocker Weekly, he gave lectures and broadcast talks; he was, in short, the 'homo academicus militans' at his best.

It is only fitting that he be honored in death as he was in his lifetime. I am happy to have the opportunity of doing so publicly in this Viaticum, for he was indeed a tower of strength and understanding, both during the war-years when I met him so often on American soil, and during my embassy in Washington thereafter. I am conscious of being only one out of very many.

A SKETCH OF THE PERSONALITY
LIFE AND WORK OF
PROFESSOR DR. ADRIAAN J. BARNOUW

by DR. J. M. JALINK[1]

Captatio benevolentiae. The writer of this sketch was taught by Dr. Barnouw from 1910 until 1915 at the Gymnasium Haganum (Grammar School of The Hague), lost touch with him after his school-leaving exam in 1915 and only in 1962 renewed contact with him, when as secretary of the Working Committee of Professors and Lecturers of Dutch Language and Literature at Universities ontside the Netherlands and Belgium, he entered into a fairly intensive correspondence with him. Of course Barnouw's official biography and bibliography were known to him, as were various of his publications. But he had no personal memories, anecdotes, etc. relating to the intervening period of nearly half a century. However the fact that very few people have known Barnouw in both the Dutch and American period of his life and that several of his friends in the United States expressed their willingness to put a number of data at his disposal, gives him the courage to risk this somewhat perilous venture.

I first met Dr. Barnouw in 1910 when, after moving with my family from Doetinchem (Geld.), in the vicinity of which we had been living, to The Hague, I had to do the entrance examination for the second form of the Grammar School there. At the time Barnouw created the impression of being somewhat reserved, but not such a person as to make things difficult for a candidate. I remember his pro-pounding an epigram to me about "rijke Kees, die veel uitgelezen boeken bezat, half uitgelezene niet één" (rich Kees, who possessed many hand-picked books, not one of which he had even half picked at). This specimen of acuity was, unhappily, entirely wasted on me, as we had not been schooled in the word-plays of Huygens or Staring at Doetinchem. Later on in class as well, Dr. Barnouw was an easy-going teacher, and the most homework he would give out was an occasional essay. Sometimes he would dictate notes to us from the

---

[1] From 1949 to 1961 Lecturer of the Dutch Language and Literature at the University of Bonn (Germany); since 1961 Secretary of the Working Committee of Professors and Lecturers of Dutch Language and Literature at Universities outside the Netherlands and Belgium.

history of Dutch literature, which we had to go over again at home. It was during such a class – it must have been in one of the lower forms – that I first heard the names of some of the famous Flemish writers such as Streuvels, Teirlinck and Cyriel Buysse. But what struck us was his aristocratic and at the same time artistic appearance, and his beautiful voice in which he read poems which were not always particularly outstanding. I still remember an unremarkable poem he read, "Huibert de Smid"[1], which I have never been able to find again since, but which was made impressive by his manner of delivery.

In general our class had, perhaps, not quite the literary bent of some of the more senior forms such as that of Victor van Vriesland or the one of my cousin Douwe Hiemstra, Dijckman van Goens and Wim Zeijdner, who read *Faust I* with our German master Dr. Kossmann in a private seminar. Yet I still recall Willem van Bylandt once producing an essay on a subject set by Barnouw: "The sword and the pen" (as symbols of physical violence set against the might of the mind) – an essay which was highly praised by the teacher. Moreover, my form-mate Leo Plemp van Duiveland, son of the editor-in-chief of the *Nieuwe Courant*, was exceedingly talented in literature, and I remember myself going for walks on free afternoons among the dunes, which were then not yet fenced off, reading with great enthusiasm the poems of Perk, Kloos, Van Eeden and Gorter, or a collection of Couperus' short stories. In those days we were still living in the declining years of the Movement of the 80's.

As became clear to me much later when reading his book *The Dutch* (1940) and especially the chapter on "The defeat of Drystubble"[2], the Movement of the Eighties must have aroused an enormous enthusiasm in Barnouw during his teens; I cannot remember, however, that this was apparent in the classroom. In the Movement of the Eighties he found his own heroes to worship such as he had previously found only among foreign authors.

"As judges of contemporary literature", Barnouw writes in the above-mentioned chapter, "Kloos and Van Deyssel were bold and aggressive. Their criticism sounded to us like a clarion call to rebellion against all that was smug and humdrum and platitudinous. They dared to use words for the voicing of passion and pride and profanity such as the previous generation had been taught to repress as indecorous and wicked. If they had been merely daring, their revolt would have been a flash in the pan. But they were inspired

[1] "Huibert the Smith".
[2] The petty-minded, hard-boiled, calculating matter-of-fact Dutch merchant caricatured in Multatuli's novel *Max Havelaar*.

prophets challenging the age in magnificent prose and verse that burnt themselves into our hearts. They fortunately addressed a generation not merely willing but eager to be saved from mediocrity and smugness. Holland was like a stuffy house with all its windows closed against the blustering winds from east and south that might blow in the dangerous germs of French radicalism and German philosophy.[1] Kloos and his fellow editors forced the windows open and enabled their compatriots to breathe in a European atmosphere".

Yet later in the same chapter he writes: "The substance of most of the contributions to *De Nieuwe Gids*[2] has lost the powerful appeal which it possessed for this writer's generation. The self-love expressed in them and its corollary, contempt for the multitude, clashed with the social feelings that stirred the generation which grew to manhood in the first decade of this century. The Labor Party came to the fore and won adherents among men of letters: Herman Gorter, a contemporary of the leaders of *De Nieuwe Gids* and hailed by them as a great poet, embraced the cause of the world's proletariat; Frederik van Eeden went in search of God in Tolstoyan love for his fellow man; and Verwey turned from self-worship to the study of man and man's self-revelation in literature. Verwey founded in 1905 a new monthly, *De Beweging* ('The Movement'), which became the rallying point of a group of younger poets who recognized in Verwey their mentor and master".

In a letter which goes deeply into the workings of Barnouw's mind, Mr. L. J. Plemp van Duiveland[3], writes to me[4]: "Apparently fearing that he might give the impression of having too much self-assurance, Barnouw would protect himself amid protestations of complete ignorance on certain subjects, whenever the occasion arose. O, he had not the slightest understanding of music, any opinion from him would be worthless . . . Yet he was well-informed about musicology and his lack of understanding was in fact confined to his inability to enjoy music. Another of his 'non liquets' he issued was on botany. Once in a lower class he asked for compounds of the Dutch noun 'look'. My contribution was 'look zonder look'[5], a

---

[1] It amazes me that Barnouw does not mention in this context the influence of the English nature poets, such as Shelley, Keats and Wordsworth, on the early lyric poetry of the Movement of the Eighties.
[2] 'The New Guide' (the periodical of the Movement of the Eighties).
[3] The Dutch degree of Master of Laws (Mr.) corresponds approximately to the English LL.M.
[4] Letter of 22.11.1968.
[5] 'look zonder look' = garlic without garlic. (the English name is garlic mustard).

piece of knowledge recently acquired in a biology lesson. Barnouw, clearly stating that he had not the slightest idea about botany either, found nevertheless that he could allow himself to be surprised by a linguistic compound whose first element was cancelled out by the last. His astonishment mounting, and his voice rising to a falsetto, he repeated 'look zonder look' several times. 'Do me a favour and ask Mr. Valk for confirmation'. I did this, adding: 'Mr. Barnouw couldn't get over his surprise . . .'. 'I'm sure he couldn't', retorted the biology teacher smiling, 'Mr. Barnouw must have been amazed that for once you actually knew something'.

In those days even less time than now was devoted to the teaching of Dutch in the Grammar School and it was not closely defined as that of the classical languages was. Particularly in the higher forms, the teacher could fill the lesson how he liked. Unconcerned about his popularity, Barnouw paid great attention in lower classes to grammar, which he considered an excellent thought-discipline. He was particular about the proper formulation of answers to his questions, and by consistently refusing an immoderate use of 'and' or repetitions preambles, he insisted on and forced the pupil to give a clear rendering of his deliberations. Barnouw was one of those teachers, even then decreasing in number, who took a serious interest in the pronunciation of Dutch of their pupils. He never relaxed his critical approach to pronunciation and there were then no current theories of 'undemocratic' or 'discriminative' to challenge his point of view.

His teaching was more inspired by learning, scholarship and scientific interest than by pedagogy. He was not a man 'whose heart went out to his pupils', but this negation in no way suggests the opposite. One could always count on Barnouw being human and accommodating in his dealings with others. His undramatic character and attitudes modelled on English lines guaranteed this. If a pupil wanted to do some particular work on his own, Barnouw stood by him with advice, study material, reference to sources – he encouraged, but never pushed. But the class as a unit of human constituents was less to his liking. His preference was for the individual, particularly the individual of his choice. Away from the school I once heard him declare that the classic method of teaching was made easy for him by the aid of a simple trick: before each lesson he would make a mental selection of three pupils, who would give him his impetus, and to whom he would be making his teaching points".

In this connection Victor van Vriesland writes to me[1]: "In Bar-

[1] Letter of 30.10.1968.

nouw's Dutch classes M. Nijhoff, Willem Wéry and I formed a trio of boys who were bad pupils, but had an ardent interest in literature; we were always to be seen together, with the result that later, at Nijhoff's wedding banquet, a song was sung to the tune of 'Daar was laatst een meisje loos'[1] with the refrain: Pom, Vic en Wéry. My reason for telling this story is that being very rebellious and non-conformist, we were always liable to start a sort of insurrection in Barnouw's periods, long before the modern outcrop of angry young students. So for instance, during the discussion of *Lucifer* and especially the chorus: 'Op, trekt op, o gij Luciferisten'[2], we stood up in our desks and spun the following yarn: Sir, here we have a metre comprising between the accented initial syllable and the unaccented final one not an iambus followed by two anapaests but an anapaest and a spondee followed by another anapaest, which should be read as following: $\acute{-}\,/\,\cup\cup\acute{-}\,/\,\acute{-}\,\acute{-}\,/\,\cup\cup\acute{-}\,/\,\cup$. Instead of throwing us out, as was to have been expected, Barnouw, the typical gentleman, went into the matter in a good-natured and serious manner and said that this was indeed possible, but it seemed to him to be a somewhat modernistic interpretation which, he thought, would never have occurred to Vondel".

Born in Amsterdam in 1877, the son of a doctor, Barnouw must at that time have been some 35 years old. With even then a certain man-of-the-world air, he was always tastefully dressed, avoiding ties or socks which did not go with the suit of the day, to the delight of the aesthetes among his pupils at a time when teacher's salaries were still not high, and when schoolmasters usually lived in one of the side-streets of Duinoord in a rented house with a little front-garden – their study on the first floor at the back, – and frequently dressed in obviously suits off the peg.

At that time, as it may be still today, it was usual for school-leavers, after their final exam, to call on the members of the staff at their homes. My friend Plemp van Duiveland and I did this together. I believe Barnouw was then living in Hollanderstraat or Van Blanken-burgstraat. It was typical of his attitude that instead of offering us a cup of tea, as did other masters, he gave us the choice of port or sherry, which gave us the exciting feeling of already being treated as students.

Indeed, I have the impression that Barnouw was never really a

---

[1] "Not long ago there was a saucy maid".
[2] "Forward, O ye hosts, Lucifer's minions; a well known line from Joost van den Vondel's tragedy (1654) in the translation by Leonard Ch. van Noppen.

'school'-man. To my knowledge he never wrote a school textbook or compiled a Dutch anthology, as teachers often do either as a hobby or as a source of additional income. Nor, when I wrote to him a few years ago that some of his former colleagues from my schooldays were still alive, did he react in his usual animated fashion. He was not primarily a schoolmaster, but rather a contemplative, even introvert artist, writer, scholar and insofar as he was a teacher, then of a higher degree, more concerned with the pursuit of knowledge, than with the curriculum of the secondary school. His period of grammar-school teaching, which was to last from 1902 until 1919, was clearly no more than a pathway to his final goal in life.

Only later did I learn that Barnouw, after his schooling in his beloved and, especially then, so picturesque birthplace, had spent the years 1895-1900 reading Modern and Medieval Languages at Leiden, where Verdam and Ten Brink were his principal teachers. In the year 1900-1901 he continued his studies in Berlin, subsequently receiving his doctorate at Leiden for the dissertation: *Textkritische Untersuchungen über den Gebrauch des bestimmten Artikels und des schwachen Adjektivs in der altenglischen Poesie*. The lectureship in English studies that he held at Leiden between 1907 and 1913 must have been for him a foretaste of his later career.

Even as early as my schooldays Barnouw was already working on the "verdietsing" of Chaucer (translation into a Dutch version), as he used to call his method of work himself, for I remember that when I was in the sixth form, he read from his manuscript of 'De Ver-tellingen van de Pelgrims naar Kantelberg' at a gathering of the League of Grammar Schoolboys in The Hague, which made even then a deep impression on us. It was later to become his life's work.

"Chaucer and Barnouw", writes Plemp van Duiveland[1], "must have been kindred souls transcending half a millennium: both wished to attain fullness of communication and power of expression by economy of linguistic and stylistic expedients. On the evening of the above-mentioned reading, the speaker placed the 'Canterbury Tales' in the context of pre-renaissance England, discussed the prosody and construction of this epic work and acquainted his audience with the people who took part in the pilgrimage. Barnouw was an excellent narrator. Part of his technique was to avoid superfluity and pay attention to characteristic detail. Once he took his sixth form, of which I was a member, to the Royal Theatre for a performance of *A Midsummer Night's Dream* which he had discussed with us beforehand at school in a few Dutch periods. Barnouw was in his element in comparative literature, he mastered the ramifications of each literary subject, he

[1] Letter of 22.11.1968.

knew its contours, relationships and foundations. He talked on this colourful material as a causeur, as a man of society, never as a scholar. He never made interpretations, for they were woven into his story. Knowledge hung upon his shoulders like a comfortable suit.

Barnouw had a strong preference for the adult element in man's nature, an element which can be manifest in both the so-called adult world and that of children. He had little sympathy for childishness which approached silliness or puerility. This was a deficiency that was bound to be exposed in his job as a schoolmaster. Observing some puerile act or clearly non-conformist behaviour he could go white with anger, 'groen wegtrekken', as it was called. This was followed by a minute's pregnant silence, an audible hush which would be lifted by his addressing one of the three favourites: 'Now go on reading'. It did not often happen, but everyone of his pupils experienced this on one or more occasions. It was a fearful and impressive human comedy".

Victor van Vriesland, who spent a few months at Barnouw's home, relates how once a week a bottle of wine was opened and Mrs. Barnouw, an English girl named Anne Midgley, then read from Shakespeare's works. "Although we were little scruffs of fifteen or sixteen, we were expected to turn up in dinner-jackets, a typically English custom". We were living then in the after-glow of the Dandyism typified by Couperus, Van Deyssel and Oscar Wilde, and the fact that its sun took longer to die in England than in Holland is perhaps the cause of the vehement reaction among the young people of that country in our times. However, to continue Van Vriesland's story: "Apart from me one other boy was living with the Barnouw family; only he was kicked out when, one fine day, Barnouw's children, two little boys of five and six, were happily sitting, dangling their feet over the Verversingskanaal, whilst the nanny was discovered with my Shakespeare-partner among the dunes. For Barnouw could get very angry indeed, as he did when he found out that Nijhoff and I had obtained an inexhaustible number of appointment chits from our dentist providing us with a reason to stay away from school for treatment in the afternoon, to fill in the date on the chit whenever it suited us". I too remember such a fit of anger when Barnouw addressed two boys sitting at the same desk: "I know that one of you two is up to no good, and I find such intrigue 'verbuizend (damright) maddening', a contamination brought into being by anger, combining the elements of the 'verduiveld' (damned) he just managed to suppress, and the more diplomatic 'verbazend' (downright). This brought the class near to choking, for the respect and affection we had for Barnouw's personality, strictly forbad us to burst out laughing.

"From as early as the first form", continues Van Vriesland, "I had one of his splendid drawings – a portrait of his mother – hanging above my bed. As far as his writing was concerned I knew him only from his masterly translation of Stevenson's *A child's garden of verses*, first a few in a reprint from *Groot Nederland*, later in book-form. In this periodical he also wrote some verses of his own, and from one I remember the splendid first lines:

> Het late licht staat op de landen
> Als koren tot den oogst bereid.[1]

To my knowledge they have never been published as a collection. His sublime translation of *The Canterbury Tales* has been a constant source of delight to me and I remember many years later Jan Campert and I deriving great pleasure from reading them to each other".

The move from the 'entrance-hall' to the 'main building' came for him 'when the days were accomplished' and, indeed, in consequence of an occurrence which was reported to the *New York Times*, after Professor Barnouw's death, as the cause of the Barnouw's moving to the United States, by the second of his three sons, Erik, at present a professor at Columbia University: an occurrence that again gives testimony of Barnouw's acuity and ability for combination. It began when Barnouw bought at an open-air market from a second-hand book stall in The Hague, a huge vellum-bound sketchbook half filled with marine sketches. The price, arrived at by bargaining, was $12\frac{1}{2}$ guilders, about $ 5 at the time. The artist's name, Albertus van Beest, was given in the volume. The drawings impressed Barnouw so much, that he was sure the artist must be represented in the museums. A search showed that he was, with a number of oil-paintings, but on the small brass plates underneath they were all ascribed to a rather fussy aristocratic painter of lesser talent, Heemskerk van Beest, the H and the A in the signatures looking sufficiently alike to make this possible. The nameplates were of course corrected. From old records Barnouw learned that the mysterious artist had fled to America in 1850 as a result of an amorous scandal. A letter of inquiry to *The Nation* elicited from a reader the information that Albertus van Beest had settled in Bedford (Mass.) and had continued his work there as a marine painter.

But another outcome of the correspondence was that *The Nation* invited Barnouw in 1913 to contribute articles on the European scene and during the First World War made him a regular foreign correspondent. In 1919, he accepted an invitation to move to America as co-publisher of the *Weekly Review*, an offshoot of *The Nation*. The

[1] The tardy light lies on the fields / Like barley ready to be mown.

new magazine failed quickly but in the meantime the Committee of the National Queen Wilhelmina Readership Foundation had appointed Barnouw as successor to the first holder of the post, the American poet Leonard van Noppen, the skilful translator of Vondel's *Lucifer*, who had in the war, after five years as Reader, become naval attaché at the American Embassy first in The Hague and later in London. Two years later, in 1921, the Readership was converted to a Chair and Barnouw was upgraded to full professor.[1] He filled this post until his retirement in 1948. Barnouw however continued to regard Albertus van Beest's sketchbook as a sort of talisman which brought a change in the destiny of him and his family. In the early 1920's Franklin Delano Roosevelt, hearing about the book and being interested in old ships, borrowed it. That was shortly before he was struck down with polio and it remained in Roosevelt's possession throughout the polio period. Under the circumstances it seemed impolite to press for its return, but later it was returned and Barnouw bequeathed it to his only daughter Elsa who lived with him after the death of Mrs. Barnouw in 1960, caring for him and standing by him in his advanced years.

It seems that Barnouw's rich and many-sided talents were able to develop to the full in this new and bigger world. He must soon have been regarded as a man of authority. In his contribution to *De Nederlandistiek in het Buitenland* his successor, Professor Dr. B. Hunningher, writes that from the start Barnouw's responsibilities were in no wise confined to his professional duties. "In those days there was no Netherlands Information Service in New York, no press council or cultural attaché at the Legation in Washington. In the absence of an ambassador, the then Chargé d'Affaires Jhr. De Beaufort repeatedly appealed to Barnouw to take his place as Holland's representative at all kinds of functions. Before long he was also participating in a tour organised by the Sulgrave Institute, at which he had to represent our country alongside delegates from England at the commemoration festivities for the landing of the Pilgrim Fathers in 1621. The journey took him to Plymouth, Syracuse, Utica, Buffalo, Niagara Falls, Cazenovia, New York, Washington, Norfolk and Williamsburgh in Virginia. At all these official banquets he was moulded as an after-dinner speaker. How many gatherings were not adorned in the subsequent years by his brilliant addresses". Hunningher goes on to speak of "the long, long list of lectures and addresses which Barnouw gave not only in the United States, but also in

[1] In this connection see Professor Dr. G. Kalff's delightful volume *A new Holland-America Line*.

the Netherlands, in what was then the Dutch East Indies, in South Africa and the West Indies. And everywhere people were enthralled by this speaker, who was as witty as he was scholarly, talking on Dutch culture.

The Institute of International Education, excellently directed in those days by Dr. Stephen P. Duggan, had organised 'International Relations Clubs' at various educational institutions in central and far-western America. At the request of the Institute, Barnouw travelled round the Clubs, conducting many round-table discussions, which often gave rise to lively exchange of thoughts".

The nice thing about all this was that these representative functions did not turn Barnouw's head at all. By nature he had a healthy self-confidence, but at bottom he was extremely unassuming. Moreover he possessed a great deal of good humour, even when directed at himself. "What do you think of the pompous attitude I'm striking here? Perhaps you will find it amusing", he wrote, when at our request he sent us his portrait for *De Nederlandistiek in het Buitenland*.

Perhaps there are more, but I know of only three dissertations written at Columbia University under Barnouw's supervision: Gerd Aage Gilhoff, *The Royal Dutch Theatre at The Hague 1804-1876*[1]; Seymour L. Flaxman, *Herman Heijermans and his dramas*[2], and Rosalie L. Colie, *Some Thankfulnesse to Constantine*.[3] These three lasted the course, but in the undergraduate studies too there seems at first to have been no overwhelming interest in Dutch as a subject. If Barnouw had few students for Dutch he had many more in the Department of English where he lectured on the History of the English Language and – with great delight – on Chaucer. In Chaucer's own words: gladly did he lerne and gladly teche. Also in the Department of Germanic Languages he sometimes taught Gothic or Old Icelandic.[4] Professor Hunningher writes: "Thus his lectures were followed by all kinds of students who then also wanted to hear him on his own language and literature, and in this way the audience of the Dutch Professor slowly grew. Nor did it shrink as a result of the Second World War. On the contrary, it grew suddenly and quickly. The U.S. Navy had at that time housed a training school at Columbia University for officers of the reserves who were intended for service as liaison-officers

[1] The Hague, Nijhoff, 1938. For this book Barnouw undertook himself the proof-reading, instead of sending the sheets to Gilhoff, who at the time was not in New York.
[2] Ibidem, 1954.
[3] Ibidem, 1956.
[4] Professor Rosalie Colie, in a letter to me of 31.10.1968 and Professor Cabell Greet, address at the Memorial Service for Adriaan Barnouw.

between the Dutch and the native population after the recapture of the Netherlands East Indies. Fifteen of them followed Barnouw's lectures. Amongst them were some who had lived in the Netherlands Indies as employees of Standard Oil, Goodyear and other American Companies. They now mastered Dutch thoroughly."[1]

According to Rosalie L. Colie, Barnouw did not make the student's choice of Dutch an easy option. "I had to ask firmly to be taken on, and was at once set to work on *Beatrijs* – no grammar, no quarter: we simply *began*". She even suspects Barnouw of trying to get rid of her by recommending Bredero and Huygens, two difficult writers. "I was so stupid then, that I didn't recognise them as impossible, and went on to write on Huygens as a thesis subject, to his horror. He told me regularly that it was impossible, that there was no subject there, and that the whole notion was ridiculous, *but* he was very pleased when the dissertation was finished and commended, and suddenly produced a folio Huygens from under the table, which he gave me as a present then and there. I had not realised till then how secretly proud he was of his few students and – in a queer way – grateful that they cared about Dutch . . .

He was rather a private man; later I came to see him and his wife, as well as some of his children, in their house. I taught at Columbia and lived nearby. Mostly we played scrabble, in a mixture of Dutch and English – and Mrs. Barnouw usually won. He remained alert always, and although to my work he usually said 'neen', no matter what – when I started work on Arminian thought he said it was completely unimportant and anyway, it had all been done – he came in the end to be quite pleased that I kept on with Dutch subjects . . . He seemed to me to live in himself a great deal and to find resources in himself which satisfied him. He was though open and amusing with his friends, and with the students who later became his friends".

I believe that it was Barnouw's felicitous combination of extroversion and introversion which made him on the one hand the 'good companion' as he is called by Professor Cabell Greet, the brilliant after-dinner speaker, the amusing conversationalist at the Century Club which, as I am told by Dr. van Kleffens, played an important rôle in Barnouw's life, and on the other hand the translator of genius, the captivating, scholarly writer, and the excellent painter and sketcher that he was.

Having indicated above something of the manner in which he held the chair of Dutch studies, I would wish, before quoting Barnouw's

[1] B. Hunningher in: *De Nederlandistiek in het Buitenland*, p. 196.

expression of thanks at the dinner-party given on his 90th birthday
– which is so revealing of his attitude to life and of the way he saw
himself – to go a little further into the three aspects of his personality
that have just been mentioned.

From Barnouw's bibliography it is clear that in 1910 he already had
started his life work on Chaucer, for in that year he delivered a
lecture to the sixth Netherlands Congress of Philologists on Chaucer's
The Milleres Tale. As we have seen, by 1914 he already had a manuscript
of *De Vertellingen van de Pelgrims naar Kantelberg*. This principal work
of Chaucer's in an eminent Dutch version, appeared between 1930
and 1933 in three groups.[1] A bowdlerized edition was published in
1954[2] and finally in 1968[3] the unabridged version was published in its
entirety to which the author had in vain been looking forward for
years and for which he himself read the proofs some time before
his death. This edition was sold out within three weeks. In the
fifties he published Chaucer's *Troïlus en Chriseyde*[4], and some ten years
later *Het boek van de Hertogin; Het Vogelparlement, twee vroege gedichten
van Geoffry Chaucer*.[5]

In addition to delivering his regular university lectures on Chaucer,
Barnouw also presided for years over a circle in which Chaucer was
read, meeting among the leather armchairs, dark panelling and subdued
lights of the Century Club, an oldfashioned building near the Central
Station. As Mr. N. A. C. Slotemaker de Bruïne informs us, Barnouw
was in 1924 elected to membership of this club which was founded
in 1847, and of which article 1 of the statutes reads: "The Association
shall be composed of authors, artists and amateurs of letters and the
fine arts". Barnouw belonged to the first two categories, but he
played a lot of billiards there as well. "Billiards, of which he was a
great lover, was made more difficult in his latter years by his weakened
eyes, but in spite of this handicap he remained a remarkably good
player."[6]

Of Barnouw's relationship with Chaucer, Professor Cabell Greet
says[7]: "Chaucer was his joy and must have been his ideal and model.
Chaucer forged a bridge between languages and linked cultures.
Chaucer had friendships in foreign lands, and understanding of men

1 Haarlem, Tjeenk Willink, 1930 group A, 149 pp., 1932 group B, D, E, 203 pp.,
1933 group F. C. B 2-7 and G.
2 Utrecht, Het Spectrum.
3 Ibidem.
4 Haarlem, Tjeenk Willink, 1955.
5 Haarlem, Tjeenk Willink, 1966.
6 In a letter to me 4.10.1968.
7 Address at the Memorial Service for Adriaan Barnouw.

in many walks of life without ceasing to be aristocratic in his own predilections. Chaucer did not belong to Adriaan's Century Club, but I think he would have been happy there. He or his friend Gower might have guided a small group of London courtiers reading Dante or Petrarch, as Adriaan led a group of downtown professional men in reading the Canterbury Tales".

How well indeed must someone have mastered a foreign language to be able to translate into it from his own mother-tongue and then, as was Barnouw's custom, in the metre of the original. To demonstrate his peerless resourcefulness in this respect, I feel I must quote his translation of the first strophe of the popular folksong about Piet Heijn.[1] What strikes one in the second line of the refrain is his nice solution of the difficulty caused by the lack of an English word for 'klein' (little) rhyming with 'Heijn'. This line reads in Dutch: 'Piet Heijn, zijn naam is klein'.

> *Know ye the defeat*
> *Of the Spanish fleet*
> *Of the silver-and-gold Armada?*
> *There was a big harvest of ore to reap,*
> *And oranges of Granada*
> *Piet Heijn, Piet Heijn,*
> *The letters of his name are nine*
> *But countless are his deeds,*
> *But countless are his deeds,*
> *Piet Heijn has captured the silver fleet!*

In his fine English rendering of the deep piety and stately rhythm of the Dutch National Anthem, he even maintains the original acrostichon throughout the fifteen verses. He makes clever use of the fact that 'William' has one letter more than 'Willem' and 'of' one less than 'van'. Here is the first:

> *William of Nassau, scion*
> *of a Dutch and ancient line,*
> *I dedicate undying*
> *Faith to this land of mine,*
> *A prince am I, undaunted,*
> *Of Orange, ever free.*
> *To the King of Spain I've granted*
> *A lifelong loyalty.*

The latter poem is included in the collection *Coming After, an Anthology of Poetry from the Low Countries*[2]; covering the period from

[1] *The Dutch*, New York, Columbia University Press, 1940, p. 160.
[2] New Brunswick, Rutgers University Press, 1948, 348 pp.

the Middle Ages right up to the moderns in the year of publication. His translation *Beatrijs, A Middle Dutch Legend edited from the only existing manuscript in the Royal Library, The Hague, with a grammatical introduction, notes, and a glossary*[1], dates from his period in The Hague. According to a letter to me from Barnouw, it was Sir William Craigie, a man who had done his utmost in the years leading up to the First World War for the study of Dutch and Frisian in England, who urged him to do the translation for the Philological Society of *Beatrijs* or of *Karel ende Elegast*. Barnouw did not remember which of them had decided that it should be *Beatrijs*. After writing in 1924 introductions to Harry Morgan Ayres' translations *An Ingenious Play of Esmoreit*[2] and *A Marvellous History of Mary of Nimmegen*[3], Barnouw himself brought out once more *The Miracle of Beatrice, A Flemish Legend of ca. 1300, translated by Adriaan J. Barnouw. Introduction by Jan Albert Goris*.[4] It was a great pleasure to the Working Committee to be able to negotiate the publication of Barnouw's *Reynard the Fox* in the Bibliotheca Neerlandica[5], and at his request we are at the moment negotiating his translation of *Elckerlyc*[6] to which he has written an introduction a few years before his death.

Barnouw took American nationality, yet until late in his life he regularly came to Holland. As he explains in *The Dutch* he remained completely loyal to both his country of adoption and his beloved country of origin. "The German invasion of Holland in May 1940 and the years of occupation", writes N. A. C. Slotemaker de Bruïne[7], "were taken much to heart by Barnouw. Not only did he share to the utmost what was happening in Holland, he also immediately took an active part in the endeavours to acquaint America with the resistance of the Dutch people . . .". The Netherland-America Foundation and its *Monthly Letters* were part of this work. Another medium was the Netherlands-America University League, of which Barnouw was one of the founders in 1940.

Professor B. Landheer, who worked between 1937 and 1952 in the United States, calls Barnouw the mentor of all Dutchmen who were attempting to make a career for themselves in the intellectual or academic life of the U.S.A.[8] "This rôle was enhanced when at

[1] Oxford University Press, 1914.
[2] The Hague, Nijhoff, 1924, 58 pp.
[3] Ibidem, 1924, 78 pp.
[4] Pantheon 144, 1944, 109 pp.
[5] Leiden, Sijthoff-London, Heinemann-New York, London House and Maxwell, 1967.
[6] "The Mirror of Salvation, A Moral Play of Everyman, c. 1490".
[7] In a letter to me 4.10.1968.
[8] Letter to me 27.11.1968.

the beginning of the Second World War at the initiative of Dr. A. Loudon, the then Ambassador, a convention was called of all Dutchmen working in American institutions of higher education, and of all Americans who specialised in the study of Holland or the Dutch East Indies. This led to the foundation of the above-mentioned Netherlands University League of which Barnouw was acclaimed president and, because of my presence in Washington at the Library of Congress, I was made secretary. I ought also to mention Professor Valkenburg of Clark University, Worcester, Mass.; Professor Fagginger Auer of Harvard University; Professor De Haas of the Harvard Business School; Professor Goudsmit from Michigan and many others. The Netherlands University League became a flourishing undertaking, thanks especially to the inspiring leadership of Barnouw, who beamed forth a sort of cultural patriotism, culminating in his well-known translation of the Wilhelmus. Barnouw interested himself in everything Dutch, but it was Dutch literature up to the Movement of the Eighties that was his special love. What came thereafter was of no more than moderate interest to him. On the other hand he was americanised, and the freedom and democracy of America in those days appealed to him. He retailed with relish how as a teacher in The Hague he had been treated in a sort of feudal manner by the governors, and the class-consciousness of Dutchmen often irritated him. Yet he was a central figure in the Netherlands Club, where the life of commerce was dominant. The meetings of the Netherlands University League, where later Dean Ten Hoot of the University of Alabama also played an important rôle, took an atmosphere of friendliness and solidarity from Barnouw which was maintained for many years. Goris was also an active participant at these meetings, as was Greshoff".

"Meetingswere held once or twice a year", Slotemaker de Bruïne writes[1], "each time at a different university. Thus I remember clearly a meeting at Princeton at which Einstein was also present. (He had formerly been attached to the University of Leiden). He did not talk about the theory of relativity, but played the violin to us".

"Barnouw could be impassioned – a quality which is rarely found nowadays", Landheer continues, "though this evaporated in his retirement. He grew together with a New York which still retained in it something of Nieuw Amsterdam, although this was probably more so in his imagination than in reality. Barnouw lived intensely and his alert opinions had a strong positive or negative charge. He was and remained the undisputed leader of the small

[1] In a letter to me 4.10.1968.

fragment of intellectual and academic Holland which managed to keep a certain identity even in the U.S.A.".

This tension between his two homelands is one of the factors that has contributed to Barnouw's enormous activity and creativity. When he sent us his bibliography at my request he added, somewhat apologetically: "My list has had the impertinence to grow long because I have had the impertinence to remain alive for such a long time". To which I replied that it was not everybody with a long life behind him who could boast of such a bibliography. It covers more than five pages not including the numerous book-reviews and articles which appeared in some forty American and Dutch periodicals and newspapers. His subjects range from the field of literature, language and history of art to that of 'Landeskunde'. Of his publications in book-form I can mention but a few here: *Holland under Queen Wilhelmina*[1], *Vondel*[2], which is still regarded as one of the best studies on this subject, *The Dutch, A Portrait study of the People of Holland*,[3] *The Contribution of Holland to the Sciences, A symposium*[4], together with B. Landheer, *The Land of William of Orange*[5], *The making of Modern Holland*[6], *The Fantasy of Pieter Brueghel*[7], *The Pageant of Netherlands History*[8] and *The Land and People of Holland*[9], translated into Persian by Moshfegh Hamedant.[10] And there was of course the *Monthly Letter* of the Netherland-America Foundation, which he wrote for 31 years (1924-1948 and 1954-1961) "both faithfully and excellently", as Professor Hunningher expressed it and through which he exercised no mean influence. "This modest little periodical was read far and wide . . . Regularly it was quoted from or reproduced in full by other publications . . . The numerous letters that Barnouw received as reactions to the *Monthly Letter* from all parts of America bear witness to the extent of its influence. Later Mr. Jerome Greene of the Harvard Corporation urgently pressed Barnouw to have the whole series reprinted in book-form. It was a flattering proposal but modestly he was quite willing to leave such an edition for the time being. With a gay laugh he much preferred to sit at his easel".[11]

[1] New York, London, Charles Scribner's Sons, 1923, 321 pp.
[2] New York, Charles Scribner's Sons, 1925, 227 pp.
[3] Columbia University Press, 1940, 297 pp.
[4] New York, Querido, 1943 (the chapter on Philology pp. 43-60 by A.J.B.).
[5] Philadelphia and New York, J. B. Lippingcott, 1944, 104 pp.
[6] New York, W. W. Norton & Co., 1944, 224 pp.
[7] New York, Lear Publishers, 1947, 100 pp.
[8] New York, Longmans, Green & Co., 1952, 370 pp.
[9] Philadelphia and New York, J. B. Lippingcott, 1961, 129 pp.
[10] Teheran, B.T.N.K., 1964.
[11] *De Nederlandistiek in het Buitenland*, pp. 196-197.

So, the Working Committee deemed it hardly possible to offer Professor Barnouw the whole series for publication. We advised him to make a selection, to which he immediately reacted by writing to me: "You are right, I have to do a great deal of pruning". By embarking on quite an extensive fund-raising scheme, the Working Committee succeeded in collecting the security demanded by the publisher. Professor Barnouw was highly delighted by our endeavours. "I am honoured and touched by your obstinate tenacity in exerting yourself to have this expensive book of mine published. Even if it comes to nothing, the memory of this act of friendship will be a consolation to me in my last years", he wrote to me on 25.10.1967. Unfortunately he did not live to see the work appear, but we were able to tell him at the beginning of July 1968 that its publication was now certain. We also sent him regularly lists of subscribers' names and it was a source of great joy to him to see the names of so many old friends and acquaintances. Meanwhile the Working Committee is delighted that the Netherland-America Foundation is having the whole series photo-copied so that it will remain accessible in toto for students in libraries.

I would wish to record here that for his contribution to the field of culture Professor Barnouw was awarded in 1957 the Golden Quill of the Royal Dutch Guild of Publishers. This was presented to him in 1960 in the presence of Dutch and American authorities. Her Majesty the Queen also appointed him Commander in the Order of the Dutch Lion.

"With my gouty legs I can climb no higher", he wrote to me, after the Working Committee, knowing nothing about this, had endeavoured to elicit a royal distinction for the occasion of his 90th birthday.

Plemp van Duiveland, recalling his grammar school years in The Hague, writes about Barnouw's love of painting and drawing which he had intended to choose as his profession, until his father advised him against it.[1] "Many a time Dr. Barnouw gave generous 'extras' to his lessons on language and literature, touching on fields which fell right outside the curriculum. His passion was painting, and within this Elysium the highest gods were the Dutch Masters of the 17th century. The name of many an artist I heard for the first time from his lips: Aert van der Neer, Pieter Saenredam, Simon de Vlieger, Joos de Momper – he would drop such names in a conversational tone, adding one or two remarks of explanation on each. In

[1] Letter of 22.11.1968.

my letter of congratulation upon his 90th birthday I thanked him belatedly for this spiritual legacy, and it was this part of the letter, he replied, which caused him most pleasure – that he had evidently succeeded in passing on to the boys something of his admiration for this zenith in the history of the nation.

Not only the paintings but also the creators of the masterpieces were close to his heart. He knew most of their life-histories, their origins, the school each had attended, their domestic circumstances. He cherished a truly 'unzeitgemässes' hatred for Campo Weijerman, the man who some two centuries earlier had written fanciful tales about the Dutch Masters. This scribbler embroidered upon the theme of the 'huishouden van Jan Steen'. Steen, according to Barnouw's introduction, left eight hundred paintings of high quality to posterity. Is such an achievement compatible with a life spent in revelry and idleness?"

Although even with his great love of art Barnouw was unable to make painting his profession, as a side-line this talent remained loyal to him, even when in later years his eyesight had greatly deteriorated. "He had already undergone some two or even three cataract operations when I knew him", Professor J. A. Goris (Marnix Gijsen) wrote to me[1]. Barnouw was to paint Goris' portrait, "and I still remember vividly those sittings during a very hot Manhattan summer. It was pitiful to see this good, cordial and sensitive man wrestling with the loss of his sight. I am positive he did not notice the tears of compassion running down my cheeks, and if indeed he did, he must have thought it was no more than perspiration".

Yet there seems to have been some improvement in his condition, perhaps after a later treatment, for in the last years of his life he sent me Christmas cards of reduced drawings he had made in the summers of 1965 and 1967 on Shelter Island, where in his old age he used to spend his holidays, drawings in which his observation of nature is still very clear and accurate.

These holiday sojourns are referred to in a letter sent to Dr. E. van Raalte[2] and contained in his reminiscences[3] published in the *Nieuwe Rotterdamse Courant* of 3.10.1968: "I am sitting in the wilderniss which surrounds my daughter's house on Shelter Island. It has a spacious veranda with a view of a bay between the trees. A pair of fishhawks which have been soaring overhead suddenly take a vertical dive into the water. This pair of birds has built itself a nest in the top of a dead tree close to Elsa's house. Their feeble, almost childish

[1] Letter of 15.11.1968.
[2] On 16.6.1962.
[3] "Herinnering aan de mens in professor Barnouw".

screeching is out of all proportions to their size. It's no pleasure to hear them, but it's a delight to watch them; and it's one of my daily joys to follow them with my eye as they go on their raids ... In these peaceful surroundings I sit enjoying Wiessing's autobiography *Bewegend Portret*. I have only reached the fourth chapter, for I read slowly and with rapt attention. It is not a book for rushing through, it enthralls, it holds you captive in its grip. Wiessing is a year younger than I. He tells of my own times and some of the figures occurring in his book are old acquaintances of mine. The meeting in Frans Coenen's museum, seldom frequented and hence wearisome, is an exquisite example of descriptive art. A play could be made of it. Wiessing is an extraordinarily shrewd writer. It is a delight to read him, and I am more grateful to you than I can say (for I do not possess his talent) for your present which gives me so much pleasure".

In his prime, Barnouw often made long journeys from which he never failed to bring back 'illuminating pictures of his eye's adventures', as Professor Cabell Greet puts it in his address at Adriaan Barnouw's Memorial Service. Many summers he spent painting in Taos, New Mexico, where his work was often exhibited and prominently discussed in *Taos and its artists*. "Painting was ever a balance in his life, a joy and a balance. His pictures, always competent and interesting, will be missed in the Century Club expositions". The day before the attack which led to unconsciousness and his death a few days later on 27 September 1968, he completed a painting that he had wanted to do for some time, intending it for his grandson as a wedding-present. It was one of his best.

"When one's old professor and friend dies", Professor Greet begins his above-mentioned oration and survey of Barnouw's life, "one naturally wonders if his life was marked by a theme. When I think of the 45 years I knew Adriaan Barnouw, I am struck most by his zest for life. This was expressed in ways characteristic of Dutch intellectuals for centuries: in letters, in the arts of good-fellowship and diplomacy, and in painting. In all these he was exceptionally talented. But the distinction he won as a scholar and teacher, as a cultural essayist in the Dutch and British tradition, and as a painter, must have been founded on habits of industry and of prudence forged in the hard competition of Dutch youth".

His daughter Elsa adds to this picture the simple comment: "He mellowed greatly as he grew older. Former pupils used to say that he was sometimes stern and angry, but he was never that way in recent years".[1] That Barnouw was not only 'the most delightful of

[1] Letter of 24.11.1968.

companions' as Cabell Greet calls him, but was also a deeply moving man will be evident from his own address, quoted as the most fitting 'last word' to this sketch of his life. These words were spoken at the dinner given on his 90th birthday on 9 October 1967, by the Netherland-America Foundation which was attended by about fourty relatives, friends and guests.

"I am deeply moved. It is always difficult for me to control my emotions. When I read a poem that strikes me as beautiful I feel a shiver creep along my spine and tears into my eyes. My wife, who came from Yorkshire, where people are of a sterner mould, thought such sentimentality unmanly. I remember an incident from the first world war that characterizes the two of us. In 1917 the Netherlands Government offered to admit and intern some 15,000 prisoners of war of Great Britain and Germany who had been in captivity for 18 months. George Clark, a nephew of my wife's, was among the fortunate ones. My wife and I went to Scheveningen where the prisoners from Germany were to be discharged at the Steamtram Station. When we saw him coming she said to me, "Should I show how I feel or should I just be British?" Well, she was just British. I was moved to tears but the meeting between nephew and aunt was quite casual. They greeted each other as if they had parted the day before, and no tears were shed.

A few years ago I read in the *N. Y. Times* a condensation of an article that had appeared in the *Lancet*, the English medical periodical. It was by a London doctor who had been intrigued by the prevalence of baldness among the men of England, whereas those of the Continent, especially in the Mediterranean area, kept their hair intact; and he had come to the conclusion that the British habit of restraining all show of emotion was a cause of baldness. Men who gave free vent to their feelings kept their hair. Those who showed a stiff upper lip lost it. If I should embarrass you tonight by dropping a tear now and then, I hope you will forgive me, looking at my well preserved coiffure, and say to yourselves "He can't help it, he's still got his hair".

I have another handicap: I am very deaf. Last summer I read an article about deafness in the *Saturday Review*. It seems that deafness is assuming epidemic proportions in America, and the writer claimed that experiments have proved that the excessive noise in this industrialized age is the cause of it. If that is true New York must be a city of the deaf, for I don't believe there is any other place on earth that is so infested with noises of all sorts. "We have two ears and one tongue in order that we hear more and speak less", according to a Greek philosopher. But my tongue is doomed to speak more and my ears to hear less. Deafness has isolated me. I shun my old companions, knowing that I am a bore and a nuisance to others. But I find consolation in the thought that it is better to be deaf than blind. I have always, from my earliest years, lived by sight, much more so than by hearing.

I was fortunate to be born in Amsterdam. The beauty of that city was apparent and a source of joy to my eyes when I was a little child. We lived on the Oudezijdsvoorburgwal in the heart of the old city, and in those days, the eighties of the 19th century, it was a dreamy, poetic, and picturesque neighbourhood. I do not feel at home in this noisy, matter-of-fact, and computerized world. I have no conception of what computers do and have no desire to know it. I am sure they cannot make people any happier, since their chief purpose, it seems, is to take all work out of their hands. A horrible ideal. For action, to me at least, is happiness. I remember that as a little boy I got impatient with my nurse when she started to dress me. "Zelf doen", I can still hear myself say; "Zelf doen", I wanted to discard my fussy computer.

I wish I could live myself back into the world of my childish imagination. All children live in a self-created dream world. Their reality is the dream, a more beautiful reality than the world of facts, in which the grown-ups live. Children are born poets, and if they could write about their dreams our literature would be much richer for it. But children are trained for the world of facts, where dream must shrivel. Small is the number of those fortunate ones in whose remembrance the child lives on unspoilt to create poetry out of the unforgotten dream.

I have remained a dreamer too long to fit into the computer world of facts. Figures and numbers have always terrified me, algebraic formulas never meant anything to me. When I have to fill out my tax papers and give an account of my income I feel I am a nincompoop.

My father used to call me a boy with two left hands; but with that second left hand, which could not hammer a nail into the wall without hitting the thumb of the other, I learned how to draw and paint. I was fond of colors and lines, not of the straight line which you cannot draw without a ruler, but the moving line in which the hand that draws it in perfect freedom expresses an inner emotion. I was fond of words with which children and poets paint, words which, like chameleons, change color and meaning in the changing context in which they occur, words which are not facts but capricious symbols. At school in Holland education did not encourage that dreamy disposition. On the contrary, it tended to choke it. You were not allowed to dream, you were not allowed to imagine, you had to know. The best pupils were the knowers of facts. I had a good memory and could hold my own in that competition, but it did not give me many happy hours at school.

During the Second World War all recent immigrants were suspect among a certain type of flagwaving patriots as people with a divided allegiance. They seemed to think that every foreigner enters America with a limited and unchangeable supply of loyalty which, as a U.S. citizen, he divided into two equal halves. But an emotion cannot be cut in two like a loaf of bread. Love is an emotion of changeable strength and content:

True love in this differs from gold and clay
That to divide is not to take away.
Love is like understanding that grows bright
Gazing on many truths.

That is equally true of the love that a man feels for his country, both for the land of his birth and for the land of the immigrant's choice. In 1945 the Holland Society of New York presented me with the Society's Gold Medal, which is annually awarded to an American the Society considers worthy of the distinction. That medal was to me a symbol of that two-fold love of country. It has two sides facing opposite directions. But who would say that these two are divided? They are joined within an unbreakable rim that holds them as one. The reverse is not separate from the medal, it is part of the medal, and the medal is part of its reverse. Neither exists without the other, In the same way, in the immigrant the loves for the native and the adopted country are not separate and conflicting affections, they are two facets of one emotion. I treasure the Holland Society medal as the American I have become and as the Hollander I shall remain at heart. And in the Netherland-America Foundation I recognize an institution dear to my heart because, like the medal, it encircles within its rims, as its name implies, the same pair of affections.

The time is not yet in which the institution of the United Nations will be true to its name. It is destined, alas, for centuries after our lifetime to remain a league of disunited nations. The Barnouws in America are showing on a microscopic scale that unification is possible. I have three daughters-in-law, one a Belgian from Antwerp, another an American from Vermont, the third a Japanese. One of my grandsons has married a Swedish girl, and another a German girl from Ulm. And within that miniature League of Nations there obtains, I assure you, perfect harmony. We form a wholeness in spite of our national diversity.

Being a linguist by profession, I like to link words that root in the same soil. *Whole* and to *heal* are closely related, to *heal* means 'to make whole', and *health* means *wholeness*. Jesus told his disciples 'They that are whole have no need of a physician, but they that are sick'. *Health* indeed means *wholeness*, and the *condition of health* is being whole. And for the attainment and preservation of real health it is necessary for a man to achieve full development of his personality in four main fields: work, play, love and worship. According to that definition I may consider myself a *whole*, that is, a *healthy* man".

MONTHLY LETTER

August-September 1946

*B*EFORE *the war Holland was to me a holiday playground. It has ceased to be that. The visitor from America·cannot help feeling somewhat embarrassed with his leisure and his supply of dollars while moving among people who are impoverished and hard at work to regain their lost prosperity. They are apt to deny that they are. If one were to believe their own appraisal of the present situation in the Netherlands, the country is in a sorry state, not so much because it is poor but because the people are lazy. Every Dutchman will tell you that the nation is afflicted with mental fatigue and an abnormal aversion to·any kind of work. The testimony of my eyes belied that self-criticism. "Have you not rebuilt your railway system in one year and are the trains not running on schedule?" I asked. They could not deny that, but this was an exceptional achievement. "And what about the polders that were flooded by the Nazis? Have the dikes not been restored and the water drained off?" That also was true, they admitted; but dire necessity forced them to that effort. It did not disprove their contention that the nation as a whole was tired and loath to work. And I was warned not to mistake the public's willingness to spend money lavishly in restaurants and theaters for a symptom of returning prosperity. They squandered it because they had no confidence in the future of the guilder. "Why should they save? They can get more for their money now than they are likely to get later on. Besides," my spokesmen complained, "the Government leaves*

FOREWORD

In December 1961 the Netherland-America Foundation brought out the last of the series of Monthly Letters that had appeared, with only few interruptions, for more than a third of a century. In explanation of my decision to discontinue their publication I wrote: "I would rather say to my readers, 'this is the last I shall write,' than hear them grumble later on, 'this is the last I will read.'" I still think it was a wise decision. It is not without serious misgivings that I attempt to stage a resurrection. The ghost of a man is never welcome to those who cared for him in the flesh, and since I deliberately buried my epistolary self some years ago, my return as a ghost writer can hardly be welcome to my erstwhile readers. Ghost writers, it is true, are popular nowadays. Most men in authority are too busy to write their own articles and addresses; there is so great a demand for ghost writers that a professor at American University, Washington, D.C., is offering a course in that useful art. Why then should this ghost writer anticipate a cool reception? Because he is a real ghost, whereas the future graduates of American University will have no right to the name. A ghost is the posthumous reappearance of a person, a deceptive semblance of him, not his late real self. Coming back to the place where he used to live is a ghost's essential characteristic. That is why the French call a ghost *revenant*, the one who comes back. Hence the present writer has a better right to the name than the Washington students will have when they have successfully completed the course. They will not come back, they will just be starting. If we were to use the term ghost writer logically we should apply it to the ghost writer's employer. The man who has his writing done by someone else is only a semblance, a ghost of the actual writer. The latter remains anonymous and never comes out into the open; but a ghost's business is to appear, a ghost is an apparition.

In all the ghost stories that I have read the apparition had a definite reason to appear. It had to fulfill some sort of mission. The dead man had gone to his grave with a burden on his conscience and could not rest in peace until he had recanted the false charges he had made and through confession to a living soul had lifted the load. Or it was the knowledge of a crime that would not let him sleep and his ghost had to haunt the spot where it occurred in hope of revealing to someone the dreadful secret and the identity of the guilty one. Or he knew of buried treasure and the apparition's purpose was to lead some living person to the spot. This writing ghost cannot plead any such mission in explanation of his reappearance. He cannot offer any better excuse for leaving the grave of his self-imposed silence than that he was summoned out of it. From several of my monthly readers I have received the request that I reprint my effusions. Let me quote one out of many, from no less a discriminating critic than Mr. Jerome D. Greene, the late Secretary of the Harvard Corporation: "The whole series should be issued in bound form or reprinted as a book; for I think they have permanent interest and great documentary value." Thus he wrote to me in 1948. I have long hesitated to rise from interment at his and other readers' bidding. That I do so at last is from a foolish but I hope excusable fear lest after my approaching demise my real ghost would haunt the attics of my erstwhile readers in a vain search for dusty copies of my neglected Monthly Letters. I shall not try to preserve the whole series as Mr. Greene suggested. This volume contains only a selection of those Letters that, in my own estimate, are least deserving of oblivion.

New York, November 1967   ADRIAAN J. BARNOUW

MONTHLY LETTERS

DUTCH CRAFTSMEN OF NEW NETHERLAND

The Metropolitan Museum of Art, thanks to the generous gift of its President, Mr. Robert W. de Forest, and Mrs. de Forest, has added a wing to its large frame and, in the treasures there exhibited, a fresh addition to the many which it holds for the lover of art. The new building is known as the American Wing, as it is devoted entirely to American art of the Colonial, Revolutionary, and Early Republican periods. The exhibits are so arranged as to give the visitor a survey of the development of the American home from the days of the early settlers until the second quarter of the nineteenth century, and the three main periods into which that historical growth of nearly two hundred years can be divided have each an entire floor of the new building assigned to them. It is a pleasure to spend an afternoon in these old-time interiors, where every detail is in harmony with the whole, and the furniture, though it be of the simplest, bears the impress of individual taste and craftsmanship. If I were offered living quarters in this wing and given the choice of an entire floor space, I should not hesitate for a moment but move my household gods into the third floor devoted to the early Colonial period. The rooms here are snug and cozy, while those below have an air of uncommodious formality. The interiors on the top floor were made to live in; the later ones seem to exist for the purpose of receiving ceremonial calls.

Still, my household gods, having come from Holland, might demur to their removal, not on aesthetic but on historic grounds. The sturdy features of Jan Strycker as painted in 1655 by his brother Jacobus Gerritsz, both of New Amsterdam, would welcome them to the place, but little else would make them feel that they came to a New Netherland home. The trusses of the roof over Jan Strycker's head repeat the structure of the Old Ship Meeting-House in Hingham, Mass., 1681, and the surrounding rooms, with one exception, are all examples of New England interiors, from Topsfield and Ipswich, Mass., from Hampton, N.H., from Portsmouth, R. I., from Newing-

I

ton, Conn. The exception is a room from a house in Woodbury, L. I., but this house was built by an Englishman as late as 1739. The Handbook of the American Wing, in its Table of Contents, defines the First Period of Early American Art as extending from "the beginnings of New England through the first quarter of the eighteenth century," and the exhibits are in accordance with that definition. One unacquainted with America's colonial history would never gather from a visit to this floor that the early American handicrafts, in the territories once comprised within New Netherland, were of Dutch origin, and that Dutch talent and skill helped to develop early American art. In the Handbook's description of the room from Woodbury we are told on page 97 that "the lowboy, chairs, tables, and looking-glass reiterate the Dutch or Flemish influences which came into England with William of Orange and were continued in popularity under Queen Anne." Had these influences to wait for William's accession to the English throne to be brought to America via England? Is it not possible that they had come here with the early Dutch settlers and had helped to develop a native American art before Stuyvesant surrendered to the British?

The writers of the Handbook have not even considered that possibility. "The beginnings of the first period of American artistic development lie in the earliest years of the permanent settlements of New England," they inform us at the very outset of their manual. In other words, in New Amsterdam under Stuyvesant, in the patroonship of the Van Rensselaers, on Long Island, in Esopus on the Hudson, in Fort Orange, were evidently no artisans at work to supply the utilitarian art for the homes of the well-to-do Dutch? Still there was comfort and even luxury in many a New Netherland home. To quote from the Handbook itself:

The inventory of Cornelius Steenwyck, mayor of New York (1668-1670), who died in 1685, shows that in the "Great Chamber were nineteen porcelain dishes and two flowered earthen pots." Margharita van Varick, the widow of the minister of the Reformed Dutch Congregation on Long Island, left behind her (1695), "Three East India cups, three East India dishes, three Cheenie pots, one Cheenie pot bound in silver, two glassen cases with thirty-nine pieces of small china ware, eleven India babyes" and one hundred and twenty-six pieces of various kinds of chinaware, bowls, jugs, flower-pots, toys, and images. Other inventories indicate that the possession of a hundred pieces of pottery and porcelain was not uncommon for a seventeenth-century New York burgher.

And of the Hollanders in Albany we read in the Itinerarium of Alexander Hamilton, the Annapolis physician who visited that town in 1744:

2

Their chambers and rooms are large and handsome. They have their beds generally in alcoves, so that you may go thro' all the rooms of a great house and see never a bed. They affect pictures much, particularly scripture history, with which they adorn their rooms. They set out their cabinets and buffets much with china. Their kitchens are likewise very clean, and there they hang earthen or delft plates and dishes all round the walls in manner of pictures, having a hole drilled thro' the edge of the plate or dish, and a loop of ribbon put into it to hang it by.

May we not safely assume that these cabinets and buffets and the rest of the furniture in these handsome rooms were the work of Dutch artisans, and is it likely that those craftsmen had no part in developing an American style of applied art? The actual existence of one Dutch craft in early New York is clearly revealed by the splendid collection of old silver loaned by Hon. A. T. Clearwater, and the Handbook, in the face of that evidence, admits that "the Wynkoops, the Boelens, Peter van Dyck, Onclebach, among many New York makers, produced superb examples of their art-craft more elaborate in decoration than those of New England." And is it likely, we ask again, that the crafts of the potter, and the pewterer, and the turner, and the joiner were not equally well-represented in the settlements of New Netherland? The emphasis laid, both in the collection and in the guide book, on the New England origin of Early American art seemed to one visitor at least to impair the historical value of an otherwise inestimable exhibit.

September 1, 1924

PALLIETERING

Labor Day is at hand, and the toilers and plodders and workers are returning to their accustomed tasks. It would be a good thing if they all came back with the gratifying feeling of a well-spent holiday. For the spending of free time so that one gets something in return for the outlay is not everybody's business. Among the ever-increasing number of subjects that are taught at American colleges and universities might be included the art of making good use of one's leisure. There is a vast difference between relaxing and loafing, but great is the number of those who believe them to be identical. He who relaxes does not cease to exert himself, but finds relief from fatigue in changing to a less strenuous and, for the time being, more pleasant occupation. He keeps going and will find it easy, when Labor Day comes round again, to get up speed for the serious business of life. The loafer, on the other hand, gets stuck fast in the mud of his laziness, and will be unable to move at the summons to return to work. Relaxation is a tonic, but loafing is a drug that makes victims of the over-indulgent.

Since the schools do not offer any training in the art of relaxation, let me recommend to you a book that can be used as a home-study course. Its title is *Pallieter*, which is the name of the hero, and its author is the Fleming Felix Timmermans, who has found an able interpreter in Mrs. C. B. Bodde of Oxford. The Flemings are an industrious and, at the same time, a pleasure-loving race. But of their industry there is little in this book, except the implied industry of its author; it is all about the love of pleasure and the art of enjoying it to the full. The book is not a story of Pallieter's life; it is a story of Pallieter's joy in life. So beautifully and convincingly has Timmermans written of his hero's zest for existence that, as Hendrik Willem van Loon informs us in his Introduction to the English edition (Harper & Brothers, New York), *pallieter* has been added to the vocabulary of Dutch Belgium and Holland and, either as a verb or a noun, is used to indicate and describe "that healthy sentiment which in the days before the war we used to call the joy of living." It is with the art of *pallietering* as with the art of the poet: one has to be born a kind of *Pallieter* to become efficient in his art, but all those who have a native sense for the spell of out-of-door life and the beauties of nature can learn from this book how to develop the gift. Pallieter, for all his happy-go-lucky mode of life, is not a loafer, for he is always on the go, eager to get the best out of every hour of the day. "A milker of days," his maker calls him, and the milk of life's kindness is his daily food. So keenly alive is he to all sensations that few are the moments which do not yield him some joy. He finds a thrill of delight in the glow of a blood-red poppy among the corn, in the spatter of the rain on his close-cropped head, in the song of a nightingale through the still evening, in the taste of old wine on the tongue, in the smell of the lush and lusty grass. In that alertness of all the senses is the secret of Pallieter's joy in life, and the author is so gifted a painter with words that he makes the susceptible reader *pallieter* with his hero.

OF WRITING AN ENGLISH LETTER

Since doctors have begun to recommend the taking of naps as a part of their health-preserving programmes, people have ceased to be ashamed of admitting their longing for a mid-day doze. I am old enough to remember the days when no self-respecting Hollander of either sex would unblushingly confess to such self-indulgence. They would actually indulge, without any doctor's insistence, but only on the sly, or under pretext of retiring from the company for serious business. No one was deceived by the pretext and the pretender did not expect that any one would be deceived. It sufficed that a means had been found which made it possible for the sleepy one to withdraw, and for the others to acquiesce in his weakness, without a feeling of embarrassment. The "serious business" was, of course, capable of variety, but there was one pretext that was so frequently resorted to as to become a recognized synonym of "taking a nap" and thereby miss its original purpose. That was the phrase, "I have to write an English letter." It was so common a lie that, by its very transparency, it ceased to be a falsehood and was accepted as a euphemistic statement of the truth. "To write an English letter" (*een Engelschen brief schrijven*) is simply a Dutch phrase for "taking a nap."

This peculiar application of the words is proof of the difficulty which the Dutchman encounters in the writing of English. In order to be done at all it has to be done in such privacy as propriety prescribes for one's slumbers. And even if he does use the privacy for the purpose and not for the doze, he will, in spite of his labors, still be caught napping by his English correspondent. For there are traps, even for the most wary and experienced Dutchman, in the garden of the English language, and though he may find his way through its labyrinth with perfect assurance and ease, he will tread upon flowers that another, to the manner born, would have noticed and gathered, and will beat about the bush while the native goes straight to the point. The present writer speaks from experience. Now and then an unusually gifted author – Maarten Maartens in England, Hendrik Willem van Loon in this country – may succeed in creating literature in the foreign tongue, but their signal achievement only brings out the more clearly the inability of the average.

One need not wonder, then, that the people of High Prairie, to whom Miss Ferber introduces the reader in her novel *So Big*, did not find a literary portraitist in one of their own kind. Their speech is not the sort of English out of which literature is made. Being tillers of the soil and living in what the author calls an "incredibly Dutch district," they had neither the inducement nor the means to cultivate the English tongue. The more grateful we are to Miss Ferber for giving us this picture of their life. She has painted them without the sentimentality that mars the story of Hans Brinker, nor has she made it a caricature in the manner of Washington Irving. Selina, the New England girl who marries and settles in High Prairie, a truck farmer's wife among truck farmers, "understood them better, though not altogether, after almost twenty years of living amongst them. A cold people, yet kindly. Suspicious, yet generous. Distrustful of all change, yet progressing by sheer force of thrift and unceasing labour. Unimaginative for generations, only to produce – a Roelf Pool."

Roelf Pool is a Dutch farmer's son who becomes a great sculptor. The author finds it difficult to account for the appearance of this impressionable, artistic boy in that environment: "Some Dutch sailor ancestor, Selina thought, or fisherman, must have touched at an Italian port or Spanish and brought back a wife whose eyes and skin and feeling for beauty had skipped layer on layer of placid Netherlanders to crop out now in this wistful sensitive boy." This is the kind of explanation that the Hollanders themselves will give for the streak of dark-complexioned type that runs through their people, especially on the Zeeland isles. They will tell you that the immixture of Spanish blood during the eighty years' war with Spain is the cause of it. But modern anthropological research has conclusively proved that this type was settled at the mouths of the Rhine, Maas, and Scheldt before the Teutons invaded those parts. The Roelf Pools belong to the Alpine race and are as numerous in South-West Holland as the blue-eyed and fair-haired Teutons. Nor is his artistic talent such an exceptional phenomenon among the Dutch that the phantom of a Spanish or Italian great-grandmother must be called up to account for it. Roelf Pool had his living counterpart in Pier Pander, the son of a humble peat skipper in Friesland who as a boy showed a remarkable talent for carving in wood. He was given his training at an Amsterdam art school, thanks to the support of the parish minister, won the Prix de Rome, and became a famous sculptor in the Eternal City. Miss Ferber's tale of the talented boy from High Prairie reads like a transcript of Pier Pander's real story. Only, Pander was a blonde, blue-eyed son of the north, whose feeling for beauty was his inheritance from generations of stolid, placid Friesians.

April 1925

OF EDUCATORS

The greatest praise one can give to a language, says Grotius in one of his earliest essays, is to call it capable of expressing one's thoughts in as short a time as possible, and that speech is, consequently, to be admired most in which fundamental ideas are expressed by words of one syllable. A living Danish scholar, the philologist, Otto Jespersen, is of the same opinion, and declares, for that reason, the English language to be the most admirable one among the many he has studied. It were to be wished that our modern speech of every day were more deserving of his praise. It prefers ugly mouthfuls of mock-Latin to its native shortness. We make our coffee in a perculator, we keep our food cool in a refrigerator, we travel from the first to the top floor in an elevator, we take the baby for an airing in a perambulator, we heat our room with a radiator, as if we were Romans with plenty of time to spend on our speech. These pompous ator-names are absurdly out of keeping with the practical purpose of the things they indicate. The ending puts them in a class with the ten immortals whom Dr. Eliot has declared to be the greatest educators of all time. And, indeed, to judge from Dr. Eliot's use of the word, an educator has something in common with an elevator. He appears to reject the matter-of-course definition of an educator as "one who educates," for, apart from Aristotle, none of Dr. Eliot's immortals made education his profession, while the names of the great ones who did are not included in his list: the Greek Socrates, the Spaniard Vives, the Hollander Erasmus, the Moravian Comenius, the Swiss Pestalozzi, the Englishman Arnold. An educator, in Dr. Eliot's use of the word, is evidently a thinker, preferably of Anglo-Saxon stock, who, through his writings, has influenced mankind and led it onward to a higher plane of knowledge and culture, an uplifter, in short, or in mock-Latin if you like, an elevator. But even among such educators there should have been a place reserved for Erasmus, "the man to whom all Europe," says Dr. Preserved Smith, "turned at the crisis of religious conflict as to an umpire." Nor should Hugo Grotius have been excluded, the man to whom, three centuries after he wrote, all Europe turns at the crisis of international conflict.

SCHREVELIUS

Having started on a discussion of educators, I feel tempted to pursue the subject and draw the reader's attention to another learned Dutchman who, a century and a half after his death, became a teacher of Greek in American colleges. Cornelis Schrevel (1608-1664) was a doctor of medicine and, for some time, a practising physician at The Hague. But in 1642 he became headmaster of the Latin school at Leyden, and it is as a classical scholar that he is now chiefly remembered, especially for his *Lexicon Manuale Graeco-Latinum et Latino-Graecum* (Leyden: 1654). This book was republished several times during the 17th and 18th centuries, amongst others by the English scholar Joseph Hill, who enlarged it considerably. The dictionary was not

7

yet out of date in the early nineteenth century, for there are American editions of 1808 (Philadelphia and Worcester, Mass.) and of 1818, 1825, 1832, all three published in New York. So many reprints seem to prove a lively interest in the study of Greek in this country. Still, the professors of that period complained of its unpopularity. "For our part," wrote one of them, John Pickering, "we can entertain no doubt that one principal reason why Greek is so much less familiar to us than Latin is the circuitous and awkward practice of studying it through the medium of a third language." To supply the need he brought out, in conjunction with Daniel Oliver, a Greek dictionary in which the meanings are given in English. The basis of this work was Schrevel's lexicon, "which, on the whole, in the present state of Greek studies in this country, was thought preferable to any other manual adapted to the use of schools." And so the first book of this kind ever published in America appeared in 1826 under the title *The Greek Lexicon of Schrevelius translated into English with many additions* (Boston: Cummings, Hilliard & Company). No other author's name appears on the title page. His American translators gave him full credit for the work he had accomplished one hundred and seventy-two years before, and generously ceded to their Dutch predecessor the honor of being the first to teach Greek to American students in their own language.

LEVE DE LAPPEN

Let me take you from the classroom of the Greek professor to the humblest possible schoolroom on the outskirts of civilization, in the northern regions of the Scandinavian peninsula. Listening, the other day, to an illustrated lecture on Lapland and the Lapps, an account of Dr. G. Clyde Fisher's travels through those parts, I was pleasantly reminded of my own country by one of the pictures that were thrown on the screen. The speaker told of a visit to a primitive school in one of these straggling Lapp settlements which, owing to the people's migratory habits, have little of the permanent about them. The day before, Queen Wilhelmina and her little daughter had inspected the school, and Princess Juliana had left a record of her visit on the blackboard: a drawing of a girl's face, evidently an attempt at a self-portrait, with underneath the Dutch words *Leve de Lappen*, i.e., "Long live the Lapps." Dr. Fisher took a photo of the sketch and the inscription before it was wiped off the board by the teacher's sponge. Thanks to his camera, the princess' charming tribute to the Lapps will outlast the little village and its schoolhouse where it graced the blackboard for one summer day.

8

DUTCH NAMES IN THE ARCTIC

I should like to refer the editors of the New York papers to the article on *Spitsbergen* in the *Encyclopaedia Britannica*. They need not read further than the middle of the second line, only the opening words: "Spitsbergen (the name being Dutch is incorrectly, though commonly, spelled Spitzbergen) ..." Why continue to do what is commonly done when its incorrectness has been pointed out? Dutch *s* seems to be out of favor with American proofreaders. Frans Hals is usually Franz Hals; why not Franz Halz, to be consistent? And New-Friesland figured in the wireless messages from Spitsbergen as New-Friezeland! Is it possible that these spellers, knowing that Zuiderzee is Dutch, put in a *z* wherever they see a chance to make the word look more Dutchy?

The wireless message to the *New York Times* giving the first account of Commander Byrd's phenomenal flight to the Pole began as follows: "The successful trip of Commander Byrd was made on a bee-line to Verlegen Hook, New Friezeland, thence West to Amsterdam Island and home. He did not follow the identical course on the return because he wanted to be sure to hit Spitzbergen, but the navigation was perfect." Amsterdam Island, Verlegen Hook, New Friezeland, Spitzbergen are all four of them Dutch names, written on the map of the arctic region by navigators from Holland three hundred years ago. The island of Spitsbergen was discovered in 1596 on the third expedition of Willem Barents in search of a northeast passage to the Far East. They sighted the island on June 19, 1596, and on the twenty-fourth Barents wrote in his log that they had called it Spitsbergen because of its being one mass of mountains and mountain peaks. He built a cairn and stuck a pole on the top of it in token of Holland's claim to the land by right of discovery. He did not live to bring the news of it to Amsterdam. For after wintering on Novaya Zemlya he left his ice-bound ship to her fate and set out with his crew in two open boats. Most of the party reached home, but Barents himself died on June 30, 1597, and was given a grave in the arctic seas.

This exploit, in spite of the limited means for distributing news, caused quite a sensation in the shipping world. In London Barents must have been the talk of the town for some time, and a fit subject for allusion on the stage. "You are now sailed into the north of my lady's opinion, where you will hang like an icicle on a Dutchman's beard," says Fabian to Sir Andrew in Shakespeare's *Twelfth Night*. The English soon discovered the importance of Spitsbergen as a base for the whale-fishery and the island became a bone of contention between

9

Hollanders and Britons. Amsterdam merchants started a Northern Company to compete with the English whalers, and appointed Hugo Grotius their legal adviser. In 1614 they sent fourteen ships north under armed convoy, but no fighting ensued. A compromise was effected under which the island was divided between the two nations. The whale fishery rapidly developed into one of the most remunerative industries of Holland.

August, 1926

ERASMUS THE BARBARIAN

A Dutch Roman Catholic missionary has discovered the existence of a sixteenth-century statue of Erasmus in Japan! Visiting the exhibition of missionary work in Rome he noticed, among the Japanese exhibits, a photo of a polychrome image of carved wood, which is preserved in a heathen temple at Azuma. It is supposed to represent a preacher of the Christian faith, but how and when it got there no one knows at Azuma. The people there call it *Hollanda Ebisu*, which means "the Dutch Barbarian." The Dutch friar, on closer examination of the photo, discovered an inscription on a banderole which the barbarian holds in his right hand. ER...MUS he read, and underneath an illegible word of which the last letter was M, followed by the year 1598. He compared it with Holbein's famous portrait of the humanist and came to the conclusion that the sculptor must have copied the picture, both the features and the drapery being alike. But how did this image of the Dutch scholar find its way into a heathen temple of Japan? The answer to that question was supplied by Dr. E. Wiersum, the learned archivist of the city of Rotterdam, Erasmus' birthplace. In the year 1598 a squadron of five ships sailed from Holland to make its way to Japan through the Strait of Magellan. Only one of the five reached her destination, was there seized by the Japanese government, and perished shortly afterwards in the bay of Yedo. This ship was called *De Liefde*, but she had formerly gone by the name of *Erasmus* and the old figure-head representing the humanist must still have adorned the escutcheon after she was rechristened. And so it happened that the great educator of sixteenth-century Europe survives in effigy as a Dutch barbarian in twentieth-century Japan.

THE BEST-INFORMED MAN OF HIS AGE

Who ever heard a foreigner observe that Americans are slow and
indolent? A rare instance of such criticism is contained in a letter
addressed, of all foreigners, by a young Hollander traveling in America
to his sister at home: "I have noticed here a general tendency to do
everything at one's ease, which is extremely surprising to a Dutchman.
If you ask for something, the usual answer is 'by and by.' Few provide
for the day after tomorrow, and the majority only for today... They
sleep very long, from ten or eleven until seven or eight. The immensity of the country makes this inactivity possible. In our country
many live on a small plot of ground, here few on large fields. This
indolence is the source of kindheartedness and peace. The people,
on the whole, are actually happy here. But that which makes them
happy, would not make a European so."

Let me add at once, in justice to the critic, that his letter was
written at Boston in the year 1783. His picture of the easy-going
New Englander of the period was, doubtless, not a caricature. In
comparison to the Bostonians the merchants of Amsterdam and
Rotterdam must have seemed fussy go-getters and busy-bodies. The
writer of that letter was himself an active, energetic youth, an
impetuous boy of just over twenty, who saw an ambitious career
ahead too full of effort and noble endeavor for him to leave anything
to be done "by and by." He knew how to use his time and did not
allow the hours to pass unproductive. The letters that he wrote home
from his travels through this country are a testimony to the wide
range of his knowledge, to his firm grasp of realities and his imaginative
foresight. They have some historical value because of the comments
they contain on various aspects of American life, because of the
writer's estimates of many prominent personalities of that period,
and also because of the prominence to which the writer rose some
thirty years later. For he was no less a man than Gijsbert Karel van
Hogendorp, one of the greatest spirits that eighteenth-century Holland
has produced.

As the name means little, perhaps, to many of my readers, the
briefest possible biography may precede the account of his American
impressions. He was born in 1762 at Rotterdam, the son of patrician
parents. When he was ten years old, his father sailed for Java, there
to restore his shattered fortune, and the boy was sent to Berlin for
military training in the cadets' corps. At sixteen, he took part in
the Prussian campaign against Austria, and three years later, having
completed his studies at Berlin, he returned to Holland and joined

the Dutch guard as cornet. In 1783 and 1784 he traveled in America, back in Holland he resigned his commission, took up the study of law at Leyden, and, having taken his LL.D., was appointed Pensionary of his native city Rotterdam, a position held by Hugo Grotius one hundred and seventy years earlier. During the French interregnum from 1795 to 1813 he held no public office, but when in 1813 the people revolted against the oppressor, it was Van Hogendorp who, with two of his friends, formed a provisional government. In the Ministry, formed that same year, he became Secretary of State for Foreign Affairs, in 1815 he was elected President of the States General, and created a count by his king in recognition of the part he had taken in the restoration.

What was it that attracted this aristocrat to the new commonwealth across the Atlantic? "I wanted to know how states were organized," he wrote to his mother, "and America is forming itself into a republic. I wanted to enlighten myself concerning finances and systems of taxation, and nowhere can these be found in a simpler form than here. I wanted to know the measure of power that the people can exercise, and never did people possess more of it than do the Americans. I was anxious to learn what are the surest avenues for a republic that is peacefully engaged in commerce, and everybody here is occupied with that same question. I have tried to inform myself a little concerning the theory of commerce, and it is here, where commerce is very little complicated and where a thousand attempts are being made to expand it, that I can best apply that theory and form correct ideas that will serve me as a foundation in the future." In other words, he regarded America as a laboratory where future statesmen could come and watch experiments in state-building, government, commerce, finance; and in his Latin doctor's dissertation on "A rational division of contributions among federated states" he devoted a chapter to the solution which the thirteen states across the Atlantic had found for that problem. He was a relative of Mr. P. J. van Berckel, the first Dutch Minister to the United States, in whose company he crossed to America, and through his influence he obtained access to the leading men in commerce and politics. Hancock entertained him at Boston, General Lincoln on his farm at Hingham, he was the guest of General Washington at Mount Vernon, Thomas Jefferson took a fancy to him and wrote him letters after his return to Holland, Robert Morris supplied him with detailed information about the Bank of North America, he was dined by the President of the Congress, who confided to him his suspicions of Mr. Morris's power, and the ladies in Boston made quite a fuss about the young Dutch officer who "looked so much like Lafayette as a brother resembles his brother."

He was much interested in the problem of equality, not because, as an aristocrat, he dreaded its implications, but on the contrary, because he admired it in principle and wanted to know how it worked out in practice. "Here one can examine best the natural inequality, with all its consequences, because it has not been mixed, or at least less than elsewhere, with inequality before the law." He found that "'gentlemen' and 'persons in lower life' is here a general distinction. 'To dress and to behave like a gentleman' is a very common description. But 'to be a gentleman' is evidently not sufficient 'to be introduced into genteel company.' The carrier who drove me from Cape Ann to Boston was a captain in the army and had been in the state's service. He was everywhere treated on an equal footing with me, he took me to the Governor, and was, in a word, 'a gentleman.' Nevertheless, he declined Mr. Hancock's invitation to dinner, and although the latter, after the man's departure, said to the company present, 'You saw that I tried my best to keep him here,' still he invited him in such an artful way as to leave the door wide open for a refusal."

Hogendorp spent fully two months in Boston, a week in New York, a month in Philadelphia, and went from there to Annapolis, "a city more given to dissipation than any I have seen in America." Congress was in session there, and Hogendorp had ample opportunity to meet the leaders of the young Republic. Jefferson was the man whom he admired most. Dr. Van Vollenhoven recently published in the *Rotterdam Yearbook* four letters from Hogendorp to Jefferson of which the originals are preserved in the Library of Congress. "The esteem of a man of your character," he wrote, "is a great reward of my endeavors to deserve it, but his affection makes me happy. A correspondence for the remainder of our life I did propose and do now accept eagerly, as it perpetuates those feelings." Jefferson's estimate of his young friend is unequivocally expressed in the short note with which he introduced him to General Washington: "This will be delivered to you by Monsr. de Hogendorff, a relation of Mr. van Berckel's. A very particular acquaintance with him here has led me to consider him as the best informed man of his age I have ever seen. Nature and application seem equally to have concurred in fitting him for important business."

Hogendorp spent a few days at Mount Vernon in April, 1784. The meeting with the great general did not come up to the young man's high-strung expectations. He was probably spoiled by the social success he had scored in Boston, Philadelphia, and Annapolis, and finding his host little responsive to his vivacious talk and his incessant questioning on all sorts of subjects, he evidently tried to soothe the hurt to his own vanity by pretending that he was disappointed in the general. "Mrs. Washington took it ill that I did not adore her husband, for she has more penetration than the great man, and she has said some very sharp things to me. But that confirmed me in my opinion, for if I had been mistaken she would have been less piqued."

It did not surprise him to find no genius in the hero. For Hogendorp, a child of that romantic era which discovered the folk song, the communal art of the people, was inclined to credit great historical happenings to the genius of the people, rather than to individual leadership. "How is it," he asked, "that we attribute great events, a mighty revolution, to the genius of a few men, and very often of one only? It seems to me that in so doing we make a sacrifice of our reason to our indolence. For it is easier to say, this is the man who did everything, and then to admire him and to adorn him with fanciful virtues, than to investigate what were the favorable circumstances, what is the genius of a nation, whence does the nation derive its distinctive character, in order to explain from various causes the event which a combination of countless causes has brought about." And when he had returned to Holland, he added to his notes of the trip this tribute to the American nation: "I now believe that the nature of the people has accomplished nearly everything, and that talents and geniuses, of whom there are hardly any, have consequently done nothing."

February, 1927

THE BLURB

From the Epistle Dedicatory to the blurb is an aspect of the progress from aristocratic to democratic society. Still "progress is a terrible thing," said William James, witness the blurb, he might have added. That word of the American thinker stands as motto on the title page of *Amerika Levend en Denkend* (America living and thinking), a collection of notes jotted down by Dr. J. Huizinga on an extensive trip through the United States. The Dutch historian came to this country in 1926 as a guest of the Laura Spelman Memorial Foundation. He might have called his stray jottings, he says, "Conflicting Reflections." For the traveler in America is swayed from hour to hour between acceptance and resistance, and even in retrospection the contrasts never fully merge into harmony. He found more to resist than to accept. He is, as a good Hollander, frankly critical, although he admits with Newtonian modesty that his observations among a people of a hundred million can never be more than the pastime of a child that with its toy pail is scooping shells, and a few shrimps, and a starfish from the ripple on the beach. "Perhaps it is the necessity," he remarks, "of finding our distance that induces so many of us Europeans to have each our say about America. For while aware of America's otherness, we hear a warning voice within us saying *tua res agitur*, your own destiny is involved." The feeling, which in Dr. Huizinga's case amounts to fear, that the process by which life is developing in America is essentially the same as that which Europe, at a much slower rate though, is destined to follow, has colored his comments on the life and thought of modern America.

Eight years ago, when he knew America only from books, he published a sketch of American life as the most typical instance of the unavoidable trend of modern society towards the mechanization of social forces. Every technical invention, he wrote, both shackles and releases human energy. The recent development of the radio has only confirmed him in that opinion. The broadcaster, it is true, unites the scattered listeners on isolated farms, on hospital beds, and in prison cells, with the crowds of town and city into a nation-wide audience, but no one who listens in chooses his own spiritual nourishment, or if one does, it is from a sadly restricted bill of fare *a la carte*. It is the same with the moving picture. By its limited means of expression, its emphasis on externals, and its appeal to the masses the film leaves numerous functions of the mind inactive, while forcing upon it a set of simplified interpretations of life which the multitude accepts as final.

In New York Dr. Huizinga was struck by the terrible waste which the unwieldy mechanism of city life makes unavoidable. Goods that are the wonderful products of ingenious techniques and human labor are scarcely touched and remain unenjoyed. Precious woods are felled every day for the manufacture of paper that litters the streets and the parks and the floors in the subways with dailies that have only been skimmed by indifferent readers. And passing on foot along the illuminated stores and theatres of Broadway, one might elegize upon all the light that burns without gladdening a soul, upon all the time that is wasted on aimless pleasures, on all the words that are never read, on all the shoes that are never worn, on all the silk that never drapes a shoulder, on all the flowers that fade behind the panes.

Dr. Huizinga quotes with approval Professor Overstreet's definition of art as "the power of selective emphasis," and he himself has consciously applied that method in sketching his picture of American life. In his selection of certain aspects for special discussion and of the illustrations that must exemplify those aspects he shows a keen eye for artistic effect. The American, he tells you, is temperamentally

15

a pragmatist, whose attitude, to quote William James, is "a looking away from first things, principles, categories, supposed necessities, and a looking towards last things, fruits, consequences, facts." In other words, he lives in the present with his mind intent upon the future, and Dr. Huizinga finds that tendency reflected in the custom of the college freshman calling his class after the year in which he will graduate. In Holland, on the contrary, the student's class takes its name from the year in which he enters college. That same attitude of mind, he observes, has brought the name of *scholar* into disrepute in America. When the papers refer to a college professor who does not teach one of the exact sciences, they usually call him an *educator*. The *scientist* requires no re-christening. His research promises fresh discoveries, new cures, better health, more happiness, greater comforts, larger dividends. But the historian and the philologist should be spared the name of *scholar*, which smacks too much of useless old books. The college professor can command prestige only as a ministering priest of the Goddess Education.

April, 1927

A LOVER OF THE PAST

"When Charles II of England heard that Gregorio Leti was writing a history of his court, he warned him to be careful not to give offence. 'I will do my utmost to obey your majesty, but were I as wise as Solomon I must offend someone,' he replied. 'Then imitate Solomon,' advised the king. 'Leave history alone and compose proverbs.' But Leti could not forbear writing his projected book. As soon as this work appeared the author was banished from England."

These lines serve as motto to Marjorie Bowen's latest volume *The Netherlands Display'd or the Delights of the Low Countries.* (New York: Dodd, Mead & Co.) Their purpose is obvious. However, after a careful reading of the book, I fail to see any ground for the author's implied fear lest she offend some Dutchman, let alone be banished from Holland. Her eulogy of the Netherlands runs from cover to cover across no fewer than 472 pages. How could any Hollander deny entrance to a visitor so appreciative of the delights of his country and so indefatigable in their praise? The average Dutchman is as much averse as the Englishman to looking a gift horse in the mouth, though I wonder whether, if he did, he would be any the wiser for what he saw. Marjorie Bowen's gift is so gracious a tribute to Holland that one feels ashamed of reading her book in a critical mood. Let us blame the publisher's proofreader for the misprints which, like a swarm of flies in a summer parlor, have stained the mirror of the author's page, and let us thank her for the vivid and colorful pageantry that she has reflected in its flyblown surface. It is a magic glass which has the power of mirroring scenes that have vanished from view. For Marjorie Bowen, while traveling through the provinces of the Netherlands, has no eye for the present. Modern life is to her a blight upon the beauty of the past, and she has wandered from place to place pretending not to see the ugly symptoms of the disease. In many an old town she had no need of pretending, for "the Netherlands are intensely individual and different from any other country in the world, and this extraordinary local atmosphere has been up till the present preserved more completely than in most parts of Europe, though it is disappearing definitely enough in the larger towns; it is studies in this atmosphere that the present book offers." In these words the author has defined her purpose. She takes her readers on a sentimental journey through the Netherlands evoking from the actual sights she visits the life and manners of a more beautiful bygone age.

Lovers of history will find the author a fascinating guide. For that bygone age is to her a living reality. The most interesting object that she has found in "the festive little town" of Arnhem is the tomb of Charles of Egmont, last Duke of Gueldres, a heroic figure of the sixteenth century who "having lost in his old age the beloved land for which he had fought so fiercely, winning, losing, winning, losing, for half a century, died of chagrin and was given those honours in death which he had just resigned in life." But even in death the old warrior seems to Miss Bowen "to remain the most vital in Arnhem!" She knows him better than does the guide who shows sightseeing parties round the church where he lies buried. For though this man assures you that Charles of Egmont was unmarried, we learn from the author that "hc wedded in 1518, when he was already fifty years old, Elizabeth, daughter of the Duke of Brunswick-Lüneberg, by whom he had no children." Guides should know their business when Marjorie Bowen is one of the party.

Composers of memorial inscriptions also come in for correction and reproof: "In the Roman Catholic Church of St. Michael, in Zwolle, is a monument to Thomas a Kempis, and on the site of the monastery is a monolith to his memory, rather heavy and dour and too much like a tombstone, which boldly claims De Imitatione for Thomas, without any hint at a possible disputation of the honor." But is this not a bit over-severe? The expression of historical scepticism is out of place on a monument. One cannot give visible shape to one's reverence for a great man and the same time warn the public that there is cause for calling his greatness in question. Hero worship can never be a half-hearted devotion. Imagine a Shakespeare society erecting a statue of the dramatist and ordering an inscription to be carved into the base which hints at Bacon's claim to the honor. It is a matter of course that one does not place a man on a pedestal unless one be sure that the pedestal is strong enough to bear him.

One thing is certain, at any rate, that Thomas need not fear the rivalry of Jean Gerson, the famous Chancellor of the University of Paris. The ascription of the *Imitation* to this prelate is founded on the flimsiest of evidence and is no longer urged at the present day, not even in France. The many Dutchisms in the Latin that the pious author wrote would be inexplicable if he had not lived in either the Netherlands or Lower Germany. There was no peace to be had, he wrote, except *in angello cum libello*, in a little corner with a booklet, of which the Dutch rendering is *in een hoekje met een boekje*. In what other language would the literal translation of those words yield a reproduction of the Latin rhyme? The author's name may not have been *Thomas a Kempis*, but his home was, no doubt, in some Dutch-speaking region. And since there is an intimate literary and spiritual relationship between the *Imitation* and writings that emanated from the Brotherhood of the Common Life in Overysel, the Dutch province of which Zwolle is the capital, there is every reason to rely on the fifteenth-century tradition that Thomas a Kempis is the author.

He had his models, to be sure, and used them with a freedom that, in our day, would not escape the charge of plagiarism. The first of the four books has been proved to be an adaptation of a Latin letter of a Dutch canon regular, whose name was Johannes van Schoonhoven. A German scholar, Dr. Paul Hagen, has brought to light an older version of the second and third books, which the author of the *Imitation* remodeled to suit his purpose, and recently Dr. J. van Ginneken has argued quite plausibly that this older version is from the hand of Geert Groote, the fourteenth-century founder of the Brotherhood of the Common Life. The *Imitation* is a composite work less expressive of an individual than a communal devotion, the purest and noblest record of that inner experience which the mystics of the Ysel valley regarded as the real life.

June, 1927

A MODERN DAVID

"And it came to pass, when the evil spirit from God was upon Saul that David took an harp and played with his hand: so Saul was refreshed, and was well, and the evil spirit departed from him." That is a very old story, but a story ever new. Let me tell you a fresh version of it, a tale of a modern harpist who became a healer of suffering souls. His name is Willem van de Wall, and Holland is his native country. He studied his art at the Conservatoire at The Hague, and was for a time a wandering musician, playing the harp in orchestras at Leipzig, Hanover, Dresden, Stettin, St. Petersburg, and in this country first in the orchestra of the New York Metropolitan Opera and subsequently in that of Mr. Walter Damrosch. His part in the orchestral music was naturally an inconspicuous one, and in the long intervals between moments when he touched the chords he had ample time to watch his colleagues and study their faces. What feelings did those features express? What mystery was concealed behind those impassive masks? Why should men apparently so unemotional take to music as a profession? What did this symphony mean to them? Did it give them oblivion of themselves and their humdrum lot, or did they give utterance in its rhythms to their subconscious ego which, without music, would remain inarticulate? These and similar questions began to absorb him to such an extent that he decided to take up the study of psychology and metaphysics, hoping to find an answer there. While playing, at Washington, D.C., in the Marine Band, he found time for a systematic reading of the principal literature on these subjects, especially the works of Freud and his school. And after three years of research he felt sure that he could make his music serve a nobler end than mere entertainment.

There is in Washington a group of amateurs that calls itself the Washington Opera Company. His association with these music lovers gave him his first opportunity to apply his ideas. He began to discuss with them, in an open forum, philosophical problems in the operas being prepared for production, but it was not long before several of his listeners began to bring their own problems to him. All that they needed, he found, was an opportunity to unburden their minds, to give vent to pent-up feelings that were too much for them. They often went away thanking him for advice he had not given, for it sufficed that they had spoken out. Their amateur efforts in music were actuated by that same craving for relief from mental anxieties. To forget for a while their ordinary daily selves, to feel their lonely minds caught up in a communal emotion, that was what music meant to them. And if those people of normal mentality found consolation in rhythm and harmony, how much greater a blessing then must music be to the stricken souls of the mentally incapacitated!

The Washington Opera Company was financed by the War Camp Community Service, and while engaged in experimental work of this kind among army recruits, Mr. Van de Wall made the acquaintance of Dr. Orlando Lewis, then General Secretary of the American Prison Association. "You have a message that we can use," Dr. Lewis said to him, and at his instigation he returned to New York to experiment there with the population of settlements, workhouses, reformatories, prisons. After an eight weeks' trial, Dr. Lewis formed the Committee for the Study of Music in Institutions, and Mr. Van de Wall was appointed its field director. The results he accomplished in this capacity were so remarkable that the work was extended to Pennsylvania and Mr. Van de Wall became a staff member of the Bureau of Mental Health, Department of Welfare, for the State, and a field worker among the various State institutions for the care of the mentally sick, the feeble-minded, and delinquent and criminal defectives.

Mr. Van de Wall does not claim that music is a panacea for the treatment of the mentally abnormal. It does not cure, but it makes the patient's mind receptive for various forms of therapy. It acts as a physical and as a psychic lever lifting submerged springs of energy into consciousness and bringing new feelings and thoughts and reactions into play. One day he visited a women's prison when force had just been used to squelch an attempt at insurrection. It would not be safe, he was told, to congregate the inmates for communal singing while they were in that ugly mood. However, he insisted that the prisoners should at least be given a chance to prove that they could behave. The cells were opened and the women swept into the classroom in a stampede. He had them start with the Star-Spangled Banner, which they roared, then followed the Battle Hymn, and by a carefully planned gradation they ended up, after half an hour with "Stars of the Summer Night" and that beautiful line, "She sleeps, My Lady, sleeps." To have started with that number would have meant failure and pandemonium. Starting musically at the point where he found them emotionally, he brought about, by a calming-down programme of emotional self-expression, a state of mental equilibrium and social order such as no force could have compelled. He respected the ringleaders in their self-assumed mastery over the others, and seeing themselves recognized and trusted as leaders, they became his assistants in restoring order. When the inmates are not in a seditious temper, he will use the texts of the songs for a talk about social and ethical principles. In the moods created by the singing, they are susceptible to the discussion of problems on which the folksongs are aesthetic commentaries. It is Mr. Van de Wall's experience that his pupils in jails and reformatories are just as eager to experience new thoughts as new emotions. They thanked him for lifting their thoughts up to the level to which the music had raised them emotionally. The therapeutic value of music lies in its power to turn the mentally afflicted from sullen resistance and morbid egotism to a receptive and trusting frame of mind, which is a prerequisite for successful psychical treatment.

Let me, in conclusion, quote one passage from Mr. Van de Wall's own writings. It is one of his sad tasks to bring comfort to those who are condemned to death. The doomed men in their agony are eager for mental relief by singing and prayer. "They listen and listen to the music with the intensity of the grip of the drowning. They pray for music. It has in some cases done what no other agency has power to effect, not even the spoken word of consolation. As for the writer of these lines, he has played music of the most elevating types on very impressive occasions, but he never felt more deeply the sacred function of music than when utilizing it to give some support and relief to those outcasts. If this support had been given to them and accepted by them before they started their career of crime, it might have moulded their moods and characters along lines of beauty."

July, 1927

CHARLES READE

An author's wife to whom I was forced to confess one day that I had not read her husband's latest novel, said in reply: "You need not be in a hurry; that book will live." She could not have given me a more felicitous answer, for it saved me from embarrassment and gave to herself legitimate satisfaction in asserting her husband's claim to immortality. I wish that I had always acted on the principle implied by her words. If I had waited for the verdict of the infallible critic Time, I should not have wasted so many precious hours on books that did not deserve, and were not destined to live. Allow a book a period of thirty years to justify its existence in print, and you may be reasonably sure to get something worth while from the author in return for the tribute that you pay him by reading his work. If his fiction can survive a generation, it bids fair to survive many more, and in reading such a book one is conscious of the tie that binds us to the dead and to the unborn. To be aware of that bond is a pleasure that one can best indulge in vacation time, for the rush and hurry of our workaday world keep our minds fixed on the immediate present. No better way, therefore, of using one's freedom from labor in a summer retreat than to read an old book whose beauty has proved to be more than a passing glitter, and which is likely to be read and enjoyed by those who come after us.

I found such a time-binding book in Charles Reade's *The Cloister and the Hearth*, the tragic love story of Gerard Elias' son and Margaret Brant, the parents of Desiderius Erasmus. It unfolds a picture of fifteenth-century life in Holland, Germany, France and Italy, which, colorful and alive with dramatic incident, holds the reader spell-bound by its convincing realism. And no wonder that the romance of Gerard's wanderings should seem so true to the life it portrays; Charles Reade, in picturing his hero's travels, was aided by the traveler's immortal son. For Erasmus, says the author, "first scholar and divine of his epoch, was also the heaven-born dramatist of his century. Some of the best scenes in this book are from his pen and illumine the pages where they come." Thus Reade makes us see the Europe that Gerard Elias' son traversed on foot through the artistic vision of Erasmus. I do not know another book in which the great scholar, estranged from our age by the lapse of time and the lapse of Latin learning, is brought so near to us, although the story ends when his own life begins. The tragedy of Gerard and Margaret's love belongs to fiction, but this fiction, so beautifully interwoven with the facts gleaned from their son's inimitable Latin, lends to our mental picture of the humanist the human touch that the biographies but seldom give.

My interest in Reade once aroused, I took up another of his novels, *It Is Never Too Late to Mend*. I wish I had known this book when I wrote my previous *Monthly Letter*. It gives a picture of life in an English prison three quarters of a century ago, where separate confinement, absolute silence, unproductive labor imposed for no other purpose than to exhaust the laborer, starvation, and physical and mental torture made up the systematic treatment of its inmates. Our time is often called an irreligious age, but when one realizes its advance in the humane care of the poor and the helpless, of the criminal and the insane, as compared to the methods employed in the god-fearing Victorian era, it seems impossible to believe in our own retrogression. Dickens and Reade teach us some self-respect. Into that den of horrors which Victorian England called a jail, Reade has introduced his chaplain Eden as the enlightened apostle of Christian fellow love. He ousts the bullies and the tyrants, gives individual care to every prisoner's needs, and wakes up the dulled minds that had been so long in want of air, of light, and of intercourse with human beings. One of those was poor Strutt, "an old man crushed to clay by separate confinement recklessly applied. So alarming was this man's torpor to Mr. Eden that after trying in vain to interest him in the garden, he ventured on a very strong measure. He had learned from Strutt that he could play the fiddle; what does he do but runs and fetches his own violin into the garden, tunes it, and plays some most inspiring, rollicking old English tunes to him. A spark came into the fishy eye of Strutt. At the third tune the old fellow's fingers began to work impatiently. Mr. Eden broke off directly, put fiddle and bow into Strutt's hand. The merry tunes as Strutt played them sounded like dirges, but they enlivened him as they sighed forth. They stirred his senses, and through his senses his mind, and through his mind his body, and so the anthropologist made a fiddle help save a life, which fact no mortal man will believe whose habit it is to chatter blindfolded about man."

I need not apologize, I believe, for this lengthy quotation. For it affords an instructive comment on the story which I told about the work of Mr. Willem Van de Wall. Notice that Reade called Mr. Eden's having recourse to the violin "a very strong measure," meaning evidently that this appeal to music was a bold innovation on his part, and also that he did not expect any faith in its effect on poor Strutt from the learned who talked and wrote about man in the abstract and devised scientific prison schemes without ever having studied a criminal's mind. Chaplain Eden and his creator Reade were forerunners of the movement of which Mr. Van de Wall is now the leader in this country. The ideas he is turning into practice were in the air seventy-five years ago. But who would claim that the Victorian era in which the Edens had to fight for a hearing was better than ours, in which a Van de Wall is given a free hand to be active in Mr. Eden's spirit?

October, 1927

OF A DUTCH CHURCH IN LONDON

Some time ago I visited a Dutch Protestant church which was different from all other Dutch Protestant churches I have seen in that it was open to visitors on weekdays. A Protestant's religion in Holland is during the week, apparently, his own concern; only on Sundays is he allowed to make it a part of the communal life. There are many old churches which, in spite of the sixteenth-century iconoclasts, have preserved some of their mediaeval beauty, and sightseers who care for that beauty can gain admission by applying to the verger and paying him the required entrance fee. If you told him that you came not for any aesthetic reasons but for an hour of prayer and meditation, he would, no doubt, admit you for your florin, but probably regard you as a crank. Who would pay that much for the privilege of being alone with his thoughts and empty pews? The exception to the rule is the Dutch church in London. The minister and elders are aware that their open-door policy is something out of the common, for there is a notice up at the church door proclaiming its week-day hospitality. In a land of open churches Dutch Protestants must follow the majority.

The London church is in the very heart of the old city, where the streets run criss-cross and narrow alleys wind their crooked ways to hidden courts and old, mysterious burial-grounds. Its location is between Throgmorton and Great Winchester Streets. Here stood, before the Reformation, a convent of Augustine Friars, a large part of which, at the time of the Dissolution, was granted to William Pawlet, Lord St. John, afterwards Marquis of Winchester. The rest of the old building was given, in 1551, to a congregation of Dutch refugees, who called it the Temple of the Lord Jesus. They had to leave it again in Queen Mary's reign. The members were dispersed, and their church was used for a time as a store house for the provision of the Navy and subsequently by the Florentine merchants to say mass in. But when Queen Elizabeth came to the throne, the former grant by King Edward vi was fully confirmed and the church restored to the Dutch who have remained in possession down to the present day.

It was not always an undisturbed possession. Early in the reign of King James a dispute arose between the Dutch consistory and the Marquis of Winchester as to which had a right to the churchyard. For several years past, says a document of 1611, the consistory had observed that the walls of their church were much damaged and its windows blocked up by the wood which John Day, a carpenter, piled up against them, and he would not allow a ladder to be put up against the wall for the purposes of repair; and on weekdays the hammering and sawing in his place disturbed the service. At the advice of some of the brethren inquiries were made as to the right the Dutch had to the churchyard. A lawyer discovered that it was not mentioned in the deeds of the Marquis, whence it was concluded that it was "concealed" land and as such obtainable from the King by supplication. The Marchioness, hearing that inquiries were being made as to her husband's right to the churchyard, became alarmed, stopped the proceedings, and caused the consistory to be summoned before her father, the Earl of Exeter, who listened to their representations in a friendly way and made an agreement with them in the name of the Marquis. The latter undertook to make the carpenter pull down the sheds if the church would indemnify the man, and to restrain him from causing any disturbance during preaching time. And further, the Marquis would grant the Dutch congregation a lease for the churchyard for the term of sixty years, for which they should annually pay him and his heirs no more than two good Holland cheeses and two gammons of Westphalia bacon at the feast of the Annunciation of Our Lady. Though this was reasonable, the Dutch were not satisfied. They were anxious to own the whole churchyard and the houses, and so a purchase was concluded in the following year by which they acquired possession of the churchyard for the sum of £ 600.

One would think that a popular history of so old and interesting a monument would be obtainable at the church. But the verger had nothing of the kind for sale and doubted whether such a book existed. It cannot have been left unwritten because of lack of material, the church possesses a rich collection of old papers and documents from which its history may be gleaned, and these are all available in print, thanks to the painstaking industry and scholarship of Dr. Hessels, who has edited them in four imposing quarto volumes. In the sixteenth century the congregation must have been much larger than it is today. There are probably more Dutch people living in London now than in the reign of Queen Elizabeth, but at that early time they were nearly all refugees from Spanish persecution who had suffered for their Protestant faith and were not likely to fall away from it in exile. Every Dutchman then living in London was, as a matter of course, a member of the Dutch church in St. Austin Friars. They were the most numerous colony of aliens in the city. According to the census of 1567, there were 4,851 foreigners living in London, of whom 3,838 were Dutch.

So large a number of strangers was a matter of grave concern to the city government, especially since they were not easily induced to forget their native country and to exchange its language and its customs for the speech and the customs of the English. The melting pot did not function well in sixteenth-century London. The authorities, however, did not seek to make up for its failure by means of a preventive immigration law but by repressive measures which caused great hardships to the immigrants who had been admitted. An Act of Common Council of October 26, 1574, stated that "strangers have come in great numbers from beyond the seas, and that the children of these that are born within the realm are by law accounted English. But experience has proved that such children retain an inclination and kindly affection for the country of their parents, and partly by the example of their fathers they have become hurtful members of this realm and especially of this honorable city." It was, for these reasons, decreed that "no citizen of London shall henceforth take as apprentice any person whose father is not born within the Queen's dominion, the penalty being ten pounds for the first offence and for the second disfranchisement and exclusion from the liberties of the city." In 1589, the Common Council of London found it necessary to renew an old decree forbidding foreign teachers of children "to write within the city or the liberties thereof, or to keep any open shop, or to hang out any sign or table, or to set up any printed or written bills." Dutch children were not only excluded from the various handicrafts, they were even prevented from learning to read and write their native language.

However, most of these decrees remained a dead letter. The exigencies of life taught the English people that they could not do without the Dutch. When James I succeeded to the throne, the ministers (there were two in those days) and the elders of the Dutch church in St. Austin Friars made their humble address to the new King, who in his answer, which he delivered in French, promised the Dutch his protection, observing "how they had enriched the realm with many arts, manufactures, and sciences useful to the public." A look at the illustrations in Sir Walter Besant's *London in the Time of the Tudors* will show that our visual conception of the city in the sixteenth century is largely, if not exclusively, dependent on the work of Dutch painters and engravers. Anthony van de Wyngaerde engraved a panorama of London, Westminster, and Southwark about the year 1543, and another by Visscher shows us the city in Elizabeth's days. Another Dutch artist, Joris Hoefnagel, did a famous picture of Nonsuch Palace. The only realistic drawing of a stage setting in an Elizabethan theatre is by a Dutchman, and the features of William Shakespeare are familiar to us from the picture by Marten Droeshout prefixed to the folio edition of 1623. In the registers of the Dutch church in London, which have been edited by Mr. W. J. C. Moens, there are several entries relating to the Droeshouts, who were a family of engravers and artists from the Netherlands. When Charles I acceded to the throne in 1626, the members of the Dutch church joined in the city's festivities by the erection of a triumphal arch, which had been designed by Bernard Janssen, a well-known mason and tombmaker among the Dutch congregation. This man was probably a brother of Gerard Janssen, who made the bust of Shakespeare on his tomb in the church at Stratford on Avon. English poetry was able to celebrate the Sweet Swan of Avon in verse that was worthy of its immortal theme, but plastic art had to rely on the skill of Dutch aliens to perpetuate the poet's mortal being.

November, 1927

A DUTCH PLAYWRIGHT

In the nineties of the last century a British politician, Mr. Samuel Plimsoll, came over to the United States on a mission of good will and peace. He was anxious to contribute his modest share to the promotion of a better understanding between the two English-speaking nations, and with that object in view he visited this country to secure the adoption of a less bitter tone towards England in the historical textbooks then in use in American schools. To judge from the pro-British bias that Mayor Thompson of Chicago has discovered in the present-day teaching of American history, he must have succeeded but too well. The writers of textbooks whom he converted to his views have evidently overshot his indistinct aim. He ought to have drawn a Plimsoll's mark to indicate the limit to which the teaching of history might be loaded with pro-British propaganda. He had drawn such a mark before for a different purpose. For Mr. Plimsoll, long before he came to America to counteract the abuse of England and the English, led a crusade in his own country against abuses in the merchant marine. He protested especially against the so-called "coffin ships," unseaworthy and overinsured vessels in which unscrupulous shipowners were allowed by the law to risk the lives of their crews. On Plimsoll's motion in 1873, a royal commission was appointed, and in 1875 a government bill was introduced, which Plimsoll, though regarding it as inadequate, resolved to accept. On the 22nd of July, Mr. Disraeli, the premier, announced that the bill would be dropped. This was too much for Mr. Samuel Plimsoll. Shaking his fist in the Speaker's face, he denounced the opponents of the bill as villains bent on stifling the proposed reform under pressure of the wealthy shipowners. He had to make an apology for his unparliamentary behavior, but the country sided with him. Popular agitation forced the government to pass a bill which in the following year was amended into the Merchant Shipping Act. This Act contained strict provisions against overloading. The mark that indicates the limit to which a ship may be stowed is generally known as Plimsoll's mark.

In Holland similar abuses existed, but the Dutch Parliament had to wait for a dramatist's voice to awaken it to its duty. *The Good Hope* is the sarcastic title of the play with which Herman Heijermans appealed to the country on behalf of the crews of the North Sea fishing smacks. That was in the year 1900. Its unprecedented success on the stage started an agitation for better government control of seagoing craft resulting in the Ships Act of 1909, which provided much needed guarantees against ships putting to sea in unseaworthy condition. *The Good Hope* was a play with a purpose, but the purpose, in this instance, did not mar the artist's picture. No play of Heijermans, nor of any other Dutch author, is as popular in Holland, and more than twenty-five years after its first production it is still capable of keeping audiences spellbound by the truth of its characterization. The unmasking of the merciless capitalist has nothing to do with this persistent success. The playgoer of today sees in the shipowner not the embodiment of a wicked system, but a wicked man as there are wicked men among his victims. And it is this triumph of the author's creation of a living character over the symbol that he intended his creature to be which lifts his play from the mass of timely propaganda literature into the realm of timeless art.

The production of *The Good Hope* by the Civic Repertory Theatre was a test of its artistic value. What should a New York audience care though the fish that are brought to the Dutch market be all too dearly paid for? The cause that Heijermans championed must leave a New Yorker cold. Besides, he is reminded of its being a past issue by the dresses of the shipowner's wife and daughter. The Katwijk coffinship that gave the play its title belongs, with the ladies' trailing skirts, to a by-gone day. The dialogue, moreover, lacks the snappiness of the "clever lines" that seem to be the chief requirement demanded nowadays from the dramatist. Yet, in spite of all these traits that mark *The Good Hope* as an out of date production, it made a deep impression on the spectators and received high praise from the professional critics. Miss Eva Le Gallienne is to be congratulated on this auspicious opening of the Repertory Theatre's Second Season. It seems safe to predict that the name *The Good Hope*, if applied to her courageous enterprise, has no sarcastic implication.

Herman Heijermans was born in Rotterdam on December 3, 1864. His father intended him for a business career, but born bohemian as he was, he loathed the prospect of spending his life in an office among account books. The street and the greenroom were more attractive haunts to him, and as a reporter for the Amsterdam *Telegraaf* he started on a literary career. Gifted with a keen observation and with the painter's memory that can re-create the scenes observed in terms of art, he began to report his impressions of life in dramatic form. His first stage venture was a failure, but that rebuff did not dishearten him. The Dutch public was sceptical about the merits of original Dutch plays. So little of any lasting value had been written for the stage in Holland that it had become a generally accepted conviction that nothing good could come out of a Dutch dramatist's brain. The success of a Russian play, produced a few weeks after his own had been coolly received, seemed to confirm the popular scepticism. How tame was Heijermans' *Dora Kremer* compared to this stirring tragedy of *Ahasverus*, which, to quote a leading Amsterdam critic, had been written with tears. The day before its first night the papers carried a pathetic story about its unknown author, a certain Ivan Jelakowitch

28

who, a fugitive from persecution under the Czarist regime, had died in abject poverty in a London slum. You could tell from the play, another critic wrote, that this gifted outcast had dramatized his own experience, for *Ahasverus* had not been written, it had been lived. M. Antoine, the Director of the *Théatre Libre* in Paris, who was then emancipating the stage from outworn traditions, obtained the production rights for France, but in Paris the play was advertised as by Herman Heijermans. Called to account by his Dutch producers for robbing the author of his due credit, Heijermans took pleasure in confessing the absolute identity of the great Ivan Jelakowitch with his humble self. However, *Ahasverus* was undeniably a better drama than *Dora Kremer*, and the success that the author afterwards won in his own name seems to vindicate the public and the critics.

In championing the cause of the victims of the existing social order, Heijermans was apt to paint the contrast between the underdog and his exploiter in consciously exaggerated colors. The facility with which he wrote proved sometimes a pitfall for his artistic conscience. Too often, also, he let his wit outrun the judgment of his taste. But when time has winnowed the chaff, enough will remain that is of lasting value, and among that residue will be found *The Good Hope*. His success as a social reformer was due to the convincing power of his art, and that art is not less great for being used to serve a social end. When Heijermans died on November 22, 1924, leaving a widow and two children in straitened circumstances, the crews of Holland's merchant marine contributed to a fund for their relief. No homage would have touched his heart more deeply. Their gratitude proved that his drama had served its intended purpose. But that he had been able so to serve was owing to his creative fancy, which under the stress of his indignation could mold a thing of beauty out of the ugly facts of reality.

December, 1927

THE WEARISOME ROAD TO AMSTERDAM'S MONEY

Current events seem to be the vogue nowadays in the teaching of history. The interest in them is akin, no doubt, to the common love of the movies. Events on the run are a more exciting spectacle than the still picture of the becalmed past. They run criss-cross in most bewildering fashion, like the shapes of things and people in a futuristic painting; you cannot make out their interrelation, for the picture is blurred by their moving so fast and so close to our view. But this very bewilderment seems to be part of the pleasure. To be mystified is better fun than to have things explained. You cannot explain the present, you can only wonder at its confusion. The man who wants to understand must be content to study the still past; and comprehension will give the student such joy as makes the fun of the mystified seem a meagre fare. For I agree with Trader Horn that "looked at from a distance the Past is often as good as fiction." It *is* fiction in so far as our mental vision of it is to a great extent imaginary. We get the facts supplied to us by the historian, but we ourselves compose from these our private picture book of bygone days. And if we have reason to believe that the historian's supply of facts is unadulterated truth, the greater pride we shall take in the seeming realism of our fiction. The imaginative reader recognizes benefactors in the so-called de-bunkers of history.

Dr. P. J. Van Winter, author of *Het Aandeel van den Amsterdamschen Handel aan den Opbouw van het Amerikaansche Gemeenebest** (The Share of Amsterdam's Commerce in the Building-up of the American Commonwealth) belongs to this charitable type of historian. He does not indulge in sentimental illusions as to the motives that induced the thirteen American Colonies to seek aid in the seven United Provinces. They were not actuated, he tells us and proves to us, by any fond recollections of Holland's past struggle for freedom. Holland was to them not yesteryear's fellow in revolt, but tomorrow's potential money lender. They did not ask for inspiration but for credits. Their official spokesmen, it is true, were fond of alluding to the glorious rise of the Dutch Republic in the ordeal of the Spanish War, but the remembrance served as a bait for the Amsterdam goldfish, not as a moral tonic for themselves. The analogy, apparent to our after-wisdom, between the Dutch and American wars of independence, could not be clear to the American Colonists. They only knew that in the Dutch Republic plenty of money was available for investment. Agents from several of the thirteen States were negotiating in the seventies with Dutch financiers and bankers, Lee for Virginia, Trumbull for Connecticut, Searle for Pennsylvania, Ridley for Maryland, and Stephen Sayre on behalf of Congress. "The wearisome road to Amsterdam's money" is the title of one of Dr. Van Winter's chapters, and to follow him as he travels over the same route that those agents took, looking for evidence of their slow passage in the past, is an instructive but not a very exciting excursion.

Dr. Van Winter has a very low opinion of Departmental archives in Washington. He found them badly preserved and negligently cared for, sometimes even in chaotic condition. Only the diplomatic and

* The Hague: Martinus Nyhoff, 1927

consular documents had been filed in such a way as to make them easily accessible. Better care was taken of Personal Papers, thanks to the prevailing interest in strong and domineering figures, which mean more to the American mind than the indefinable, abstract State. I wish that the writer, during his visit to this country, had caught the infection of that love for the personal. We get glimpses in his story of Dutch merchants in America of whom we should like to know more than Dr. Van Winter cares to tell us. There is Alexander Gillon, of humble Rotterdam parentage, who, having risen to affluence and power in South Carolina, turned up again in Amsterdam as Commodore of the frigate *Union*. There is W. H. Van Hasselt, who abandoned his country estate and his attempts to grow silk and emigrated to Charleston, where he resumed his ill-fated experiments with silkworms. There is Henry Hope who, as Boston agent for his two brothers in Holland, laid the foundations for the great banking house of Hope and Co. which is still first among its peers in Amsterdam. There are the Amsterdam merchants De Neufville, father and son, both ardent promoters of American interests in Holland, who after the collapse of their great financial schemes found a refuge in America, the father with his wife and daughter in some village in the neighborhood of Boston, the son in Albany, where he earned a scanty livelihood as a glassblower until he fell a victim to religious mania and ended his days in an asylum. Here are the elements of adventure, romance, and tragedy which an historian with the novelist's sense for the personal might turn to account.

February, 1928

NOT WONDERFUL BUT MIRACULOUS

The word *wonderful* is no longer adequate to express our amazement at happenings that are full of wonder. It has been used so often in praising what is merely nice, or beautiful, or interesting that, when a wonder does happen, we must avoid the Anglo-Saxon term and call it miraculous. Our age has need of the Latin word, for miracles do happen nowadays. Aviation and radio are miracles to the layman, although he knows that no super-natural agency controls them, and radio is the greater miracle of the two. I base that comparative estimate on the manner in which our ancient ancestors imagined their realization. To imitate the birds and explore the sky seemed to the early Greeks a possible achievement for man; even to imitate the fish and explore the submarine world did not seem an impossibility two thousand years ago. Alexander the Great, says the Greek legend, made a large framework of iron, like a cage, wherein he placed a thick glass vessel, and in the bottom of the vessel was a hole large enough for the hand to go through. This opening was closed from inside, so that when the whole apparatus was submerged, the traveller might be able to open it quickly, and, putting his hand through, might draw in whatever he saw on the ground. To the cage he attached a chain 200 cubits long, and he ordered his men in the ship not to draw him up from the sea unless the chain was set in motion. But no fable or myth of the ancients ever imagined that man could speak to man across the seas. It was only the voice of a God which could accomplish that miracle. Daedalus and Icarus are the mythical precursors of Lindbergh, Alexander of legendary lore anticipated the exploits of William Beebe, but human imagination in the remote past never fancied that wonder to be humanly possible which Marconi has actually accomplished in our age. And his discovery enables even the humblest layman who has no notion of how it is done to avail himself of the miracle. Man will never learn to fly with a bird's native ease; it will remain to him a difficult art to be practised at the danger of his life. But he can speak, as the gods spoke of yore, from coast to distant coast across the ocean, without the need of acquiring a god-like utterance. On Monday, January 30, at half past nine in the morning, that miracle happened to me in an apartment of the Savoy-Plaza. There and then His Excellency, Mr. Richard M. Tobin, United States Minister at the Hague, inaugurated radio telephone service between this country and Holland, and by his kind invitation I was privileged to be present and exchange a few words in Dutch with Jonkheer F. Beelaerts van Blokland, the Netherlands Minister of Foreign Affairs at The Hague. It was wonderful to hear his voice come across as distinctly as if he had spoken from somewhere in New York. It was more than wonderful, it was miraculous.

A GREAT HYDRAULIC ENGINEER

Hollanders do not like "to go over one night's ice." With this picturesque simile they describe their native caution in accomplishing the things they undertake. In the year 1641 the engineer Leeghwater draughted the first plan for the reclamation of the great Harlem lake, but not until 1852 was that inland sea laid dry and turned over to the cattle breeder and the farmer. Mr. J. P. Amersfoordt, a gentleman farmer and a PH. D. and LL. D. of Leyden University, was one of the first to buy a large farm in the new polder, and at the very spot where in former days the Amsterdam people had come to bathe, he began to drive the first steam plough ever seen in the Netherlands through the rich soil that was once the bottom of the lake. *Badhoeve*, Bath Farm, he called his place. Satisfaction with his new experiment made him an enthusiastic advocate of a still more ambitious scheme of reclamation. In 1849 Mr. B. P. F. van Diggelen proposed a plan for the drainage of the Zuiderzee, and Mr. Amersfoordt became one of its most ardent supporters. He designed, and made out of wood, a geological relief map to serve as an exhibit at the world exhibition held at Philadelphia in 1876. The map bore this rhymed legend,

> Harlem Lake is drained
> And drained is the Y,
> If peace is maintained,
> Zuiderzee gets dry.

As a matter of fact, it was just because peace was not maintained that the plans for its reclamation are now being carried into execution. The enormous expense at which the Dutch army was kept mobilized during the World War, made the Hollanders realize how little, comparatively speaking, the drainage of the Zuiderzee would cost them. The total expenditure, according to optimistic estimates of ten years ago, would amount to no more than half the sum the country had to pay in one year for the maintenance of its neutrality during the war. If the taxpayers could bear the burden of those costly years of armed preparedness, they could certainly bear the smaller expense of an enterprise that would yield profits to the next generation. And so it happened that, while the Great Powers were at war, the Dutch Parliament passed a bill for the reclamation of the Zuiderzee, which was estimated to turn 890,000 acres of turbulent water surface into a harmless inland lake. Only those parts of the new lake where the bottom is of a loamy composition were to be reclaimed and added to the surrounding mainland, the portion that was to be left undrained being destined to serve as a fresh-water reservoir.

Dr. C. Lely, in whose inventive mind this great scheme took birth, will arrive in New York for a short visit to this country, during which he will deliver a number of lectures on the reclamation of the Zuiderzee. No Hollander is more competent to speak with authority on this subject. As long ago as 1886 he was called in as an expert by the Zuiderzee Association, on whose behalf he published a reclamation scheme in 1891. The plan that was finally adopted in 1918 was an elaboration of that earlier draught, and Dr. Lely himself was the Minister of Waterways during whose tenure of office the reclamation bill passed into law. Dr. Lely has served his country in other capacities, as a member of both Houses of Parliament, as Governor of Dutch Guiana, which the Hollanders call Suriname, as Commissioner of

Public Works at The Hague, and as President of the Royal Institute of Engineers. But he will be best remembered in days to come as the originator of that great feat of hydraulic engineering, the solution of the Zuiderzee problem.

OF CIVIC SELF-RESPECT

South of Amsterdam, in a beautifully wooded section of the country, lies the rural town of Baarn, where many wealthy commuters have their homes. The town council and the burgomaster take a justifiable pride in the community for which they are responsible. They see to it that no street within its precincts has its aspect spoilt by a garbage heap on a vacant lot or by the unsightly spectacle of an empty tenement falling into ruin. Even a haunted house must keep up a show of respectability. Hence the Council passed an ordinance in 1926 declaring it unlawful for the owner of a house destroyed by fire to leave it in its disreputable condition and authorizing the town police to compel him either to demolish or to rebuild it within a specified period. But the Executive Committee of the Provincial States, to whom this ordinance had to be submitted for approval, objected to it on the ground that its enforcement would restrict the owner's right of property and would give too large a scope to the subjective taste of the town police. Hence the Committee advised the Crown to veto the ordinance. But there is in Holland a State Commission for the Preservation of Monuments — the word monument to be taken in the sense of relic of the past that for its beauty or its historical value deserves to be saved — and this body, having been consulted by the Minister of Arts on behalf of the Crown, dug into the past and found that the Baarn ordinance was not a freakish innovation but in line with a well-established tradition, which could be traced back as far as the fifteenth century. In two ordinances of the seventeenth century the right of the city Magistrates to interference was definitely based on aesthetic grounds; where negligence of a property owner was deemed to spoil the architectural beauty of the town, he could be compelled to remove the eye-sore at his own cost. To judge from the aspect of the average American city, the Baarn ordinance would find little favor in this country, and it may be that the property owner's liberty is a more precious principle than the aesthetic sensitiveness of the public at large. But since that liberty is already restricted in so many ways, the question might be asked whether a further limitation in the name of civic self-respect would entail a serious injustice.

JANUS DOUSA

Janus Dousa is probably an unfamiliar name to most of my American readers, unless they retain a clear recollection of the pages which Motley devoted to the episode of the siege of Leyden, for he played a hero's part in that historic tragedy. Nature had not intended him to be a man of action. The Latinized name by which Jan van der Does liked to call himself is evidence that his own inclinations were towards study and retirement. He was a nobleman by birth and a scholar by profession; he wrote Latin verse and edited classical texts, he was an authority on the early history of Holland, and published an edition of a rhymed chronicle composed by a Dutch monk about the year 1300. There is a portrait of him in the Municipal Museum at Leyden, which shows him, with his wife, in the midst of their family of nine children. It was painted about 1592, when the perilous days of the siege were long past. Even the eldest children in the group do not seem old enough to have retained any personal recollections of the stress and strife that their parents had passed through. They look a serious family, though, as if the unremembered past had bequeathed to them an instinctive knowledge of the perils and vicissitudes of life and, with it, a bold determination to face them with their father's fortitude. *Ante Omnia Musae* was Janus Dousa's favorite motto, but when his country was in danger he abandoned the Muses for a time and served Mars instead. He was a champion of Dutch freedom from the very beginning of the revolt against the Spanish King, was sent by Prince William on a diplomatic mission to England to implore Queen Elizabeth's aid, and was commander of the forces within the city of Leyden during the harassing months of the siege. And having helped in saving Leyden with his sword, he served it no less devotedly with his pen. For when Prince William of Orange decided to reward the city for its endurance with a university, Jan van der Does was foremost in helping to lay the foundations and the first to be appointed on its Board of Trustees. And when the University Library was established, Janus Dousa again took charge of the books. It was a small but precious collection, to judge from an early print of 1610, showing a double row of eleven one-shelf cases with reading desks underneath, to which the books were attached by chains. Four arched windows on either side let in sufficient light to read by. Strange to say, the students, by the testimony of this early print, were allowed to bring their dogs with them into this sanctuary of learning. I love to imagine Janus Dousa ruling here as librarian and finding peace among books after the stormy years of his early manhood. Those dogs disturb the tranquillity of that mental picture.

Americans, accustomed to seeing a new college, fully equipped, rise out of the ground in a few years, will be interested in the account of the haphazard way in which Holland's first seat of learning was established. No special buildings were erected for the housing of the young institution. There were several abandoned monasteries within the city walls that could serve the purpose. The convent of St. Barbara seemed to meet the requirements, and, to judge from the accounts of student life in those early days, the name was not inappropriate for a building where young barbarians had to be taught the essentials of culture. Two years later, however, the university, for unknown reasons, removed its headquarters to the vacated Beguinage, and in 1581 it took possession of the former church of the White Nuns, of the Order of St. Dominic, which is still its central building at the present day. The male sex invaded the quarters once occupied by women only, and for three hundred years the old church of the White Nuns remained closed to girl students. Not until the last decade of the nineteenth century were women admitted to the lecture rooms, and now they form so large a percentage of the student body that the spirits of the White Nuns must feel satisfied that their ancient rights to the building have been vindicated.

Few changes have occurred in the general plan and architecture of Leyden in the course of the past three hundred years. The old ramparts have been turned into parks that circle the city with pleasant avenues, beyond which the city keeps expanding into the surrounding polder land, but the old town that Dousa knew, within its ancient ring of walls and moats, looks very much the same as it did at the time of the siege. Even the *Burcht* is still standing, which was a venerable antiquity to him and his contemporaries. They believed it to be an ancient Roman stronghold, and claimed for their city, on the strength of that relic, a dignity surpassing that of any other Dutch city. As a matter of fact it cannot be much older than a thousand years, and was probably erected by the inhabitants of that part of the Rhine delta to serve as a refuge and fortress against raids of marauding vikings. They chose a strategic point for its erection at the confluence of two arms of the Rhine which hold an island in their embrace. Any ship sailing up the river from the North Sea could be seen from this vantage point and barred from further progress up the stream. At the time of the Spanish siege, six centuries after its erection, it had long ceased to serve any military purpose. Civic pride, however, kept the old stronghold intact that it might serve as evidence of

Leyden's antiquity. There are aristocrats and plebeians among the cities of Europe, and the city that can trace its origin to a Roman settlement belongs to the highest rank of nobility.

THE STATEN-BIJBEL

On Sunday, December 9th, at four o'clock in the afternoon, a service was held in the Cathedral of St. John the Divine which had a special interest for Hollanders and friends of Holland. The Netherlands Minister, Dr. J. H. van Roijen, on behalf of Her Majesty Queen Wilhelmina's Government, presented to the Cathedral a copy of the first edition of the *Staten-Bijbel*, the official version of the Scriptures in Dutch, which was published in 1637 by the order of the States General. Dr. Henry Evertson Cobb, Senior Minister of the Collegiate Reformed Protestant Dutch Church of the City of New York, dwelt in his address on that occasion upon the influence of this book on the lives of the Dutch colonists in New Netherland. The Dutch settlers probably read little else besides this Bible. It was the anchor by which their native speech in its isolation was kept from drifting and retained its contact with the speech of the Netherlands. In the language of the *Staten-Bijbel* they heard Peter Stuyvesant issue his orders and Reverend Megapolensis preach his sermons from the pulpit of the church in the fort. It was a language very similar to the Dutch of present-day Holland, and yet, how different it sounds to us who are living today! There is a grandeur of style in that old version that is no longer ours. We are sensitive to its eloquence, but it is an eloquence no longer suited to our needs. To the large majority of Hollanders in the seventeenth century the Word was the only word they knew. But the word, in this present age, has become more vociferous and all-intrusive. Then every household used to listen at the breakfast table to a reading of a lesson from the Bible, but now the morning paper spreads the word. At night, before retiring, again a chapter from the Book was read aloud and a prayer spoken in its language; a stranger's voice coming over the radio now holds the attention with a bedtime story. The word has gained in volume a hundred-thousandfold, and the hundreds of thousands who broadcast it by print and sound wave are different beings from the orthodox Calvinists who rendered the Bible from the original Hebrew and Greek into seventeenth-century Dutch. One-book people are scarce nowadays. The eloquence achieved in modern Dutch literature is a composite thing, a prism of many facets, whereas the grand style of the *Staten-Bijbel* reflects the unruffled tranquillity of a mind that knows no doubts. No Hollander of the present day could write a history of Governor Stuyvesant's time in Staten-Bijbel prose.

It is a different time as we see it from the time it was to him and his contemporaries, and a different style must give expression to our more sophisticated mood.

A DEBUNKER OF HISTORY

Mr. Hendrik Willem van Loon's *Life and Times of Pieter Stuyvesant* is a characteristic illustration of this truism. He writes in English, to be sure, but his English smacks as little of the King James version as a modern Dutch translation of it would resemble the prose of the *Staten-Bijbel*. Mr. Van Loon's manner is adroit, colloquial, witty, informative, and absolutely unemotional. It is the readable and fluent style of American journalism, reporting, or rather exposing, the foibles and follies of the past. The book is a tale of incompetence and failure, for which of course not Mr. Van Loon but the incompetent Directors of the Dutch West India Company are to blame. But one cannot help feeling that their failings are the making of the book. Mr. Van Loon's wit feeds on their folly. He is at his best when he can show them at their worst, and since they can seldom be shown to have acted wisely, it follows that the story is good reading throughout, except for those Hollanders who take a touchy pride in their country's past. There is more of the times than of the life of Pieter Stuyvesant in Mr. Van Loon's story. He accounts for this lack of proportion in his characteristic manner, saying, "We really are better informed about several Egyptian kings who have been dead and buried for more than thirty centuries than we are about the obstinate Frisian who tried to start a one-man Dutch Empire on the American continent and whose pear-trees were bearing fruit until a few years ago." The allusion to those long-lived pear-trees is of a piece with Mr. Van Loon's pen-and-ink illustrations. It makes us realize the old Governor's nearness to ourselves as compared to the remoteness of the mummified pharaohs. But although something living that belonged to him has survived into the twentieth century, very little is known about the man himself. Hence the story of his life, which to judge from the Foreword was the theme the author had originally in mind, became through lack of material a history of New Netherland, to which he prefixed a rapid survey of the growth of Holland's international commerce. Mr. Van Loon, who takes so much delight in debunking history, has let a good occasion for indulging that pleasure escape him. Anneken Jans, whom he styles the "great-grandmother in extraordinary to the whole of Knickerbocker New York," did not hail from Holland, as he appears to believe. Masterland, which he mentions as her native village, is not a Dutch placename, but the form in which the early records naturalized

Marstrand, the name of a village on an island off the coast of Sweden, not far from Goteborg. Mr. A. J. F. van Laer, who pointed this out in his edition of the "Van Rensselaer Bowier Manuscripts" (p. 56), has thereby disposed of the silly legend which, to the doubtful glory of her Knickerbocker progeny, made Anneken Jans the illegitimate daughter of a Prince of Orange.

March, 1929

A GREAT ACTOR

On January 20, 1929, Willem Royaards died at Menton, in the south of France. The name will not mean much to my American readers, for the art of the stage through which he rose to eminence among his people was limited in its appeal by the foreigner's ignorance of the Dutch language. The actor must speak the language of the country; there is no Esperanto of the stage. Hence Royaards played all his life to an audience whose diminutive size was out of all proportion to his real greatness. His first start in life was in search of adventure in a wider field. He wore a midshipman's uniform before he dressed up for his first part in the play. But the discipline that went with the uniform robbed the adventurous life that he sought of its romance. He soon found that the stage behind the footlights promised him more adventure than the deck of a man-of-war. Had he remained on board, he might have become a popular commander, but would never have achieved the fame that became his on the boards.

As an actor, however, he retained the sailor's love for a roving life. He tried to surmount the barriers of the native speech and to seek applause abroad. He obtained an engagement at Berlin, where he appeared in the role of Svengali, a successful performance which he subsequently repeated at St. Petersburg. From there he returned to Germany, where he played at Berlin, at Dresden, at Leipzig; from Germany he moved to Great Britain, but there he met with less applause, it would seem, as he was soon back again in Germany, playing under the direction of Max Reinhardt. Reinhardt's inspiring example was of great moment in the shaping of his subsequent career. Realizing, no doubt, that he would never master German as he did his native tongue, he returned to Holland; but while resigning himself to the narrowing of his field of action, he conceived the ambition to rise to undisputed leadership within that narrow area. He would be the Max Reinhardt of Holland. With irrepressible persistence he succeeded in persuading a number of patrons to furnish the capital which he needed for his dramatic venture. He called his new company

Het Tooneel (The Stage), and gave his first performance at Amsterdam in September, 1908. It was Royaards' aim to raise the drama from a mere form of amusement to an art, an aim which is difficult of attainment, but especially difficult in Holland, where even as an amusement the drama is little appreciated. The Hollander never was an enthusiastic playgoer. Orthodox Calvinism, which was the ruling religion in the seventeenth century, has always frowned upon the stage as a den of wickedness and abomination, and the actor's profession has not yet fully succeeded in living down the evil repute which the hostility of the Protestant Church has cast upon it. The theatre in Holland, moreover, never enjoyed the patronage of a royal court, as it did in Paris and London, nor was there a powerful nobility to take it under its wing. In short, the drama in Holland has always been a Cinderella among her sister arts, until Prince Royaards came and raised her from her low estate. He did not court her as an indulgent lover; on the contrary, he proved a severe master, enforcing among his company a discipline as strict as he would have maintained on board ship, had he become a commander in the navy. His profound respect for a poet's work would not allow an actor even the slightest departure from the context, nor would he suffer one of his players to outshine the rest of the cast and unbalance the drama's poise and proportion. Each had to be satisfied with being an organic part of the whole. His stage settings were in accord with this striving after unity of style. They remained subordinate to the act, the beauty achieved by the simplest lines and colors being a plastic accompaniment of the story.

His great services to the nation and the national stage were recognized by the University of Utrecht, which conferred on him the degree of honorary Doctor of Literature. I cannot help feeling that there is something presumptuous on the part of organized scholarship in believing that they can honor a great artist by making him one of their own. It would be more fitting for the organized actors to elect an eminent teacher of literature an honorary member of their guild, for an artist's creation is a thing of higher order than the learning of a university professor. But Dr. Royaards did not see it that way and felt pleased with his scholastic distinction, which proves that I am wrong and that the university authorities were right. They were more than justified, for they bestowed by this election greater honor on their institution than they could bestow upon the actor. If they were actually prompted by that selfish motive, one would be altogether mistaken in sensing anything presumptuous in their action.

My personal recollections of Willem Royaards take me back to the early summer of 1923, when he visited New York and made the round of its theatres. I had many a chat with him during those days, and I treasure the letters that he sent me from the Plaza, where he was staying. In one of these he wrote, "On my return from Coldspring Harbor, I received the news of Couperus' death. I have been miserably depressed ever since. On the day that I sailed from Holland, Geo. Breitner died, and now this indubitably great one among our countrymen has departed for good. Our generation born in the sixties is thinning considerably. Whose turn will come next?" He promised me before he sailed that he would come back the following year and give a recital for the Institute of Arts and Sciences at Columbia University. But he postponed that second visit from year to year, until it was too late. His turn has come all too soon. He has made his exit, leaving to his people the memory of a heroic part magnificently played.

May, 1929

AN EARLY ENVOY TO CHINA

Early Relations between Holland and China was the subject of an interesting talk which, on April 25th, Dr. J. J. L. Duyvendak, of the University of Leyden, gave to the members of the Foundation at the home of Mr. and Mrs. G. Evans Hubbard. Dr. Duyvendak is well known among Sinologists as the translator and editor of the Diary of His Excellency Ching-shan, containing the inside story of the Boxer rebellion as told by a high Manchu functionary, an historical document of extraordinary interest. He is, furthermore, the author of "The Book of Lord Shang, A Classic of the Chinese School of Law," which he published in English, and of a quarto volume in Dutch on "China against the Western Horizon." If any members allowed the splashing rain to deter them from attending the tea at Mr. Hubbard's home, they bartered a great intellectual treat for a little physical comfort. Dr. Duyvendak told a romantic story of the attempts of the Dutch East India Company to enter into trade relations with the Chinese. One episode had particular interest for his American hearers. This was the account of the Embassy sent by the Dutch East India Company to the Emperor of China in 1794. An American citizen, Andreas Everardus van Braam Houckgeest, was appointed second in this Embassy, and, on his return to this country, published an account of his mission which he dedicated to President Washington. Mr. Van Braam Houckgeest was born at Werkhoven, in the province of Utrecht, Holland, in 1739. He served his country in the navy, in which two of his brothers rose to the rank of admiral. But he himself left the service in 1758 and sailed for China as supercargo on a ship of the

Dutch East India Company. He resided at Macao and Canton until 1773, except for two short voyages to Europe, on one of which he married, at the Cape of Good Hope, a daughter of Pieter Baron van Rheede van Oudtshoorn. Having returned to Holland in 1773, he settled in the town of Zutfen, in the province of Gelderland. But after ten uneventful years in this quiet little place, his roving disposition lured him to fresh adventure. In 1783 he emigrated to the new American Republic and made his residence in Charlestown, S. C., where he engaged in business and laid out a rice plantation. He was naturalized as a citizen of the United States in the following year, and would probably have ended his days in Charlestown, if death had not robbed him there, in the course of one single month, of his two only sons and two of his daughters. This tragedy, added to the loss of a large part of his fortune, induced him to accept an appointment by the Dutch East India Company as Chief of its Factory at Canton. And so it happened that Mr. Van Braam, being on the spot and well acquainted with Chinese affairs, was made second envoy in the Embassy that went to visit the Emperor in 1794. He returned from this mission to America, arriving in Philadelphia on April 24, 1796, accompanied by several Chinese, who were the talk of the town, and bringing with him a rich collection of drawings and curios. Among the many visitors who called to make his acquaintance and inspect his Chinese treasures was the French exile Moreau de Saint-Méry, who, two years earlier, had established a bookstore and printing press at Philadelphia. He was introduced to Van Braam by Talleyrand, and on his first visit he made arrangements for an edition of Van Braam's account of the Dutch Embassy to Peking which appeared the next year in the French language in a two-volume edition. A London publisher brought out an English translation of the book in 1798, in which the dedication to His Excellency George Washington, President of the United States of America, is retained. It reads as follows in the English rendering:

Sir, Travels among the most ancient people which now inhabits this globe, and which owes its long existence to the system that makes its Chief the Father of the National Family, cannot appear under better auspices than those of the Great Man who was elected, by the universal suffrage of a new nation, to preside at the conquest of liberty, and in the establishment of a government in which everything bespeaks the love of the First Magistrate for the People. Permit me then to address the homage of my veneration to the virtues which in your Excellency afford so striking a resemblance between Asia and America. I cannot show myself more worthy of the title of Citizen of the United States, which is become my adopted country, than by paying a just tribute to the Chief, whose principles and sentiments are calculated to procure them a duration equal to that of the Chinese Empire.

Three years after these words were written, Van Braam left his adopted country for good. It is not clear what reasons induced him to return to Holland. His second wife, whom he married in Philadelphia at about the time when his book appeared in print, was an American of Dutch descent, Miss Johanna Egberta Constantia van Schuler. But in spite of this fresh tie that might have bound him more firmly to the country of his adoption, he bade it farewell in 1800. He seems to have parted with Moreau on anything but friendly terms. On August 1, 1798, the latter wrote in his diary, "In order to conclude my dealings with Mr. Van Braam, I was obliged to have recourse to arbitration. In this connection let me quote M. de Cazenove, who, in a letter of July 22 last, says with regard to Mr. Van Braam that he has the pretense rather than the substance of wealth, and that Americans are more astute than Hollanders." Financial embarassments may have caused him to repatriate. He did not long enjoy the pleasure of home life among his own people. He died in 1801 in Amsterdam. Moreau, who slights his old friend in the words just quoted, the last passage of the diary that refers to Van Braam, gave him a different character in an entry of five weeks earlier. On June 21, he recorded that the Directoire in Paris had been foolish and careless enough to disregard Van Braam's generous offer of his entire Chinese collection as a present to the French Republic. "Voilá de l'insouciance française bien condemnable." Moreau himself states that in France the value of the collection would have been one and a half million francs. Could the wealth of so rich a collector be justly called more ostentatious than substantial? Voilá de la légèreté française bien condemnable!

July, 1929

BILLOP HOUSE

The name of Staten Island puzzles me. What tenacity is there, I wonder, in the Dutch plural *Staten* that saved it from translation into English? To my Dutch and, presumably, prejudiced ear it has a kindlier and more beautiful sound than the monosyllabic *States*, which, beginning with *st* and ending in *ts*, strikes me like a hissing summons to be silent. The trochaeic lilt of the name ($\acute{\smile} \smile \acute{\smile} \smile$) is more melodious than the abrupt rhythm of its English equivalent ($\acute{\smile} \acute{\smile} \smile$). It is, perhaps, this musical quality that accounts for the survival of the

Dutch plural in the speech of an anglicized community. Rhythm is an erratic preserver of linguistic antiquities. The adverb *enough* is the only word in the English speech of every day that has retained in its initial syllable the ancient prefix *ge-* still so common in modern Dutch and modern German. Why did it survive in this sole instance? The repeated use of the word in connection with a preceding monosyllabic noun such as *bread*, *meat*, *food*, *salt*, *milk*, *beer*, *wine*, *et cetera*, seems to have saved the prefix from total extinction. *Bread enough* comes more easily across the lips than the close succession of even beats that would result from its omission. Even so, I imagine, did the name Staten Island owe its immunity from naturalization to the people's ear for rhythm and euphony.

How many Manhattanese know more about the island than its name? I have a suspicion that to the majority it is an undiscovered land. It forms part of the city of New York, and most people do not expect much adventure from the exploration of their home town. I must confess that I myself do not belong to the inquisitive minority. I never realized that one could go into the country without going out of town until I paid a visit recently to Tottenville, S.I. It was not on my own initiative that I set out on this exploring expedition. I had received an invitation from the President of the Borough of Richmond and the Directors of the Conference House Association "to be present at a celebration to be held at the Conference House, Tottenville, Staten Island, N.Y., on Saturday afternoon, June 29, 1929." The name Conference House meant nothing to me. My ignorance on this point was apparently anticipated as a matter of course, for along with the invitation came a printed account of the early history of the mansion. From this I learnt that it is also known by the name of Billop House; and an incomparably better name it is. It is shorter, it is exclusive, and it commemorates the man who had the old mansion built. Christopher Billop needs the help of the English speaking inhabitants of Staten Island to save him from oblivion, since the editors of the new Dictionary of American Biography have, for obvious reasons, decided to ignore him, his achievement being of merely local importance. In 1664 the Duke of York became proprietor of the newly erected province of New York, and by his grant in the same year to Berkeley and Carteret of all that portion which lay west of the Hudson River, Staten Island became properly a part of New Jersey. But in 1668 the Duke decided that all islands within New York Bay which could be circumnavigated in twenty-four hours should be adjudged to New York. Captain Christopher Billop made the trip within the time limit, and thus it happened that the island was incorporated with the State of New York and was, more than two centuries later, included within the limits of this city. But for Christopher Billop there would be no Hylan Boulevard on Staten Island. The skipper was rewarded with a grant of 1,163 acres at the south end of the island. He turned this property into the Manor of Bentley, and the manor house which he had built still stands in the village of Tottenville. It was in this house that Lord Howe, on September 11, 1776, held a peace conference with Benjamin Franklin, John Adams, and Edward Rutledge representing the Continental Congress, which meeting gave to the Billop House its alternative but less attractive name.

This house has now become a historic shrine, thanks to the munificence of Mr. Wm. E. Harmon, who has deeded it to the City of New York; the city, in its turn, has placed it in the custody of the Conference House Association, which is at present engaged in restoring the building. There is an old kitchen in the basement, the floor of which is paved with bricks imported from Holland in the seventeenth century, and with a view to restoring the cellar with the same kind of bricks, an order was placed with the firm of Van Lookeren Campagne, of Zaltbommel, Holland, for an adequate supply of similar bricks made in the same moulds as those in the seventeenth-century kitchen floor. The arrival of these bricks was the occasion of the ceremony on Saturday, June 29th. The presiding officer was Mr. Cornelius G. Kolff, a born Staten Islander and the son of an immigrant from Holland. Escorted by a bodyguard of two little urchins dressed up as Dutch fishermen, he received the official guests, representatives of the British, French, and Netherlands Governments, with old-time cordiality and ceremony. He informed his audience that the house was haunted by the ghost of a young lady who died of a broken heart within its walls, and as proof of his veracity he actually produced the apparition – and a lovely ghost she was indeed – and made her act as announcer and interpreter of a historic pageant which presented scenes from the life as it was lived on Staten Island in Indian, Dutch, and English days. But the crowning event of that afternoon was the auction of the Zaltbommel bricks. These were knocked down, one by one, to the highest bidder, the proceeds of the sale being destined to swell the funds for the restoration of the house. Mr. Kolff, who acted as auctioneer, certainly knew how to sell his ware. The bricks went for $ 5.00 a piece, a record price, as the books of Zaltbommel firm will be able to testify. The buyers were, of course, free to carry their bricks home as mementoes, but they all preferred to dedicate them to the house for use in the restoration of the cellar, and to inscribe their names in a book of donors as a lasting record of their presence at the ceremony. Beautiful weather favored the occasion. The heat of the sun was tempered by a strong breeze from across the water, such a breeze as must have swelled the sails of Christopher Billop's craft when he saved Staten Island for New York.

HELLEGAT

Government white papers and similar official publications are not the kind of literature that lends itself to discussion in these Monthly Letters. The Foreign Office at The Hague has just published the Correspondence which has passed between the Netherlands and Belgian Governments since the rejection of the Dutch-Belgian Treaty of April 3, 1925, and these documents are no exception to the rule. One of them, however, contains a passage that will be of interest to New Yorkers, as it sheds light upon the etymology of the well-known name Hell Gate. The Belgians demand from Holland the right to dig a canal across the province of Brabant by which Antwerp would receive a shorter and, as they claim, safer connection with the Rhine than the existing one along the natural waterways; Holland, on the other hand, insists that her international obligations do not compel her to more than the amelioration of those natural routes so as to make them answer the requirements of modern navigation. But these channels are not, and never will be, safe, is the Belgian contention, witness the ominous name of Hellegat, by which one of them is marked upon the map. But the Netherlands Government does not admit the soundness of this argument. The infernal character of the channel in question cannot be demonstrated from its name. Hellegat, it is explained, does not mean Hell Gate; popular etymology has given it that meaning, but the original name was Hillegat, meaning Hill Gate. The hill from which it took its name is still in existence on the Brabant side of the channel. The same old word occurs in the name of the Dutch town of Hellevoetsluis, which means, of course, the Locks at the foot of the Hill. For who has ever heard of the foot of Inferno? It would be just as unfair to condemn this old harbor as inaccessible on the strength of its seemingly ominous name as it is wrong to believe that you can prove Hellegat unnavigable by shouting its name to the mast tops. There is no such word as *hil* in modern Dutch. Its disappearance from the language gave rise to the erroneous etymology which connected the channel with the terrors of the lower regions. No Charon is needed to navigate these waters, as the experience of the past has amply proved. It does not follow, however, that our own Hell Gate does not deserve its evil reputation either. It was probably named by Dutch sailors after Hellegat in the province of Zeeland, and to them the name did actually have the ominous implication which popular etymology has given it. New York's Hell Gate cannot be cleared of its stigma by the linguistic evidence the Foreign Office at The Hague has produced to prove the innocence of Holland's Hellegat.

September, 1929

AN ASTRONOMER WITHOUT A TELESCOPE

If a painter were asked to do a picture of an astronomer, he would, of course, represent him with his eye at the telescope under the dome of an observatory. The observatory would seem to be the astronomer's natural habitat. Without it he must be just as helpless, one would think, as a baker without an oven or a farrier without a smithy. Or he might be compared to a starving Tantalus of science, forever tortured by his inability to come near enough to the wonders that he hungers to observe for the satisfaction of his scientific craving. But this appears to be an ignorant layman's notion, long since exploded by the achievement of a Dutch astronomer who, without the traditional equipment of his profession, made the modest University of Groningen, where he studied and taught, a sacred shrine of astronomy. The Frenchman Baillaud, who presided in 1922 at the astronomical conference in Rome, said in the course of his opening address, "Three factors, during the past half century, have revolutionized astronomical research: photography, the giant telescopes, and the Groningen Laboratory." In that laboratory, without the tools that are the usual attributes of the astronomer, was developed the modern conception of the structure of the world which is known among scientists as "the Kapteyn Universe." Can there be greater honor for a scholar than to have given his name to the vastest concept of which the human mind is capable?

I have been reading the biography of J. C. Kapteyn by his daughter, Mrs. H. Hertzsprung, a work of love and devotion performed with admirable restraint. No overstatement mars the effect of this simple and beautiful narrative. It is the story of an apparently uneventful existence. "O for a life of emotions rather than of thought," she once said to her father quoting Keats. "Child," he replied, "do you think that a life of thought knows no emotions?" The provincial town of Groningen, in the north of Holland was, indeed, a rather dull place to live in. He was appointed to a full professorship at the age of twenty-six, and he remained in Groningen for forty-three years, leaving it at the age of seventy to retire to a home in the country in the neighborhood of Amsterdam. Occasional journeys to attend

47

international congresses in Europe, South Africa, and the United States and, in later life, an annual visit to the Mount Wilson Observatory in California, broke the monotony of the professor's life in Groningen. But he never found it dull or uneventful. In his laboratory he made discoveries that were more wonderful than the strangest things that travelers brought back from unexplored regions. It was there that he conceived, to quote his own words, "a first attempt at a theory of the arrangement and motion of the stellar system." He expounded it in the *Astrophysical Journal* of May 1922, his last contribution to the literature of astronomy. He died on June 18 of that same year, seventy-one years of age.

When the Groningen Laboratory was inaugurated on January 16, 1896, Kapteyn himself explained, for the benefit of his lay audience, how astronomical research was possible without observatory and telescope. "Photographic observatories," he said, "are counted by the dozen. These workshops collect more data than they can possibly turn to account ... The curse of most observatories, especially those where they work hardest, is the constant accumulation of nonproductive material. Precious observations are amassed in their archives without yielding any fruit to science because the number of scholars who can utilize them is not commensurate to that of the observers and photographers. It is about time that the balance between the work of the latter and that of the theoretical astronomer should be restored. That is the purpose of this laboratory. Here we shall devote ourselves to the task which Darwin has called 'the grinding of the facts into law'." He was, indeed, dependent for the facts on others, on the workers in the observatories all over the world, and on their disinterested collaboration. Science that seeks itself does not get anywhere. But Kapteyn did find willingness to cooperate in abundant measure, so much so that he once wrote to the Director of the Greenwich Observatory, "I sometimes cannot help thinking that you must take me for the most troublesome man alive, the man who has always something to ask and has never something to offer in return. I hope you will consider that it is not all my fault. It is the one thing that makes such an institution as an astronomical laboratory objectionable which must live on the materials furnished by other institutions." His correspondent knew that there was no need for him to apologize, for if there ever was a self-forgetful scientist, that man was Kapteyn. After the completion of the *Cape Durchmusterung Catalogue*, a work in three imposing quarto volumes to which he had devoted twelve years of his life, Simon Newcomb, the great American astronomer, wrote, "This work of Kapteyn offers a remarkable example of the spirit which animates the born investigator of the heavens.

Although the work was officially that of the British Government, the years of toil devoted by Kapteyn to it were expended without other compensation than the consciousness of making a noble contribution to knowledge, and the appreciation of his fellow astronomers of this and future generations."

His own country was slow in recognizing his greatness. At a time when he had won for himself worldwide distinction, the legislature at The Hague questioned the value of the work that he was doing in Groningen. He had applied to the Government for additional equipment that was needed in his laboratory, and the Second Chamber, which had to vote the necessary appropriations, found it appropriate to enquire "whether the Groningen laboratory was not a superfluous institution, since there were already two observatories in the country." Kapteyn, therefore, was asked to explain the usefulness of his laboratory before the Chamber was willing to grant him the equipment that he needed for his work. If he felt grieved, he did not show it. In all modesty he supplied the information; it was not recognition and honor that he wanted most of all, but the means for continuing his research.

Kapteyn never taught astronomy to his daughter. He evidently was of a mind with his friend Sir David Gill, the Cape of Good Hope astronomer, who, on being asked by an admiring lady, "I suppose your wife knows all about astronomy?" replied in his uncompromising way, "Not a word, thank God!" Mrs. Hertzsprung's ignorance of her father's science lends charm to the story that she tells of his life. There is no exposition of his learning in these pages; his greatness as a scholar is revealed indirectly, by the tale of his friendships with the heroes of science, who saw in him their peer, if not their master: Sir David Gill, Simon Newcomb, George E. Hale, the Director of the Mount Wilson Observatory, Eberhard, Eddington, Einstein, and many others whose names will share immortality with his. Sir David stands out in Mrs. Hertzsprung's narrative as her father's twin spirit. When the news of his death reached the Kapteyns in Groningen, they at once went to London. They found Lady Gill lying down in a state of prostration, waiting for the arrival of her husband's most intimate friend. Kapteyn knelt at her bedside, and solemnly she laid a hand on his head, blessing him and thanking him for all that he had been to her husband. Sir David was buried in his native town of Aberdeen. In London, at the same time, a memorial service was held at St. Mary Abbot, Kensington, which Kapteyn and his wife attended. The organ played Tennyson's "Crossing the Bar," and a boy's clear solo sang the words of comfort. They never forgot that poignant moment.

Every Sunday morning, Mrs. Kapteyn has played that same dirge in memory of the friend who had crossed the bar.

Life, Kapteyn used to say, had been good to him, and he did his best to make life good for others. He wanted to see people happy, and was always ready to help the destitute and to alleviate distress. He never turned a poor woman away who came to hawk her paltry ware at the door of his laboratory. The shelves were full of worthless stationery and pencils, pathetic tokens of his goodness of heart. His grandchildren adored him. He was never too tired to listen to their stories, he devised for their future, and made provisions for their college education. On his last sickbed, shortly before his death, he pictured himself surrounded by them in the country home to which he was going to retire. Each child was to plant a tree in the garden, he would teach them all about birds and plants, and he would read with them the books they loved. One of them, who was getting her first instruction in history at school, was asked by her mother the meaning of A. D. The child did not know; the teacher, evidently, had failed to tell from what event our chronology took its start. So her mother explained; "Nineteen hundred and twenty years ago a great man was born, and from the year of his birth we begin to count the years down to the present day. That man was the best and noblest and wisest man that ever lived. Can you guess who that man was?" The child did not hesitate for a moment; she knew at once. "Grandfather, of course!"

THE CAUSE AND CURE OF BERI-BERI

One of the scientists who shared in this year's Nobel prize award is the Hollander, Dr. C. Eykman, of the University of Utrecht. His work has resulted in the saving of human life from the ugliness of disease by demonstrating the importance of various kinds of vitamins for a health-preserving diet. Before he was called to the University of Utrecht, he was a military doctor in the Dutch East Indies. There he discovered the cause of beri-beri, a disease widely prevalent in tropical countries. He observed that chickens, if fed on polished rice, developed symptoms similar to those of beri-beri, but if given rice in the husk remained immune. The entire pericarp and germ, which are absent from the milled and polished article, appeared to contain the substance that secures this immunity, a substance so minute that there are no more than ten grains of it in a ton of rice. Vitamin is the name that was given to this particle by Dr. Casimir Funk of the Lister Institute. This discovery led Dr. Eykman on to an ever deepening study of vitamins, which has earned him, at an age at which professors in Holland must retire, the high distinction of a Nobel prize.

It was also a Hollander who gave the first scientific description of beri-beri and its symptoms. This was the Dutch physician Jacob Bontius, who had himself suffered from the disorder during a four years' residence in Java. He died at Batavia in 1631, leaving in manuscript the results of his studies in the fields of natural history and medicine. These were published by a brother of his in 1642. In this volume called "De Medicina Indicorum," of which an English translation appeared in 1769, occurs an accurate description of beri-beri, or the barbiers, as it is called by the English translator, who had evidently practised medicine on the coast of Malabar. Bontius derives the name from a native word signifying sheep, explaining that "those who are seized without, from a tottering of the knees and a peculiar manner of walking, exhibit to the fancy a representation of the gait of that animal." But the word is now more convincingly derived from a Sinhalese word meaning weakness. A general lassitude is, indeed, its chief symptom, but at the same time that it impairs the sensation of the feet and hands and sometimes even of the whole body, it induces a sort of palsy or tremor and obstructs the patient's power of speech. Bontius himself, when suffering from it, had so feeble a voice that people sitting close to him could hardly hear what he said. He believed that beri-beri was caused by a chill in the night, when people, after being fatigued by the heat of the day, unwarily throw off their bedclothes. Later writers attributed it to malarial poisoning or infection, but no bacillus could be discovered. And so the disease remained a scourge in tropical countries until it was found that a rice diet is detrimental to the people's health, unless the rice is eaten in the husk. It is said that God sends the cure with the disease. But in this case the disease was of man's own making. He refused to eat the rice as Nature prepares it; he wanted to improve upon Nature's product by polishing her gift. And it took man three hundred years from Bontius to Eykman, to find the remedy for this self-inflicted plague.

BEGUINES AND HIGHLANDERS

There was in mediaeval Amsterdam a Beguinage such as may still be seen in many a town in the Flemish part of Belgium. There are no Beguines in present-day Amsterdam, but the sheltered court round which they used to live can still be visited. It is close to the Kalverstraat, a narrow and very busy street of stores and cafés; its proximity to this noisy thoroughfare heightens the impression of peace and retirement that still prevails in the old Beguinage. The Sisters were not expelled after Amsterdam had been won over to the cause of the Reformation. The city government was tolerant enough to let them continue their harmless mode of life undisturbed. Their church, which occupies the centre of the court, was taken from them, however, and given to the English Presbyterians who were numerous at that time in Amsterdam. But the Beguines retained the right of burial in the church. An old etching by J. van Meurs shows a view of the English church in the sixties of the seventeenth century with, in the foreground, a funeral procession of Beguines, twelve of whom carry the body of their sister to the church that once belonged to them and where they recovered a place for themselves by dying. A few weeks ago the quiet court of the Beguinage was the scene of an even stranger procession. Sixteen members of the clan of Mackay, in kilt and tartan, and preceded by two Highlanders blowing their bagpipes, marched across the court to the church, there to present the copy of an old flag under which Mackay's Regiment had fought in the service of the Dutch Republic. This regiment of Scots, under the command of members of the clan of Mackay, served in the Netherlands from 1572 till 1782. In 1855 the Dutch Government presented the old flags of the regiment to the eleventh Lord Reay, the head of the clan, who, in his turn, made a present of them to St. Giles Cathedral in Edinburgh. It was a copy of one of these that was recently dedicated to the English church in the Beguinage, where so many of the Scottish soldiers must have worshipped in the days of the Dutch Republic.

Many Scottish officers who served in the armies of the Dutch States General married and settled in Holland and started Dutch offshoots of the clans to which they belonged. The late Lord Reay, of the clan of the Mackays, was a Hollander born and a prominent landowner in the land of his birth. Another Dutch member of that clan, Aeneas Baron Mackay, was Prime Minister at The Hague from 1888 till 1891. There are Dutch MacLeods and Macdonalds and Macneils and Macgillavrys; there are subjects of Queen Wilhelmina who bear the un-Dutch names of Balfour of Burleigh and Hamilton of Silverton Hill. Holland has no reason to complain of Scottish stinginess. The Highlands have been generous to the Low Countries in sending them some of the bravest of their sons to fight for Dutch Freedom and to fuse with the Dutch race.

PIETER JELLES TROELSTRA

On Monday, May 14th, Pieter Jelles Troelstra, the grand old man of Holland's Social-Democratic Labor Party, passed away at his home in The Hague. His death was a loss not only to the host of workers whose leader he had been for a generation, it was a cause for nation-wide mourning and regret. For Troelstra was more than a mere party man and politician, he was a national figure respected and admired, however reluctantly, by even his bitterest opponents. The very passion which, in his fiery moments, made him throw all political caution to the winds, won him a grudging esteem from the cautious and the level-headed. A man of such daring and impetuosity could not be a wily schemer, and his critics, while calling him a dangerous man, gave him credit for mental honesty and courage. A noble idealism carried him over many an obstacle both in domestic politics and in his work for the organization of the Internationale. His success in that wider field added to his popularity at home. It gratified Dutch pride to see a Hollander play so important a role on the international stage, though the majority of the people did not approve of the show. During the war Mr. Troelstra was undeservedly accused of being a pro-German meddler. By his persistent efforts to bring about a meeting of Socialist representatives from all the belligerent States, at a time when the Central Powers were hard pressed and more immediately in need of peace than their opponents, he unfortunately incurred the suspicion of being a Germanophile through thick and thin. He was nothing of the sort. Troelstra's aim was not to come to the rescue of Prussian militarism, an absurd charge to make against the leader of the Dutch Socialists, but to revive the Internationale, in which he saw the only power that could restore peace and brotherhood to the world. This unshaken trust in an organization which the war, at its very outbreak, had shown to be of small avail against the dissolving elements of national greed and chauvinism was characteristic of the man who, all through his active life, had been fired by a fervent belief in mankind.

On the day of Troelstra's funeral, thousands from all parts of the country traveled to The Hague to pay their last tribute to the leader. For hours they filed in impressive silence past the bier at the open grave, lowering their banners as they approached the body. It seemed, said one who watched them march, as if those banners were swept down, like corn in the wind, by the sighs that rose from the never-ending procession. There was one wreath on the coffin that bore the Frisian inscription *"Wy berntsjes fen è fryske greiden roppen oan Piter Jelles en lest farevol ta fen't alde Heitelan."* (We children of the Frisian pastures call a last farewell to Pieter Jelles from the old fatherland.) Friesland, in the north of Holland, was the land of his birth, and Frisian, which is a closer cognate of English than of Dutch, his native tongue. When he wrote poetry, he wrote in Frisian. He was a poet before he became a politician. But in 1890, at the age of thirty, he bade farewell to his Frisian Muse. In 1897 he was returned by the Frisian capital, the city of Leeuwarden, which he represented in the Second Chamber for nearly twenty-eight years. At that time he was the leader of but a small following; in this year of his death, the party numbers 66,000 members and is supported at the polls by 800,000 voters. While building up this powerful Labor organization, he found no time for the writing of poetry. However, in spite of his strenuous work as a member of Parliament and as editor of *Het Volk*, the chief Labor organ, he returned, after nineteen years' defection, to his neglected Muse. A Frisian brother poet's challenge made him break his silence. Mr. Troelstra had thrown cold water on the national joy at the birth of Princess Juliana by making the stereotyped Socialist declaration as to his party's attitude towards the ruling dynasty, and the indignation among non-Socialist circles was voiced by the Frisian poet J. B. Schepers, who pitied the statesman in whom the poet had grown old and cold. The appeal touched Troelstra's heart, and he answered in verse: "In these great, splendid times an epic sounds through the world, an epic of truth overcoming falsehood, of new life, new suffering, new battles, an epic of slaves wrestling for freedom, an epic of the first human brotherhood." The reply was a justification of both the poet and the statesman. The poet had not grown old and cold, but had given nobler expression to the inner life by mingling his mighty voice in the chorus that chanted the new epic of freedom and democracy throughout the world. To Troelstra the fight for a better humanity was poetic creation, and his own life the best of his poems.

Some twenty years ago Mr. Troelstra visited the old village where he had spent his youth, and the villagers assembled in their ancient church to hear him recite a selection from his own poetry. That day must have seemed to him to foreshadow a new era in which the poet, the politician, and the preacher would no longer be the exponents of three different and often antagonistic views of life, an era whose political practice would be guided by the preacher's sense of righteousness and the poet's unfailing instinct for truth.

GUIDO GEZELLE

The ancient city of Bruges will witness this summer the annual passage of hordes of sightseers from the United States. They will visit the Beguinage and buy from the old women lace handkerchiefs that will come in useful next Christmas, they will be awed, or pretend to be, by the beauty of the Memlings in the Hospital of St. John and ask questions from the caretaker about that incredible legend of the eleven thousand virgins who were massacred wholesale at Cologne by Attila's bloodthirsty Huns, they will do the city by water in puffing little motorboats, and watch the artists at their easels painting the picturesque architecture along the canals; and having left a memento of their hasty visit in the guest book of Hotel Memling or one of the other hostelries, they will rush on to the next stage of their fast-moving itinerary. The guides that take them round never show them the place where Guido Gezelle was born in 1830. The guides do not know it, and if they did, there would be no sense in pointing it out to sightseers who are strangers to the country's language. For Gezelle was a poet, and the truest interpreter of that Flemish soul which travelers imagine they have sensed when doing the sights of "Bruges la morte." Gezelle's birthday is the first of May, that favorite day of the mediaeval poets, Geoffrey Chaucer among them, who, devoted as he was to his studies, never left his books for any game,

> save, certeynly, whan that the month of may
> is comen,

for then it was "farewel my book and my devocioun." On that day of the poets, the greatest Dutch poet of the nineteenth century came into God's world, which he was to love so intensely and would celebrate so abundantly in melodious verse.

The story of his life is simple and uneventful. He was trained for the priesthood, and, shortly before his ordination, was appointed instructor at the Roman Catholic Seminary of Rousselaere. He was fond of children; they were to him kin of the flowers and the birds and the butterflies, all beautiful creatures of the Maker. He was like a child himself among them, entering wholeheartedly into the fun of their games and being as quick and alert in their sports as the quickest among them. There were always English boarders at the school, and Gezelle, who spoke and wrote English with ease, had supervision over these boys when they stayed on during vacation time. He spoke with them in their own language and knew how to cheer the homesick. His study was always open to his boys, and those who showed poetic talent were encouraged by the master to come and show him their latest efforts in verse. He was an inspiring teacher of literature. He had read all that is best in ancient and modern letters, and had read each work in the original tongue. For he was an exceptionally gifted polyglot; he had not merely a reading knowledge of several foreign languages, he had mastered them so as to speak and write them. He corresponded with his favorites among the alumni of the seminary in English, German, and Italian; to one of them he wrote occasionally in Hindustani. It was like going on an exploring expedition to traverse, with him as a guide, the vastness of international literature. And the gifted among his pupils, spurred on in this quest for beauty by his enthusiasm, discovered the creative impulse in themselves. He established a school of poets, and from a mere schoolmaster became the leader of a poetic revival.

But his very success as an inspiring teacher of the talented became the tragedy of his life. Gezelle was too much of an individualist to conform to the rules and doctrines of traditional paedagogy. No one had ever taught as he was teaching at Rousselaere. His superiors frowned on his novel methods, which seemed erratic to them. The average student could not reach as high as Gezelle expected him to do. They wanted facts which they could commit to memory, and he gave them ideas instead, which they could not understand. He wanted them to think, and the best they could do was to learn by rote. His passionate love of his Flemish speech was another grievance against him. The literary elite among the boys, who rallied round Gezelle as their leader, made bitter earnest of the master's language cult and refused to speak French during recess in defiance of a long-established practice of the school. Even Gezelle's authority, who did not approve this effect of his teaching, could not repress their Flemish zeal. Rebellion could not be tolerated in a Roman Catholic Seminary. For the good of the school Gezelle's influence on the students had to be curbed. The class in poetry was taken away from him and given to his chief opponent among the faculty. The pupils were forbidden free access to the rooms of the instructors, a ruling that applied to all but which was meant to strike a special blow at Gezelle. It did strike him cruelly. Deprived of the intimate contact with his boys, deprived of the courses in literature in which he could give them the best and the noblest that was in him, he saw his gifts degraded and debased. The following year he was transferred to an English seminary at Bruges, still later he was appointed chaplain in one of the parishes of his native city, and subsequently called to Courtray in that same humble capacity, which he retained until his death in 1899.

From the year 1860, in which he left Rousselaere, until his arrival at Courtray, twenty years later, Gezelle did not publish any poetry. It seems as if the students whom he had inspired were as indispensable to him in kindling his poetic fire. However, when he recovered his voice, it gave expression to nobler poetry than he had written at Rousselaere. "Tijdkrans" (1893) and "Rijmsnoer om en om het Jaar" (1897) are the two volumes that have placed him among the ranks of the great poets. A masterly rendering of Longfellow's "Hiawatha" also shows the best characteristics of his uncommon talent. He was original to a degree as an interpreter of nature's music. His poetry is a mass of magic sound and color welded into word. All the innumerable voices of nature, from the soft rustling of the reed on the water's edge to the mighty roar of the thunder re-echo in his verse; all the variegated hues of his Flemish country, the blues of its summer skies, the grays of its November days, the scarlet of its winter sunsets, are described with an inexhaustible splendor of words. The love of words was a passion with him. He collected them as an eighteenth century virtuoso collected rare cameos. He gathered them out of old books, forgotten gems of speech which he set again in the bright surface of his verse, out of the rough speech of the day-laborer by the roadside, no matter where he found them, as long as he thought them beautiful. "Old words are of more value than old jewels," he used to say. And thus he created an artistic language, from the speech of several periods and all the country dialects of Flanders.

A MYSTIFICATION

Mr. Hendrik Willem van Loon, of the town of Veere, which is in Zeeland, has done me an unexpected service, for by editing in English the highly interesting memoirs of his ancestor, Dr. Joannis Van Loon, which are, in effect, an account of the last years and the death of Rembrandt van Rijn[1], he has unwittingly shed light upon a somewhat obscure document among my family papers. It is in the handwriting of a certain Pierre Barnou, who was the first of my Huguenot ancestors to settle in the Netherlands, and it was evidently written as a draft for a letter which his employer intended to address, or did address, to a certain Mr. Van Loon. I cannot decipher his first name, it is written so indistinctly, and to make matters worse, the writer must have smeared his sleeve across the wet ink, thereby turning the Christian name into a pagan hieroglyphic. But now that I have read H. W. van Loon's R. v. R., I have no longer any doubt as to the identity of the Van Loon for whom the letter was intended. Old Dr. Joannis was

[1] R.v.R. *The Life and Times of Rembrandt van Rijn.* New York: Horace Liveright.

mistaken in believing that the manuscript he left behind would have no interest for his son. What was the boy's name, by the way? I cannot remember his father in the memoirs ever calling him anything but "my son" or "my boy," which is a great pity, for if the name did occur anywhere in the book, I could substitute it for the dash which above takes the place of the undecipherable hieroglyphic. For I am positive that the addressee was no other than the chirurgeon's sole offspring. His father did him an injustice in supposing that he would not take any interest in the old man's memoirs. He actually did his best to have them brought out in print, for the document in my ancestor's handwriting must refer to the book which, two hundred and fifty years later, was to see the light in an English version. Pierre Barnou (the *w* at the end was added in the eighteenth century; he himself spelled and, no doubt, pronounced his name in the French fashion) was a native of Lyon, and would probably not have left that delectable city for our damp polderland, if the dragoons of King Louis XIV had not persuaded him in their humane way that life under the clouded skies of Holland was preferable to a living death in the sunshine of *le Roi Soleil*. When he composed the letter to Mr. van Loon, he had been a resident of Amsterdam for more than a dozen years, and by that time had mastered the Dutch language sufficiently well to act as secretary and general factotum to old Mr. Andries van Damme, publisher and bookseller, at the sign of the Polar Bear, on the Rokin by the Kromelleboogsteeg. As a matter of fact, he wrote a more fluent and intelligible Dutch letter than the average Dutch businessman (and statesman, I might add) was capable of writing in those days, the Frenchman's native sense for clarity in thought and diction standing him in good stead when he expressed himself in the unmanageable syntax of his adopted language.

Monsieur Van Loon, On behalf of Mr. Andries van Damme, who is lying in bed with an attack of the stone and suffering so much pain that he cannot even dictate this letter, I am writing to explain why my master, to his great regret, must decline to print the manuscript which you were good enough to offer him for publication. He has read it from cover to cover with as much interest as children take in those Stories of Mother Goose, which have lately come out of France. The boss was many an evening so absorbed in the book that he became unconscious of his pain, so you see, even years after his lamented death Dr. Joannis continues his noble work of alleviating human suffering. In his fascinating style he has left us an effective anaesthetic. The more is the pity that Mr. Andries does not see his way to marketing this pleasant pain-killer. He realizes that he would benefit mankind by making it widely available, but charity, as you know, begins at home. He has not forgotten yet what happened to old Dominee Balthazer Bekker, who had the audacity to tell us in a book of two quarto volumes that devils do not exist. You remember what happened! All his dear colleagues got after him and harassed the poor man with such infernal mental torture that he had to admit, there were at least as many devils left as he had brethren in the consistory. If that could happen to a minister of the Word, what can a humble bookseller expect in the way of mercy, should the dominees find him guilty of printing a book so full of heresies as that of your father's? When Mr. van Damme was in the employ of Mr. Daniel Elzevir, more than twenty-five years ago, an Englishman walked into the office one day and handed Mr. Elzevir a manuscript which he said he could not get printed in England, because it would cost the publisher his liberty, if not his head. The visitor's name was Skinner, and the book was some sort of treatise on the Christian doctrine by a man whose name I think was Milton. I do not know why it was considered such a dangerous book, unless it were for its unblushing defence of polygamy, for which the author claimed to have found abundant sanction in the Bible. Anyhow, Mr. Elzevir undertook to publish this scandalous treatise, but the English Government got on his track (they have their spies all over the Continent) and in some way or other compelled the old man to surrender the manuscript to their agent at The Hague. So the poor publisher always gets into trouble, if not by the meddling of the dominees, then by the interference of some secular authority. And for this reason Mr. Andries van Damme respectfully declines to publish this very precious manuscript, and would advise you to keep it under lock and key until more liberal notions, such as your honored father sets forth in the pages of his memoirs, have gained headway among the majority of our nation. That may not happen in this century, nor even, maybe, in the next. However, your father's book can afford to wait that long, for it is of the sort whose value is increased by the passage of time. It is akin, in that respect, to the pictures of the great master whom your father loved and admired so much. With my best wishes for your continued health and prosperity, I am, dear Sir, your obedient servant, Pierre Barnou. P. S. Mr. van Damme wishes me to state that the reference to Rembrandt in the closing paragraph does not reflect his sentiments. In his opinion, your father made a mistake by putting that painter on a pedestal and making him loom so large both at the beginning and the end. The doctor, he says, should have left that spendthrift alone and restricted his story to his own adventures, which will interest posterity more than those irrelevant chapters about a painter whose murky pictures, absurdly overpraised in his own lifetime, have lost the power to please this more enlightened generation of ours. P. B.

There is no date to this document, but it is possible from internal evidence to determine approximately the year in which it was composed. I find that Daniel Skinner came to Amsterdam in 1675, the year after Milton's death, to arrange for the printing of certain of the latter's manuscripts, including *De Doctrina Christiana*, and since the letter says that this happened more than twenty-five years previously, Mr. Van Loon, Jr., must have submitted his father's manuscript to Andries van Damme in the early years of the eighteenth century. There is one thing that puzzles me not a little. Opposite page 164 of R. V. R. is a facsimile reproduction of page 1437 of the manuscript, on which Dr. Joannis, in his almost illegible Dutch (his handwriting, by the way, was just as modern as were his ideas), makes the surprising statement that "This book is not genuine. It is entirely fictitious. The diary of which this is supposed to be a page does not exist." That must be a joke of the old chirurgeon of which the point escapes me. He might as well have said, "This painter Rembrandt never existed, he is a fiction of my brain." His diary is genuine (or Pierre Barnou's letter is not genuine either) and is no less astir with the real life of seventeenth-century Amsterdam and the Dutch Republic than is Rembrandt's immortal painting known as the Nightwatch.

February, 1931

A DUTCH GRINGO

I have just finished reading, for the second time, a Dutch gringo's story of his life as a ranchman. Gringo was, of old, the Spanish colonist's contemptuous nickname for the later settler of the Nordic race, a justifiable quid pro quo: gringo for dago. This gringo from Holland spent five years of his life on horseback in the service of the biggest cattle company in the Far West. There may have been many more of his race and mettle who rode the bronco across the plains, sharing the hardships and the pleasures of life in the open with roughnecks of all nations, but I know of no other Hollander who had the gift of words to make literature of his experience. He started his career in the West as a fruit farmer. But the orchard they sold to him as first-class land proved a barren waste on which no peaches would ripen. But being a Dutchman as well as a greenhorn, he would not give in at the first disappointment. He thought he might be able to force his gardens to yield fruit if he enlisted the strong aid of science; he took up the study of horticulture and entomology in order to learn how to grow trees against odds. To this new knowledge he owed his appointment as Horticultural Commissioner of his county and, subsequently, as State Quarantine Guardian for his district. But his titles looked better than did his trees. They would not thrive, expert farmer though he had made himself. At last sour sap struck his orchard and ruined him. Then it was that he accepted employment in the cattle farm which he served with so much distinction for fully five years. Its president was one of those powerful empire builders who, armed with an iron will and an unshakable belief in themselves, wrested a whole province from the wilderness, a man of boundless energy who never spared himself and never spared any one else. In comparison to the vastness of his vision, individuals were to him of no importance. Scruples he had none. The author, who remembers his former master with profound admiration, tells an amusing instance of his indifference as to the means by which he attained his end. He once testified in court that "he rode in a boat all over the land," thereby making good his claim to certain admirable grass lands under the swamp and overflow act. Only too late was it ascertained that indeed he had, but that the boat had been placed in a wagon and pulled over the dry soil by four of his sturdy mules.

Our Dutchman, Hendrik van Doorne, was the youngest manager on the corporation staff and at that the overseer of its most important division. He was, consequently, very often in confidential contact with the president, and thanks to this opportunity for close observation he has succeeded in painting a lifelike portrait of the Empire builder, stressing his greatness without sparing his shortcomings. Their collaboration was bound to become strained to the breaking point, for the younger man, for all his admiration of the master, could not stand for the autocrat's relentless disregard of human rights; and as his sense of responsibility grew with his age and experience, he felt less and less justified in abdicating his own judgment at the dictates of this corporation head of the old school. But as long as their relationship lasted, Van Doorne managed the company's affairs to the master's entire satisfaction. The secret of his success lay, apparently, in his gift for reading character, which enabled him to get along with all sorts and conditions of men. The stories that he tells of his adventures as a ranchman supply ample evidence of his mind-reading skill, and of his intuitive knowledge how to turn this insight into character to good account in his endeavors to gain people's confidence. There is the delightful tale of Daddy Logan, a pretentious and blustering humbug, who under Van Doorne's tactful handling turns into a meek, and even grateful, debtor; there is the story of the young Scandinavian, whom he taught, more by suggestion than persuasion, to be ashamed of becoming a skunk and a quitter; there is the tragic account of Martinez Toralles, the slave of ungovernable passions, who, a lifer in prison and longing for escape through self-inflicted death, entrusts the care of the little child he will leave behind to the only friend he knows, Hendrik van Doorne. The central part of the book is taken up with the account of a perilous railway journey from Chicago to Sacramento, on which the author had charge of a shipment of blooded breeding bulls, an excellent piece of story-telling. The book's jacket shows the portrait of a California Ranch Superintendent in the early nineties, a photograph, no doubt, of Hendrik van Doorne himself. It is not difficult to recognize in this dapper, mustachioed young man the features of Mr. H. A. van Coenen Torchiana, the Netherlands Consul General at San Francisco, who confesses himself to be the author of this delightful little book of recollections.[1] He warns the reader in a note prefixed to his memoirs that "in the descriptions of each person, fiction is mixed with reality and the reality is part of a composite recollection of memories; he who will look for a biography of some one known to him will therefore be disappointed, for there is none." But I like to think that this warning does not apply to the portrait of the hero, Hendrik Van Doorne. Knowing the Consul General of the Netherlands in San Francisco and holding him in affectionate regard, and having twice read from cover to cover *California Gringos*, I have no hesitation in saying that the young, daring ranchman is one and the same as the Consul General, and has every reason to be proud of the identity.

March, 1931

A FACETIOUS HISTORIAN

The Dutch and Swedes on the Delaware 1609-1664 by Christopher Ward[2] deals with a period in the history of Delaware that one might call its nursery days. It would never occur to a biographer to write a book of nearly four hundred pages about the babyhood of George Washington or Abraham Lincoln. He would find it difficult to make an interesting story out of such stuff as the first smile, the first distinctly articulated word, the cutting of teeth and the fevers attending it, and measles and whooping cough and toys and nurses. But that is exactly what Mr. Christopher Ward has tried to do and, I admit at the outset, has

[1] *California Gringos* by H. A. van Coenen Torchiana. San Francisco: Paul Elder and Company.
[2] University of Pennsylvania Press.

succeeded in doing much better than would seem possible at first blush. His story ends when the region settled by Swedes and Hollanders was just beginning to outgrow the nursery. New Sweden had laughed its first smile of prosperity under Governor Printz, a very faint and only passing smile, it had feverishly cut palisade teeth out of the forest and given itself a false sense of security, it had suffered from the measles of internal discord, had played at soldiering and housebuilding and shop-keeping and trading, and had changed nurses repeatedly, Swedish sometimes and at other times Dutch. Doctor Stuyvesant had called, now and then, to inspect the baby and scold the nurses, but since he lived so far away and was never expected to repeat his visit very soon, the negligence and sloth that he rebuked were seldom subdued for very long. And when Mr. Ward takes leave of the child, it is a limp, anaemic, and undernourished little patient, for whose life indignant Dr. Stuyvesant on his Bouwery north of New Amsterdam has given up all hope.

This limitation of his story to the infancy of the Delaware region has had an unfortunate effect upon the manner in which Mr. Ward has seen fit to present his subject. He is too much aware of his own intellectual superiority over this infant society of settlers and traders and officials, and in telling us about them assumes that condescending tone of good-humored raillery with which grown-ups discuss the pranks of their troublesome but amusing offspring. "At last Rising was convinced that Stuyvesant's intentions were hostile. He rolled five barrels of beer into the fort and called a council of war." That sentence is a fair sample of the burlesque spirit in which Mr. Ward has conceived the history of the Dutch and Swedes on the Delaware. "The funny darlings" he seems to say, "all their fighting was done with stoups of beer!" His attitude of amused superiority is extended to the rulers in the homelands of the settlers. The Directors of the Dutch West India Company are referred to, on one occasion, as "the Noble Lords Directors, Masters, and Poltroons in Amsterdam." What cowardice on their part suggested this cheap pun on the title Patroon? They had heard from Stuyvesant that he had granted to the Swedes on the Delaware the right to have their own military organization under their own officers, and this news, according to Mr. Ward, caused almost a panic among the Honorables. "It would have been better, they thought, to disarm the whole nation there, than to provide them the weapons which they will know well how to use against us not only upon the arrival of the slightest Swedish succour, but also on other occasions." On the very next page the writer tells us that, very soon after, the Swedes and Finns together were "overwhelmingly superior in number to the Dutch," and on page 330 he admits that "there can be little doubt that during the years of their submission to the rule of the Dutch, the Swedes and Finns cherished always the hope, even the expectation, of deliverance from bondage, that some champion of the oppressed would come out of Sweden and free them from the hated rule of the Dutch." Was there not some ground, then, for the anxiety felt by the Directors? They did not know, as the historian Christopher Ward in his after-wisdom knows, that "there could not have been found in America a more peaceful, law-abiding and obedient group of colonists than those Swedes and Finns on the South River." They only knew that the Swedes considered the Dutch as usurpers and they naturally questioned the wisdom of Stuyvesant's liberal policy. This much, however, Mr. Ward must admit, they made no further objections when the Director General had given them good reasons for his decision. If this is poltroonery, I wonder what hyperbolical term Mr. Ward would be able to invent for the motives that prompted the recent invasion of a perfectly harmless Finnish club in New York?

Mr. Ward, who, to judge from the way in which he spells and translates Dutch words, is as innocent of any knowledge of that language as a new-born babe, has nevertheless a keen sense of the music that resounds in them. "Patroon," he tells us, "is as sonorous a title as ever issued from the lips of a monarch at the moment of accolade. There are drums and trumpets in the word." This will be a revelation to his Dutch readers. The word is familiar to them as a common synonym of "boss." Dutch butchers and bakers and candle-stickmakers will be pleased to know that when they talk about their "patroon" it is as good as a brass band to the sensitive ear of one musical American. And what about "poltroon," we feel tempted to ask? The two words are so similar in sound, being within punning distance from each other, that Mr. Ward is bound to hear the drums and trumpets in "poltroon" as well. From which it would follow that "poltroon" must also be as sonorous a title as ever issued, etc., etc. This sort of snappy writing may be delectable in the columns of the *New Yorker*, but it is out of place in a scholarly work such as Mr. Ward has written. His persistent attempt to be amusing will not make his book enjoyable for the superficial reader, and it irritates the serious one who is capable of appreciating its excellence in spite of this annoying inducement to mirth.

WILLEM BILDERDIJK

Holland commemorates this year one of her great poets, Willem Bilderdijk, who at the age of seventy-five passed away one hundred years ago. He was born in 1756. Dutch literature in the eighteenth century had fallen upon evil days. The writing of verse had become a polite entertainment, and the result was a polished kind of rhymed verbiage that charmed no one but the self-satisfied rhymester. The romantic revival of Germany and England made something of a stir in Holland, but it was not strong enough to arouse the general apathy to a new life. Bilderdijk was the only poet in whom the romantic spirit proved an inspiring passion, and he had to atone for his uniqueness by lifelong solitude and isolation. He was a strange, exotic animal in the well-regulated menagerie of Holland, a gloomy dean of letters, a bitter and unpleasant critic of his age, a preacher of morality who, in his private life, boldly defied the conventional moral code, an arch-conservative in an age that made democracy its gospel, a mystic among rationalists, and a great poet among a crowd of petty rhymesters. He was born in Amsterdam, the son of a prominent physician. At an early age he suffered an injury to his foot, which confined him to his bed for twelve years. Growing up without the friendship of playmates and with no other companions than books, he became a shy, self-centered misanthrope, rich in the knowledge of book-learning but devoid of all knowledge of his fellow men. His encyclopaedic mind took a passionate interest in nearly every field of human endeavor. "The study of Roman law is my chief delight ... poetry only an inter-mittent paroxysm," he wrote to one of his friends. He taught history for a time at Leyden, he published a book on geology, he took himself for an expert in linguistics, and engaged in polemics with a Leyden philologist on the proper spelling of the Dutch language; he studied genealogy and heraldry, and corresponded with German scholars on questions of philosophy and religion. His passionate nature was never satisfied with a partial yield; he demanded the utmost from everything and everybody. Disillusionment was, consequently, his lot. He loved his country passionately, but expecting too much from it, he found himself sadly disappointed. It was the only country in which he could endure life, but even in Holland he found it at last endurable only in Leyden. His first wife left him equally disillusioned. When in 1796 he refused to swear allegiance to the Batavian Republic and preferred banishment to disloyalty to the Prince of Orange, she refused to follow him into exile. He took that refusal for an act of abandonment. In London he became acquainted with a Dutch painter, whose two daughters took private lessons from him. The younger one, Catharine, fell in love with her teacher, and he took her to wife, though legally he was still a married man. The couple went to Brunswick in Germany, awaiting an opportunity to return to Holland. But to his growing vexation the release from his exile was postponed from year to year. The long delay embittered him, he satirized the Duke of Brunswick, who had supported him financially, for not supporting him enough, he reviled German life and German manners, and made himself disagreeable to all who came in contact with him. His second wife, however, was a patient Griselda to this erratic Count who had married her. Count of Teisterbant was the name by which Bilderdijk called himself, not in order to conceal his identity, but because he honestly believed that he had a right to this title, proclaiming himself a descendant of that mediaeval house and, through it, of the Knight of the Swan, who was the son of a Byzantine emperor. In 1806 the Count of Teisterbant was readmitted to his native country, then a kingdom under Napoleon's brother Louis Bonaparte. The romantic believer in feudalism and in royalty by the grace of God could reconcile himself with this new state of affairs. He became the King's instructor in Dutch and his librarian, and spent a brief period of happiness in the sunshine of his royal favor. But in 1810 the Kingdom of Holland was incorporated with the Napoleonic Empire, Louis Bonaparte was dethroned, and Bilderdijk relapsed into his former state of hypochondria. The closing years of his life were brightened for him by the affection and worship that he received from a group of younger men who had sat at his feet in the lecture rooms at Leyden. Among these was Isaac da Costa, son of a Portuguese-Jewish family of Amsterdam, who became the leading poet of the next generation and the apostle of the ideas that his master and converter had taught in his lectures and his poetry. His devoted Griselda passed away before him; he followed her two years later to a grave in the Church of St. Bavo at Haarlem.

The poetic oeuvre that he left is as incongruous and erratic as the life he led. He was cursed with a gift for versification, and succumbed too readily to the temptation of turning everything he wrote into rhyme. The result was an appalling mass of verse of very unequal quality, exquisite lyrics touched with a passionate mysticism and dull didactic poems which smell of eighteenth-century pedantry and dusty folios, imitations of Ossian and of ballads from Percy's *Reliques* and classical drama in the manner of Voltaire, sensuous love songs and biblical epics, intemperate invectives and patriotic odes. Much of it is hollow rhetoric, but among it is some of the finest and noblest poetry that has been written in the Dutch language. The Bilderdijk centenary is being sponsored by an imposing group of men and women more numerous, I have no doubt, than the number of readers the poet still has among the present generation. How many of these Bilderdijk admirers would be able to recite one of his poems, I wonder? Not a single quotation from his works has become a winged word in the Dutch language. The best service these commemorators can do the great poet is to reduce the fifteen tomes of his collected poetry to one slender volume containing the purest essence of his verse. The little that would make up such a volume would demonstrate his indubitable greatness.

August, 1931

THE POWER OF SONG

There seem to be people who, in the grip of a terrible fright, feel strangely impelled to burst forth into song. Bontekoe, the Dutch skipper who wrote a popular storybook of his sea adventures, describes an episode in which he was seized, and miraculously saved, by that impulse. He was at the mercy of two Malayan savages, who were paddling him down stream in their prau. To left and right of him was the impenetrable jungle of Sumatra; far ahead, at the mouth of the river, was his shipwrecked crew. He had gone inland with two of his men to look for a native settlement and to bargain with the savages for food. They had found a village, they had bought a cow from the inhabitants, but the stubborn beast resisted all their attempts to lead her away. Bontekoe, therefore, had left his two comrades behind in charge of their recalcitrant purchase. They would bring her down as soon as she became amenable, and he had enlisted the aid of two natives to paddle him back to the rest of his crew. He felt ill at ease in the company of two wild creatures with whom he could converse only by signs. The signs in which they spoke, while steering their little boat down the current, were as plain to him as his own Dutch speech. They wanted money, and still more money. The ease with which their menacing gestures produced silver coins from the depth of Bontekoe's pocket increased the eloquence of their hands and faces. He began to read a sinister meaning in their greedy eyes. They were intent upon murder and robbery. And in the fear that seized him on realizing that his life was in danger, he suddenly began to sing at the top of his voice. Song followed song, and the echoes from the woods along the banks made a chorus. The savages listened open-mouthed in dumb amazement. The seaman's repertoire acted as an incantation, which robbed them of the power to do harm. The prau glided down the stream, while Bontekoe's song held the savages in check, and returned him safely to his crew on the beach.

Bontekoe was not a writer of fiction. One would give him credit for more talent than he possessed, if one were to take this story for a yarn of his own invention. Still, the old skipper's manner of reacting to the sense of fear has always seemed to me a very rare, if not unique, kind of reflex. I never met anyone who confessed to having confronted a perilous situation in his vocal fashion. The other day, however, I read a story which supplied a striking analogue to Bontekoe's and made me more convinced than ever that he had described an actual experience. Julian Duguid, in his admirable narrative of an adventurous trek across "Green Hell," as he calls the jungles of eastern Bolivia, tells of a lonely ride through the forest after nightfall. He had dropped off to sleep in the saddle, and was in the middle of a pleasant dream, when suddenly the horse was on its hind legs, snorting with fear. The rider, wide awake at once, discovered the cause of the horse's fright in a couple of yellow lights about five yards away from him. A jaguar was evidently crouching in the darkness. Suddenly the author had the kind of inspiration that came to Bontekoe in his extreme peril. "I began to sing," he tells us; "not that I have a beautiful voice, but it is powerful, and has a terrifying habit of changing into low gear when ascending the gradient of a song. So with a certain heartfelt feeling I gave the tiger two verses of 'Show me the way to go home.' At first these raucous noises did nothing beyond startling Green Hell, who laughed, and the horse, which reared. The tiger went on blinking. However, towards the end of the second verse, the lights disappeared quite silently into the forest and the horse for obvious reasons stopped trembling. Once again we proceeded on our sleepy way." Is this bursting into song in the face of imminent danger a kind of mad bravado, a subconscious urge to dare death by a pretence at unconcern and mirth? The unexpectedness of the victim's uncanny reaction to the menace may well startle the assailant, be he man or beast, and throw him off his guard. In Duguid's case his fear was unfounded, as we learn from the sequel to his story. There was no jaguar crouching in the dark. But that does not detract from the value of the episode as an analogue of Bontekoe's case. The Dutch skipper may also have been mistaken when he believed himself to be in danger of his life. The thing that matters is that both, by a subconscious urge, daunted death by flinging a challenge of song into his face.

In a previous Letter I had occasion to mention the extinct game of
kolf, which was exported to Scotland and came back to the Netherlands
as golf. One of our members has asked me for information as to how
the game was played in the Low Countries. That question is not
easy to answer, for the Dutch, being better artists than writers, have
left many a picture of people playing *kolf*, but hardly any description
of the game in writing. A miniature in a Book of Hours made at
Bruges in the early sixteenth century and now owned by the British
Museum shows three players putting at a hole in the turf. The turf
of the churchyards seems to have provided an ideal link to the mediaeval *kolf* fans. Municipal ordinances of the late Middle Ages forbade
repeatedly the use of the cemeteries for that frivolous purpose. "The
Council of our town," says an ordinance of Amersfoort of 1436,
"forbids old and young to play *kolf* or ball or any other game in St.
John's Churchyard at a penalty of one pound, and if children should be
found guilty, the Council will hold the parents responsible." The
turf, however, does not seem to have been essential to the game; a
hole between the flagstones of a church would serve the players' purpose just as well. A fifteenth century ordinance of the little town of
Naarden, south of Amsterdam, forbade the abuse of the church by *kolf*
and ball players. A common name for the game in mediaeval Dutch
was *sollen metter colve*, i. e., to "sole" with the golf club, to "sole" being
a word of French origin which was in use in England in the seventeenth
century. The club, called *kolf* or *klik* in Dutch, was often reinforced
at the head with a mounting of lead or iron, but the use of these was
repeatedly prohibited by the authorities, who would allow no clubs
that were not made entirely of wood. The ball was small and very
hard; it was stuffed with feathers and had a leather cover. The purpose
of the game was to drive the ball to the goal in as few strokes as
possible. This goal was not necessarily a hole in the turf; it might also
be a little stake that stuck out an inch or two above the ground. This
stake was the regular goal when the game was played on the ice. One
may see the players in action in many a winter scene by landscape
painters of the Holland school such as Hendrick Avercamp and Aert
van der Neer. Six van Chandelier, an Amsterdam poet of the seventeenth century, refers to the game as it was played on the ice in a
passage that is scarcely intelligible to a modern reader. I understand
this much of it that the players drew lots for partners. They stood on
skates or wore nails under their shoes to stand firm on the ice. The
club was made of aspen wood and loaded with lead, or, if it was a
Scottish cleek, it was made of palm wood, three fingers broad at the

head and one finger thick. The feather-stuffed ball was placed upon a tee called *druifje*, meaning grape, which was so small that it was hardly visible when the ball was lying on the top of it. Each player carried a twig for a tally, which he stuck into the button-hole of his jacket. The winner's prize was either money or free beer. The best picture of a *kolf* player on skates that I have seen is an engraving by Romeyn de Hooghe, to be found in a series of "Figures a la Mode" published in Amsterdam at the end of the seventeenth century. In the eighteenth century the game began to be played on a specially prepared *kolfbaan* or mall, a change which gave it an entirely different character. These malls were usually covered by a tiled wooden roof, but open on the sides. The length of the course was no more than eighty feet, and its width seldom more than twenty. A stake in the shape of a huge nine-pin stood at either end, and the ball was driven from one to the other across a course of loam mixed with mortar and beaten into a hard, smooth surface. The balls were larger than in the previous century, and the clubs were made of brass with a mounting of iron at the head. The game had become an indoor sport, as a result perhaps of ordinances that forbade it in churchyards, on the street, and on the ice. But within the narrow limits to which it had been banished it soon lost its popular appeal. A writer in 1814 described a *kolf* game on a village mall as a rare survival of past days, and predicted its total extinction within the near future. Even the simple craftsmen and the peasants in the rural districts at that time were quitting the mall for the billiard table. There was a *kolf* course still in existence, when I was a little boy, in a village near Alkmaar in North Holland. But that was more than seventy years ago. I do not believe that a single one has survived into the twentieth century.

November, 1931

ST. MARTIN'S DAY

The celebration of Armistice Day in Holland has given a new meaning to a very ancient custom that has come down from pre-Christian times. The eleventh of November is St. Martin's Day, dedicated to the memory of the holy warrior who, finding a shivering beggar at the gate of the city of Amiens, cut his mantle in two with his sword and covered the poor wretch with one half of it. On St. Martin's Day it is a common practice for little children to march through the streets carrying Chinese lanterns or candles. You will not find them doing this at The Hague or Amsterdam, but in the south and the east of the country, especially in places where St. Martin has given his name to the church, the custom still prevails. The candles that they carry are all that is left of the fires which, in the people's pagan past, were lit in the fields as a sacrifice to the Gods in whom heathen mythology personified the forces of fertility and vegetation. They danced around the flames, jumped over and across them that the glow might give them immunity from sickness, and carried a burning brand home as a protection for man and beast against disease. It is not quite clear how St. Martin became a patron of this pagan practice. Perhaps the Church of Rome, finding the torch-light procession to be an ineradicable ceremony, substituted for the heathen Gods this Christian paragon of charity, and made the flames rise up to him like so many prayers for the health of man, beast, and crop. The firebrands have dwindled into insignificant candles, and the children that carry these are unaware of the original purpose for which the procession was held that they repeat year after year. But since the eleventh of November has received a new consecration through the Armistice having been concluded on that day, the candles have begun to shine forth with a new meaning. In the city of Groningen, whose principal church is dedicated to St. Martin, the children's procession carries the candles in lanterns that are shaped as doves, or angels, or bells of peace, and adorned with appropriate pictures and inscriptions. Thus St. Martin, the warrior who used his sword to cut a cover for a poor, naked beggar, has become the patron saint of the disarmament movement. The annual march of the little pacifists through the streets of the city of Groningen should have its counterpart in every village, town, and city of Europe and America, forming an impressive children's crusade against the Anti-Christ War.

February, 1932

A ROYAL ARTIST

The chief topic of conversation at The Hague is, strange to say, not the depression, which they call Crisis in Holland, but an uncommon artistic debut. The Kleykamp Galleries, opposite the Peace Palace, have become a place of pilgrimage for thousands of visitors who are eager to see the latest exhibition put on view. The show is worth seeing for its own sake, but its interest to the public is enhanced by the prominent personality of the painter. For no less a person than Her Majesty Queen Wilhelmina is the artist who has filled the walls of three spacious rooms on the second floor with paintings and sketches from her hand. It was no secret to any one in Holland that Her Majesty was fond of sketching and drawing, but few people realized that her

71

devotion to art was more than a dilettante's pastime. The collection on view at the Kleykamp rooms is not the work of an amateur, and the Queen's subjects owe it to the Crisis – the depression *must* be mentioned after all – that she is thus revealed as an accomplished member of the painters' craft. For only the Crisis could have induced Her Majesty to exhibit the artistic achievements of her leisure hours. The admission fee and the returns from the sale of the catalogue are a part of the Queen's contribution to the Emergency Relief Fund. By revealing herself as an adept of the art that is most essentially Dutch she makes a most effective appeal to the generosity of her subjects. They know a good picture when they see it, and they know a good artist when they see his work. Having gone to the exhibition to view the Queen's paintings, they were surprised and delighted to discover a painter in their Queen.

Landscape is Her Majesty's favorite genre. There is a tiny pen sketch of peasants mowing and making hay, which is conspicuous by its uniqueness. Scenery unenlivened by figures is her forte. On her travels in Norway, Bavaria, and Switzerland the Queen has sensed the beauty of mountain solitude, and rendered it on canvas under various light effects. She has painted the rising sun when it flooded the valley with radiance from behind a dark mass of drifting clouds, she has observed the wooded slopes through a silvery mist after a heavy rainfall, and the dusk that gathers late in the day in the depth of a Norwegian fjord. Some of the sketches with pen and ink show her talent at its very best. In these she has rendered a simplified vision with bold and vigorous craftsmanship. The catalogue, a booklet to be treasured by lovers of art and admirers of Queen Wilhelmina, contains a few reproductions of these sketches that will confirm the praise bestowed upon the originals. Few Hollanders, however, will be satisfied with a glance at these photographic copies. Requests from other cities are coming in to have the Queen's collection shown within their walls. Thus Holland will witness a royal progress in novel fashion, a Queen being hailed by her people for her talent and for the charity which turns that talent to the benefit of the suffering poor.

RHODES THE DREAMER

Thirty years ago today, the twenty-sixth of March, Cecil Rhodes died in his cottage at Muizenberg, the popular seaside resort at the Cape. In Holland his name is anathema. Over there he is popularly believed to have been the evil genius of SouthAfrica, the ruthless imperialist who trampled upon the rights of the Boers, who was behind the iniquitous Jameson raid, and threw SouthAfrica into the welter of the Boer War. But it is forgotten, if it is known at all, that this same man, at the height of his phenomenal career, was the friend and associate of Jan Hofmeyr, 'Onze Jan' as he was popularly called, who was the leading representative, in the eighties of the past century, of Dutch South Africa, and one of the foremost men in the Cape Parliament. This statesman, the very antithesis of the wicked schemer that Rhodes is supposed to have been, saw in a political alliance with him the means of realizing his own hopes for South Africa. The two became united by their common conception of a future in which a SouthAfrican nation, within the compass of the British Empire, would shape and control its own destinies, a nation not of English race that had absorbed the Dutch or vice versa, but one in which Briton and Boer would live together as equals, each respecting the other's individuality and valuing its distinctive traits as assets in the building up of a bilingual Union. Rhodes's fervid longing to see the materialization of his dream was largely responsible for the fatal errors of his later years. "How old are you?" he asked Sir Percy Fitzpatrick one day, when the two were discussing the steps that had to be taken to bring about a Federation of South Africa. "On the right side of forty," answered Sir Percy. Whereupon Rhodes almost indignantly exclaimed, "To think that you will see it all ... and I shall not!" Baffled impatience made him, towards the close of his career, the reckless schemer who thought he could ride roughshod over every obstacle that he met in his way. It is the Rhodes of that period who left a sad caricature of his real self in the minds of my Dutch countrymen. The Union of South Africa as it is today, a generation after his death, is the realization of his vision. As far back as 1883, Rhodes foreshadowed this development in the course of a speech in the Cape Parliament. He drew before an audience partly sceptical, partly carried away, the picture of a British Empire of the future, the component parts of which would be independent nations, but all of them partners in the privileges and advantages derived from cooperation with the Empire. When in the early nineties he had become Prime Minister of the Cape Colony with the backing of Hofmeyr's Afrikaner Bond, he defined his policy as aiming at "the government of South Africa by the people of South Africa with the Imperial tie for defence." On the Kerkplein, the Church Square, in Cape Town, in the center of his native city, Onze Jan stands on his pedestal in bronze, facing the Dutch Reformed Church where he worshiped. High up on the mountain slope above Groote Schuur Rhodes' bust stands enshrined in a colossal monument. His eyes stare into the north across veld and mountains as if they encompassed in their gaze the united South Africa of his hopes. Each has been given a place appropriate to the man and his ideals. Hofmeyr was the realist to whom statesmanship was the art of organizing the party under his control to the fullest advantage of the country. His place was among men in the centre of the city. Rhodes was a lonely dreamer to whom statesmanship was the grouping and organizing of nations, a visionary whose genius set him apart from his fellow men. Still our knowledge of the dreamer is incomplete unless we think of him also as the friend and associate of the realist. The real Rhodes is revealed by his partnership with Onze Jan.

OF OSTRICHES

Ostriches are said to be the inventors of the policy of averting danger by ignoring it. It is a pretty story, for which all credit is due to the ancient fabulist, whoever he may be, that gave it vogue. But he did not give due honor to the birds, for their astuteness exceeds his ingenuity. Instead of making themselves unseeing by burying their heads in the sand, they practice the magician's art of becoming invisible. I wonder why I was never told this true ostrich lore in my young school days. I have no fault to find with the teacher who told me the age-old head-in-the-sand fable; it is too good a tale not to be perpetuated. But it is not fair to the birds that the real story of their sagacity was withheld from us children in school. I had to come to Oudtshoorn, in the Cape Province, to learn the truth about the ostrich. Oudtshoorn is the centre of a once prosperous district of ostrich farms. The birds seem to thrive there, and a generation ago the Dutch farmers throve with them, supplying the millineries in Paris, London, and New York with costly white and black plumes. They amassed large fortunes that counted for fabulous in those days, and built themselves palatial mansions in late-Victorian taste. But a change of fashion brought distress to Oudtshoorn. When Sargent lost vogue as the painter of elegance, the Dutch farmers saw the value of their ostrich herds reduced to nothing. During the boom they had paid from £300 to £400 a morgen, which is about two acres; after the crash they were glad if they could dispose of their superfluous land at one-tenth of that price. The most stately of the Victorian palaces is now in use as a hostel for the women students who attend the classes at the State Training College for Teachers in Oudtshoorn. Some farmers, who husbanded more cautiously, succeeded in weathering the storm, and turned from ostrich to cattle farming. They still keep a small flock of birds, more as a hobby than an investment. We visited one of these, and it was from him that we learnt the truth about the ostrich which sounded stranger than the fabulist's fiction. It was new to me, at any rate, that the ostrich, when she sits upon her nest of eggs, is almost invisible. For her feathers, of a greyish brown color, make her seem to be part of the sand or the parched grass, and, as she lays her eggs in a hollow her body does not break the even surface of the ground. We found one sitting on her nest but did not notice her until we were close upon her. The long neck lay flat upon the ground, the head looking like the nozzle of a garden hose, and the eyes, far from being buried under the sand were keeping sharp watch. Thus she sits for forty-two days, a picture of patience. But at sunset she is relieved by the male, who faithfully takes her place at night. His feathers are black, and being part of the darkness he keeps his neck and head erect without fear of detection. The turtle dove has, from time immemorial, been the poetic emblem of conjugal fidelity. He is fabled to perch on a withered branch mourning for his lost mate. But the true test of conjugal devotion is not in sorrow for the dead mate but in service to the living one. The black ostrich guarding the family eggs from sunset to sunrise for forty-two nights is a nobler mate than the tenderly cooing turtle dove on his barren branch.

We attended a society wedding at Oudtshoorn, which was a grand and lavish affair, reminiscent, said the local paper, of the good old days of the ostrich feather boom. The emblem of former prosperity was much in evidence on this occasion. The bridal couple drove to church with beautiful white plumes on the radiators of the automobiles, and at the reception several ladies wore their hats trimmed with ostrich feathers. The sight of the beplumed radiator made me realize that the ostrich feather is obsolete in these motoring days. They are beautiful on a horse's head; on the head of our modern steel horse going at the rate of thirty miles an hour they looked like a helpless tuft of grass on a windswept kopje. And all the ladies' hat plumes blew in the same direction pointing like weather vanes the way they came from. The waving plumes lent beauty to an age of dignity and repose; storm-tossed on the radiator they would not grace but only stress our modern speed. There are still flocks of ostriches in Oudtshoorn, but I am afraid that they will never again be an investment.

A PRODIGAL'S PROGRESS

On May 17, 1807, the American brig Abigael sailed from Amsterdam for Philadelphia with only six passengers on board. They were an aged Swiss physician and his daughter, a Dutchman in his teens and his Mulatto wife, and two colored servants of the young couple. Neither the Swiss nor the Hollander were men of any consequence. The doctor's right to his title was subject to doubt in view of the lack of medical skill that he betrayed during the voyage, and the husband of the Mulatto bride had no other claims to distinction than the wealth into which he had married, his wife, a precocious young lady aged twelve, being heiress to a large plantation in Berbice. The boy was the son of a clergyman, who was minister of the Dutch Reformed Church at Naarden, a small garrison town south of Amsterdam. The marriage of his scapegrace of a son with the dusky offspring of an illegitimate union was a terrible blow to the Reverend Swaving. His small parish must have been humming with amused gossip at the dominie's expense. To ship the prodigal off to his Berbice plantation was the only way of saving the family from further ridicule and disgrace. The boy went only too gladly. A born adventurer, with the wanderlust itching in his blood, he did not fit into the respectable middle-class life of his native land. At the age of twelve he had enlisted as a naval cadet on a Dutch man-of-war and had grown up among a dissolute crew recruited from the slums of Holland's seaports. What good could be expected from a boy who had gone to school in the forecastle? When father and son parted on the stoop of the vicarage, each knew that it was to be for good. The ne'er-do-well had no intention of coming home to roost, and the old man foresaw that the yellow fever of Berbice and the boy's own excesses would cut short his worthless life and silence the scandal mongers at home. But ill weeds grow apace instead of dying. That this Monthly Letter gives a passing thought to the Reverend Swaving is owing to his scapegrace son, who left a printed record behind which is doubtless more readable than the most edifying sermon of the Naarden pastor. In the year 1827, when the younger Swaving was earning a living in London as a language teacher and translator, the Dordrecht publishing house of Blussé and Van Braam brought out in two volumes "*Swaving's Reizen en Lotgevallen door hem zelven beschreven*' (Swaving's Travels and Adventures described by himself), a copy of which recently came into my hands. As several chapters of this book deal with his experiences in the United States, a brief account of these may be of interest to readers of this monthly sheet.

The voyage from Amsterdam to Philadelphia lasted one hundred and eighteen days. Young Swaving paid six hundred guilders ($ 240) for his cabin on starboard. The saloon served as a sleeping place for six members of the crew and as a store room for part of the cargo, which consisted chiefly of gin and cheese. The foul atmosphere, the close quarters, the slow progress, and the stale food conspired to turn the crossing into a physical and mental torture. The bible which a customs man gave them to kiss on landing was a greasy old book, but they must have kissed it in rapture as a token of their release from torment. Their miseries, however, were not yet over. They soon found that no hotel would take them in, on account of the bride's complexion. Swaving at last prevailed upon the manager of the General Washington to admit them on condition that he should never appear at the table d'hote accompanied by his wife. The Dutch consul, who bore the German name of Lechleitener, next day found a room for them in a grocer's house, where they paid $28 a week including meals. Life in Philadelphia was twice as expensive as in Holland, rents being even four times as high. While waiting for a ship that would take them to the island of Barbados, they made an excursion in a buggy to Germantown, Chestnut Hill, Clement's Tavern, Quakers Town, Bethlehem, Nazareth, and Belvedere. The landlord at Clement's Tavern was the son of the man who gave his name to the place. His father, he told them, was a native of Amsterdam, Holland, and had amassed a fortune as a merchant in Philadelphia. But his ventures having gone awry, he had the keel of a ship that he had saved from his ruin removed to the top of this hill, and had retired on board from the hazards of commerce and trade. From Belvedere, "a heavenly place," where they spent a full week, they returned to Philadelphia to set sail for Berbice via Barbados.

Swaving was back in New York in the summer of 1810. His child wife was no longer with him. She had died after giving birth to a still-born child, and had left him heir to the plantation. As a man of means he took rooms in Mechanics Hall on the Park, where they were building a new City Hall. The sights to be seen in those days in New York included, according to his itinerary, the Institute for the Deaf and Dumb, the Picture Gallery in the building of the American Institute, the New York Lyceum, the American Museum, the Botanical Garden, the Dissecting Room of the Medical Institute, the Arsenal, the House of Correction, the State Prison, the principal Hospital, the Orphanage, the largest of the eleven banks, the French and English theaters, some of the fifty-six places of worship, among which there were six of the Dutch Reformed Church, and some of the eight city markets, where he heard almost nothing but Dutch spoken. By the newly invented steamboat he traveled up the river to Albany. This city, at that time, was still entirely Dutch, but finding it a somber place devoid of amusements, he left it the following day to visit the Cohoes Falls. On his progress north he passed a settlement of Hollanders and Germans called German Flats, the most fertile spot he had ever seen, and a village called Rotterdam, where he was the guest of a countryman called Hendrik van den Broek. He visited the Oswego and Niagara falls and returned by the same route to New York.

A year and a half later he left his mismanaged plantation for good, a much poorer but hardly much wiser man. He disembarked at Baltimore in January 1812. It amazed him to see how rapidly this town was expanding. During the six months of his stay there about seven hundred houses shot out of the ground between Fell's Point and Baltimore. There were still some old Westphalians living in the town who had known the place when it consisted of hardly more than half a dozen wooden huts. At the time of Swaving's visit Baltimore numbered more than 45,500 inhabitants. The larger part of the lower classes were illiterate, but there was a strong movement on foot for the spreading of education among them. In Philadelphia, where he stayed at the Mansion House, he saw in the theater Jerome Bonaparte with his wife and child sitting in one of the boxes. In New York he took a room in the City Hotel, which he describes as an immense hostlery. While he was dining there at the table d'hote, he was arrested for a debt of twenty thousand Spanish piasters, which he owed to the ship brokers' firm of Lehman & Co. In the debtors' jail, next to the City Hall, he made the acquaintance of a Dutch Jew, who had posed for a time as an apostle of Christ, proclaiming by means of huge posters at the street corners that, invested with divine power, he had come to the United States to save sinners from perdition. Dressed in purple and attended by footmen in gorgeous livery, he had driven from place to place in a carriage and four, until an accumulation of unpaid hotel and stable bills had landed the saviour of sinners in jail. This fellow, who was on the point of being discharged on Swaving's arrival, smuggled a flask of poison into his cell. A frustrated attempt at suicide attracted the attention of charitable people to Swaving's plight. The firm of Bayard & Macever (McKeever or McIver?) sent him money, someone else supplied him with books, and visitors came to cheer him in his confinement. At last he found a way out by signing up for the United States army. Soldiers were needed for an expedition to Canada, and jailed debtors were baited into enlistment by the promise of release from prison. His physical condition, however, was such that the medical officer who examined him recommended him for discharge from military service. While awaiting the decision of the War Department at Washington, Swaving served as clerk to a recruiting officer, who took up headquarters at the Golden Cock in New Haven, Conn. His employer soon collected the one hundred men that he needed to claim for himself a commission as captain of a company, and by that time the War Department gave its fiat to his discharge, on condition that he should report to the Court at New York for recommitment to the debtors' prison. Swaving, however, first paid a visit in full uniform to the firm of Lehman & Co., hoping to impress his creditors by his martial appearance and to soften their hearts by a realistic account of his past sufferings. But these gentlemen would not relent towards him. On the contrary, they threatened to keep him in jail for the rest of his life, and after his death they would have his dead body on exhibit at their door until the garbage collector would take it away. That interview convinced him that his only hope was in absconding. Instead of reporting to the court, he paid a visit to his old friend, the discredited saviour of lost souls, who was now a saviour of old clothes in the Jewish quarter. He exchanged his uniform for a suit of plain clothes, obtained passage on a ship bound for Holland by handing the owners a draft for $100 on his brother, a physician in good standing at Amsterdam, and sailed that same evening towards liberty and his native land.

June, 1933

THREE GUIDES TO HOLLAND

Three books on Holland are lying on my desk, *An Indiscreet Itinerary* by one who was actually born there and whose name is Hendrik Willem van Loon (Harcourt, Brace & Co.), *Holland* by Karl Scheffler (Alfred A. Knopf), and *Letters from Holland* by Karel Capek (G. P. Putnam's Sons). Mr. Van Loon, being a native Dutchman, offers to act as the reader's guide, Mr. Scheffler, being a German, addresses him as a philosopher, and Mr. Capek, who has no axe to grind, wants to be just his friend, that is all. The three together are to the foreign traveler in Holland what Bolingbroke was to Alexander Pope. The guide, in this case, is really a railway guide, for Mr. Van Loon confesses to the reader that it was the New York representative of the Netherlands Railways who persuaded him to write this little book. This Dutch official, by the way, bears the un-Dutch name of Ravelli. It seems to be the fashion nowadays for European countries to employ special envoys whose visiting card does not reveal their actual nationality. When Italy needs a financial expert to discuss economic matters with President Roosevelt and his brain trust, she can find no better man than Herr Jung. France speaks to the Assembly of the League of Nations through Signor Massigli, and even the Nazi Government employs at Geneva, as spokesman for the racially purified German Reich, a gentleman who bears the un-Nordic name of Nadolny. So Holland is quite up to the latest fashion in having her railways represented in New York by my good friend Signor Ravelli. He is the right man in the right place. Mr. Ravelli knows his business, he knows his American public, and he knows also that the Made-in-Holland publicity stuff is no good for distribution in this country. English as it is written in Holland is very seldom pleasant reading to one who is born to the language. E. V. Lucas, in *A Wanderer in Holland*, first published in 1905, was kind enough to say that most Dutch guides were written in good English, "albeit," he added, "of Dutch extraction." But it is the extract that spoils the flavor. Lucas's irony has not convinced the Dutch that English cannot be written in Holland. They have a firm belief that their linguistic talent, which is indeed highly developed, can overcome all difficulties. It is an old delusion that can be traced back to the early sixteenth century. In the year 1537, Richard Grafton, writing to Thomas Cromwell, complained about the wretched English of a Bible translation then being offered for sale in England. "Douchemen dwellynge within this realme go about pryntyng of ytt, which can nether speke good Englyshe nor yet wryte none." The passage that Mr. Lucas quotes from a guidebook entitled "Through North Holland" gives a specimen of the kind of English that results from such ignorance. But a guidebook writer must have more strings to his bow than a good command of the language he uses. He must also have literary skill and a thorough knowledge not only of the country he describes but also of the people whom he proposes to guide. Mr. Van Loon fulfills all these requirements. I believe that he knows his Americans even better than he does his native countrymen. He treats them exactly as they like to be treated. Before taking them on tour he entertains them with a lecture. It is a lecture that digs deep into the past, excavation being the popular sport of the would-be intellectual in this country, to judge from the headline excitement over Tut-Ankh-Amen and the dinosaur eggs from the Gobi desert. So *An Indiscreet Itinerary* starts from those pre-historic days when England was geologically connected with the Continent and the Thames was a tributary of the Rhine, and takes the audience in thirty pages across the ages to a present in which Holland is telephonically connected with Java. Having thus speeded his personally conducted party from prehistoric to modern times, he allows them to sit down and catch their breath, while he draws a delightful little pen sketch of a Dutch breakfast table. And then he takes them on a leisurely sightseeing trip through the country. He knows that his method of travelling is not at all like the system practiced by the usual agencies of mass transportation. "But what earthly use," he asks, "in merely 'seeing' a country? You must feel it, sense it, if you want your travels to be of lasting value to you." Mr. Van Loon himself, after having become completely Americanized, went back to live in Holland and learnt to sense it more impartially, and therefore more accurately, than a stay-at-home Hollander can. He has remained a Dutchman, however, in his love of moralization. "And what is the moral of the story?" he asks. "Well, there is not any," is his answer. But his closing words belie that modest denial. When he wrote his little guidebook he was thinking of that rapidly increasing number of his fellow citizens "who have learned some sort of lesson during the last four years … and who are now seriously endeavoring to find some way out that should provide us with a 'mode of living' rather than a chance to 'make a living'." And the moral of his guidebook story is that those who seek such guidance may find it in the self-possessed, peace-loving people of Holland.

Our friend Mr. Karel Capek has much in common with our guide Van Loon. He also illustrates his book with his own drawings. Van Loon's clever sketches are naturalistic snapshots; Capek sees everything simplified and running into patterns. The picture of a Dutch high-road lined with trees and the accordion player on the jacket are good examples of his manner. He must have visited Holland in the summer, for he refers again and again to the reflection of the landscape in the water of *grachts* and canals. "The towns appear to be standing, not on the earth, but on their own reflections; these highly respectable streets appear to emerge from bottomless depths of dreams; the houses appear to be intended as houses and, at the same time, as reflections of houses." On winter days, however, the mirror looks usually dull under a sunless sky, or it is hidden under a sheet of ice and snow. Mr. Capek was amazed at the number of bicycles he saw everywhere. "I saw nuns on bicycles and farmers on bicycles leading cows. People eat snacks on bicycles and courting couples go pedalling along, arm in arm, on bicycles, towards a blissful future; a nation on bicycles, in fact." But he did not see the nation on skates which is a rarer and just as amazing a sight. He was struck by one other conspicuous feature of street life in Holland: the ubiquity of the dog. "They have no muzzles and the consequence is that they keep on laughing almost out loud; nor do they quarrel or bite or growl at each other with that Central European touchiness; which only shows that freedom without a muzzle does not cause either dogs or human beings to go to the dogs, but is a paramount gift of God. Amen."

I said that Mr. Capek had no axe to grind. But that was somewhat hastily spoken. He does do some grinding in the final chapter, which is entitled "A Small Nation." Since Czechoslovakia has been an independent state its people have been asking themselves questions. What does this small nation of ours amount to? Did we not count for more in the world's affairs when we formed part of the Hapsburg Empire? Some citizens of the new Czechoslovakia complain of their petty surroundings, while others daily warn them of the big, evil world which is preparing to swallow them up. So there is trouble among them, and Mr. Capek, being interested to find out "how they deal with this trouble in other places where the Lord of Hosts has assigned to the people the same sort of small scale national undertaking as He has to us. And that – next to Rembrandt – was the first thing I looked for when I went to Holland."

He did not get the impression that the Hollanders worry very much over the smallness of their country. But he did notice that they have developed a technique of living that is harmoniously adapted to the diminutive scale assigned to them. "There is a certain cosiness and frugality with regard to size which constitutes nothing short of an ingrained formal law." Nothing in Holland is overdone either in architecture or in the people's way of living. Quality is stressed rather than quantity. "The national ideal does not aim at sizes but grades. You will discover this in everything: work, way of living, and even in nature itself. If you had to say on the spur of the moment what the Dutch are distinguished for, you would not think of anything huge, but of the fine, unusual and almost perfect quality of most they produce." That is the lesson and the consolation that Capek wants to convey through these letters to those countrymen of his who are worried by the limited size of their country and the national insignificance that they fear will result therefrom. Stress quality, he tells them, not only in material production, but also in the realm of ideals. "I cannot help feeling," he concludes, "that this small nation on the Rhine delta has acted like Mary in the Bible: it has chosen the better part."

Karl Scheffler's *Holland* is an entirely different kind of book. It is a guidebook in a way, but not the sort that you carry under your arm to pick information from at odd moments. It is a book for the thoughtful and the studious, who have both time to read and time to linger. If you go to Holland for a few days' sightseeing, *An Indiscreet Itinerary* will serve your purpose better, though Mr. Van Loon denies that he has written for such as you. You can consult him, anyway, and be much the wiser for what he tells you. But if you really want to know something more than surface information on Holland's history, the aspect of her landscape, the character of her cities, the mind of her people, the range of her art, Karl Scheffler is the ideal instructor. Capek's *Letters* are interesting reading, not for anything of value that they may add to your knowledge of Holland, but only because they reflect the impressions made by that country upon a discerning and artistic mind. It is the personal note that lends them charm. Van Loon writes from a profound knowledge of his subject, but the audience that he addresses compels him to stay on the surface. Scheffler does not obtrude his personal views, nor does he strive to be popular. Solidity of knowledge, a keen sense of the beautiful, and force of expression lend this book authority and style. It is the finest estimate of my native land and people that has come to my knowledge. His love of Holland does not blind him to her shortcomings. He does not love the country because he knows it so well, he knows it so well because he loves it. Affection is the source of understanding. This philosophic observer of the Dutch has come to the conclusion that "from the traveller's viewpoint Holland is not really a land for youth. Nor have women much of a chance. Romanticists – and the young are naturally so – are rather out of place. It is a country for men. Only those who love the everyday things of life are at home in it – who prefer the rule to the exception, weekday to Sunday. But those who have learned to know and love Holland are held very close. To them it becomes the loveliest land of Europe."

AN OUTPOST OF PROGRESS

In one of his grimmest short stories, which he gave the sarcastic title of "An Outpost of Progress," Joseph Conrad describes the tragic lot of two derelicts of civilization, who have been left in charge of an isolated trading post somewhere in the wilds of Africa. Among the belongings of their predecessor, who had died of the fever, they found some old copies of an English paper featuring an article, in highflown language, on what the Editor was pleased to call "Our Colonial Expansion." It expatiated on the rights and duties of civilization, on the sacredness of the civilizing work, and extolled the merits of those who went about bringing light, and faith, and commerce to the dark places of the earth. The writer's oratory flattered those two simple fellows with a vision of future fame preposterously inconsistent with their incompetence. Said one to the other one evening, "In a hundred years, there will be perhaps a town here. Quays, and warehouses, and barracks, and – and – billiard rooms. Civilization, my boy, and virtue – and all. And then, chaps will read that two good fellows were the first civilized men to live in this very spot." The story of their tragic end is Conrad's bitter comment on the journalist's oratory and on the ambitious dreams it evoked.

TWO PIONEERS

I cannot read that story without thinking, by way of contrast, of two Hollanders who, facing hardship and solitude in the wilds of Sumatra, were sustained by a similar vision of future greatness and saw it realized beyond their most sanguine expectations. Their names were Nienhuys and Cremer. They were the pioneers who started reclaiming the jungle of Deli, on the east coast of Sumatra, for the cultivation of tobacco and, incidentally, for the expansion of the white man's civilization. That happened in the seventies of the past century. The Deli Company, of which they were the founders, became a power in the land. Sumatra wrapper soon was the most highly priced tobacco in the Amsterdam market, yielding returns on the original investment such as had not been recorded since the palmiest days of the Dutch East India Company. The two pioneers, still in the full vigor of life, returned to Holland, Nienhuys to enjoy in leisure the wealth that his youthful enterprise had brought him, Cremer to go into politics and try his hand at statesmanship. He was an efficient Minister of Colonies, for which high office his experience in the tropics stood him in good stead, and, towards the end of his life, represented his country as Her Majesty's Minister in Washington, D. C. Deli is now one of the most prosperous regions of the Dutch East Indies, and Medan, the capital, with its harbor Belawan, has grown in less than three quarters of a century into a modern city not only of quays, and warehouses, and barracks, and billiard rooms, but of beautiful homes in spacious gardens, of hotels, and clubs, and stores, which together constitute a piece of Europe transplanted among the luxuriant vegetation of the tropics. "Civilization, my boy, and virtue, and all!"

AN UNCOMPROMISING REALIST

White Money, A Novel of the East Indies by Madelon Lulofs, translated from the Dutch by G. J. Renier and Irene Clephane (New York: The Century Company) tells a story of life as it was lived by the planters in Deli during the boom years preceding the present-day world-wide depression. If the author had written in Conrad's sarcastic mood, the translation might have been entitled "Civilization and Virtue." But Madelon Lulofs is in bitter earnest. She is indignant with the conditions she describes, and sarcasm, which is the mood of the cold intellect, cannot breathe in the tropical heat of indignation. The planters have subdued the jungle, and the rich Deli soil they have reclaimed is yielding them rich harvests of tobacco and rubber, which, in the boom market of the post-war decade, fetch prices unheard of in any previous period. Money is plentiful and is recklessly spent. In former days few planters were married. They lived with a native or Japanese housekeeper, abiding the time when they could retire with a comfortable fortune and settle down to a life of leisure and domesticity at The Hague or in some other garden city of Holland. But in the period which Madelon Lulofs describes the majority are married, and it is the advent of white women that instills into this primitive society the poison of demoralization. The continuous grind of the daily work, which knows no intermission even on Sundays, keeps the men's physique and moral fibre intact, but the women, with plenty of native servants at their beck and call, and doomed to inactivity and leisure, seek an escape from boredom in a hectic hunt for excitement. Illicit love affairs, drunken orgies, shameless promiscuity are the result. In the old days a rough comradeship had been the basis of a social order notorious, no doubt, for wild drinking bouts, but with unwritten laws of loyalty and honesty. But now suspicion, hostility, envy, intrigue are rife. The white man's society in that remote spot of Sumatra is disintegrating as it is breaking down all over the world in the post-war period. And when the Wall Street crash knocks the props from under the world's commerce, and the price of rubber comes down with a bang, the isolated jungle community in Deli is involved in the general collapse. Sobered by the sudden turn of fortune, the jobless planters drift back to Holland, which was to them the land of promise while they were in the Indies. But they find it hard to strike root again in the native soil. There is something alluring in that strong, cruel life of the tropics that keeps haunting them in the homeland where they no longer feel at home. Madelon Lulofs is an uncompromising realist. She allows her readers no relief from the depressing tale she has to tell. But she has told it with great force and talent. *White Money* is a literary debut that makes one hope for more and better from her hand.

January, 1934

OLD PLAYBILLS

While hunting for a rare publication in the New York Public Library card catalogue – a thrilling pastime that may lead you on to pleasant discoveries – I found that the library possesses a precious collection of playbills of the Dutch Theatre at The Hague covering the period from 1819 till 1860. They are bound together in eleven stout volumes and constitute a valuable record of dramatic production in Holland during the first half of the nineteenth century. To look through these files of forgotten performances is like going to the theatre with one's great-grandparents. It is a more genuine entertainment than the one to which Christopher Morley invited us a few years ago at a Hoboken playhouse. For those of us who went there pretended to be their grandparents only in order to pull grimaces at the reflection which they saw in the mirror of the stage. The perusal of these handbills recalls to the mind's eye not only the scene behind the footlights but the audience in front of it and the picturesque little town that The

Hague then was. Its limited size may be inferred from the Directors' manner of addressing their patrons, which seems to imply a personal acquaintance with the individual playgoers and a genuine anxiety to please them. Each bill is phrased in the form of a letter, which was probably handed in at the door a few days in advance of the performance. "Mijnheer," say Messieurs Hoedt & Bingley at the top of the bill, "on Monday next we shall have the pleasure of presenting ..." and they conclude the announcement with the formula, "In the hope that this representation may be honored with your presence, we have the pleasure of calling ourselves respectfully yours Hoedt & Bingley." On special occasions they introduced themselves as benefactors of their custom, ever anxious to please, even to the extent of yielding the playhouse to rivals from out of town. In the second week of March, 1820, the announcement read that "the Directors, always zealous and inclined to provide the honored public, by means of variety, with those pleasures which they may find at their command, have accordingly signed a contract with the Köbler family, who have aroused general admiration by their excellent talents during a three months' engagement at the Amsterdam theatre." These Köblers were vaudeville artists combining song and dance with pantomime and acrobatics. Their appearance seems to have scored an unusual success, for ten days later the bill made known to Messrs. Hoedt & Bingley's patrons that "at the flattering request of the general public" the Köblers would give "a fifth and positively final performance, to wit, The Deceits of Harlequin, Great Comical Ballet and Pantomime."

Five performances was indeed a record number. For as a rule no show could be put on twice in the same week, and only popular plays were offered to the public twice a year. Plays never had a run, they just stood one performance and were taken off the boards for six months at least. When Hoedt & Bingley announced the forthcoming production of "Jean Calas or The Innocent Condemned, Famous Tragedy by M. Victor," they added, as a telling proof of its excellence, that it had run in Paris more than eighty times to the applause of continuous throngs. The Dutch actors at The Hague, playing for an audience drawn from a small community, must have envied their fortunate colleagues in Paris who could repeat a successful show night after night. Hoedt & Bingley's company had to work hard to vary their repertoire from day to day. And they gave the playgoer more than he nowadays gets for his money. Each performance consisted of two plays, a serious one followed by something light, a one-act comedy, farce, or vaudeville. That was a very old tradition, which went back to the practice of the late Middle Ages. Only on very special occasions was the lighter entertainment omitted. On February 22, 1820,

86

Hoedt & Bingley featured "The Dead Uncle or The Frustrated Deceit, from the German of F. W. Gotter." "This play," says the programme, "is one of the most classical comedies of entire Germany, and on account of its greatness nothing extra will be shown after it." The same distinction was given to "Cabal and Love or The Victims of Ambition and Jealousy, Famous Tragedy by Germany's foremost author, the great Schiller." Just as rare as the one-play performance was the one-title play. The twin title was a set feature of the drama of that period. I wonder what purpose it was meant to serve. Was the substitute name tagged on as a reserve force wherewith to capture the curiosity of the public in case of the first one's failing to catch it? And was its interest won by the enlightening or the mystifying character of the substitute? It is clear that there was no sense in its addition, unless it improved upon the first title; it had to partake of the nature of the adjective, which colors the grey meaning of the noun by putting on touches of the personal and the actual. "Edward of Scotland, great and very famous Drama from the French of Duval" was one of the attractions on Hoedt & Bingley's repertoire. Its second title, "The Night of a Fugitive," is a good example of the species; it limits the story in time and reveals the predicament in which its hero finds himself. But there are many twin titles that are mere juxtapositions of grey nouns, the second adding neither light nor color to the first. "The Merchant from Riga or The Lady in Waiting" gives us a choice between a hero or a heroine but nothing definite for the chooser to go by; "The Shipwreck or The Heirs" tosses our imagination, like the ship, from sea to land but leaves it a wreck on the shoal of uncertainty; "The Skeleton or The Knights of the Lion" suggests a scene-shifting from a cupboard to a castle, but little else to stir our fancy. Such titles are meaningless pairs, of which either half tells us just as much or as little as the whole.

The overwhelming majority of the plays that were produced were translations from the German. Dutch children growing up at The Hague in the twenties of the past century must have got the impression that the land of the Hohenzollerns was the nursery of the true drama, and that the greatest of its nursery-men was August von Kotzebue. No fewer than forty-three of his plays were put on by Hoedt & Bingley from 1819 till 1821, and several of these were performed twice in the same year. His name appears on these handbills almost every week, and often two Kotzebue plays made up one evening's programme. He seems to have been the idol of the playgoing public and the favorite playwright of the Court. For on November 13, 1821, the Directors announced that they would stage by Royal Command "The Inheritance" and "The Confusion" both from the pen of "the celebrated Von

Kotzebue." English plays, on the other hand, were seldom seen by Hoedt & Bingley's audiences, and the few that were produced had passed through French or German versions on their way to The Hague theatre. Among the novelties that the management offered their patrons in 1820 was "The Teasers or Much Ado About Nothing, after H. Beck's adaptation of a play by Shakespeare!" "Hamlet" was acted in a translation of the French version by Ducis. "Still Waters Run Deep" was featured as "A famous Comedy from the German based on Beaumont and Fletcher's Rule a Wife and Have a Wife."

This neglect of English drama is the more surprising as Mr. Hoedt's partner was of English extraction and must have been acquainted with the successes of the London stage. The latter's father, Ward Bingley, the son of English parents who were residents of Rotterdam, made his debut on the Amsterdam stage in 1779. Soon afterwards war broke out between Great Britain and the Dutch Republic, and anti-British sentiment was aroused to such a pitch that the young actor with the English name had to face hostile audiences in the first months of his novitiate. But gradually his great talent overcame the popular prejudice. One of his most applauded parts was that of a comical character in Garrick's "Miss in her Teens," which Bingley himself had translated into Dutch. In 1796 he left Amsterdam and founded the *Nederduitsch Tooneel* (the Dutch Stage) in his native city Rotterdam. After his death in 1818 his son Willem took over the management of the *Nederduitsch Tooneel*, in partnership with the actor Jan Hendrik Hoedt, who had married Ward Bingley's only daughter. The two brothers-in-law moved their headquarters to The Hague, although they continued to give performances in Rotterdam. Hoedt & Bingley remained "respectfully yours" until the death of the latter in 1843 dissolved the partnership, and Hoedt made his exit three years later. In their honest attempt to please and to make profit, they had, without any ulterior purpose, brought French and German culture to their patrons at The Hague and Rotterdam.

There is good reason to doubt whether the profit of the partners and their company was commensurate with the pleasure of the patrons. It is clear from these handbills that the *Nederduitsch Tooneel* relied for its support on monthly or annual subscriptions. The play season ran from the middle of October until the end of April, and the price for a season's subscription for the most expensive tiers was sixty guilders ($24.00), or seventy if one were willing to pay for a reserved seat. The charge for a monthly subscription was fifteen or, for a reserved seat, sixteen guilders. These prices were reduced for the less expensive tiers to forty or fifty, and eleven or twelve. The charges for admission to a single performance were not listed on these handbills, which, as appears from the phrasing, were primarily missives from the Directors to the subscribers, though they may also have been handed to the casual playgoer at the door of the theatre. The curtain rose at six o'clock, and there was a long interval between the two plays, in which the audience adjourned to the coffeeroom to partake of refreshments, an old-established rite that was held to be an essential part of the evening's entertainment. We know from the contemporary testimony of reliable critics that the overworked and underpaid actors were, in their art, better craftsmen than the playwrights to whose romantic imaginings they gave an ephemeral life upon the boards, better craftsmen also than the average playgoer was able to appreciate. Spectacular shows, gaudy pageantry, and mechanical marvels were more in demand than the protrayal of human passions and emotions. One of the chief attractions on Hoedt & Bingley's repertoire was "Love in the Lazaretto," a coarse farce by a seventeenth-century Dutch rhymester. It was not its ribaldry that drew the crowds but the shows that went with it between the acts, and which could be varied from year to year. In 1821 the intermezzo between the first and second acts consisted of "the Royal Cabinet of Wax Figures, all beautifully modeled from life and presenting striking likenesses of several well-known characters." Between the third and fourth acts appeared "The Automatic Domino Player, Historical and Comical Dramatic Trifle of the Nineteenth Century, equipped with the necessary mechanisms." And before the curtain rose upon the fifth act, the audience was treated to a performance by "The Mechanical Statue," which the handbills declared to be both artistic and comical. And of course, on account of the greatness of this representation, nothing extra was to be given after it. "Love in the Lazaretto" was on a par with "Cabal and Love, by Germany's foremost author, the Great Schiller."

February, 1934

THE STORK AND THE PELICAN

The stork is called *ooievaar* in Dutch, an ancient word of obscure origin, but probably meaning "bringer of luck" The little children that were blessings to their parents knew that the *ooievaar* had brought them. But little children, in these days of depression, are no longer so sure of being blessings, and the luck-bringing bird's popularity has consequently suffered a decline. On the Campus of Columbia University they tell a story of an Instructor in the English Department who, having explaining to her class of Oriental students the meaning of the phrase "penny-wise pound-foolish," enquired whether there was an equivalent idiom in any of the languages that her students spoke. "In my country," said a stolid Chinese, "we say, 'You go to bed to save a candle, and you beget twins'." Now, if in China the arrival of twins is deplored as the costly effect of penny-wisdom, one need not wonder that in Holland, with its high standard of living, the birth of one child is not always a case of single blessedness. Dutch farmers used to invite a couple of storks to spend their summer honeymoon on the place. They laid a cart wheel on the roof or on the top of a high pole for the *ooievaars* to build their nest on. But these perches are becoming very rare, and a stork's nest on a housetop is a thing of the unhygienic past. The bird still graces, in effigy, the coat-of-arms of The Hague, and its live counterpart still stalks, or used to stalk until recently, among the slithery offal of the fish market opposite the Hague City Hall. But to be employed as a scavenger is a sad degradation for an erstwhile accoucheur. The heraldic honors still accorded him cannot counterbalance that disgrace. In short, Mr. *Ooievaar*, who in the past was held to be the national bird of Holland, has fallen upon evil days. And what little prestige he had left was taken from him recently by the sudden ascent of a rival to national fame and to first place in the affection of the people.

The usurper is the pelican. There is some comfort for the stork in knowing that he has not been supplanted by a worthless upstart. The pelican has an honorable record. She is that noble bird who fed her starving young with her own heart's blood and thus became the symbol of Christ shedding His blood on the cross to atone for the sins of mankind. In December of last year a Pelican flew from its nest at Schiphol, the airport of Amsterdam, to the Dutch East Indies to bring them the Christmas greetings from the mother land, and before the year was out she was back at Schiphol with New Year messages from Java. From Amsterdam to Batavia in one hundred hours and thirty minutes, from Batavia to Amsterdam in one hundred hours and forty minutes, a distance of twice 15673 kilometers covered in almost a week's time. In the days of the Dutch East India Company a ship that did the voyage from Amsterdam round the Cape of Good Hope to Batavia in one hundred days had an auspicious passage, and voyages that took from four to six months were nothing out of the common. Now the Pelican, with a crew of four, has reduced the one hundred days to as many hours. When these flights began, ten years ago, they took from twelve to fourteen days. Better engines, improved landing facilities at the intermediate ports, and the accumulated experience of the last decade have made this four days' trip to Java possible. The four men of the Pelican's crew will be the first to admit their indebtedness to the precursors who blazed the trail; but all honor is due to them for the courage and the skill with which they beat all previous records. The Dutch nation has paid a tribute to its heroes such as few Dutchmen have ever received from their countrymen. They were welcomed with an impressive outburst of national enthusiasm, and the Pelican, sharing in the honors of her masters, was proclaimed the symbol of Holland's conquest of the air.

In the early evening of December 30, when the four flying Dutchmen were reported to be heading for Schiphol, the narrow highway from Amsterdam to the airport poured thousands into the aerodrome. Automobiles, bicycles, pedestrians passed for hours by the quaint old farmhouses that line the winding road. The waiting crowd on the landing field clustered round huge open fire pots, and those who could not come close enough to the warming glow tried to keep their circulation going by stamping their feet on the frozen ground. Some one began to sing, "*Diender, o diender*!" (*diender* is one of the many Dutch names for a policeman), the waiting crowd took up the popular ditty, and turned it into an ovation for the mounted guardians of the peace. Suddenly, at twenty of ten, the ground lights flooded the flying field. A surge of excitement drowned the singing, then silence and breathless suspense, all ears on the alert to catch the first purr of the plane. There she was, not visible yet, for a fog enveloped the airport. The roar overhead dwindled down again to a distant purr. The flyers were evidently circling round to get their bearings. The purr grew again to a roar, the Pelican suddenly pierced the fog, and settled gracefully down upon her nest. Hats flew up in the air, hands waved frantically, shouts of joy greeted the flyers, the national anthem rose above the tumult. But many, overwhelmed with emotion, could not sing.

May, 1934

OF HAZING

Belly Fulla Straw by David Cornel De Jong[1] is the first novel of a young American author who, born in Holland twenty-eight years ago, came to this country when he was in his early teens. He has had the good sense to write about familiar things, for his book is the story of an immigrant Dutch family which settled shortly before the Great War at Grand Rapids, Mich. Newcomers in an established community are usually felt to be intruders. They are received with silent reserve, or derisive contempt, or open hostility. Such treatment is the price they

[1] New York: Alfred A. Knopf, 1934.

must pay for admission. Among certain social groups the penalty is imposed, and the suffering endured, as part of a silent pact, which, as a matter of course, is lived up to by either party. Thus hazing, in school and college, has become a mere convention, which, as such, has lost most of its cruelty. The novice who seeks admission recognizes in his tormentors the indispensable instruments of his initiation. He needs them more than they need him, and he knows that what they force him to do and to suffer will in the end be the making of him. But within the Dutch-American community of Grand Rapids there are no conventions that regulate the hazing of newly arrived immigrants. There is no concerted plan, no fixed time limit, nor a name for the trial. If you told the good people of Grand Rapids that they indulged in the pastime of hazing the newcomers from the land of their own origin, they would stare at you in surprise and ask, "What do you mean?" They are not even conscious of putting them to the test; they are just helpful and anxious to be kind, and to tell the poor creatures a few things they ought to know. But that is just it. The very indefiniteness of the mode of reception exposes the novices to all kinds of injuries that range from gentle pinpricks to festering wounds. To be regarded as "poor creatures" and to be told condescendingly how to behave is gall and wormwood to the proud and independent. Harmen Idema is one of these. He has been a master builder in his native town on the sea coast in the far north of Holland; he is good at his craft, he has an eye for the right proportions in architecture, a sense of beauty, a love of solidity. The cheap, tawdry homes which jerry-building real estate agents have inflicted upon this country are a horror to him, and to be treated by the owners of such despicable dwellings as a helpless ignoramus is more than his proud sensitiveness can endure. For these Americanized Dutchmen of the second, third, and fourth generations have a way of discussing the old mother country as if they pitied the man who was born there. They like to boast, indeed, of their Dutch descent, and they swallow with relish the flatteries of the local papers which, not being run by Hollanders, see political gain in praising the solid Dutch traits of their constituency. But anybody coming from those parts is, in their eyes, a backward individual who needs help and advice in adjusting himself to the saner and more enlightened American standards. This smug contentment with their trite and commonplace existence will not allow Idema to find American salvation in his own way. He must follow theirs, otherwise he cannot succeed. And from that conflict springs his tragedy: DUTCHMAN, DUTCHMAN, BELLY FULLA STRAW

Their way leads through the Church, and the Idemas are strangers on that road. Harmen is not a Church member, his four children have not been baptized, nor taught to say their prayers before meals. Mr. Kuyper, the grocer and hardware dealer, to whom Idema has an introduction from a mutual acquaintance in Holland, is duly shocked on discovering their godless state. However, he takes the abandoned family in hand, shelters and feeds them for the first day and night, and palms off on Idema a ramshackle house that has long stood vacant. They soon discover that the water supply is polluted. Mrs. Jansen, the next-door neighbor, knows all about it. The previous tenants always got their water at the livery stable, eight houses further up the street. No, she would not let them draw hers. "I told the landlord, I can not be bothered letting his renters use my water." "Aren't we neighbors and Hollanders?" asks Idema meekly, but inwardly seething with indignation. "I can't help that," is the bland answer. They receive more kindness from other neighbors who are not Dutch. The children especially feel drawn towards the good-natured Italians and Poles. And there is an old American lady who treats them to cakes and sends them home with little presents. She is crazy, they are warned by the Dutch-American children, and they begin to feel that craziness is somehow akin to kindliness. Those Dutch kids that call her crazy cannot be crazy themselves, for they are far from kind. They bombard the Idema children with tin cans, destroy their sand castles, call them nasty names, and yell after them in the street,

> Dutchman, Dutchman, belly fulla straw
> Can't say nothin' but ja, ja, ja.

It is a curious fact that Hollanders in this country do not feel drawn towards one another as Dutchmen, but only as members of the same denomination. The bond between them is not the common fatherland, but the language in which they pray to God. Idema the Hollander can lay no claim to the help of his Dutch-American neighbors; but Idema as a member of the Dutch Reformed Church is assured of a welcome among them. Detjen, his wife, insists on their joining. She hankers for peace with her neighbors, she is for compliance and compromise. And Harmen gives in, grudgingly admitting that dishonesty is the best policy. So Detjen makes her peace, not only with the Dutch community, but with her God. Her great ambition is to make her family a pattern for the neighborhood to follow, "especially since people are bound to recall that they are only foreigners." She has discarded all pride in her native country, and has put on a new pride in the American family that she is trying to mould. But Detjen is taken away before her task is half fulfilled, and Harmen is left with a family that has lost the old intimacy and is groping blindly for new contacts with the unfamiliar environment. The children slowly grow away from their father. Their youth is malleable and takes the form of the American mould more readily. The two older ones, a girl and a boy, get married and become estranged from him. He despises their contentment with the standardized, humdrum home life to which they settle down. They have made good in the opinion of the community, and that means more to them than his approval. They fade away from his consciousness as part of the dull, colorless mass that absorbs them. One day, while he is rowing on the lake, the rhythm of the oars recalls to his mind some lines of a Dutch poet which seem to give poignant expression to his grief. On the cadence of his strokes he repeats them over and over again. But it angers him that he gives way to his despondent mood in this unmanly fashion, and in order to break the charm of the verses he begins to translate them into English. In the rendering all the flavor of the poetry evaporates, and with it the melancholy and dejection. "There was nothing then, only something transplanted which cackled idly, with an empty belly, with a belly full of straw." Thus it is with Harmen Idema himself. He is a strain of Dutch poetry translated into American terms, and talking, with an empty belly, with a belly fulla straw. As a practical craftsman he has prospered materially. His sterling qualities insured him employment, and by dint of hard work and careful saving he has laid aside enough for his old age. He need not worry over his physical well-being. But the Dutch soul that is in him is starving. And when the only real friend that he knows in Grand Rapids has passed on, he decides to return to the old country. "You see," he explains to the dead friend's widow, "I'm a man of fifty now; at that age your biggest leaps are done. Nothing new to start on. For that reason I may as well go back to those things which I left when I was young, and return emptier than I went when I started out." "And the children?" she asks. "It doesn't matter." "No, it doesn't matter, I suppose. I don't know." "No, we don't know."

Mr. De Jong has created in Harmen Idema an unforgettable character. This honest man, so tenacious of old loyalties and capable of deep, though inarticulate, tenderness for his wife and children, leaves his features impressed upon the reader's mind. We look forward to greater things from the young painter of this fine Dutch portrait. Will he tell us in the next novel the story of Ka, Harmen's younger daughter, and of Dirk, the talented Benjamin, who is a freshman at Cornell when the father sails back to his native land? Ka is a chip of the old block. She has inherited from Harmen his loyalties and finest instincts; but, more fortunate than he, she has the youth and the vigor and the unhampered freedom that will enable her to go her own free way towards her American destiny.

VINCENT VAN GOGH

It was poor judgment on the part of Mr. Irving Stone to give his novel of Vincent van Gogh the title of *Lust for Life*.[1] The word *lust* connotes an overmastering desire for the satisfaction of the senses, an avid enjoyment of physical rather than spiritual values. Mr. Stone's own story belies its name. The tale that he has drawn from the letters that Vincent van Gogh wrote to his brother Theo is the record of a mystic's search for the perfect life, for the life, as Vincent defined it, that is in harmony with the rhythm of nature. Through disappointment and suffering and defeat he attained at last the discovery that only by his art could he bring his own life into tune with the universal rhythm. To call his passionate love of painting an unbridled reveling in self-expression would be to misjudge the artist and the man. Dr. Gachet, of Auvers sur Oise, who knew him as a patient and admired him as a painter, understood him better: "The word 'love of art' does not express his devotion," he said of Van Gogh; "faith is the correct word, faith unto martyrdom." Long before Vincent had become aware of his own talent, he dreamt of high achievement through self-denial. "In order to accomplish something in this world, one must become dead to oneself," he quoted from Renan in a letter that he wrote to his brother Theo from London. He actually tried, in the late seventies, to follow the example of Christ and to obey the Master's lessons to the letter; and although he outgrew the saintliness of his early years, he never lost the conviction that he had a mission to fulfill among his fellow men. In 1890, when he had lost Vincent, Theo wrote of him to their mother, "A volume of his letters would reveal how much he has thought and how consistently he remained true to himself."

His very earnestness made Van Gogh a difficult man to live with. He had a craving for companionship, but he found that few could endure his presence for long. It was not that people did not like him; on the contrary, he met with sympathy and affection wherever he went, but even those who loved him devotedly could not bear the strain of his continuous nearness. His indomitable faith in the justice of a course of action he had chosen made him self-willed and stubborn and intolerant towards all who did not share his belief. Theo van Gogh, who adored his older brother, once wrote in a mood of despondency, "It is as if there were two beings in him, one marvelously gifted, tender, and gentle, the other self-loving and hard. He

---

[1] *Lust for Life*. The Novel of Vincent van Gogh by Irving Stone. New York: Longmans, Green and Co.

makes life difficult for himself and others." Hence his passionate longing for affection met with rebuff at every turn. Thwarted in love and without an abiding friendship he would have lived an empty life if his ecstatic love of art had not filled the void. She came to him, as the Maya of Mr. Stone's allegory, and surrendered herself to his genius. "Why should you love me?" he asked. "Women have always despised me." "You were not meant for love, you had other work to do," was Maya's reply. Art alone was destined to be his mistress, but he did not win her for his own until eight years of fierce study and struggle reached their crowning achievement in Arles.

The allegorical Maya incident is Mr. Stone's only departure from the actual story as revealed by Vincent's letters. It is the poet's prerogative to mingle fiction with fact, but where the warp and woof are taken ready-made from the loom of reality one single thread of fiction looks like a flaw in the pattern. It is not a conspicuous flaw, however, for Mr. Stone's stretch of fiction bears a surprising resemblance to the historical episode of Margot's love for Vincent. If he could inspire such ardor in a Dutch girl of the misty Brabant heath, we do not wonder at his meeting another Margot in Maya under the blazing sky of the Provence. But the duplication of the incident detracts both from the realism of the Nuenen girl's story and from the symbolism of the later episode in Arles. The author gave his allegory the name of Maya, Goddess of Earth and its fertility, because Vincent's art was, to himself, the visualization of the throbbing life of Nature, the rhythm of growth realized in impassioned color and line. "When I paint a sun I want to make people feel it revolving at a terrific rate of speed, giving off light and heat waves of tremendous power. When I paint a cornfield I want people to feel the atoms within the corn pushing out to their final growth and bursting. When I paint an apple I want people to feel the juice of that apple pushing out against the skin, the seeds at the core striving outward to their own fruition ... When I paint the portrait of a man I want them to feel the entire flow of that man's life, everything he has seen and done and suffered." This definition in the master's own words of the scope and the meaning of his art is sufficiently clear and convincing to make its transposition into allegory superfluous.

With Maya eliminated from the story, Mr. Stone's novel is an admirable biography. The three volumes of letters edited by Theo van Gogh's widow contain so full a record of the painter's vicissitudes and mental processes that no fiction was needed to turn it into an absorbing tale. That collection of 652 letters is unique in Dutch literature. I know of no other Hollander who has laid bare his soul to a confidant as did Vincent to his younger brother. Theo, the Paris art dealer, who was the recipient of these outpourings, was the only one among Vincent's relations who never lost faith in him. He paid him a monthly allowance on which the penniless painter, who never made a living by his art, subsisted for the last ten years of his life. Vincent accepted this support without any apparent scruple, believing, or pretending to believe, that the work which he gave Theo in return would one day repay him a hundredfold. He had no ground for such optimism except in the consciousness of his own power. When he left his native country for good, he left many studies and paintings behind in the parsonage at Nuenen. They were packed in cases and stored with a carpenter at Breda, who subsequently sold the whole lot to a junk dealer since no one seemed to care about them. In Arles Vincent painted a portrait of Dr. Rey and gave him the picture as a souvenir. The good physician took it home and used it to cover a crack in the wall. A few years ago "The Late Christopher Bean," adapted by Sidney Howard from René Fauchois' "Prenez garde à la Peinture," was among the most successful plays of the season. How many theater-goers realized that the dead hero of that delightful skit on the art dealers' trade owed his shadowy stage life to the cruel realism of Vincent's life in Arles? That tragic episode supplied the background for M. Fauchois' lighthearted comedy. The satire that he leveled at the professional art trade leaves Theo van Gogh unscathed. When he buried his brother in the little cemetery at Auvers, he fully realized the extent of the loss to himself and the art world. It is painful to imagine what would have become of Vincent if Theo had not sustained him with his firm belief in his genius and had not acted as guardian to the gifted brother, who was a helpless child in the practical affairs of this world. The guardian did not long survive his ward. Theo's mind broke under the strain of his grief, and six months after he had laid Vincent to rest, he followed him into death. They are joined forever in the grave among the cornfields of Auvers. "And in their death they were not divided." That word from Samuel ii, 1, 23 was placed by Theo's widow as motto on the title page of her edition of Vincent's letters to his brother. They are indeed a monument to them both.

Mr. Stone acknowledges in a postscript his indebtedness to Van Gogh friends and enthusiasts in Holland and France. He seems to know Vincent's native country very well and to have visited the Brabant villages where the artist's father was a minister of the Dutch Reformed Church. He might have known then that the peasants of Etten do not speak French. The author's constant reference to francs and centimes as the currency of Holland is equally surprising. This was deliberately done, as is thus explained in the postscript, "I have utilized a few devices for the sake of facility, such as the use of the franc as the unit of exchange during Vincent's trek over Europe." The painter's wanderings were limited to Holland, Belgium, and France; it requires a stretch of the imagination to call them a "trek over Europe," and to represent Vincent as constantly changing his scanty resources from one foreign currency into another. He lived on guilders in Holland, and on francs in Belgium and France. By ignoring that simple distinction for the sake of facility the author, in the eyes of one Dutch reader at least, has detracted somewhat from the local color of his picture. The use of the term Flemish as descriptive of Dutch architecture is another peculiarity that strikes a native of Amsterdam as rather odd. I lived for many years on the Keizersgracht, but never saw there "the long row of narrow Flemish dwellings" that Mr. Stone claims he discovered. He has given us such an excellent picture of Vincent's native country that one wishes it were free from even these slight blemishes.

DUTCH NAMES ON THE MAP OF AMERICA

I wonder by what name the Barnstable peninsula was known to the good people of New Amsterdam and to the crews of Dutch West-Indiamen. They must have called it North Holland, I should think. For it was sandwiched in between the Noord Zee, now called Cape Cod Bay, and the Zuiderzee, better known as Nantucket Sound, just as the Dutch peninsula that forms the Province of North Holland is washed on the West by the North Sea and on the East by the Zuider Zee. The coast line of that Province, north of Den Helder, is broken through by narrow straits, which form the islands of Texel, Vlieland, and Terschelling. The first two of these names were also transferred to the Western hemisphere. Martha's Vineyard was the Dutch sailor's American Texel, and Vlieland, lying farther north from Holland, had its namesake in the remote island of Nantucket. I was told the other day by a Nantuckian – if that is the correct term – that these islanders speak of the mainland as "America," and that visiting there is to them tantamount to "going abroad." Dutch Vlieland has remained just as much a world to itself, which proves that the Dutch sailors used good judgment in drawing an analogy between the two. Statenhoek was their name for Cape Cod, the Connecticut River was the Versche Rivier, and the Housatonic was to the seventeenth century Hollanders Rodenberghs Rivier. These and many other Dutch names occur on the map which N. J. Visscher designed in 1650. An excellent reprint of it has appeared in the Historical Atlas of the Netherlands which is in course of publication at The Hague. Another leaf contains reproductions of plans of New York and Albany in 1664, of New York in 1730, of Albany in 1763, and of the environs of New York after an English map of 1776. A third leaf shows the distribution of later Dutch settlements that are scattered all over the Continent, all colonized by immigrants who came over in the forties and following decades of the past century. A brief commentary goes with the maps, from the hand of Dr. J. van Hinte, the learned author of *Nederlanders in Amerika*.

PROVINCIAL SELF-APPLAUSE

After the memorable flight from London to Melbourne the *New York Times* declared editorially that Americans had reason to be proud of the showing that their engineers made in the race. "The American contribution demonstrated with a commercial load that London is now but four days distant from Australia." That sounds as if the wonderful Douglas air liner, like a robot of the sky, had itself piloted its commercial load across three continents. I yield to no one in respect for the engineers of the Douglas Aircraft Corporation, and subscribe wholeheartedly to the *Times* editor's eulogy. But to represent their achievement as the decisive factor of that successful flight is going a bit too far in provincial self-applause. The Dutch pilots who finished second in the race have deserved better from America's leading newspaper. It was the skill and endurance of K. D. Parmentier and J. J. Moll that brought demonstration of the Douglas airliner's superiority, and no praise of the shipbuilders should go forth without due mention of the crew that manned the ship. Was it confidence solely in the craft and its Wright cyclone motors that gave the three passengers courage to undertake the hazardous voyage? Or was it their trust in the two men and in their skill to ride the cyclone? "Some English editors," said a dispatch from London, "considered the methodical flight of this plane, until almost within an hour of Melbourne, as the most sensational achievement of the whole race." And I would ask the *Times* editor, Was the method the engine's or the men's?

March, 1935

WE GATHER TOGETHER

Dutch people's heads are not richly stocked with poetical quotations, but the opening line of the old Thanksgiving Hymn is familiar to every Hollander who cares for music: *Wilt heden nu treden voor God den Heere.*

And every Hollander knows, besides, that it is one of the hymns from *De Nederlantsche Gedenckclanck* by Adriaen Valerius. The word defies exact translation into English. Memorial Strain comes, perhaps, nearest to it. The book was published in Haarlem in 1626 with a dedication to the States of Zeeland. For its author was a citizen of Veere, a little seaport on the isle of Walcheren, in the Province of Zeeland. The town has changed but little since the days when Adriaen Valerius was a notary there and a member of the Municipal Council. The tall church round which the low houses are huddled together as if for shelter from the sea-blown storms, the plump tower that stands at the water's edge as a beacon for sailors, the harbor with its sailing craft, and the quay lined with quaint crowstep gables form the picturesque setting to the scene on which Adriaen Valerius acted his part as notary and town Councillor and where, three hundred years later, Hendrik Willem van Loon used to entertain American visitors at his home in one of Veere's ancient houses. Life in a seaport, small though it be, is never dull. Every ship that runs into harbor brings news from another shore and food for talk and meditation. The sea, in its tempestuous moods, keeps men busy in the town's defence, and lures them to its edge for play and enjoyment in the calm summer season. And beyond the town walls lies the fertile island with its pastures and gardens and its blonde fringe of dunes, and with the beautiful city of Middelburg, the market and shopping centre of that sea-enclosed community. Mr. Valerius owned a country-house within walking distance from Veere, and loved to spend there the early spring mornings watching the birds that found a sanctuary in his garden. He loved them and studied their habits with an expert eye. In a long and somewhat laborious poem, he has described an early walk along the seadike to his country-place, Sandijck. Gulls and curlews, oyster-catchers and sandpipers were his companions along the edge of the sea. But when he reached his garden, he found it alive with a veritable Parliament of Birds. He gives each kind its name and descriptive epithet: nightingale, lark, raven, kite, sparrow, cuckoo, wagtail, starling, swallow, titmouse, quail, turtle dove, jackdaw, goose, swan, turkey, peacock, and a few others whose names are puzzles to the dictionary makers. Melchior d'Hondecoeter, half a century later, was to paint such gatherings of birds in gorgeous colors. Valerius's verbal picture lacks the brilliance of that great master's works. He was Melchior's inferior in execution, but had evidently as intimate a knowledge of birdlife as the painter. And to their rich variety of song he probably lent an equally observant ear. For Valerius was a lover of music. Under his parents' roof he must have listened as a child to his father playing the organ. François de Valery, clerk to the captains of the civic guard at Middelburg, who in 1575 bought the cast-off organ of the demolished Westmonster Kerk, was doubtless Adriaen's father and first music teacher. By latinizing the family name the son had no intention of disowning his parentage; on the contrary, he lent it distinction by the change, for it proclaimed him a man of letters and learning, of whom his parents had reason to be proud. He mixed with the literary and social élite of the island, entertained them at Sandijck, and contributed verse to a poetical miscellany which the beaux esprits of Walcheren published under the title, "The Zeeland Nightingale." There is not a single poem in this collection that deserves to be compared with the song of Philomela. "The Walcheren Parliament of Birds" would have been a more appropriate name. It is a medley of very uneven performance, in which the croak of the raven and goose-like cackling can be heard more distinctly than the notes of pure warblers. We cannot count our friend Valerius among the latter. His name would not have survived down to the present day but for the posthumous publication that his heirs brought out in 1626, a year after his death. That book alone has secured for him a place among Holland's immortals.

The Gedenckclanck is a history of the Netherlands struggle against Spain as it reveals itself in popular songs. The stirring events of that great epoch were celebrated in ballads, in battle hymns, in lyrical outbursts that expressed the feelings of the inarticulate mass of the people. The Introduction to the volume gives a brief account of the rise of the Spanish power in the Netherlands. The outbreak of the revolt and the story of the war that ensued supply to Valerius his theme, and into his prose narrative he inserted the songs which were occasioned by the events that he describes. The Thanksgiving Hymn belongs to the year 1597, when special days of prayer and thanksgiving were held throughout the Netherland Provinces for the glorious victories of Prince Maurice of Nassau over the Spanish armies. It is uncertain, and I would say even unlikely, that the words are by Valerius. The melody is certainly not his. He deserves small, if any, credit as a poet and composer. His merit is in that he has preserved for us the tunes of these songs, seventy-six in all, in musical notation, exactly as they were sung in his lifetime. Some are written in parts, and all have lute or cithern accompaniment, and these arrangements may be due to Valerius himself. But the melodies are of various origin: Dutch, German, French, English, and Italian. The initial words of the song from which the melody is taken are faithfully quoted in each case. Among the English tunes occur Sweet Robert, Come Again, Come Shepherds Deck Your Heads, Farewell, Sweet Margaret, Woddecot, whatever that may mean, and several others.

The tune of the Prayer of Thanksgiving was taken from an older Dutch ballad, which has been preserved in full in a sixteenth-century manuscript from the hand of Bartholomew Boeckx, a rhymester of Lier, a little town south of Antwerp. Its subject matter forms a strange contrast with the solemn prayer to which it lent its tune. It is the doleful complaint of a young bandit over the faithlessness of his mistress who has betrayed him to the authorities.

> "Ah, wilder than wild, what man could tame me?"
> I used to be boasting early and late.
> Now may I well sing a song to shame me,
> Since Fortune has left me to my fate.

Like an old broom that they sweep the floor with she threw him away, he complains, when she had no use for him any more. And he invites her to come to the place of execution and bring a stoup along that she may fill it with his warm blood. "I bid thee adieu," are his final words,

> I bid thee adieu, Prince, death will part us.
> The hour for me to die has come.
> God have my soul, who cares may have my carcass.
> I have to thank my sweetheart for my doom.

The Prince thus farewelled was not the Prince of Orange, but the presiding officer of the Chamber of Rhetoric, a kind of sixteenth-century writers club, of which the balladist was a member. It was the custom, in those days, for a poet to address the Prince in the closing stanza of his composition, and the author of the ballad, by making his luckless hero pay this tribute, added a touch of poignant realism to the story at the risk of being mistaken for the scapegrace himself. Such ballads were the news stories of an age that was not blessed yet with daily papers. The rhyming reporters sang the latest sensations into the ears of the people, and no printed editorials ever had so wide and so long a vogue. For generation after generation repeated the thrillers until no other memory or record of the incident survived than the song alone. "Ah, wilder than wild!" could still be heard in the streets of Flemish towns in the early nineteenth century, three hundred years after the bandit's execution. The patriotic songs that Valerius collected were winged birds of similar feather. What their makers said in verse would now be said in headlines, front-page stories, and editorials. If we bear this in mind, we shall understand more easily how the poet of the Prayer of Thanksgiving could suffer it to be sung to the tune of a ballad that told so sordid a story. To the rhyming reporter an execution on the scaffold, a victory on the battlefield, the capture of a fortress, a skirmish at sea, all partook of the nature of news. The man who first intoned the Thanksgiving hymn to the tune of the convict's complaint took no cynical delight in the contrast. He was not aware that there was any contrast, just as little as we are shocked by the juxtaposition on the front page of our morning paper of the stories of a kidnapper's trial, a divorce scandal, a Presidential message, the latest news from Germany, and revelations about a New York vice ring. To the rhyming reporter tunes were the means of circulating his stories, and in choosing his tune he did not ask what purpose it had served before, but only whether it would suit his present purpose. And thus it came about that the bandit's melodious complaint gained worldwide vogue as a church hymn. Its international currency dates from the late seventies of the past century. It became popular in Europe after it had been sung by a male chorus in Vienna under the direction of Eduard Kremser in 1887. In its German translation by Joseph Weyl it struck the fancy of the Emperor William II, who in 1893 ordered it adopted in German schools as a patriotic song, to be sung especially on the annual festival commemorating the victory of Sédan. Imperial favor secured it a welcome among the Germans in this country, who made it popular throughout Protestant America.

May, 1935

A KIDNAPPED PAINTING

Pictures have their histories like human beings. The common run of them lead dull and uneventful lives and die an obscure death by accident or through neglect. But the great ones attract the limelight of public attention; they are the stake of litigation, the victims of criminal attacks and of kidnapping plots, the subjects of historical research and the heroes of fiction. Rembrandt's Nightwatch is supposed to have suffered mutilation at the hands of callous guardians, who were anxious to fit it into a frame too narrow for its size, and books and articles have been written as to the truth of that story and the extent of the damage done. Some fifteen years ago a madman, who believed that the Government had done him an injustice, informed the public at large of his grievance by the novel method of slashing Rembrandt's masterpiece with a butcher's knife. A surgeon was rushed to the victim's side and sewed him up with such expert skill that only those who know where the wound was inflicted can discover the scar. All the world knows the story how Leonardo's Mona Lisa was kidnapped from the Louvre and kept in hiding for several years. In April 1934 great consternation was caused by the discovery that one panel of the Adoration of the Lamb, the famous altar piece by Jan van Eyck in the Church of St. Bavo at Ghent, had disappeared. It bore on one side a representation of the Just Judges, on the other the figure of John the Baptist. A few weeks after the theft the Bishop of Ghent received a letter from a man who claimed to have the picture in his possession. He offered to restore it to the cathedral in return for an exorbitant ransom. He warned the bishop, however, that the police should be kept out of this, as otherwise the precious panel would be destroyed. Was the letter a hoax? The writer soon brought undeniable proof that he was in earnest. He sent the Bishop a receipt for a package left in the parcel room of the Gare du Nord at Brussels. It contained the picture of John the Baptist. The thief had sawed the thick panel in two, had kept the side with the Just Judges, and returned the Baptist to act as intermediary. St. John had no difficulty in convincing the ecclesiastical authorities that he came from the kidnapper, but no ransom money passed through his hands. No further clues were discovered, and the public began to despair of the missing Judges being rescued. Recently, however, the police came upon the trail of the criminal. On November 25 of last year there was a trade union meeting at Dendermonde, which was attended by leaders of the Catholic Democratic Party. One of these got so excited in the heat of the discussions that he suffered a stroke and died an hour afterwards. He was called A. Goedertier and a resident of Wetteren in East Flanders, where he was president of his party's club. No one suspected him of criminal tendencies. But among the papers in his desk were found rough copies of the letters received by the Bishop from the thief, and on the desk stood the typewriter on which he had written them. He appeared to have been heavily in debt. The Just Judges were to have squared his accounts with his creditors, if John the Baptist had succeeded as a go-between. But the Bishop was apparently not willing to negotiate with the perpetrator of the crime, and while he was vainly pinning his hope on the Judges, the Supreme Judge called him to account. Did he destroy the other half of the panel when he found that his plot had failed? The picture has not been found among his belongings. But he seems to have had accomplices, for the man who left the package at the Brussels station did not resemble Goedertier. Here is rich material for a mystery story. The hero a sacristan of the church in his native town, who employs his leisure time with drawing and painting. He becomes so proficient in his avocation that he is appointed Director of the local art school. He becomes active in politics, joins the Christian Democratic fraction of the Catholic party, rises to leadership in his home town, and is elected President of the Party Club House. People respect him as a pillar of church and society. But he has a dual personality. The other man in him is unknown to his fellow citizens. They have no suspicion of the spendthrift career that leads him by devious paths on to bankruptcy and crime. Detective stories, of which he is an avid reader, suggest to him an escape from financial ruin. He plans the crime that must save his respectability. Then follow the theft, the flight, the extortion letters, the suspense, the frustration, the imminent downfall, the gnawing anxiety, the failure of his tortured heart, the sudden death. And then the search starts for the missing half of the panel. And in the midst of the excitement, St. John the Baptist quietly resumes his place in the altar piece turning his back to the vacancy left by the missing Judges.

A MODERN JONAH

Among the many possessions of Great Britain that are scattered across the globe is a small group of islands far south in the Atlantic Ocean which is known by the name of Tristan da Cunha. They may be found on the map about half way between Buenos Aires and Capetown, but their exact location was not known until recently, not even to the Admiralty in London. On November 14 of last year a Netherland submarine, the K xviii, left Holland on a voyage to the East Indies, which took her all the way down to Buenos Aires, then straight east to Capetown, and thence, via Mauritius and Fremantle, Australia, to Java, a cruise of 23,000 miles, the longest ever made by a submarine. When the British Government learnt that the K xviii would touch Tristan da Cunha, it requested the Netherland Government to charge her commander with the task of determining the longitude and latitude of the island group, and so it happened that a Netherland naval officer, Lieutenant D. C. M. Hetterschij, was the first to find out for the British Government where it must look for one of its colonies in the south Atlantic Ocean. A Dutch geologist, Professor Vening Meinesz, well known in this country for his deep-sea research, was on board to study the formation of the submarine crust of the earth and the effect of cosmic rays at various depths. I feel deep admiration for both the scientist and the crew, who could endure living, like Jonah in the belly of the whale, not three days and three nights but for six times three months. But they had this advantage over Jonah that they knew where they were going and could steer the monster that had swallowed them to their distant goal.

SILVER TEAPOTS

President Roosevelt paid tribute, the other day, to an early Dutch family which settled first in New York and subsequently moved up the river to what is now called Hyde Park. On Sunday, September 15, he unveiled in St. James Episcopal Church, Hyde Park, a marble tablet in memory of Jacobus Stoutenburgh, who, says the inscription, "became the first white resident of record on the Flatts, south of Crum Elbow creek, where subsequently the village of Hyde Park was built." It was probably Stoutenburgh who gave the creek its name. But he called it Kromme Elleboog, meaning crooked elbow, a very common name in Holland for a street or a water course with a bend in it. There is a Kromelleboogsteeg, Crooked Elbow Alley, near the Royal Palace in Amsterdam, and in Capetown Krom Elboog Lane has resisted, down to the present day, the general trend towards anglicisation that prevailed there in the past century. The crooked elbow that sticks out when the hand rests on the hip is an attitude of challenge, and the name that describes it, to judge by its stubborn survival in English-speaking environment, seems to partake of its defiant nature. There must have been a streak of stubbornness and defiance in Stoutenburgh, too. We know what he looked like, for he and his wife, Margaret Teller, had themselves painted in their wedding clothes in 1717. These portraits are now in the possession of Miss Caroline Thorn Wells of Rhinebeck. The two look strangely alike, so much so that it is difficult to tell the man from the woman. Both express determination in the straight line of the thin, compressed lips; both pairs of eyes stare coldly at the world, the woman's with a faint twinkle of amusement or mockery. Their noses are absolutely identical; it looks as if the artist, having succeeded in painting one, traced it and transferred it to the other face, rather than risk the portrayal of as good a second nose from nature. If they resembled one another so closely on their wedding day, they must have looked like a pair of twins after fifty years of married life. For it is said that husband and wife show the imprint of their community of thoughts and interests in each face reflecting more and more the other's features. They remained partners for more than half a century. For Jacobus made his will in 1770 and his widow survived him. Their eight children, six sons and two daughters, were all alive at the time of their father's death. That will is a curious document. The old man seems to have thought that a Dutch household's respectability in the Hudson valley depended on the possession of a silver teapot. He was anxious to leave none of his children without one. "I leave to my eldest son, Tobias, besides what

I have already given him by deed, the sum of twenty-five pounds and a silver teapot ... Whereas I have given my daughter Antje a silver teapot of the value of fourteen pounds, I give to my daughter Margaret a silver teapot which is now in the family; and I order a silver teapot of the same value to be made for each of my sons." Yet tea drinking was not such a solemn rite among those Dutch Americans as it has since become in Holland. The Swedish botanist Peter Kalm, who made a journey through the American colonies in the forties of the eighteenth century, has described the frugal fare of the people in Albany, which was then an entirely Dutch town. Their way of living was similar, no doubt, to that of the settlers on Crum Elbow Creek. Kalm was not an admirer of the Albanians and what he tells us about them is anything but flattering. But he does praise them for their sober way of living. Their breakfast consisted of bread, smoked meat, and tea; the midday meal was bread soaked in milk or buttermilk, and sometimes boiled or roast meat. And supper was again bread in milk, and thin beer or water. Lettuce was the stock accompaniment of each meal, and they seasoned it with quantities of vinegar, but very little oil. Hence tea was drunk only at breakfast, unless they observed the custom so common in rural communities in Holland of having the tea simmering over a little flame or a pot of live coals so as to be ready for the reception of any chance caller. Kalm also observed the manner of their drinking it. They did not put the lump of sugar into the cup, but laid it on the tongue and poured the tea over it. The fisher folk along the north seacoast of Holland still take their tea that way. It is the ingenious invention of a thrifty people. Not an atom of the costly sugar is left in the cup and thrown away; the lump was good to the last grain. Jacobus and Margaret Stoutenburgh, with their family of eight children, must have practised the same economy.

PALING

A Dutch friend of mine in New York, who spent the summer in his native country, has come back with an amazing Zuiderzee yarn. The fisherfolk along its shores foresaw the decline of their industry by its transformation into a freshwater lake closed off from the sea. But it now appears that the Zuiderzee has become a favorite haunt of *paling*, for which they get much better prices than they used to be paid for their salt water catch. Paling are a kind of eel that live in freshwater lakes and pools; but when the spawning season comes, which happens, it seems, only once in a paling's lifetime, they seek the Atlantic Ocean, where, at great depth and at great distance from the European coast, the new generation is born. The older one never returns, according to the ichthyologists, but the young fry, by some mysterious intuition or guidance, find their way to the old haunts of their progenitors. "But how," I asked my informant, "do they get into the Zuiderzee now that the Dutch engineers have botled it up?" "Oh," he said, "they crawl across the dike; they are used to traveling over dry ground. In former days they swam up the rivers that flow into the Zuiderzee, and found their way through fields and meadows into the pools and lakes that dot the Dutch landscape. But now the Zuiderzee offers them a spacious freshwater basin, and the fisherfolk no longer curse the reclamation scheme."

Dutch paling has been a popular article in the London market ever since the Middle Ages. The Dutch fishermen who brought their catch to Billingsgate were known there by the name of palingmen. In an act of Parliament of the year 1495 it was ruled that "Noe such marchaunte nor paling man shuld sell nor put to sale any Elys by barell." The word thus officially adopted into the King's English has puzzled the dictionary writers for centuries. Where did the word come from? The etymologists came to the rescue. "Palingman," said Blount in his Law Dictionary, published in 1670, "seems to be a merchant Denizen; one born within the English pale." That settled the question. Blount's cautious "seems to be" became "is" in the definitions of his copyists, and as late as 1864 Webster's dictionary stated that a palingman was "one born within that part of Ireland called the English Pale." So easy it is to make Irishmen out of true-born Hollanders and Frisians.

December, 1935

VINCENT VAN GOGH

In October of the year 1920, some seventy paintings and drawings by Vincent van Gogh were on view at the Montross Gallery. It was the first opportunity that was offered to New York art lovers to become acquainted with the painter's work. He was received with cool indifference. The more amazing, then, that the collection now exhibited at the Museum of Modern Art is drawing such multitudes to Fifty-third Street that on Mondays, when admission is free, one has to stand in line on the pavement and wait one's turn for a glimpse of the pictures over the shoulders and heads of a milling crowd. What is the explanation of this sudden popularity? The cynical call it the fruit of clever advertising. Paintings insured for a million dollars? An artist's work that can be worth that amount must make a stunning show. Let us go and see it! The advertised money value of the collection may partly account for the popular interest, but it is not the sole nor the chief explanation. The painter himself was unwittingly the best propagandist for his art. He wrote the story of his own life in letters to his younger brother Theo. The three volumes of these Letters form a unique document in the literary and artistic history of Holland. I know of no other Dutch painter who has so unreservedly made confession on paper of his yearnings and trials, his hopes and disappointments, as did Vincent in his messages to Theo. They form an illuminating commentary to his art, and high praise is due to Mr. Alfred H. Barr, Jr. for enriching the catalogue of the exhibition with well-chosen quotations from the Letters, which illustrate the text even better than the excellent reproductions can. It was the man of Letters who, a generation after his death, aroused a diffident or indifferent public to recognition of his other self the artist, and the artist, once having been recognized, keeps the interest in the Letters alive. They were the making of his fame. The eleventh edition of the Encyclopaedia Britannica, which was published in 1911, twenty-one years after Van Gogh's death, contains no information about him. There is, indeed, a casual mention of his name in the article on Impressionism, but the General Index, which should refer to that, ignores him. Not long after the Montross Gallery exhibition, I did my best, at the instance of Theo's widow, Mrs. J. van Gogh-Bonger, to interest some publisher in New York in an English edition of the Letters. One whom I had approached wrote in justification of his refusal, "The letters of a really eminent American statesman in three volumes would hardly be considered at this time, not to mention a foreign painter known only to a very small though distinguished American audience." I do not know what happened to the letters of the really eminent American statesman, but those of the foreign painter did appear, after all, in an English translation; they were published, in three volumes, by Constable in London and Houghton Mifflin in this country. Thanks to the Letters the "very small though distinguished American audience" has grown to tens of thousands of eager, though perhaps less distinguished, Van Gogh admirers and enthusiasts. The surest measure of the artist's present popularity is his reception into the light verse department of the *New Yorker*. Now that he is the talk of the town, the pronunciation of his name has become a matter of popular speculation and inquiry. Hortense Flexner's couplets give the readers of the *New Yorker* a choice of four possibilities, rhyming Gogh with flock, or stroke, or woe, or fog, whichever you like. She might have added another couplet to give the sticklers for correctness a chance to try their throats on the true Dutch utterance, something like this,

> Only the Aquarium showing the Loch
> Ness monster could vie with Vincent van Gogh.

The artist himself would have been gratified by the growth of the small though distinguished élite into a less distinguished multitude of tens of thousands. Not because he shared the naive American delusion that bigger and better are synonyms. But he loved the simple folk far better than polite society, and he liked to believe that his art would appeal to the undistinguished many. "It is very true," he once wrote, "that the common people, who are content with chromos and melt when they hear a barrel organ, are in some vague way right, perhaps more sincere than certain men about town who go to the salon." Madame Roulin, the postman's wife, who was the model for the Woman Rocking a Cradle, was one of those common people who had the true artistic instinct. Van Gogh did three portraits of her and let her choose one as a present. "She had a good eye and took the best." To capture the direct and simple taste of the Roulins, the Tanguys, and their like, Vincent used his colors in the arbitrary way he did. If art is a symbol, not a copy of nature, that symbol will be more easily understood as art which does not seem or pretend to be a copy. One might compare Van Gogh's style with the style of primitive literature. To the primitive mind that language alone is poetry which by its rhythm and its uncommon vocabulary is far removed from the common speech of every day. Primitive poetry has a language of its own, and the primitive paintings of Van Gogh have a color language all their own. Color, to Van Gogh, expressed something all by itself. The fierce dissonants of red and pink and yellow and green of his night café expressed, he said, "that this is a place where one can ruin oneself, where one can turn mad and commit crimes." Of his Bedroom in Arles he wrote, "Here color is to do everything, and giving by its simplification a grander style to things, is to be suggestive here of rest or of sleep in general." It was his hope that such color paintings would delight the common people and give them something better to look at than the chromos that they loved. For his art was to be a gift to the poor. In the early eighties he was full of the idea of doing lithographs of types of workmen, a sower, a digger, a woodcutter, a ploughman, a washwoman and such like, drawings from the people for the people, and of spreading these in a popular edition as a work of duty and love. He dreamt of a future in which the artist should again be a craftsman, working like the smith and the carpenter in all simplicity, as he had done in the Middle Ages.

He liked to live as a workman among workmen, and used to say that he would gladly labor for a fixed weekly wage as every other member of the working class. Art, which the Renaissance had taught us to adore like a mystic god revealed only to the initiated, was to come down to earth and become human, as God had become human in Christ, to bless the simplest and the poorest. "The Notre Dame," he once wrote, "is beautiful in the Fall, at night between the chest-nuts. But there is something in Paris even more beautiful than the autumn and the churches, I mean the poor."

People speak of the tragic life of Vincent van Gogh, and they think of his poverty, his lack of appreciation, his consciousness of the mental derangement that darkened his final days. But those were not the real tragedy. The real tragedy is this that, when recognition and fame did come at last, a generation after his death, his pictures attained values that made them accessible only to the very rich and the specu-lators. To the common people for whom he liked to paint Vincent van Gogh remained a stranger. The Museum of Modern Art, there-fore, has done a good work in bringing these paintings and drawings together from private collections so as to put them nearer to the common people whom he loved.

COENTIES SLIP

The New York papers of November 25 announced the death of Mr. John C. Ten Eyck, one of the pioneers of golf in the United States. According to a notice in the *Times*, the first Ten Eyck in this country was Coenraet Ten Eyck, who came from Holland to New Amsterdam in 1640. "In his new home," said the *Times*, "he acquired the nickname of 'Coenties,' which is found today in Coenties Slip, from which this seventeenth century New Yorker ran a ferry to Long Island." Coen-ties, however, was not his nickname, nor did he acquire it in this country. It is the genitive case of Coentje, which is the diminutive of Coen, the common abbreviation in Dutch of Coenraet. Coenraet's mother must have called him Coentje in the old country, except when she was angry with him, for the diminutive, besides expressing small-ness, serves as a term of endearment, and a naughty boy is made to feel his disgrace by mother's refusing to call him her little one. Since Coenraet Ten Eyck, as a grown-up man, was still known as Coentje among his New Amsterdam fellow citizens, he must have been either small of stature or a very popular character who had made himself beloved among the early Dutch settlers. Hence Coenties Slip means Coenraet's Slip or Wharf. The family name Ten Eyck belongs to a type that might be called address names. In the olden days family names were not in common use. People were called by their Christian names, and an easy way of distinguishing one Jan or Hendrik or Willem from other Jans, Hendriks and Willems in the community was to describe him as the one living at such or such a place, at the mill (Ter Meulen), at the swamp (Ten Broeck), at the wood (Ten Bosch), at the oak (Ten Eyck), etc., and the next generation retained the address as a surname, though they might have moved far away from the old homestead. *Ten* and *Ter* are contractions of *Te den, Te der,* in which *te* is a preposition, the Dutch equivalent of English *at*, and *den, der* are the dative cases singular of the masculine and feminine genders. Hence the Dutch word for mill is a feminine noun, that for oak a masculine noun. The English counterpart of Ten Eyck is the family name Noakes, strange and incredible as it may seem. Noakes is the genitive case of Noak, meaning originally son of Noak, and Noak is an abbrevation of Attenoak, i.e., at the oak, the *n* in the name being the old dative case ending of the definite article, which in the spelling of the name Ten Eyck still retains its proper position. Another English example of an old address name in which the preposition is still extant is Atterbury, meaning originally At the borough; here again, as in Ter Meulen, the *r* is the ending of the dative case singular of the feminine gender.

January, 1936

A CHESS CHAMPION

They tell a story in Holland about a little old man who followed a match between two professional chess players with never flagging interest. He arrived, every day, ahead of time and captured a seat close to the table so as to make sure that not a move should escape him. One day the game did not begin punctually. One of the players sent word by telephone that he had been detained and might be half an hour late. His opponent, on receiving the message, turned to the wizened old watcher and invited him to try his hand at a game while they waited for the other's arrival. "No, thank you," he answered, "I don't know how to play checkers." I am like that old man: ignorant of the game, though I do not misname it, yet keenly interested in the contest for the world championship that ended in a victory for Dr. Euwe. This is less absurd than it would seem at first blush. A man may be avidly reading the dispatches from the front without a scrap of the strategic knowledge that enables the war correspondent to report the fighting intelligibly. To know that those two players were waging a battle on that small board was sufficient to stimulate the old fellow's interest. The purpose of each move was enigmatic to him, but to wait for the outcome of the game gave him the thrill of suspense that he craved. The Dutch people, whether chess-conscious or not, watched for the result with the same tense expectancy. Dr. Euwe was fighting Holland's battle, and when he came out victorious, the country was prouder of him and more jubilant than if he had been a general triumphant in war. He suddenly found himself famous and the object of journalistic curiosity. The papers printed stories about his early childhood, how, at the age of eight, he angered his father by beating him at chess and how, two years later, he won his first public victory; they printed interviews with his parents, his wife, his pupils, and pictures of Dr. Euwe the paterfamilias feeding milk to his baby, and of Dr. Euwe the schoolman teaching mathematics to his class at the Girl's Lyceum in Amsterdam and being entertained at dinner by his pupils. And Hollanders abroad, to judge from my own experience, must have been answering, day after day, the phonetic question, "How do you pronounce the name of that new chess champion?" Last month I had to teach my American friends to say Van Gogh, now I keep saying, "*eu* as in French jeu, and – *we* as in English jewel." Thank God that he calls himself Max as an easy substitute for the name under which he is registered at the city hall in Amsterdam. For Machgielis is an even tougher phonetic problem than Van Gogh. Machgielis Euwe's victory has proved a boon to the manufacturers of chess sets in Holland. Every Dutch youngster seems to be studying the game. The city of Utrecht has made instruction in chess an optional subject in its schools, and the Commissioner of Education in Amsterdam has expressed his intention to place it on the curriculum of one of the city schools by way of trial. The crop of Dutch candidates for the world's chess championship will be prodigious ten years from now.

February, 1936

GERMANTOWN

Germantown, Pa., was not settled by Germans, and Pastorius was not the leader of its pioneers. That is the conclusion reached by Dr. William I. Hull, Howard M. Jenkins Research Professor of Quaker History in Swarthmore College, in his latest publication entitled *William Penn and the Dutch Quaker Migration to Pennsylvania*. The first Germantownians came from Krefeld, a town on the left bank of the Rhine, in the Country of Mörs, which in the seventeenth century belonged to the House of Orange-Nassau. The present political frontiers do not correspond with those of nearly three centuries ago, and the Dutch language, in those days, was spoken far beyond the border line of modern Holland. Krefeld, under the rule of the Prince of Orange, Count of Nassau, was essentially a Netherlandish town. The speech, at any rate, of the first Germantown settlers was Dutch. That is clear from a document in the possession of Mrs. Benjamin K. Kirk, Drexel Hill, Pa., which bears the signatures of nearly all the grown-ups in that small group of pioneers. It is a marriage certificate for Dirck Isaacsz and Nöleken Veiten, who were united in wedlock at a Meeting of the Krefeld Friends shortly before the emigration to Pennsylvania. The document was drawn up in Dutch, and most of the witnesses bore unmistakably Dutch names. Seven of the eleven men who signed it were among the thirteen who, two years afterwards, settled Germantown. Three of the other four arrived there a year later; only one stayed behind. Pastorius, who went to Pennsylvania as an advance agent of the "German Society" or "Frankfort Company," landed a few weeks ahead of the Krefelders, and on October 25, 1683, the latter met with him in a dug-out cabin that was his preliminary home in Philadelphia. There they drew lots for the sites of their future homes, William Penn having issued to them a warrant for three thousand acres. Pastorius continued to live in Philadelphia until the summer of 1685, but the thirteen from Krefeld began to build at once in the new settlement assigned to them. Their community numbered thirty-four in all; nine of the men had their wives with them, there was one youth and one unmarried girl in the group, and there were ten children, two of whom were small infants born at sea. It is clear from the list of newcomers down to the year 1709, which Dr. Hull has derived from Pennsylvania and European sources, that this humble settlement retained its Dutch Quaker character for a generation. Before the great German immigration of 1709 and following years the bulk of the townspeople consisted of Dutch Quakers, with a sprinkling of Dutch and German Mennonites, English and Welsh Friends, and German Lutherans and Pietists.

In 1688 three of these Dutch Quakers of Germantown, together with Pastorius, signed a petition for the abolition of slavery, which they submitted to the Monthly Meeting of Friends. "We who profess," they wrote, "that it is not lawful to steal, must likewise avoid to purchase such things as are stolen." It was their duty as Christians to put a stop to this stealing of human beings, to deliver them out of the hands of the robbers, and set them free. The Monthly Meeting, however, found this a ticklish matter and referred it to the Quarterly Meeting, which passed it on, in its turn, to the Yearly Meeting. And here it was decided that it was not proper for this Meeting to give a positive judgment in the case, as it had "so general a relation to many other parts." Slavery was a general problem of all the Colonies, and the Friends, being a minority, did not deem it wise to antagonize their neighbors by endorsing the protest of a few Dutch idealists in their midst.

The petitioners based their argument against slavery also on practical considerations. It would bring Pennsylvania into disrepute among the Friends in Europe and stop the flow of immigration. William Penn's chief agent in the Netherlands would have agreed with them. This was a Hollandized merchant of English birth in Rotterdam by the name of Benjamin Furly. He was a man of wealth and social importance and had a proper sense of his own dignity. He was not a subservient employee of the great man, but felt free to remonstrate with him as Friend to Friend. Furly protested against the proposed Frame of Government that Penn had signed on April 25 and against the Laws agreed upon on May 5, 1682. He suggested to Penn that the importation of slaves from Africa should be prohibited and that slaves brought into Pennsylvania from the other Colonies should be emancipated within eight years. He was in charge of Penn's publicity campaign on the Continent, and he doubtless felt, with the Germantown Quakers, that the report of Friends' buying and selling men like cattle would impair the success of his advertising. Furly was an indefatigable propagandist. He sold for Penn some 50,000 acres before 1700, he translated Penn's writings into Dutch, and had renderings made into Dutch and German of letters from contented colonists, which were transcribed in his office and forwarded to several correspondents in towns and villages of Holland and Germany. The most flattering accounts were given a more enduring form in printed editions. Dr. Hull's book contains a photostat copy of the title-page of a little pamphlet of 1684 containing two Missives from Pennsylvania, one written by a Hollander in Philadelphia, the other by a Swiss in Germantown. The Hollander was Cornelius Bom, a baker from Haarlem. "I have no servants," he wrote, "except one negro whom I bought. I have no rent or tax or excise to pay. I have a cow which gives plenty of milk, a horse to ride around, my pigs increase rapidly ... I have many chickens and geese, and a garden, and shall next year have an orchard if I remain well; so that my wife and I are in good spirits and are reaching a condition of ease and prosperity." The exemption from rent, tax, and excise, reported immediately after the mention of the bought negro, may have neutralized the damaging effect that this reference to slavery might otherwise have had upon prospective Quaker emigrants.

Benjamin Furly had been acquainted with William Penn since the latter's first visit to Holland in 1671. Penn came again in 1677 for a protracted tour through the Netherlands and Germany, and came back a second time in 1686. Dr. John Northleigh, a London physician, heard him address a Quaker Meeting at Rotterdam. That an Englishman should presume to hold forth to a foreign audience seemed to him, at first, "as preposterous as prayers in public in an unknown tongue." But Penn was fortunate in having a dexterous interpreter, who, "being elevated with him and standing by his side, by paragraph translated his English to his Dutch auditors without the least hesitation." This interpreter was doubtless Benjamin Furly, and the Meeting was probably held in his house, maybe at the very address that is given at the end of Furly's Dutch edition of Penn's *Account of the Province of Pennsylvania*. "Further information," says this postcript, "may be obtained in Amsterdam from Jan Roelofs van der Werf, in the Heerestraat, at the Vergulde Vijfhoek (the Gilded Pentagon) and in Rotterdam from Benjamin Furly, English merchant, who lives at the former Brewery of the Crown, on the Scheepmakershaven (Shipbuilders Harbor)." Furly himself did not sail for the Colony which he had helped to populate. He purchased four thousand acres in Pennsylvania, but never went across the Atlantic to take possession of his property. His business affairs, his literary interests – he was a great book collector – and perhaps the comforts of his Rotterdam home bound him to Holland. When his library was sold after his death, a Dutch printing firm acquired the "very accurate Chart of Pennsylvania, with all its Rivers, Bays, etc. done in ink on parchment," on which he must have marked the lots that he sold to the emigrants when they called at his office on their passage through Rotterdam to the New World.

In 1696 the Monthly Meeting of Philadelphia proposed that the Quakers of Pennsylvania should establish a printing press of their own. The Yearly Meeting approved of the plan, a press and letter types were purchased in London, and Reynier Jansen, a Dutch Quaker, was appointed in February, 1699, official printer of the Friends of Pennsylvania. Jansen was a newcomer, for in May, 1698, he was still living in Alkmaar, Holland. He calls himself, in the Dutch documents, a *vetermaker*, which Dr. Hull supposes to mean lace maker; "but since lace was not too much in vogue among the Germantown and Philadelphia Quakers at that time, he was doubtless glad to turn his hand to printing." Dr. Hull has, apparently, only a dictionary knowledge of Dutch, and dictionaries are often treacherous interpreters. The word *veter* means lace, though not Brussels lace but bootlace, and bootlaces, I suppose, must have been just as much in vogue in Pennsylvania as in Holland. Jansen was probably a Jack of all trades who willingly turned his hand to any work that was offered to him. He never became an accomplished craftsman. Caleb Pusey apologized for his shortcomings as a compositor in the preface to one of the books that he published. "The printer," he wrote, "being a man of another nation and language, as also not bred to that employment, is consequently something unexpert both in language and calling." In spite of his mediocre craftsmanship he also became the official publisher for the Province and printed its laws in the year 1700.

Dirck Isaacksz., the bridegroom of the Krefeld wedding, bore the family name of Op Den Graeff. Two brothers of his sailed with him to Pennsylvania, and the Op den Graeffs became a prominent family in Germantown. Dirck and Abraham were among the four who signed the anti-slavery petition of 1688. In 1689, Penn granted a charter for the "German Towne" to "Dirk Isaacs Opte Graeff Linnenmaker" and his ten associates, and appointed him and three others first burgesses. The same charter named Dirck's brother Herman Town President. And Abraham was a member of the Colonial Assembly in 1689, 1690, and 1692. Dr. Hull, with the aid of his treacherous friend the dictionary, has attempted to explain the name Op den Graeff, and supposes that the brothers were so called "because they came into Krefeld from the county." For the dictionary told him that *graaf* means count, and *graafschap* county, which to Dr. Hull does not seem much different from country. But if they came from the county, they would have been called Van den Graeff instead of Op den Graeff, which would mean On the Count, if count were the correct translation. But Graeff in this name means ditch, or moat, and is a cognate and synonym of *gracht*, both being derived from the verb *graven*, to dig. The family must have been so called because their house stood on the moat or canal in the place from which they came originally. One of the witnesses at Dirck's Krefeld wedding was Tunnes Keunen, i.e., Anthony, son of Koenraad. One of his sons was again called Cunrad after his grandfather, but Cunrad, or Cunrads, or Kunders, – all sorts of spellings were in use – became the regular family name. It survives, according to Dr. Hull, in the form Cunard, Samuel Cunard, the founder in 1838 of the first regular steamship service across the Atlantic, having been a descendant of Tunnes Keunen.

April, 1936

A STUDENT OF BI-RACIAL RELATIONS

In the current issue of *Travel* an American scientist, Dr. Victor Heiser, tells of his experiences in Java, where he went to offer his services in the fight against the hookworm plague. Simultaneously, the Viking

Press, New York, brings us a book by a Dutch scholar from Java, who came to America to study the plight and the problems of her aliens of non-European extraction. Dr. Heiser went to Java uninvited. The Rockefeller Foundation, ever zealous to make its resources available to suffering humanity in all parts of the globe, sent him out on this mission to the Netherland East Indies. Dr. B. Schrieke, the author of *Alien Americans*, undertook his study at the request of the Board of Trustees of the Julius Rosenwald Fund and spent nearly a year in this country as its guest. The American was not received in Java with the cordial welcome that his native country gave to the Hollander. The Dutch officials in the Indies were jealous of the reputation their own doctors had gained in fighting tropical diseases. Dutch medical science had stamped out beri beri and cholera, and needed no American assistance in conquering other plagues. Dr. Heiser does give the Dutch credit for what they have accomplished in that field. "In their laboratories they developed the smallpox vaccine, sought vainly for so many years, that would remain effective for long periods under tropical temperature. They were the first to experiment with cholera vaccine on a large scale, testing it on the inhabitants of each alternate block in Batavia. Practically no cases occurred in the blocks protected by the vaccine." Hence Dutch officialdom turned the cold shoulder to the Rockefeller scientist and his staff, whom they regarded as meddlesome intruders. "We had the feeling we were being allowed to make our demonstration only in order that they might demonstrate to us how wrong we were." But they were not guilty of pig-headed obstinacy. "When the Dutch civil service was finally converted, it entered the field of health education of the natives with every bit of its abundant energy."

The case of Dr. Schrieke's visit to America offers a striking contrast to Dr. Heiser's experience in Java. Americans are less cocksure of their own infallibility and more receptive to suggestions and ideas from abroad. Scholarship in the United States is just as hospitable to foreign science as the country has been, in the past, to newcomers from abroad. When Mr. Edwin R. Embree, the well-known writer of *Brown America*, was traveling in the Netherland East Indies, he was impressed by the excellent work that was being done there in the field of native education, and it was at his suggestion that the Julius Rosenwald Fund invited Dr. Schrieke to come to the United States and make a study of Negro life in the South. Mr. Embree chose the right man for this important mission. Dr. Schrieke has had the training and the experience that eminently fit him for the difficult task of evaluating relationships between dominant white and subdued dark races. He studied oriental languages at Leyden, and served for eighteen years in the East Indies in various official capacities, as Assistant Commissioner of Native Affairs, as Director of the Museum in Batavia, as Professor of Social Anthropology and Sociology in the University of Batavia, and finally as Secretary of Education and Religious Worship. The Malay Archipelago is a vast territory inhabited by a heterogeneous mass of peoples. The name Malayan covers a multitude of skins. To govern these many millions, about nine times as numerous as the population of Holland, and maintain peace and contentment among them is not an easy task. For the very education that the Hollander is bringing to the natives supplies them with the knowledge and the desire to supplant the teacher and shift for themselves. Infinite tact and patience and psychological insight into the native mentality are the prerequisites for the successful discharge of the administrator's function. "In the extremely difficult situations that confronted them," says Dr. Heiser, "the Dutch seemed to possess to an unusual degree the ability to combine the scientific with the practical." His praise refers especially to their achievement in the field of public hygiene, but it holds good as well for other spheres of colonial government. Dr. Schrieke the ethnologist and linguist is also a practical administrator. He knows the native psyche, both from the study of books and through personal contact. No wonder that the call from the Board of Trustees of the Julius Rosenwald Fund attracted him. Here he could study the white men and the colored in different relationships under different conditions, and watch them work out their problems in ways offering suggestive contrasts and analogies to those he was familiar with. His volume *Alien Americans* contains the gist of his research and the conclusions drawn from his findings.

Dr. Schrieke did his work thoroughly. In order to grasp the peculiar character of the problems facing black and white in the South, he found it necessary to make a preliminary survey of the full range of the American background and study the American reaction to other biracial relationships. Hence the pivotal chapter on The South and the Negro is preceded by brief discussions of the Chinese and the Japanese in California, of Mexicans and Indians, and of America and the Alien. Dr. Schrieke is an impartial and dispassionate observer. His sympathies, no doubt, are with the Negro in his striving for betterment and education. But this does not blind him to the white man's problems in the South. As a promotor of native education in Java, he is naturally inclined to look with favor upon college training for the Negro, but he does not conceal his disapproval of the use that is being made of the opportunity. "In my opinion," he writes, "attention is given too exclusively to Negro problems in most of the Negro colleges and universities. It is natural; but the danger is – and in my judgment that danger is not consciously or at least not effectively avoided – that the Negro problems are not studied in their relativity, in their world aspect, without which they are apt to increase resentment and not to serve to liberate the mind and the individuality. The only way to mental freedom is analysis. Only in this way can the pathological self-centredness, resulting from the oppression psychosis and the repression of self-determination, and the spell of uniqueness be broken, and the obsession realized to be the product of general laws." It is a cumbersome and ill-constructed sentence, but its meaning is clear and goes to the heart of the problem. The main argument of Dr. Schrieke's brilliant study is that the Negro can overcome his sense of futility and hopelessness by learning to view his own plight in the perspective of human history. When he realizes that he is not the unique victim of circumstances especially created for his oppression, but that his case is the fatal result of forces which, in other climes and under other conditions, have similarly victimized other races, brown, yellow, and white, as well as black, he may be able to recover the self-respect that he needs for his progress towards a better future. In his survey of bi-racial situations in America the author found prejudice everywhere, against the Chinese, the Mexicans, the Indians, the East-European Jews. But all these race relations were in a state of flux. The first immigrants moved from their colonies to zones of second and third settlement, and were gradually submerged in the American mass. Indians and whites are now living at peace, and efface their different types by intermarriage. American-born Chinese and Japanese mix with Italians, Mexicans and others and blur the dividing lines between the alien colonies. In the South, on the other hand, he found black-white relationships in a state of petrifaction. There is no hope for the South, in his opinion, unless there also the barriers be let down and prejudice yield to forbearance. Dr. Schrieke sees the South heading for a serious economic crisis. The cotton belt is moving westward, to Texas, New Mexico, Arizona, and Southern California. The tide of migration towards the cities has come to a stop and is ebbing back to the land. How will these millions survive with their source of erstwhile prosperity drying up? The author sees no other solution than the development of a new peasantry. In parts of America other than the South the author found already symptoms of a new rural economy evolving. Peasant communities are emerging, consisting of a village or a town as its centre and the open country as its tributary territory. The new peasant produces his own food and the feed for his stock. He is not a serf, but a hardworking tiller of his self-owned land. There is hope for the South, in Dr. Schrieke's judgment, if it will allow and encourage the Negro to become the white man's fellow peasant. "As a basis of the new South, the building up of a peasant economy is as vital to the whites as it is to the blacks and requires the co-operation of all."

June, 1936

MARIA VAN RENSSELAER

The Correspondence of Maria van Rensselaer 1669-1689, translated and edited by A. J. F. van Laer and published by the University of the State of New York in 1935, is good reading in the Editor's rendering. I wish, though, that he had printed the text with the original Dutch on the opposite page, for Maria's correspondence reflects the speech of one who was born in the Colony, and so little is known of native New Netherland Dutch that a collection of this kind is a precious linguistic specimen for the philologist. Maria was born at New Amsterdam on July 20, 1645. Her parents were Oloff Stevensen van Cortlandt and Anna Loockermans. She must have received her education in the local school, which could teach her little more than the three R's. She never learnt to spell correctly, but for that very reason her writing is instructive to the linguist, for since she was guided by her ear rather than by orthographic convention, the text of her letters reveals the actual speech that was heard in the Van Cortlandt family. Mr. Van Laer gives all proper names in Maria's spellings, which are often curious and puzzling. Especially foreign names are apt to acquire a Dutch appearance when she puts them to paper, Cartwright becoming Catrick, Leisler Lasselyr or Lyselaer, Livingstone Levenstone or Leuvesteyn, Pattishall Padderschal. She probably never learnt to speak English, though all the letters printed by Mr. Van Laer were written after the British occupation. Her younger brother Jacobus was evidently eager to learn the language of the new rulers. While on a visit to Boston, which Maria spelled Baston, he wrote his father a letter in English, and Oloff Stevensen thought his son's performance sufficiently remarkable to report the fact to Maria in Albany. The letter was probably a schoolboy's exercise; perhaps he had been sent to Boston for the very purpose of learning the language. As a businessman he would have to know it. But Maria, living on her own estate among an entirely Dutch community, had neither inducement nor opportunity to study English.

Maria married Jeremias van Rensselaer in 1662. Four years previously he had succeeded his brother Jan Baptist as Director of the Colony of Rensselaerswyck. Jeremias died in 1674, leaving her the care of four sons and two daughters, the youngest child, Jeremias, being born after his father's death. As there was no one immediately available to take the late Director's place, his widow took temporary charge of the administration, relying for assistance and advice on her brother Stephanus van Cortlandt in New York. There was, of course, no regular postal service between the settlement on Manhattan and Albany; the correspondents had to rely on carriers who happened to go up or down the river. "My last letter was by an Indian by way of the Esopus," wrote Stephanus in one of his early epistles, but the usual way was to charge a skipper with the delivery. There was good reason, in those days, for starting one's message with some such formula as "I duly received yours dated May 14th," or "I wrote you at length, which letters I hope duly received in good health." Most of the letters did arrive safely, with how much delay it is impossible to infer from their contents. They suffered damage some two hundred and fifty years later, when they were salvaged, badly burned along the edges, from the Capitol fire of 1911. Hence the dates of many of the letters were destroyed, and internal evidence only could guide the Editor in arranging them chronologically.

They do not tell us much about the social and domestic life in the Colony. Maria never wrote for the mere pleasure of writing; she was apparently incapable of a chatty letter. She discussed business affairs, contracts, debts, claims, rents, litigation, labor troubles, disputes with neighbors, in short, all the worries and cares that wealth is heir to. Maria never thought of herself as a wealthy woman. "If you examine the receipts of the Colony, you will see that one year with another it could not produce enough to cover the expenses," she wrote to her brother-in-law Richard van Rensselaer, the Treasurer of the manor of Vianen in Holland. Her husband, she complains, had left her an encumbered estate. "Dear brother, you will know yourself how ..., whenever any one of importance came from New York, we had to entertain him to keep up the dignity of the Colony. You also well know that brother Jan Baptist wrote that one should not be particular about one or two thousand guilders." She planned, in 1675, to send her son Kilian to Holland, "for I do not know how he can earn his living here." She changed her mind because of the war then raging between Holland and France, and apprenticed the boy "with a silversmith in this country." Four years later he was in Boston, apprenticed to the silversmith Jeremy Dummer. "It seems," wrote his uncle Stephanus to Maria, "that Kilian is not used to living so plainly as they do there." No wonder the boy was spoiled, being the son of parents who, as hosts to distinguished guests from New York, had to keep up the dignity of the Colony. Perhaps the plain living among the English of Boston had a wholesome effect on Kilian. In a letter to Richard van Rensselaer of 1683 she reports, with evident pride, "He can get along very well with the farmers and also knows the patroon's cattle, yes, down to the calves, so that he pays due attention to them. This year I let him settle with the farmers about the tithes. He is a diligent young man. I made him set up his silversmith's shop outside the city limits of Albany. He makes good use of his time. He is also a member of God's church. May the Lord let him grow up in virtue and grant him His blessing as to soul and body."

Maria was fond of complaining, in her letters to the Van Rensselaers in Holland, about the burden of responsibility that was weighing her down. But when the Dutch relatives decided to appoint Nicholas van Rensselaer, a younger brother of her husband, Director in her place, she strongly protested. Her brother Stephen sided with her in opposing the new management. Nicholas was apparently willing to let her retain an important share in the administration, for he consented to an arrangement under which Maria would be treasurer and Stephanus van Cortlandt bookkeeper, three hundred bushels of wheat being set aside for their salaries, of which the Director was to receive one half and the other half was to be divided between the treasurer and the bookkeeper. This arrangement lasted until Nicholas died in November, 1678. Stephanus succeeded him in the Directorship, but as he resided in New York, the actual management remained in Maria's hands until her death in 1689. She must have been an able, courageous, and energetic woman. She was never in good health, had to support herself on crutches, and died at the youthful age of forty-four, but she seems to have possessed a strong will-power that could overcome her physical handicap. She was not given to sentimental effusion. Her environment was hardly calculated to develop the softer side of human nature. She had to deal with impertinent farmers, quarrelsome neighbors, scheming relatives, and doubtful friends. "It is here at present so sad, one does not know whether one deals with friend or enemy. One dares not even trust one's own brother." Of Nella Maria, daughter of Johannes van Rensselaer, she wrote, "I never thought that the patroon's sister was such a vile woman," and speaking of Philip Pietersen Schuyler she called him "that interloper and his bitter family." Of her parents Maria wrote with genuine affection. This is from a letter of November 12, 1684, addressed to Nicholas van Rensselaer. "On the fifth of April it pleased God suddenly to take out of this world my dear father, while he was in his prayers and in good health, in the presence of myself and of my dear mother, who would have liked so much to keep me with her a while longer. Having been home but a short time, I received a letter that I must come down again. I therefore went down in all haste. God granted us a favorable wind, so that we arrived at New York the next day, but I found my dear mother in the place where my father's bier had stood. She had died on the twelfth of May."

On June 7th, 1678, the Duke of York issued a warrant to Governor Andros to grant a patent for the Colony of Rensselaerswijck, but for some unknown reason, says Mr. Van Laer, no action was taken by the Governor, although the Van Rensselaers in Holland did a lot of wirepulling at the courts of the Prince of Orange and St. James. They renewed their efforts when Colonel Thomas Dongan succeeded Governor Andros in 1683, and petitioned him for a patent that would include the town of Albany, which Governor Stuyvesant had severed from the Colony by an arbitrary decree of 1652. Governor Dongan, however, refused to rescind his Dutch predecessor's action, judging it to be "not to his Majesty's interest that the second town of the Government, which brings his Majesty so great a revenue, should be in the hands of any particular men." The Van Rensselaers, accordingly, had to sign a release of their claims to the town and the surrounding country within a radius of sixteen miles, before the Governor could be persuaded to grant a patent to Kilian, son of Johannes, and to Kilian, son of Jeremias, the representatives of the Netherland and American branches of the family. Thus the Colony of Rensselaerswyck was erected into an English manor, and its first lord, Kilian, son of Johannes, came over from Holland and married Maria's daughter Anna. Their union was of brief duration. Anna's husband died in February, 1687, and was succeeded by his cousin Kilian, the former silversmith apprentice. When Maria was lying on her deathbed, late in January of 1689, she had the satisfaction of leaving the patroonship which her husband's father had founded in charge of her eldest son as lord of the manor.

JUFFERS

The city of Amsterdam is an inverted forest. Its pine trees do not rise from the ground, they bore into it, crown downward. The terrain is so soggy that each house must be built on a solid foundation of piles driven into the mud. The Hollander has a strange name for these subterranean trees; he calls them *juffers*, young ladies. I wonder why. The reason for the comparison is perhaps in a similarity of posture. A compliment to the erect build of Dutch girls may be implied. No woman can demur at being called as straight as a pole. However that may be, the Hollander, in calling a pole a lady, is less offensive to the fair sex than the German who calls his women folk female timber, *frauenzimmer*. That is inverting the comparison into a downright insult. It took 13,659 *juffers* to lay the foundation for the imposing city

124

hall, which was inaugurated in 1655. Every Amsterdam school child knows the number by heart. It is easy to remember: you take the number of days there are in a year and sandwich it in between a one and a nine. If so many pine trees were needed for one building, it is clear that the whole of underground Amsterdam is a dense forest of millions of timber. But above ground it is a mass of brick and stone, with spare fringes of foliage along its canals and here and there dots of green parks; and where the city ends, the flat country begins, deep-lying polders with a crisscross pattern of ditches lined with dwarfish pollard willows that do not obstruct the endless vista of pasture. There are no woods in the immediate neighborhood of Amsterdam to lure the poor away from the crowded city. The well-to-do have the means to spend their weekends and vacations in Utrecht or Gelderland, or farther away in Switzerland or Germany. But those who can afford no more than a tram ride for an outing, must find the pleasures and the benefits of rural life vicariously in the dusty city parks. Since the larger part of the city's population cannot be brought to the distant woods, the municipal government has decided to bring the woods to the city. Amsterdam, built on a forest, will soon be belted by a forest. A thousand men will be employed during the next five years in planting trees on the very outskirts of Amsterdam. Rather than have them come to the city hall each week for their dole, the author-ities will pay them for making the city a healthier and pleasanter place to live in for their fellow citizens and themselves. The plans for this huge enterprise have been made by a committee of experts on forestry, landscape gardening, and botany. But the authorities count chiefly on the assistance of Nature, whose genius for landscape architecture will be given free rein after her human adepts have done the planting. The swampy parts of the city's environs will not be drained but left intact for the recreation of anglers and lovers of water sports, who will find greater beauty in their favorite haunts when pools and lakes will mirror sheltering girdles of foliage. The botanists and landscape artists will go hunting all over the world for trees of the new Amster-dam forest. The Far East, Siberia, Caucasia, and the North American continent will all contribute saplings to the polder landscape. A seventeenth-century poet pitied the "worry-sick" merchants on the Exchange, who with all their wealth lacked oak in Amsterdam. Twen-ty years from now the poorest slum dweller will be able to go pic-nicking of a summer Sunday in the shade of oak or beech or maple or whatever forest growth his fancy prefers.

The University of Leyden paid tribute, last month, to the memory of Jan Swammerdam, on the three hundredth anniversary of his birth. He was born at Amsterdam on February 12, the son of a well-to-do apothecary, who was a collector of precious porcelain, curios, minerals, exotic plants, and stuffed animals. His Cabinet, as such private museums were called in those days, was one of the sights of Amsterdam, and visitors who showed an interest in naturalia were always welcome to inspect his collection. The son was a chip of the old block. He was a trained naturalist before he came of age. He loved to wander through the polderland around Amsterdam collecting and studying the tiny live stock of pools, swamps, and ditches. Thus he acquired the knowledge which enabled him to publish, in 1669, his General Treatise of the Bloodless Animalculae. He studied medicine at Leyden, and obtained his doctor's degree in 1667 with a dissertation on the respiratory organs. But the study and practice of medicine never claimed the whole man. Biology was his passion, and in that field he did pioneer work that bears the stamp of genius. He was the first to study insect life in its circular course from egg to egg, and devised a classification of insects on the basis of their various metamorphoses which retains its value to this day. It was generally assumed in Swammerdam's time that insects came to life by spontaneous generation from mud, manure, and putrid matter. He proved this to be a superstitition and taught that "just as all vegetation evolves from a perceptible and fertile seed, even so all other creatures and animals spring from a seed or egg." He wrote about snails, which he discovered to be hermaphrodites, about bees, describing their anatomy and the distribution of labor in the hive, about ink fish and other creatures that had never been studied scientifically. Swammerdam was a deeply religious man. Behind the natural phenomena that he discovered and described he looked for the divine power which alone could explain them. In 1675 he published a little book on the mayfly, which he prefaced with "An earnest admonition to the truth-seeking reader." "Do not think," he wrote, "that the insect which I describe in the following pages is merely an ephemeral creature that runs its course of life pleasantly and without discomforts. On the contrary, it is perhaps the most miserable creature alive in the world, being subject, more than any other species that I know, to dangers and difficulties. Indeed, water, air, and earth seem uniformly armed to destroy it before, during, and after its birth. For this reason I have not hesitated to present this insect as a truthful emblem of human life, which is no more than a dark and very brief night, considering the manifold and endless miseries that surround man during his brief career. And these sorrows, which he foolishly learns to love, darken his view to such an extent that he becomes wholly incapable of beholding the rays of the eternally shining days, let alone of loving them and following their light as his sole beacon." His health, which never was robust, was undermined by malaria and too much study. He was cursed with an avaricious sister, who despised him for wasting his time on useless and unremunerative studies, and tried to deprive the wastrel of his due share in their father's estate. Preferring peace of mind to physical comfort he did not care to put up a fight, but the financial worries that ensued aggravated his melancholy. "Among the various traits that we have observed in the story of the may-fly," he wrote, "nothing seems to me more remarkable than that it does not try to postpone the time of its metamorphosis. It casts off as soon as it can the shape of a creeping and swimming worm to assume the figure of a flying creature. This teaches man that he should quickly and readily leave the wet and cold waters of this muddy vale of tears and raise himself on the wings of Hope and Love, which are the two arms of Faith, into the air of Divine affections." His transformation took place on February 17, 1680. Boerhaave, who brought out an edition of Swammerdam's biological oeuvre on the centenary of his birth, gave it a title which did justice to the scholar who had served science to the glory of God. He called it *Biblia Naturae*.

August-September, 1937

AMSTERDAM'S JEWISH QUARTER

Some twenty-odd years ago the City Council of Amsterdam decided on the demolition of the old Jewish quarter, which, picturesque to a degree in the artist's eye, had become an eyesore to the hygienist. The Council's verdict did not outrage Jewish feeling, for the Jews themselves had, in more than one respect, begun to loosen the ties which held their community together. A less strict adherence to the old ritualism and dogma, the spread of radical and socialist ideas, the closer contact with the Gentile by the increasing frequency of intermarriage were the agents of a dissolution which the Council simply emphasized by giving it official recognition.

A ghetto in the proper sense of the word never existed in Amsterdam. At no time were the Jews forced to live together in a separate quarter walled off from the rest of the city, nor were they compelled to wear badges by which they could be recognized as Jews. They stuck together voluntarily, they formed their ghetto themselves. The first comers, in the late nineties of the sixteenth century, settled on the right bank of the Amstel, south of the medieval part of Amsterdam, and this section of the city has remained the Jewish quarter down to the present day. It was here that Rembrandt built himself a sumptuous house on the Jodenbreestraat, the Jews' Broad Street, in the very heart of the ghetto. On summer days the population, like the Hebrew tent dwellers of ancient Palestine, lived in the open, on stoops and pavements, gossiping and squabbling, transacting business, and settling family affairs. The scene in front of his house was to Rembrandt a resuscitation of New Testament life. He needed but to open a front-parlor window to find suggestions right and left at his own door of scenes from the life of Christ and illustrations of the parables.

The States of Holland, by a resolution of 1616, left the cities of the province free to decide for themselves whether to admit or exclude Jewish immigrants. This gave the individual cities supreme power over their Jewish residents. The Jews were regarded as subjects of the burgomasters, not as aliens liable to expulsion. They benefited from this arrangement. For Dutch commercialism saw the advantage of attracting wealthy Jews with business relations in foreign countries, and the cities vied with one another in conniving at the non-enforcement of their own regulations restricting the life and activities of Jewish residents. The Jews possessed no civil rights under the Dutch Republic. The craft guilds were closed to them, so that they were limited to such professions as were not organized in corporations. First among these was the diamond industry. Rich Portuguese diamond dealers became the employers of the poorer Portuguese, German, and Polish Jews. In 1748 their Christian competitors made an attempt to check their ascendancy by requesting the City Council to organize the industry into a guild, to which Jews should pay dues without the right to vote, to forbid the employment of new Jewish apprentices, and to prohibit the Jews from working on Sundays. But the city Government refused to comply with their request, because "the Jews had established the diamond trade in Amsterdam." They retained a virtual monopoly of the industry until the year 1870. About that time the first Cape diamonds were brought to Amsterdam, and the rapid growth of the import from South Africa caused such a rise in the demand for skilled labor that the cutters and polishers were no longer recruited exclusively from among the Jews. From that date Jews and Christians were seen working side by side in the mills, the latter forming about two-thirds of the total of hands employed. This fusion of labor was another factor in the emancipation of the Jew from his seclusion in the self-made ghetto. A realistic picture of this

128

latter-day life in the diamond mills is given in *Levensgang* (Life's Way), a naturalistic novel by the late Israel Querido, who in his early days was a diamond cutter himself and a sharer in the life and the hardships of the ghetto and the trade.

The jewelry business was not the Jews' only means of livelihood. There were, in seventeenth-century Amsterdam, Jewish silk manufacturers, sugar refiners, printers, bookdealers, tobacco merchants, brokers, physicians, surgeons, apothecaries, grocers, innkeepers, money lenders. Wealthy Jews played a part on the Amsterdam exchange. In 1687 an Amsterdam lawyer, Nicholas Muys van Holy, published a pamphlet advocating the imposition of a tax on time speculations in shares of the East and West India companies. His special point was an attack on the bear market, which he considered to be harmful to both the companies and the commonwealth. "The trade in shares," he wrote, "is mostly in the hands of the Portuguese nation, which enjoys more freedom in this land than in most regions of the world." With the limited facts at the historian's disposal it is impossible to determine whether Muys van Holy's contention was well founded or inspired by an anti-semitic bias. Several pamphlets disputed his charge, and one anonymous author retorted that, if Jews were guilty in this respect, they were in the good company of many prominent Christian gentlemen, who traded in company shares whenever they saw a chance of making money.

The history of Jewish participation in the economic life of the Netherlands is yet to be written. A solid foundation for such an undertaking has been laid by an American scholar in a recent volume entitled *The Economic Activities of the Jews of Amsterdam in the Seventeenth and Eighteenth Centuries*, a dissertation with which Rabbi Herbert I. Bloom, of Kingston, N. Y., obtained the doctor's degree at Columbia University. The author modestly admits that his task was limited to clearing the ground for further research. He restricted himself to seeking an answer to this question, "Did the Jews contribute to the rise and growth of capitalism in one of its focal points: the city of Amsterdam, and if so, how great was their contribution and what was its nature?" He has come to the conclusion that Amsterdam, without the Jews, would have prospered just the same. They did not materially alter the course and the manner of the city's growth, capitalism being a plant of native origin, not a Jewish import from Spain and Portugal. "The Jews," says Dr. Bloom, "with all their cultural and economic affluence, were but a drop in the commercial bucket of the great metropolis." Amsterdam gave them more than it received in return. It offered them a haven of refuge from a world universally hostile to the Jew, and a sphere of capitalistic activity in which their race was in its very element, highly trained as it was by age-long experience in the manipulation of money, that being the only remunerative pursuit left open to them by Christian intolerance. Still, considering their numerical insignificance, their share in the industry and commerce of Amsterdam was considerable. The number of Jews engaged in the credit business, in brokerage, and speculation formed a larger percentage of the Hebrew community than did those of any other element of the population. Jewish capital was heavily invested in the Dutch West India Company. Civil and political rights were more freely extended to the Jews in the American colonies than they were in the home land, hence Jews became plantation owners in Brazil, Dutch Guyana, and Curaçao, whence many, subsequently, emigrated to the United States. The Jewish trend towards the Dutch colonies in the Far East was less pronounced. They found less scope for their commercial talents in Java, the Chinese having entrenched themselves in the very positions for which business acumen fitted the Jews. It is true, all the same, that wherever Dutch enterprise went pioneering for profit, in the Baltic, on the Barbary Coast, in Turkey, in the Levant, in America, in the Far East, Amsterdam Jews followed in its trail and contributed to Holland's commercial and colonial expansion.

The Portuguese Jews, the Sephardim, were the leaders of their race in seventeenth-century Holland. The Ashkenazim, the Jews from Germany and eastern Europe, far outnumber them at the present day, but the Portuguese community still retains its social prestige and prominence. The Sephardim form the aristocracy of Dutch Jewry. They were the heirs of Spanish and Moorish culture; they brought with them refinement, a love of letters, learning, and philosophy, which gave them distinction among the Dutch and leadership over the Ashkenazim. The names of these Sephardic families have a musical cadence and sonority that sound exotic in Dutch ears: Orobio de Castro, Mendes da Costa, Lopes Suasso, Teixeira de Mattos, Da Costa Gomes de la Peña. Men and women bearing such names have been Dutch residents for ten generations and full-fledged citizens for nearly a century and a half. For in 1796 the Jews, both Sephardim and Ashkenazim, were emancipated and accorded full citizens' rights. The bulk of them are loyal subjects of Queen Wilhelmina. But their political equality with the rest of the nation does not tend to efface their racial distinctness. On the contrary, the more the Jew becomes politically absorbed in the civil community, the more distinctly his Jewishness becomes accentuated in all he does. It almost seems as if the gradual process of naturalization were a challenge to the Jew to assert the virtues of his race. Since the beginning of this century it has become customary to talk and write about Jewish literature and Jewish art, as the work of Jewish authors and Jewish painters was felt to be intentionally expressive of racial idiosyncracies. Josef Israels, in his later days, was not unconscious of this tendency. From the portrayal of the North Sea fisherman at home and on the beach, he turned, in his old age, to the study of ghetto scenes, such as the ragged pawnbroker on the doorstep of his mysterious store, a Jewish wedding ceremony, and episodes from the Old Testament. The recrudescence of anti-semitism in other parts of Europe and its corollary, the Zionist movement, are strengthening this tendency towards self-assertion. The late Jacob Israel de Haan testified in his poetry to the longing for the ultimate return to Palestine and to his faith in the invincibility of his race. He went to Palestine himself and found martyrdom in the land of promise at the hands of assassins. Though he was a prophet of the people of Israel in their dispersion, Dutch was the language in which he wrote his verse. Zionism, in the field of letters, is doomed to remain a national and polyglot movement, enriching each separate literature rather than adding force to the international action. For Yiddish is not a fit instrument, it seems, for the prophet's inspired song. In Holland the gain which her literature derives from Hebrew poetry and fiction is acknowledged with gratitude.

October, 1937

ILLEGITIMATE FRANS HALSES

The city of Haarlem has called its municipal picture gallery Frans Hals Museum. Hals was indeed the greatest painter that ever lived and worked in Haarlem and deserves the honor of fathering the home that shelters, besides some of his own magnificent paintings, panels and canvases of many lesser Haarlem masters. During the past summer these others had to make room for a host of invaders, all Frans Halses loaned to the Gallery by public collections and private owners both in Holland and abroad. For three months Frans Hals was in sole possession of his Museum. If his spirit haunts the place, he must have been happy in the midst of one hundred and sixteen children. But were they all his? A Dutch art critic, Mr. M. M. van Dantzig, looked them over carefully and found eighty-three of them to be either bastards or changelings.[1] The Museum building was in former days the city's orphanage. Mr. van Dantzig, by robbing eighty-three supposed Halses of the master's paternity, restored the old house, for

[1] *Frans Hals Echt of Onecht* door M. M. van Dantzig, Amsterdam: H. J. Paris, 1937.

the time being, to its previous use. There they were, eighty-three orphaned treasures, which will go back to their fond guardians as disowned, nameless waifs. This is an object lesson to collectors. They should not loan their precious paintings to retrospective and memorial exhibitions. At the gathering of the clan each reunionist is mercilessly scrutinized, and those who do not show the characteristic family features run the risk of being sent home with the stigma of illegitimacy.

What tests does Mr. van Dantzig apply to ascertain the genuine Hals strain in a picture? He starts from a preconceived conception of what constitutes a genuine Frans Hals. There is first of all the manner in which he posed his models; or it would be more correct to say, in which he caught his models in action. For he did not allow them to be in repose. A portrait by Hals is a study of movement. The gesture of an outstretched hand, the laugh that enlivens a face, the zigzag line of the folds in a sleeve, the vibrancy of the brush stroke, the play of the light on the texture of skin and draperies, all combine to create that impression of mobility. Mr. van Dantzig has drawn up a catalogue of forty peculiarities which he claims to be typical of the master's technique. These constitute his canon of authenticity. Each exhibit has been checked up with this catalogue of essentials, and when the result shows a preponderance of discrepancies, Mr. van Dantzig is satisfied that the ascription to the master is a blunder of the experts and a deception of the public. There are a dozen heads of fisher boys and girls which the author suspects to be the work of a nineteenth century English painter. They do not show any of the canonical features and resemble one another in several traits that betray their common provenance from a studio that was not Hals's. These are deliberate forgeries. But there is a fine gradation in illegitimacy. There are studio pictures by the master's pupils to which he gave the finishing touches, there are contemporary copies of authentic works, and seventeenth-century originals by other painters erroneously attributed to Hals. Mr. van Dantzig claims that his method of procedure can distinguish between these varieties of factitiousness. It may be so, but I for one am not inclined to follow him unreservedly. The method is too mechanical. It treats each picture as an algebraic formula. Frans Hals cannot have been the faultlessly functioning machine that evolves from the author's analysis of his technique. An artist is a man of moods, erratic, spasmodic, incalculable, defying all attempts to divide his talent inventorially. He must have had his weak moments, when he worked against the grain and his hands did the work without the heart's guidance. In moods of storm and stress the inner turmoil may have overthrown the law that governed his genius, supposing always that Mr. van Dantzig's canon is not a fiction of his brain but an actual code of Hals's art. Mr. van Dantzig may be right in his elaborate analysis of the master's technique, but his pernickety collation of the paintings with the canon has led him astray into hazardous and unwarranted conclusions.

I do not mean to imply that Mr. van Dantzig's suspicions are unfounded. It is an open secret that the picture trade has foisted many fakes upon collectors, and the production of forgeries is still proceeding at a merry pace. Some twelve years ago a false Frans Hals was on trial at The Hague. It was the portrait of a gentleman painted on panel, and looked so much the genuine article that a well-known firm of art dealers at Amsterdam was misled into buying it for *f* 50,000. Besides, the picture was certified to be an authentic work of the master by a leading authority on seventeenth-century Dutch art. But it was proved that this great expert was not infallible. For a professor of chemistry of the University of Delft examined the paint and found the artist had used pigments that were unknown in the seventeenth century, and photography revealed, under the layer of paint, an iron nail embedded in the panel, of a kind that was not manufactured before the second half of the nineteenth century. Among art circles at The Hague the identity of the real painter was a matter of common knowledge. He was less to blame than the wealthy collectors who buy pictures not for their beauty but for their name. A modern artist who can paint a deceptive Frans Hals must be a man of uncommon talent. If he cannot make a living with his own paintings, one can forgive him for succumbing to the temptation to make easy money by impersonating Frans Hals. Would any collector have bought that same picture if the artist had signed it with his own name?

MASCOTS

Last summer I spent a few happy days in the city of Münster in Westphalia. For a native of Holland a visit to this ancient episcopal seat is in the nature of a pilgrimage. For it was there that, in 1648, the peace was concluded which gave the Dutch Republic official recognition of its hard-won independence. Nothing has been changed since that day in the room where the document was signed; the very cushions that made the wooden seats along the walls less hard for the delegates to sit on are still there, moth-eaten and faded. Gerard Terborch painted a picture of the ceremony, which is now in the National Gallery, London. With a clear recollection of that painting in my mind, I could easily reconstruct the historic scene. The Guild House of the Merchants, where the Netherland delegates were lodged, is still one of the most admired samples of Renaissance architecture of Münster. The Dutch envoys kept a stork there as a mascot. One day the bird escaped, to the joy of the Münster children, who chased it across the Principalmarkt and the Domplatz into the Bergstrasze, where it found refuge in the house that lodged the Spanish delegates. These took such good care of the stork that it refused to return to its Dutch owners. The people of Münster saw in this incident a sign of a speedy peace between Hollanders and Spaniards. The Franciscan Chronicle, in which the city archivist of Münster found this story, asserts that none of the delegations was without its mascot: the French had brought a wolf, the Emperor's representatives a fox, the Spaniards a sheep. The annalist does not call them mascots. The universal use of the word is of recent date. Edmond Audran's opera La Mascotte, produced in December 1880, started it on its international career. From obscurity and humble usage in provincial French it rose, in a few decades, to world-wide adoption. But the belief in such bringers of good luck must be as old as the human race. It was news to me, though, that our forefathers used to carry mascots along to their peace conferences. The practice ought to be revived in the present age. Beneficial animal magnetism might be able to effect a cure of the war infection where international assemblies have failed. Since Aesop's days the wisdom of the beasts has offered guidance to their human betters. Why should they not try it at Geneva? Besides, a League of Nations Menagerie would greatly add to the amenities of that pleasant city.

December, 1937

CRANBERRIES

On my last year's visit to Holland I was told a Dutch cranberry story that will bear repeating this turkey season. A century ago, a beach-comber on the island of Terschelling found a barrel washed up by the North Sea. He broke it open and found it to be full of inedible berries. Cursing his bad luck, he shook them out on the beach and left them there to rot. But the discarded berries were not so easily disposed of. They had not lost their vitality during their long imprisonment on the transatlantic voyage. The west wind blew them inland, they found the dune sand congenial, and rooted themselves in that salty soil. And now these Terschelling berries are thoroughly at home in their new habitat, and enjoy the distinction of being unique on the European Continent. For the barrel had contained American cranberries, which are not indigenous anywhere outside America. Cranberries are a divided family. Those in Great Britain and northern Europe form a clan by themselves, which, it is true, has its offshoots on this continent as well. But the typical American cranberry is different. The botanists call it *vaccinium macrocarpon*, big-fruit blueberry, and the common European kind *vaccinium oxycoccos*, the sharp-seed variety. The early American colonists, who were familiar with the latter, gave its Low German name to the fruit they found in this country, cranberry meaning crane berry, according to the etymologists. Cranes and their like, maybe, are fond of the fruit, but the Low German *Kranbeere* is apparently not fit for human consumption. At any rate, you need the American big-fruit variety for cranberry sauce. Hence the island of Terschelling had a windfall when the beachcomber abandoned his find on the sands. The islanders used to export the berries to England, but since the British tariff, for the promotion of Imperial autarchy, has begun to favor Canadian over Terschelling cranberries, the Hollanders themselves have developed a liking for cranberry sauce.

AN ISLAND CUPIDO

This is not an old wives' tale, but a well authenticated story. We even know the identity of the beachcomber who, unwittingly, became benefactor to his island. His name was Pieter Sipkes Cupido. The Cupidos are a numerous Terschelling clan. One of them has the monopoly of the insular auto bus service. We went to a dance, one evening, at an isolated pavillion on the dunes, far away from the villages. Many went there, as we did, on bicycles, but the girls who thought their dresses too good for conveyance by foot power had their sweethearts take them to the dance in Cupido's bus. The driver actually functions as a binder of hearts. For in pre-motor days, when East and West were connected only by the Zuiderzee dike and a muddy footpath, there was no love lost between the inhabitants of either part, and marriages between them were rare. They did not, and do not yet, speak the same language, the speech of West Terschelling being a dialectical variety of Hollandish, whereas the East speaks Frisian. The linguistic border line runs, strange to say, across the village of Formerum. It seems almost incredible that one half the population of a small island village should speak a language different from that of the other half. The explanation may be found in the peculiar shape of the settlement. The centre of most Dutch villages is the parish church, but the kernel of Formerum is arable land. The settlers on the eastern edge of the rye fields had moved up from the Frisian side, those on the western edge from the Dutch-speaking part of the island. The two sections were never united into one parish, and that also may account for the tenacious bilingualism of Formerum. Although a difference in speech still prevails, the old racial hostility between Dutch-speaking and Frisian Formerumites no longer divides the villagers. Even the extreme East and West have ceased to hate and fight each other. The old antagonism is not proof against the locomotive power of Cupido, who by his daily rides from one end of the island to the other is promoting intercourse and better understanding between them and matching girls and boys whose grandparents were traditional enemies.

TERSCHELLING

Terschelling is one of a row of islands that lie north of the province of Holland and form a badly broken barrier between North Sea and Zuiderzee. The inroads of the North Sea cut them off from the mainland, but it gave them a firm protection against itself in the rampart of dunes which the tides threw up in the course of the ages. Each receding tide left its deposit of sand upon the beach, the west wind blew it further, it settled among plants, which struck root into that nomad soil and built it into a storm-proof wall. Sea, wind, and plant life are the architects of Holland's dunes. The lover of solitude finds here his paradise. You can sit on the top of a dune, the endless beach at your feet, behind you the duneland undulating towards the flat pasture and arable land along the island's south shore, and never see a soul or hear a sound reminding you of human life. The stillness is broken only by the distant roar of the breakers, and by the shrieks of gulls and other kinds of sea birds, which seem to be in sole possession of the scenery. They know that these dunes are a sanctuary, where only photographers may take shots at them. There were said to be three thousand summer guests last year, but the beaches are so wide and stretch out to such length that the bathers seemed a few specks upon the sands. And the extreme east end of Terschelling will always remain virgin territory. One third of the island is uninhabited dune and beach, thousands of acres of sand that no plough has ever cut. An East end farmer will take you into this desert in his covered wagon. Nothing has changed here since the days when Pliny, in the first century of our era, looked upon some such scene as this and wondered whether he should call it land or a part of the sea. In the days of the Dutch Republic West Terschelling was a thriving port, for the seaborne traffic of Amsterdam and other Zuiderzee harbors passed there on its way in and out. In the nineteenth century Amsterdam built itself a canal straight west to IJmuiden, which gave it readier access to the sea. Thus navigation was deflected and the island was left in its present isolation. But formerly it was in touch with all parts of the world. Its own sailors were at home on the seven seas and brought treasures back from foreign countries that still adorn the parlors of many a lowroofed Terschelling farmstead, pictures of Naples and Mt. Vesuvius in eruption, sea shells and conches, buffalo horns from Africa, Chinese knicknacks, and batiks from Java. Though these islanders knew the five Continents and the manner of life of other peoples, they never showed any inclination to ape foreign manners. Their hazardous, insecure life perhaps created a craving for an anchorage in ancient tradition. Besides, the women seldom, if ever, left their isolated home and were, consequently, the natural custodians of island customs. The steamboat, the auto bus, the movies, and the radio have made the youngest generation aware of their otherness. The girls have become ashamed of their Terschelling costumes, they dance the fox-trot rather than the old-fashioned *skotse fjour* (scottish four) or the zevensprong (seven hop), and prefer international music hall tunes to the stock of old folksongs that were still current a generation ago. When the women did their own spinning, the girls of the village used to go round in bevies to help the farmers' wives prepare their wool. *Spinfeemen* was the island name for those hen parties. They served at the same time as singing classes, for while the wheels were purring, the girls went through their rich répertoire of songs and ballads, singing from morning till sunset. At dusk the wheels were put aside, and the boys were admitted into the circle, when lovemaking and courtship were transferred from song into fact. For the spinsters were all unmarried girls, as they still are in all the dictionaries of the English language. Home spinning has gone out of fashion, the spinning wheels have been sold to antique dealers, and now adorn the drawingrooms of the rich in Amsterdam and The Hague. Only the songs linger on in the memory of a few who once were, or who have remained, spinsters. A musicologist, Mr. Jaap Kunst, has collected a hundred of them and published texts and melodies in a charming book on Folk Life in Terschelling (*Terschellinger Volksleven*), of which a second edition appeared this year.

Mr. Kunst's book is not altogether cheerful reading. He describes an ancient island society that is fast shedding its characteristics. The people themselves are not aware of the precious beauty of which they are the custodians. In the second half of the past century the villages were despoiled of medieval monuments, which were replaced by styleless modernities. A magnificent twelfth-century church at Midsland was demolished at the instigation of the minister, who preferred to preach in a less forbidding looking house of prayer and – fortunate coincidence – happened to know a cousin of his who was willing to build one. And so the walls that had stood for seven centuries and could have lasted another seven hundred years were levelled with the ground, the old tombstones were cut up and the fragments made into thresholds, and the fifteenth century bronze bell, too heavy a load for the new structure, was sold to a Roman Catholic parish somewhere on the mainland. At Hoorn, further east, they burnt, half a century ago, the entire church archives to get rid of the dusty rubbish. Mr. Kunst calls this vandalism. But vandalism is wanton destruction, and these people did not destroy for the pleasure of it. They meant to make their island more beautiful. The word *schoon* in Dutch has the twofold meaning of beautiful and clean. Tidying up is an act of beautification, and the removal of ancient piles, be they of medieval stone or of more recent dust, is consequently a meritable undertaking. One must not expect the people of Terschelling to look at their island with the eyes of the historian, the artist, and the folklorist.

April, 1938

SS NIEUW AMSTERDAM

The Nieuw Amsterdam, the new flagship of the Holland America Line, will soon be fully equipped for her maiden voyage to New York. She was born on January 3, 1936, if the laying of the keel may be called the birth of a ship. She was conceived on twice the scale of the largest vessel ever launched before her from any shipbuilder's wharf in the Netherlands. That made her a favorite with the Dutch public, who took a national pride in this bigger and better Nieuw Amsterdam, and wanted to be kept informed of every new phase of her growth. Queen Wilhelmina performed the christening ceremony on April 10, 1937, and on February 13, 1938, the baby giant made her first attempt to escape from her cradle of the Rotterdam Drydock Company. She had to be held in leading strings, for, being still without steering gear, she had no control yet over her motor nerves and muscles. A swarm of Lilliputian tugs crowded round her to pull her out, their whistles shrieking raucous signals to each other that impressed the onlookers along the river banks with the dangers and difficulties of the manoeuvre. It was a Sunday afternoon, when the river traffic is at its lowest ebb, and the unwieldy Gulliver was least likely to sprawl dangerously across the path of navigation. The tugs, after much puffing and straining of hawsers, pulled her clear of the quay and into the river, and brought her to face west, in the line of the traffic. Her new berth, Dock 4, at Wilton-Feyenoord, the largest drydock in Europe, was ready to receive her. Here she remained until she was ready to leave under her own power and submit to the trial trip prior to her maiden voyage. That trial trip took place on March 21. She stood the test triumphantly. And now the finishing touches are being put on that must prepare her for her New York début.

A TENDECKER

The Nieuw Amsterdam is a tendecker. On top, of course, is the boat deck. It surmounts three layers of promenade decks, the main one being sandwiched in between an upper and a lower. Then follow, in downward and alphabetical order, decks A, B, C, D, E, and F. The boat deck, though it carries twenty-two lifeboats, does not press heavily upon its substructure. For the boats are made of aluminum, each weighing about 3300 pounds less than the type of lifeboat that the late namesake of the Nieuw Amsterdam was burdened with. The potential seasick are charitably assisted in deluding themselves with the pleasant notion they are not on the sea, but only within view of the sea at some fashionable beach resort. For all the comforts that city life affords and all the attractions that take one's mind off the troubles and ailments that flesh is heir to will be within the traveler's reach. He will be able to take the receiver off his bedside telephone and call up his own physician in Kalamazoo, Mich., or wherever his home may be. If it is not the sea and the ship's motion that have upset his appetite, but his annoyance over the course the ship of state is steering at Washington, he can vent his spleen in a letter to the editor of the ship's daily newspaper and find relief, at breakfast next morning, on seeing his sarcasms in bold print and his fellow passengers chuckling over them. Dog lovers with pets will have no need to worry about their darlings. For they will not be in the hold but well provided for in up-to-date kennels on the boat deck, and may take their daily constitutionals and indulge in their canine recreations on territory especially set aside for them. Sun worshippers will have their solarium, and athletes their gymnasium. The natatorium, on the other hand, goes by the common name of swimming pool. Sun bathing is evidently a superior method of body culture deserving the embellishment of a Latin designation for the tannery. The sedate and the studious who practise aloofness and love the quiet and privacy of a comfortable fauteuil in the drawing-room will not be expelled, as happens on so many liners, by the after-dinner crowd that wants to go to the movies. The picture fans on board the Nieuw Amsterdam will not inconvenience anyone, for the ship has a spacious theatre that can seat the full cabin-class passenger list at one showing. Every precaution has been taken for the safety of the travelers and the crew.

Every week of the year is fire-prevention week on the Nieuw Amsterdam. All bulkheads between staterooms, all hangings and carpets, the very paint on the walls are made of fire-resisting materials, and the slightest ignition will call the Grinnell automatic fire sprinkler and alarm system into action. Four thousand of these sprinklers are distributed all over the ship. Any passenger on board can re-enact the miracle of Moses striking water out of the rock; he need but hold the burning tip of a cigarette close to the sprinkler and the water will rush forth and flood his room. The ship's power equipment consists of eight turbines developing 34,000 horse power. Her contract speed is twenty-one and a half knots. In short, the Nieuw Amsterdam offers to her patrons comfort, beauty, entertainment, safety, and speed, at the risk of finding that many, though not wishing that the comfort be greater, would gladly have the speed be less.

May, 1938

HER MAIDEN VOYAGE

On May 10th the Nieuw Amsterdam left Holland on her maiden voyage to New York. The arrival of the new flagship of the Holland America Line may reawaken the slumbering interest in the city's origin and early past. For she is the godchild of the small township on Manhattan Island which grew into the city of New York. She will carry more people than lived in Nieuw Amsterdam at the time of the town's surrender to the English. The liner has accommodation for 568 cabin passengers, for 455 in the tourist, and 210 in the third class. Add to these figures a crew of six hundred and fifty, and we get a total of 1883, which is about three hundred more than the number of inhabitants of Nieuw Amsterdam at the close of Peter Stuyvesant's governorship. Commodore Johannes J. Bijl will reign over his floating republic with no less absolutism than Stuyvesant claimed for himself over Nieuw Amsterdam. His will must be law in the lonely community cut adrift on the ocean, there being no power above him except the Almighty. Old Governor Peter was not always successful in enforcing his commands. His fits of rage were a kind of argument that did not convince the recalcitrant of his better judgment. Commodore Bijl is his predecessor's superior in dignified self-restraint. His proven skill as a navigator and quiet, gentle bearing command respect and reliance on his authority such as Stuyvesant was more anxious than able to inspire. He has spent forty years at sea, twenty-eight as master, without a mishap or accident of any kind. Accumulated experience handed down from father to son creates the qualities that make a good sailor. He who wants to be trained for the sea must be born a seaman. Many a shipboy's first experience of life on board is less a revelation of a new world than a realization of inherited subconscious knowledge. It was that to Commodore Bijl. For he is the son of a seafaring father and felt the call of the sea long before he was out of his teens. He joined the Holland America Line in 1898, as an eighteen-year old cadet. That was on the Rotterdam, the second of that name. Ten years later he rose to his first command as skipper under God of the Soestdijk. The dijk-ships, as everybody knows, are the freight carriers of the Line, the dam-names being reserved for the passenger ships. To move from the dijk to the dam is a promotion for a Holland-America skipper, though no Dutch landlubber would think so. For a dijk, which runs along the water's edge, seems to him a more stable place to be on than a dam, which is thrown from edge to edge across the water. But landlubbers are poor judges of what is right and proper on board ship. When Captain Bijl was called from the Sommelsdijk to the Spaarndam, he gladly stepped from the deck of the dijk to the deck of the dam. He was the last skipper of the Nieuw Amsterdam that was. She was a fine ship. I remember her well, for it was she who brought me over when I emigrated to the United States. The last I saw of her was in the harbor of Durban, in the spring of 1932. She was on her way to Japan and the scrapheap.

A HOSPITABLE CITY

The line on the map that represents the transatlantic course of the Nieuw Amsterdam and her sister ships is a hyphen linking Holland and America together. The old town on Manhattan was a symbol of the flight away from Europe and European civilization. Its first settlers were the forerunners of that ceaseless stream of immigrants from all parts of the old world who wanted to escape from its despotisms. To them Nieuw Amsterdam was only a port of call at the entrance to that uncharted sea of mountain, wood, and prairie that lured ever larger numbers westward. But this very desire to leave Europe as far behind as possible stimulated American ingenuity in devising means of accelerating travel. The vastness of this Continent was a challenge to inventive genius to defeat distance. The descendants of the pioneers who wanted to cut themselves off from Europe for good and all brought the old Continent nearer and nearer to the new, until the distance between them, which used to be measured by days, is now measured by hours. Hence the name Nieuw Amsterdam is no longer a symbol of the flight from Europe, but is now borne by a ship that, like a shuttle, carries to and fro the threads that are gradually woven into a harmonious pattern of Dutch-American friendship. The loom was set up as long ago as 1873. On April 18 of that year the Holland-America Steamship Company was incorporated in Rotterdam. The shuttles then employed were called Rotterdam and Maas. They moved but slowly across the loom, each taking from fourteen to sixteen days. Since that modest beginning the Holland-America Line has steadily expanded its fleet, in spite of occasional vicissitudes and setbacks. Its new flagship has twenty times the size of the two vessels that sailed from Rotterdam sixty-five years ago. She is the last word in modernity. It almost seems as if the Directors, justly proud of their modern creation, were anxious to ban from the public's mind all association with the old township that gave the new flagship its name. For in the A deck foyer two murals, painted by Adriaan Lubbers, depict views of modern New York, one the city skyline as it looks from the top of Rockefeller Center. If instead of the latter Mr. Lubbers had painted Nieuw Amsterdam as we know it from the engraving on the Visscher map of New Netherland, Commodore Bijl might say to his dinner guests, "Look upon this picture and on this." The same spot changed beyond recognition from its Dutch beginnings in less than three hundred years. The fort with the church and the windmill, the Governor's mansion, the Company's storehouse, the town hostel, the jail, and the brick houses of the burghers with their triangular gable tops are all accurately depicted by Claes Visscher. It looks like a Lilliput community compared to the Brobdingnag towers that have arisen on its site. No traces are left of the old Dutch town except in a few names. And yet, something more precious than what strikes the eye has been preserved from those early days. I mean the tolerant spirit of the founders. They knew that only peace and goodwill create the atmosphere in which commerce can thrive. They threw their own city wide open to all who were willing to come, no matter what they believed or refused to believe, to the separatists from the Anglican church, the Huguenots from Wallonia and France, the Jews from Spain and Portugal. Intellect, enterprise and labor which other countries ejected, enriched the city of Amsterdam. And they pursued a similar policy in Nieuw Amsterdam. In theory the Company allowed no other religion than the Dutch Reformed, but the Directors would not have any bars put up against the admission of dissenters. As early as 1644, when the French Jesuit missionary, Father Jogues, visited Nieuw Amsterdam, he was told by the Director General that "on this island of Manhattan and its environs there may well be four or five hundred men of different sects and nations speaking eighteen different languages." In that statistical picture of early New York we recognize the Manhattan of today. In it our after-wisdom sees the seeds of the future for which Nieuw Amsterdam was predestined. In the intention of the first Dutch settlers it was to be a transplanted Holland, but Manhattan soon became a transplanted Europe, reflecting in its composition the heterogeneity of the old world.

That spirit of tolerance and interracial goodwill is the inheritance that New York owes to its Dutch past. And if that spirit still prevails, it is due to the city's devotion to international commerce, which broadens the minds of those who engage in it. For it brings the merchant into contact with foreign peoples and teaches him to cultivate their friendship. It is not an accident that the founder of international law was a native of Holland. Hugo Grotius could not have conceived his vision of international rule of law in a country that had no commercial contacts with the outside world. The closing years of Peter Stuyvesant afford an instance of the truism that knowledge engenders forbearance and peace. The fiery old man must have cursed Colonel Nicholls with all the wealth of expression of which he was master, when he was forced to surrender his town to the English commander. But when he was living in retirement on his bouwerie, and the colonel had command in the fort, the two became fast friends. I love to picture the old fire-eater stumping applause with his wooden leg on the tiled floor while listening to the colonel's stories and shaking hands over a stoup of beer with his former enemy, the Englishman.

Nieuw Amsterdam's latest godchild has inherited that spirit of hospitality and goodwill. She will be a floating counterpart of the old town Father Jogues described as harboring different sects and nations speaking eighteen different languages. On her decks, in her smoke-room and dining room, at her bar, in her palm court, men and women of various lands and languages will fraternize, and foreigners will become friends.

June-July, 1938

MUSEUMS

The Netherland Ministry of Education, Arts, and Sciences has published a useful little book on the museums of Holland[1], containing in brief outline information on their whereabouts, the hours of admission, the dates of their founding, the nature of the exhibits, publications concerning them, and the average number of visitors per year. A table at the end gives an instructive survey of the steady increase in

[1] *De Nederlandsche Musea.* Uitgegeven vanwege het Departement van Onderwijs, Kunsten en Wetenschappen. The Hague.

the number of museums. Only nineteen collections date back to a period prior to the nineteenth century. In the years from 1800 to 1875 thirty-two were added to that original number, the last quarter of that century witnessed an increase of thirty, in the first two decades of this century fifty-one museums were established, and in the past eighteen years no fewer than one hundred and seventeen new ones opened their doors to the public. They are to be found in the most unexpected places, in small villages that even most Hollanders have never heard of, in churches, almshouses, hospitals, schools, townhalls, and private homes. Private collections, however, must be open to the public, otherwise the Netherland Ministry does not recognize them as museums. For its definition of a museum is "a collection which, either in its entirety or in part, is on permanent exhibition for the public benefit and accessible to visitors at stated intervals or upon request, either for a fee of admission or gratuitously." The New English Dictionary omits accessibility to the public from its more elaborate definition. But I agree with the editor of the Netherland Ministry's museum manual that it constitutes the essential character of what is called a museum. The word came into vogue with the rise of public collections. Before the nineteenth century collectors of books, pictures, curios, and objets d'art were wealthy capitalists, not the State or the municipalities. Holland in the eighteenth century was rich in private collections. Their proud owners were always glad to show them to connoisseurs who came to them with reliable credentials. But they did not admit callers indiscriminately. The current name for such a private treasure house was not museum but cabinet. The small nucleus was first locked up in a cabinet, and though the collection outgrew its space and gradually overflowed into several cabinets and finally filled the house from attic to cellar, it retained the name of its original depository. The word is still in use in isolated cases. The Dutch name for printroom is *prentenkabinet*, for numismatic collection *kabinet van munten en penningen* (cabinet of coins and medals), and the picture gallery on view in the Mauritshuis at The Hague bears the official name of *Koninklijk Kabinet van Schilderijen* (Royal Cabinet of Paintings).

The nineteen museums whose origin antedates the year 1800 were not known by that name and were not museums in the sense of the Ministry's definition. Among them are collections belonging to art schools and universities, royal cabinets and palaces, treasure rooms of medieval churches, almshouses, and ancient townhalls with well preverved interiors. These all existed before 1800, but not as museums. They became museums by being made accessible to the public. And that did not happen before the nineteenth century. Americans may wonder what there is about an almshouse that could make it a showplace for tourists and sightseers. They preserved their early homes and furniture for generations, until the things of daily use, unvalued in the past, became precious samples of primitive handicrafts highly prized in an industrialized age. And then the public gained admission to these homes to view treasures that were never collected for show but solely for the utilitarian purposes of every day life. There are four of this type among the early nineteen, and they are the most attractive kind of museum. For each is the survival of a domestic unit presenting a picture of home life of an earlier age preserved intact. The collector's storehouse is like the dictionary of a dead language. It contains all the things, as the lexicon contains all the words, that were in use in a bygone period. But neither can show us how the things and the words were arranged for the purposes of social life. These ancient alsmhouses and townhalls that became museums by no collector's effort but as it were automatically, by virtue of their well preserved old age, are like plays by Plautus and Terence, which show the use and arrangement of old things in daily life. There are, to be sure, Latin scholars who can imitate Terence and compose a Latin play from the words in the lexicon. And even so there are learned museum directors who can piece together an early living room from scattered exhibits in their collections. But these composite reconstructions of the past lack the charm that invests the genuine survival. They instruct, but cannot convince.

For the guidance of the specialist who is interested in only one subject the editor has drawn up an alphabetical list of all the various categories represented in the Dutch museums. Each collection is given its number, and the name of each category is followed by the numbers of those collections that are partly or entirely devoted to that special field. A highly specialized kind of museum is that which is dedicated to the memory of one man such as the Spinoza House at Rijnsburg, near Leyden, the very same house where the philosopher lived in the early sixties of the seventeenth century. It was opened in 1899. Copies of the books Spinoza is known to have read have been collected by the founders, and this reconstructed library is the chief attraction of this modest place of pilgrimage. Another is the Rembrandt House in the Jewish quarter at Amsterdam. These two are not survivals but restorations. After the great men moved out, they were occupied, for more than two centuries, by generations of tenants who did not care for, or were ignorant of, the mighty presence that had once pervaded the rooms they occupied. Rembrandt's house, after he left it, was divided in two and each half was raised by one story. Mr. K. P. C. de Bazel, a leader among modern Dutch architects, undertook its restoration in 1908, and rebuilt the two parts into the one house that was the master's from 1639 till 1660. Etchings, drawings, and paintings by Rembrandt and contemporary artists who influenced his style are hung upon the walls, and furniture of the period creates a semblance of a home. But the life is gone from it. On one visitor, at any rate, the Rembrandt House made the same impression that spoilt his pleasure in a pilgrimage to Williamsburg, Va. The faultless restoration of eighteenth century architecture aroused his respect for the designers and builders, but in wandering through this reconstructed village he felt like inspecting a stage set and waiting for the play to begin. But the play was performed, and the actors made their exit, long, long ago, and an artistic make-believe takes the place of the scenery on which they did not act but lived their parts.

I much prefer the picture galleries that do not pretend to be anything but showrooms. They do not, it is true, bring out a picture to its best advantage. The large majority were not painted for wholesale exhibition. Rembrandt's portrait of his mother would be far more impressive if we could still see it hanging in the living room of his parents' simple home than it is on the wall of a gallery where, among the crowd of other scenes, the essence of its intimate beauty is lost. Still, Johannes Vermeer's famous Milkmaid in the Rijksmuseum now gives joy to untold numbers, whereas it used to enchant only the few who were privileged to see it in the intimacy of the Six home. What man would deplore that the sun shines upon all and every one, though he may love it most for the beauty it adds to his own garden? I am not one of those who repeat the cynic's sneer that museums are mausoleums of art. The crowds that visit the museums of Holland do not regard them as burial places. If the Mauritshuis at The Hague were a home of the dead, it would not attract fifty thousand visitors a year. Besides, Dutch individualism and local pride protect the art lovers against the deadening effect of centralization of the country's art treasures. The Rijksmuseum, richly stocked though it be, is only the largest among a host of lesser collections scattered all over the country. No gifted peasant boy need die a mute, inglorious Rembrandt. In the nearest market town he will find inspiration and guidance for his budding talent in the treasures on view in the local museum. The maligned mausoleums of the cynic's sneer will rob dumb forgetfulness of its prey.

A SKIPPER WITHOUT A CREW

The past few months have produced a crop of dramatic news items about daring transatlantic flights. Mr. Hughes hopped from Mr. Grover Whalen's right to his left around the top of the globe, Mr. Corrigan, bound for California, landed in Ireland, and a German plane swooped down under the smoke of New York before the smoke of secrecy that screened its departure had lifted in Berlin. All these flights were sensational because of their unprecedented rapidity. The time involved was in each case almost negligible. If the record-breaking race continues at this rate, man will soon rival the genii of the Thousand and One Nights, who can fly anywhere in the wink of an eyelash. In an age that has so little patience with time that it seems bent on killing time altogether, one cannot expect the reading public to take much interest in a man who hugs time to his sailor's chest and makes her his companion on the transatlantic voyage. To take ten months in crossing from IJmuiden, Holland, to Staten Island seems a preposterous waste of precious time to a generation that worships speed. But if time is so precious, why then should we try to kill her? Jacob Kuyt of Zaandijk, Holland, took her to himself in a nutshell of a boat and sailed, ate, and slept with her in close intimacy without ever growing tired of her on the slow voyage from Holland to the west coast of Africa, thence across to South America, and northward through the Caribbean and along the east coast of North America to Staten Island. For sailing to Jacob Kuyt is a pastime, not a kill-time.

When he left IJmuiden, in the early morning of August 22, 1937, his plan was to sail to the Netherland East Indies round Cape Horn. He made his escape almost as secretly as did the German airplane from Berlin. He wanted to avoid all the hullabaloo that attends the hectic activities of press reporters and photographers. At the crack of dawn he slipped out of the harbor, waving goodbye to his wife and two little sons and to the parents of Dirk Hofman, who was all the crew he took along. Dirk was a young fellow from Amsterdam, in his early twenties, with a love of adventure but no experience of the sea. The voyage was to teach him the art of navigation. His presence on board made Kuyt change his original plan and steer for the West Indies instead of Java. For the boy fell sick and had to be taken to the hospital in Paramaribo, in Suriname, or Dutch Guyana. The story of their adventures is a mixture of comedy and tragedy. It gave me a thrill to hear Kuyt tell it in his racy, picturesque Dutch. True poetry in speech often comes from the lips of people who are not spoiled by literature. School education and literary training make the cultured afraid of trusting to impulse in speech. Jacob Kuyt possessed that spontaneity of utterance which creates words and similes from personal vision and feeling, because his mind and memory had not been exposed to the inhibiting effect of literary models. He could recount conversations with Dirk in a manner that turned the dialogue into vivid drama. One day the boy told him about his grandmother. He was terribly homesick on the long crossing from Africa to the West Indies, and found relief from his nostalgia in talking to the skipper about his own people. "Grandmother always carried something in her pocket for me when she called. She never came to see us without a little present. Yet she was awfully poor. But she never complained. She had faith in God, and that made her happy." Jacob Kuyt saw his chance of improving the occasion. "Don't you think, Dirk, that you might give a thought now and then to the Great Skipper who has been our help and protection so far? Fold your hands, boy, and let us thank Him." Dirk had been desperately ill. For three weeks he had lain in his narrow bunk, suffering from the effects of a sunstroke. Skipper Kuyt nursed him back to health with the Great Skipper's help. There were anxious days when he did not expect the boy to live, and he was tormented by the question what he should do with the body. He could not drop it overboard. For a huge shark accompanied the boat while the boy lay sick, apparently scenting the prey that was to come to him. There was plenty of salt in the storeroom. Better sew him up in a sack full of salt and thus preserve him for burial on land. But Jacob Kuyt was spared the bitter necessity of deciding that dilemma. He even had the satisfaction of catching the over-sanguine shark. "Don't drop your faith in the Great Skipper into the wastepaper basket when you are back in Holland," he said to Dirk one day after their evening prayer. "You never know when you may need Him again, and it would be awkward to have to search for it among the rubbish."

While they were lying in the harbor of Lisbon, a Portuguese sailor came on board and asked to be taken along as far as Brazil. He had lived in Rotterdam, had gone to evening school there, and had learned to speak Dutch. Would the skipper allow him to bring his wife along too? The skipper would if she was a good sailor and would do the cooking. She proved, subsequently, to be neither a good sailor nor the good sailor's wife. Still, she was useful as a cook and as a weather prophet. For nature had endowed her with barometer toes, as Skipper Kuyt called them. They actually were infallible in their forecasts. An itch in the big toe of her left foot was a storm signal, a ticklish big toe on the right was a sure sign of calm weather. But Kuyt did not enjoy their company and connubial quarrels, and decided to give them the slip on the African coast. He did get away without them, but also without the bill of health and sailing permit from the Portuguese harbor master. That got him into trouble with the French authorities at Cayenne. Why had he no papers? "Lost them. The French were to blame. They made such marvelous wines." What had that to do with his having no papers? "Well, this is what happened. On my way from the Portuguese harbormaster's office to the quay I passed a French tavern. A bottle of wine would do me good, I thought, in this infernal African heat. The wine was delicious; so I ordered another. And when that was finished I found that I had just enough Portuguese money left for a third bottle. When I jumped into the sloop that had to take me to my ship, I lost the little balance I had left. I seized hold of both sides of the boat to steady myself, and dropped the papers overboard. I was too drunk to care what happened to them. Never mind the damned papers and row me to the ship, I told the boy. And that is how I landed here without them. Your French wines are to blame, don't blame me." This piece of extemporaneous fiction had the desired effect. The officials gratefully accepted the praise of the national wine in lieu of the missing documents, and Jacob Kuyt as a welcome visitor from foreign parts in their uneventful isolation. A gift for telling stories is a useful passport anywhere. Kuyt was a master of invention and delivery. I do not mean to imply, though, that his account of the voyage was the product of his inventive brain. He spoke of his adventure with such straightforward simplicity and earnestness that his audience could not doubt his veracity. The early Dutch navigators who sailed the seven seas and brought the first news to Holland of the Orient, and the East and West Indies, must have been men of the type of Jacob Kuyt. That is how they must have told their yarns in the taverns and along the quays of old Amsterdam, I thought, while I listened to him one evening at the Netherland Club in Gramercy Park. He and Dirk are now on their way back across the ocean. Early in November Jacob Kuyt will celebrate his sixtieth birthday, and he wants to be home for the feast. May the Great Skipper protect him and return him safe and sound to his wife and children.

MICK FIRST

David Cornel de Jong's *Old Haven* – a Houghton Mifflin Fellowship Novel – is dedicated "To my Father and my Mother and all my brothers except Mick." That exception seems to give Mick a bad character. The black sheep of the family, is the natural inference. But don't let us be hasty. Take De Jong's first novel, *Belly Fulla Straw*, from the shelf, and you will see that the author's debut was "For Mick," and for Mick only. His exclusion from the present dedication is a signal honor. For him it would have been a step down to share the gift with his parents and brothers. Mick came first, and came alone.

WITSUM

Belly Fulla Straw was advertised on the jacket as "The picture of a family – the portrait of a father." *Old Haven* might be described as "The picture of a town – a family's portrait gallery." The new book has the same pictorial qualities that distinguished the writer's first novel, but it is richer in subject matter, wider in scope, and far superior in its portraiture. The children of Mr. Idema in *Belly Fulla Straw* seldom step out from the family group as clearly defined individuals. That first book was, indeed, the portrait of a father, with het mother and children dimly seen in the background. But in *Old Haven* each member of the Mellema family is a distinct character. These Mellemas are the most prominent family in the little town of Witsum. But there runs a queer streak through them all. They are apt to run counter to social conventions, to defy proprieties, and do as they please, no matter what the town gossips may whisper. Old Beppe Mellema, the widowed grandmother, shocks everybody in town, including her four spinster daughters, by opening a saloon. Women don't run saloons, old women, at any rate, don't, especially not dignified old women like Great Beppe, of the best family in town. Her only son marries a girl of humble station. The women of the Mellema clan wear golden helmets and golden-helmeted women do not mingle with the kind that Gosse Mellema takes to wife. And Gosse's three sons again kick over the traces. Maarten marries a fisherman's daughter, an unheard-of offense; for landfolk and seafolk do not intermarry, though they live together in the same town. And Tjerk brings a bride home from way south in Gelderland, a stranger who does not speak Frisian and refuses to dress and to behave in the proper Witsum manner. For Witsum is in Friesland, where people speak a language that is more like English than Dutch. And Klaas, the youngest, is a charming scapegrace, who goes poaching and seduces the girls, both of the landfolk and the seafolk. He comes to an untimely end. In a ship's collision he is thrown overboard and drowned. The body is sent home in a black coffin, and the girl whom he left with child claims, and obtains, the right to be the only one to walk behind the bier from the station to the bridge. That is to be her wedding ceremony. And from the bridge to his parents' home she will be joined by all the other mourners, and that will be her husband's funeral procession. Only Gosse's daughter Jantje is all for conformity. She takes after her maternal grandfather, who lives in the fear of the Lord and makes his fellow beings live in fear of himself. The Bible is his book, Jehovah of the books of Moses is his God, and to be a Jehovah in his own home to his children and grandchildren his chief glory in life. When his grandson Tjerk came to visit him one day, "his long, drooping nose lifted defiantly, as if he were daring Tjerk to greet him kindly." One should not be kind to Jehovah. He is the epitome of all things stern, his eyes are "cold as rain-washed macadam."

LAND'S END

Witsum is land's end, "cool and gray and lovely." That's how Tjerk describes it to a fellow recruit. "But terribly far away. Way up there, hugging nothingness and the sea," says his friend. "You never saw the sea." " Not much, the other admits. "Then you don't know what you're talking about. The sea makes the land a nothingness." In that remark Tjerk has epitomized the whole philosophy of the isolated community in which he was born. The story opens with the account of a tidal wave that suddenly rose like a leviathan, strode across the dike, and swooped down upon the town in the depth of night. "And all the poor souls asleep there, and nobody to warn them." "The sea is our Foe" is the title of the first book. Living close to that foe and in the fear of his menace, these people cling to their heritage of custom and tradition as the only safe anchorage for their insecure lives. The seafolk of Witsum hold on to the superstitions of their pagan ancestors; the landfolk to the letter of Holy Writ, and both enforce upon the next generation the inhibitions and don'ts that not reason but antiquity has hallowed. The minister won't let the children draw with crayons on Sunday because that is sin, but drawing with black pencil is no sin. It is sinful to take pleasure in colors. Still all the houses of Witsum wear red-tiled roofs both Sundays and weekdays. There is no sin in that, for red they have been since time immemorial. Only the new Mellema house has a blue roof, but that proves again that the Mellemas are non-conformists. And high above that cluster of red-capped houses rises the stumpy church tower, which is a dull gray. Its bells call the townfolk back from their fields, the seafolk back from their voyages, to lie buried in its shadow. The drowned who find no grave in Witsum's churchyard will haunt the tower and the town with their wandering spirits. The fisherfolk do believe in God's word, but they get their faith all tangled up with pagan lore. They cannot help it if they see spirits, hear devils shrieking, and see werewolves prowling. Those have peopled the town so long. There is no sin in such beliefs. Sin is not to live according to the Witsum code. Tjerk's young wife, who comes from Gelderland, does not conform, an unpardonable offense. Wise old Beppe Mellema, who has a sneaking affection for her, warns her to behave for her own and her husband's sake. "You are walking with the devil in broad daylight on our streets. If you walked with God on the street and kept forty devils in your house and in your heart, you'd be forgiven. That's Witsum's code; why don't you learn it?" It would have been easy enough, for walking with God on the street meant wearing longer skirts, abstaining from swimming in the canal, and not showing her affection for her husband by walking with him arm in arm. People have to be strict about such things when they live in terror of the sea. Its ever-present menace, which makes life hazardous and insecure, must be counterbalanced by rigid conservatism in everything that belongs to the land. But Mellemas cannot remain there. Tjerk takes his wife and children across to a wider life in America. The stubborn, the dull, and the inert who do not reason and rebel, they stay behind. Tjerk's sister Jantje, the only one of Gosse Mellema's children remaining in Witsum, tries to comfort her father. She takes her little son's hand and leads him to Gosse, "See, Father, here's the boy who'll some day step in Tjerk's shoes ... He'll carry on where Tjerk left off." And old Beppe Mellema, hearing her speak, has a sudden vision of all places invaded, the whole land populated, by righteous Jantjes and their correct children and children's children.

"Nowhere in fiction can one find a more beautiful picture of Holland today," says the publishers' blurb. *Old Haven* is not a picture of Holland, nor of Friesland either, but of a small and isolated Frisian town. There are many such towns, both in Holland and in Friesland, but only along the North Sea coast. You may find similar communities on the islands and the coast of Denmark and German East Friesland. It is the sea, not its Dutchness, that gives Witsum its character. Its conservatism is sea-born, and strong and relentless as the sea. Its beauty and picturesque charm are part of that conservatism. It would vanish if rebellious Mellemas invaded all places and turned all the roofs blue. The author, though his sympathies are clearly with the rebels, understands and appreciates the charm and beauty of conservative Witsum. That makes his picture of the old town such a convincing human document.

April, 1939

PHOENIX

The phoenix, that fabulous bird of antiquity which rises to new life from its own ashes, is the subject of one of Rembrandt's etchings. It has long been among the most enigmatic of the artist's compositions. For the phoenix lends itself to many allegorical interpretations, and has served various figurative purposes from the days of Herodotus down to our own. In the Middle Ages it was a symbol of Christ's resurrection and the immortality of man. And its present day usefulness is attested by the New York Telephone Directory, which lists more than eighty commercial concerns that take shelter under its wings. Not only fire insurance, which is by right its specialty, and asbestos, which may claim kinship to the phoenix, are dedicated to its protection, but also brushes, candy, carpets, coal, drugs, hosiery, leather goods, sportswear, stationery, towels, underwear, and what not. A wonderful bird is the pelican, but, in spite of the limerick's praise, it does not seem to have the same ad appeal. Only one New York firm takes its name from the pelican. There is good reason for its boycott by the commercial world. The pelican of medieval iconography was the symbol of self-sacrifice, above all of Christ's death on the cross. For the bird was fabled to have fed her young, in time of dearth, with her own heart's blood. Self-sacrifice, however, has no place in the economic plan of this materialistic world of ours. The merchant needs the buoyant belief in self-restoration. If he has failed in the hosiery business, he may have better luck in underwear. He must retain his trust in the phoenix-like resilience of human endeavor.

REMBRANDT'S PHOENIX

Rembrandt's phoenix was, doubtless, not intended for a commercial trademark. We can tell from his presentation of the bird that he was not commissioned by an Amsterdam business firm to advertise their wares under its wings. In that case he would have portrayed the phoenix in its traditional aquiline splendor. Instead, he drew a pert, long-legged fledgling that has nothing imposing except the impetuosity with which it spreads its young wings. It stands on a festoon of palm twigs held by two cherubs who, blowing their trumpets, carry the

153

bird on high. The flames from which it has arisen are still ablaze on a high pedestal that looks very much like an anvil. In the background, to the right, trees are visible in the distance, to the left high houses suggesting that the miracle is taking place in a city square. In the left foreground a dense multitude is looking on with upturned faces which are on a level with the base of the pedestal. A woman lifts a baby in swaddling clothes high up above the milling crowd. In front of the pedestal the figure of a man, strongly foreshortened, is lying on his back, as if thrown over by a blow or a sudden fright. Dr. Jan Veth, the Dutch portrait painter and art historian, discovered that this composition was strikingly similar to a ceiling piece in the Vatican by Lauretti Tommaso. But there a crucifix occupies the place of the phoenix, and the recumbent figure in the foreground is clearly a pagan image which has been thrown down from the pedestal. Tommaso painted an allegory of antique culture dethroned and superseded by the Catholic Church. Rembrandt may have known it from a sketch brought home by a Dutch brother artist who had visited Italy. But the meaning that he gave to his borrowing is less transparent. It has long defied all attempts at interpretation. However, the year of its composition, 1658, combined with the substitution of the phoenix for the crucifix of Lauretti Tommaso, supplied Mr. Jac. Zwarts with a clue to the mystery.[1]

After the conquest of Portugal by Spain in 1580, the Jews were expelled from the country. Many found a refuge in Amsterdam. They established there a synagogue in 1597 and adopted the phoenix as its emblem. From the ashes of their martyrs who had died at the stake in Spanish *auto da fes*, Jewish faith sprung to new life in the free air of Amsterdam. A second Portuguese congregation was formed eleven years later, and this also took shelter under the wings of the phoenix. A third chose the pelican instead, but when the three became united in 1639, it was the phoenix that hovered, spread-eagle fashion, over the fusion. Its senior rabbi was Haham Saul Levy Morteyra, a friend of Rembrandt and, for many years, his near neighbor. It must have been Morteyra who suggested to Rembrandt the subject for his phoenix etching. He painted the rabbi's portrait in 1658 – the picture is now in the Galleria Pitti at Florence – and from what happened in Portugal in that same year we may infer the meaning of the strange composition.

Spain and Portugal had not expelled the Jews because of their race. The invention of that objection to them was reserved for a more civilized northern nation. They drove them out on account of their

1 *Oud Holland* 1926, pp. 61-73.

religion. Those who embraced Catholicism were allowed to stay. These converts were known by the name of Maranos, the accursed. The exiles in Amsterdam kept in touch with their unfortunate brethren in the Spanish peninsula. When in 1655 two Jews had been burnt at the stake in Cordova and Santiago, prominent members of the Amsterdam synagogue published a memorial volume of 172 quarto pages under the title *Elegios que zelosos dedicaron*. Three years later news reached Amsterdam that another Jewish martyr had died in an *auto da fe* at Porto. It may well have been a subject of conversation between the painter and the rabbi while Morteyra was sitting for his portrait. Rembrandt's generous soul must have burned with indignation as he listened to the story and saw with his mind's eye the inhuman scene it evoked. He felt drawn towards the Jewish community at that time of his life. For he himself had passed through fire. Bankrupt, deprived of his beautiful home, forced to sell his art collection, he had moved to a different quarter of the city. He had become an exile in his own Amsterdam, an outcast among his countrymen. But the artist's self-assurance, the consciousness of his power and genius bore him up in his humiliation. He rose from the ruin of his life to new and greater effort, creating between the bare walls of his denuded workshop paintings that rank among the very greatest of the world's art. The exile in the humble home on the Rozengracht felt a certain kinship with men such as Morteyra, in whom the spirit of the Jewish race burned with inextinguishable intensity. Their Christlike resignation to suffering, their trust in God's ultimate justice, and the strength it gave them to begin a new life among strange people in a foreign land appealed to Rembrandt who, more feelingly than any other artist, had interpreted the gospel and taught in images Christ's blessings upon the meek, the mourning, and them that have been persecuted for righteousness' sake. When he had heard the story of the martyred Jew in Porto, he sat down before his copper plate to fortify the Jewish community in Amsterdam with another image of divine justice. The phoenix etching was his message of comfort to Morteyra's congregation in their affliction. The scene portrays the *auto da fe* in Portugal. The little baby in swaddling clothes is held up by its mother to witness the death of an accursed unbeliever. But it will remember for life a different spectacle: Out of the burning pile a strange bird has leaped up, the executioner who has been fanning the flames has fallen backward in terror, and the two cherubs who carry the bird aloft proclaim with trumpet blasts the victim's victory over persecution and death. The etching was printed on precious Chinese paper in a limited edition that was evidently intended for distribution among a select circle of intimate friends. They will have understood its twofold meaning. For the phoenix exemplified not only the regeneration of Jewish worship in Amsterdam; it was at the same time an allegory of himself transcending frustration and defeat by the strength of his genius. Nor is its hopeful Easter message lost on this age of ours. We can use its comfort in these sad days that witness on all sides appalling manifestations of man's inhumanity to man.

May, 1939

AN HONEST IRASCIBLE DESPOT

Peter Stuyvesant's wooden leg has been an asset to his memory. The stump on which he hobbled through the streets of New Amsterdam has added a picturesque touch to the imaginative picture that posterity has conceived of him. His must have been an iron constitution that could survive the loss of a limb in those days of primitive surgery and no anaesthetics. He was wounded in the right leg during an attack on the island of St. Martin, a Portuguese possession in the West Indies, and gave the amputated limb a decent burial in Curaçao. Its loss was, in his own estimate no doubt, but a small sacrifice to the fatherland that he loved and served with a single-minded devotion, so small indeed that it does not deserve the distinction of being singled out as his most striking characteristic. He possessed other traits that were not due to accident and outward circumstance, but the native marks of his personality. He proved himself a loyal servant of the West India Company, and was a God-fearing Calvinist who demanded from the burghers under his rule the same unquestioning obedience that he willingly gave to the Almighty. The God he bowed to was the Old Testament Jehovah, rather than the merciful Father of the gospels, and Peter himself would sometimes emulate the Hebrew deity in outbursts of wrath and denunciation. Who can blame him for losing his temper once in a while? The community that he was given command over was not a host of angels. There were troublesome elements among them who were apt to abuse, in this isolated outpost of civilization, the freedom from the restraints and conventions of Holland, where life ran smoothly through straight-cut grooves and channels, as straight and placid as the ditches that make checkerboards of the Dutch polders. There were no conventions in New Netherland except those that the settlers themselves had brought over and were willing to maintain. However, since the community on Manhattan numbered many of un-Dutch stock who were ignorant or scornful of conventions imported from Holland, the Dutch themselves became lax in the maintenance of social restraints which they saw disregarded or ridiculed by their fellows and neighbors. Hence, when Stuyvesant took office in 1647, he found the colony badly in need of discipline and reform, and having neither fear of his subjects nor any doubt of his own righteousness, he won for himself the reputation of an honest, irascible despot.

He was the son of a minister of the Dutch Reformed Church, the Rev. Balthazar Janszoon Stuyfsant. That is how the father spelt the family name. A rigid orthography of proper names is a modern fetish. In those early days people felt free to choose from as many variants as the sound of the name suggested to the writer. The reverend Balthazar's parish was the village of Scherpenzeel, in Stellingerwerf, a wooded section of the province of Friesland. Twenty years later he received a call from the parish of Berlicum, in the northern part of that same province. The simple burghers of Berlicum do not seem to have known that a written invitation to the preacher of their choice did not make him their minister. The newly established Dutch Reformed Church insisted on the observance of certain formalities which evidently were disregarded in this case. The classis of Leeuwarden, at any rate, aggrieved that the proper procedure had not been followed, declared the call null and void. But the Berlicum congregation was not properly contrite for its careless cutting of red tape. It protested to the States of Friesland against the interference of the classis and requested this highest secular authority in the province to override the veto upon the minister's acceptance of the call. The classis, in its turn, appealed to the executive committee of the Provincial States for an endorsement of its action. The upshot of this dispute was a victory for the Berlicum burghers. The classis of Leeuwarden was told that it had exceeded its authority, and Berlicum was given the minister it wanted. Such perseverance implied a compliment to the Reverend Balthazar's gifts as a pastor and preacher. He arrived in his new parish on July 19, 1622, accompanied by his wife and child. The child was doubtless his daughter Anna. Peter, by that time, was old enough to have left his father's patronage and shift for himself. No record has been found that throws any light on the events of his life prior to 1635. On October 11 of that year, father Balthazar petitioned the Amsterdam Chamber of the West India Company for preferment of his son Peter, who was then going to be transferred from the island of Fernando Noronha to Pernambuco. The young man's birthday was in the offing, and Stuyfsant senior may have thought that promotion to a higher rank was the best present his son could hope to receive. How long he had been in the company's service is a matter of conjecture. It had been founded in 1621, the year in which the war against Spain, after a twelve years' truce, was resumed. Peter Stuyvesant may well have enlisted for employment in the West Indies in the very first year of its existence. A fourteen-year record was a solid ground on which his father could base a plea for preferment. We may be sure, at any rate, that old Balthazar had no reason to be ashamed of his adventurous son.

The father did not live to see Peter attain to the high rank of Director General of New Netherland. He died in 1637. Ten years later, on May 11, 1647, the son arrived on Manhattan to assume control of the colony. The crowd of burghers who watched him disembark included men who were soon to turn against him and his dictatorial way. When they aired their grievances, a few years later, his proud bearing was recalled as one instance of his despotism and arrogance. He had strutted like a peacock, with great state and pomp, and had shown himself as thoughtless of others "as if he were the Czar of Muscovy." In spite of his despotic tendencies, he was not a reactionary. He was one of a host of Dutch pioneers who carried European civilization to other continents. Although he was personally intolerant of other creeds than his own Reformed religion, he suffered Lutherans and Quakers and Jews to settle in New Netherland under orders of the Company that was his master. The cause which he served was infinitely greater than himself, and the city that grew from Stuyvesant's New Amsterdam has inherited its tolerance from that spirit of moderation that informed the colonizing work of the Hollanders.

December, 1939

THE PLAYFUL WHALE

One of the earliest seascapes of the Netherland School is a magnificent picture in the Vienna Museum. The master who painted it must himself have been in danger of his life on a storm-tossed vessel. Towering, whitecrested waves rock a small two-master, whose full-blown sails proclaim the terrific force of the gale. Other craft are riding the tempest in the distance. A coastline with low-roofed houses is vaguely seen on the far horizon. White gulls, distinctly visible against the dark sky, swarm above the tumultuous scene. The sea is dark too. Only in the middle foreground is its darkness pierced by a pointed blade of eerie light. The two-master in distress stands clearly silhouetted against it. At some distance on her right a whale is disporting himself, and between the monster and the ship a barrel floats upon the waves. Until recently the painting was thought to illustrate the story of Jonah. If that was the artist's intention, he must have been a humorist, for he left the prophet out of the picture. Look for him in the monster's belly! But the critics are now agreed that no section of the whale is needed to discover the solution of the riddle. They are unanimous in attributing the picture to Peter Brueghel the Elder, and Brueghel's well-known love of proverbs makes it highly probable that this picture too images some gnomic bit of popular wisdom. It was Ludwig Burchard who explained the painting convincingly. He found in Zedler's *Universal-Lexicon* (1732-1750): "When the whale plays with a barrel the sailors have thrown to him, and thus allows the ship time to escape, he is an emblem of the fool who, for the sake of empty nothings, neglects his true profit." It must have been a widespread practice among seafaring people, including the English, to throw a barrel to the whale. In the first part of "The Troublesome Raigne of King John" (1591) occur these lines:

> the mariner
> Spying the hugie Whale, whose monstrous bulke
> Doth beare the waues like mountaines fore the wind,
> Throwes out an emptie vessel, so to stay
> His fury.[1]

And recently a Belgian scholar, George Marlier, found a reference to this mariner's ruse in a Flemish chronicle of Brueghel's time. Marcus van Vaernewyck, a patrician of the city of Ghent, wrote in the late sixties of the sixteenth century an accurate account "Of the Troublous Times in the Netherlands and chiefly in Ghent 1566-1568." He relates how the iconoclasts shattered the stained-glass windows of the churches at Ghent and then marched across country to Courtray destroying church property everywhere. But the bishop let them rage hoping that Ghent might be spared if they cooled their fury outside the city walls. "Even so they throw a barrel to the whale to prevent him from toying with the ships that come his way." W. K. Marriott says in the Introduction to his translation of "The Prince" that Machiavelli, in 1520, "received a commission at the instance of Cardinal de' Medici to write the "History of Florence," a task which occupied him until 1525. His return to popular favor may have determined the Medici to give him this employment, for an old writer observes that "an able statesman out of work, like a huge whale, will endeavor to overturn the ship unless he has an empty cask to play with."

---

[1] I have taken the liberty of slightly altering the text so as to make it intelligible. In the printed text of 1611 the fourth line runs thus: "That throwes out emptie vessels, so to stay" etc.

It is strange that among the many art critics who have discussed the meaning of Brueghel's picture there is none who has noticed its resemblance to the frontispiece of Jonathan Swift's "A Tale of a Tub." This shows a thick-lipped and beady-eyed whale gracefully curling himself around a barrel and venting his pleasure over the new toy by shooting up two water spouts that look exactly like ears of wheat. In the background a rococo ship, a cross between a viking's dragon boat and a Victorian sofa, escapes across a neatly curled sea. In the Preface Swift explains the allegory: "At a Grand Committee, some days ago, this important Discovery was made by a certain curious and refined observer; That sea-men have a Custom when they meet a Whale, to fling him out an empty Tub, by way of amusement, to divert him from laying Hands (sic) upon the Ship. This parable was immediately mythologiz'd: The *Whale* was interpreted to be *Hobbes' Leviathan*, which tosses and plays with all other Schemes of Religion and Government, whereof a great many are hollow, and dry, and empty, and noisy, and wooden, and given to Rotation. This is the *Leviathan* from whence the terrible Wits of our Age are said to borrow their Weapons. The *Ship* in danger, is easily understood to be its old Antitype the *Commonwealth*. But, how to analyze the Tub, was a Matter of difficulty; when after long Enquiry and Debate, the literal Meaning was preserved: And it was decreed, that in order to prevent these *Leviathans* from tossing and sporting with the *Commonwealth*, . . . they should be diverted from that Game by a *Tale of a Tub*. And my genius being conceived to lye not unhappily that way, I had the Honor done me to be engaged in the Performance."

If only those modern leviathans, the U-boats, could be distracted from their preys by the same simple device! But there is nothing playful in a U-boat. The monsters that man creates are creatures without a soul and know not how to gambol and to curl themselves like kittens round a skein. They are more vicious even than Cerberus, who let himself be placated by a sop. But neither is the barrel as harmless a toy nowadays as it was in Peter Brueghel's time. Hitler threw Finland in Soviet Russia's path to divert the leviathan's menace. But the barrel appeared to be loaded to the brim with dynamite and studded on all sides with sharp spikes. What modern Brueghel paints an allegory of that gruesome scene: the Finnish barrel exploding in the coils of the Russian leviathan, while the German skipper, himself in danger of foundering, turns loose a swarm of robot whales to deal death and destruction all around.

A FLYING DUTCHMAN

Anthony Fokker has crossed into the beyond from which there is no return flight. He left a world that seemed a wilderness when contrasted with the one from which, a generation ago, he winged himself up in his self-made plane, a daring boy of twenty, happy in his hopeful vision of mankind finding release from stagnancy and boredom and overcrowding in the free, uncharted regions of the sky. He was a genial, kindhearted man, without a grain of ill will towards any one. That his inventive genius made modern warfare the infernal torment that it is in this year of craze must have saddened his soul. The quickening of peaceful commerce among nations was his chief concern. To build bigger and better transport planes for transatlantic passenger service was Fokker's ambition. He took pride in having created the huge F-36 for the Royal Dutch Air-lines, and the Josephine Ford that carried Floyd Bennett and Byrd to the North Pole. To unite distant peoples, to explore the unknown was his aim. In the year before the outbreak of the World War, Colonel House saw "a man named Fokker" perform incredible evolutions over a flying field outside Berlin. But more incredible is the evolution that the Fokkers which he built passed through in the ensuing years. The German Government pressed him into its service. He won for his new masters superiority in air combat by his invention of the interrupter mechanism permitting a machine gun to fire through the whirling blades of the propeller. Thus he revolutionized modern warfare. His Fokkers grew up into birds of prey sowing death and destruction among innocent peoples. But the begetter of this evil brood could not recognize himself in his offspring. When the German high command sent him up into the air to demonstrate his invention, he refused to fire at a Frenchman who was at his mercy. Release from German service must have been for him a return to freedom. He found a wider field and his true element in America. He came here in 1922. He passed away before his fiftieth year. His was a meteoric flight through history. And one that will not easily be forgotten. For the name that he inherited from his Dutch parents has been enshrined in the English language. The Fokkers may die out in Holland, but fokkers will cross the continents and the oceans, long after this mad age of ours, to promote commerce and friendly intercourse and peace among nations.

REMNANTS OF DUTCH IN AMERICA

While reading H. L. Mencken's *The American Language*, the other day, I came across a new name for Dutch. You will not find it, though, in the publicity about Holland House, for the Dutch themselves know better. Mencken quotes on page 622 a passage from an article by Dr. J. Dyneley Prince on the Jersey Dutch dialect. This relic of the Dutch language is now almost extinct, but a generation ago it was still spoken by some two hundred persons. Dr. Prince, then Professor of Semitic languages at Columbia, became interested in it and published in 1910 an excellent monograph on the Jersey Dutch Dialect (Dialect Notes Vol. III, Pt. VI). It was originally, he says, "the South Holland or Flemish language, which in the course of centuries (c. 1630-1880) became mixed with and partially influenced by English." No Hollander would describe it in those words. For South Holland is the name of a definite and very limited area, that particular province of Queen Wilhelmina's kingdom in which The Hague, Rotterdam, Delft, Leyden, Gouda, and Dordrecht are situated. And the language spoken in that province has never been called Flemish. In this quotation from Dr. Prince the term Holland is not interchangeable with Netherland. He did not mean South Holland, but South Netherland, that is that part of the Low Countries which was formerly called the Southern Netherlands and is now known by the name of Belgium. There the people speak Flemish, which is, indeed, a variety of the Dutch language but cannot possibly be described as Holland Dutch. Hence what he meant to say was that the people whose speech he had studied were descendants of settlers who had come from the southern Netherlands.

Dr. Prince thought that contact with English had worn off the original Dutch inflections. The mixture of languages always has that effect. But the orthography of Netherland Dutch misled him into assuming that those inflections were still audible in its spoken form and that their disappearance in Jersey Dutch was a striking feature of that dialect. "The definite and indefinite articles, *de* and *en*, became uniform for all genders, ... in the comparison of adjectives the superlative affix decayed from *-st* to *-s*." Both articles are also uninflected words in spoken Dutch. The only typically Jersey Dutch trait is the use of *de* also for the neutre gender, for which Dutch has a separate article, *het*. And the dropping of final *-t* after *-s* is equally common in the speech of the vulgar in Holland and Flanders. That is why the educated Hollander adds a *-t* to the Dutch word for rice and calls it *rijst*. In his anxiety not to join the vulgar in dropping his *-t*'s he pronounces a -t even where the -s is legitimately final. Hence there was closer similarity between Jersey Dutch and its mother tongue than Dr. Prince suspected. "An intelligent Fleming," he wrote, "or South Hollander (meaning South Netherlander) with a knowledge of English can make shift at following a conversation in this Americanized Dutch." Of course he could.

A large number of words in daily use were borrowed by the Jersey Dutch from English. Among these Dr. Prince listed *smoke*, *since*, and *blaubääse*, which he took to be a literal translation of blueberry, "the standard Dutch word being *heidebes*." I wonder how many among my Dutch friends in New York are familiar with *heidebes*. I must admit that I have never heard it in my life. I do not find it listed in Koenen's *Verklarend Handwoordenboek der Nederlandsche Taal*, nor in Van Dale's *Nieuw Groot Woordenboek*. But I do know *blauwbes* and remember a short story by E. J. Potgieter which had for its title the street-cry *Blauwbes, Blauwbes*! And *smoke* and *since* are just as good Dutch as English. Dr. Prince spells the latter word *säns*, which doubtless indicates a pronunciation that is commonly heard in vulgar Dutch. Hence Jersey Dutch shows also in its vocabulary a closer affinity to the parent language than one would gather from Dr. Prince's study. These comments are not made here in a faultfinding spirit. I have the greatest admiration for his work and wish I possessed one tenth of the linguistic knowledge that he has gathered in his lifetime. There is scarcely a language in Europe that he does not speak. Whenever I have the pleasure of meeting him we converse in Dutch. As a Hollander I feel indebted to him for his interest in my native language. The day is near when not a trace will survive of the Jersey Dutch speech except in the pages of Dr. Prince's precious monograph. The few corrections that are offered here are made as a tribute to his scholarship.

The wanderings, transformations, and disguises of words have a fascination for me that never palls. In a footnote on page 109 of *The American Language* Mencken quotes a list of words noted down near Kingston, N. Y., by Mr. Karl von Schlieder of Hackensack, N. J. He is not sure whether all of these are of Dutch origin. *Surallikus* (so-so) certainly does not look Dutch, yet I believe it disguises a Dutch diminutive adverb *schraalkens*. I do not know what to make of *haidang* (nothing), *brigghity* (impudent), and *pietje-kamaakal* (unreasonable). If *haidang* is used, like English "don't mention it," in reply to an expression of gratitude, I suspect that it is the Dutch phrase *geen dank*. *Brigghity* may be Dutch *prachtig* (splendid) for splendor paraded may easily change into impudence in the eyes and the speech of the envious. *Pietje* is good Dutch for little Peter, but *kamaakal* nonpluses me. The rest, however, can easily be identified in spite of weird changes in spelling and meaning. *Zwok* (soft, slippery) is Dutch *zwak* (weak), *connalyer* (crowd) is *kanalje* from the French *canaille* (rabble), *klainzaric* (untidy) must be Dutch *kleinzeerig*, though it is hard to account for its connection with disorder. I do not know an English word that can exactly render *kleinzeerig*. It describes one who cries out at the slightest hurt or sense of pain. Crybaby, perhaps, describes a *kleinzeerig* person best. But what can be the relation between sensitiveness to pain and slovenliness? *Onnozel* (outlandish) meant innocent in early Dutch; it is now in general use in the sense of simple-minded. Contempt for the ignorant stranger may account for the change in connotation. *Poozly* (whining) is Dutch *poezelig*, which describes the softness of a baby's body. How came the softness of its flesh to be confused with the softness of its whine? *Feaselick* (undesirable) is from *viezelijk* (dirty). *Kanaapie* (child) is vulgar Dutch *knapie* (little lad). *Aislick* (no-account) means awful in Dutch. Awful things are despised and treated as of no account. *Bahay* (confusion) is doubtless identical with *boehá* or *boehaai* meaning fuss about nothing, hot air. These words are stray remnants of a speech that was the prevalent language of northern New Jersey in the eighteenth century. Their scarcity makes them precious to the philologist.

May, 1940

A RAIN OF MEN

It has been raining men from the sky in the Low Countries, men in Dutch and Belgian uniforms, German men seeking shelter in disguise. They were brave men offering easy targets to sharpshooters during their drop to the ground, but willing to take the risk for the glory of their fatherland. Or were they perhaps glad to die and thus escape from slavery at home, from the spectacle of their country's infamy abroad, and from their own evil conscience? For many of these men were nurslings of the land that they invaded like thieves in the night. When German children were starving during the world war, they were shipped to the Netherlands by the thousands to be cared for and nourished in Dutch homes. They learnt to speak the language, they learnt to live in the Dutch way, they made themselves familiar with the lay of the land. They were the very boys that Hitler needed for his long-planned invasion of the Low Countries. Nazi education easily extirpates the roots of gratitude from tender souls. It is a weed that chokes the free growth of nobler plants indigenous to the Nazi soil, such as will to power, contempt of the weak, joy in frightfulness, racial purity, worship of the state, and other exotic growths that thrive in the Nazi hothouse. Don't let us call the descent of those parachutists upon the land that saved them from starvation an act of vile ingratitude. They had never been taught the virtue of gratitude, they had been taught to despise it as a vice of the weak. How then could one expect them to be grateful? The best we can hope for is that some at least, in the face of death, were stricken with a sudden consciousness of guilt, a sickening disgust with their own selves.

A RAIN OF BOMBS

It has been raining bombs from the sky upon the Low Countries. Their fair cities are bleeding from deep gashes, peaceful homes have been shot into ruins, clouds of smoke rise up from the holocausts that Nazi culture dedicates to its pagan gods. In the midst of this welter Red Cross processions of stretchers carried the dead and the wounded, men, women, and children, to the hospitals. Meanwhile the water was seeping in through the opened dikes to embed the bleeding land under its cool protective sheet. But that old standby of former days could not save Holland this time. The little country, so vulnerable because of its dense population, succumbed to the onslaught of the ruthless German air force. The Nazis always clamor about their need of *Lebensraum*, living space. The Low Countries have less *Lebensraum* than Germany. However, the slaughter of civilians by strafing bombers is a simple way of creating living space. In the prison into which the Nazis have transformed their own land reigns the stillness of the tomb. The voice of noble indignation cannot speak out there. The prison silence is broken only by the thud of the jailers' boots, by the echoes of their *Sieg Heils*, and by the rumbling of their strafing machines that keep the prisoners subdued. And yet, from the cowed silence of the imprisoned German herd seems to emanate a quiver of disgust that the Nazi rulers cannot afford to ignore. How else can we explain Herr Von Ribbentrop's attempt to justify the invasion of the Low Countries by accusing them of having plotted with England and France to invade the Ruhr district? He knew too well that not a single soul abroad would give credence to that stale pretext. His statement was not made for the enlightenment of the foreign diplomats and journalists who were invited to the treat of hearing him deliver it. It was prepared exclusively for home consumption. The inarticulate indignation that is simmering in the pent-up hearts of decent German men and women had to be doped into drowsy insensitiveness. That speech of Von Ribbentrop had one beneficial effect. It gave assurance to friends of the German people abroad that the German spirit which they used to love and admire has not yet been choked to death in the Nazi grip.

The Nazis pay a lot of romantic lip service to the sanctity of the German soil. It is clear from their practice that they deny other people's right to similar soil worship. One would think if any nation had a just claim to its soil, it was the Dutch, whose title to the land was not acquired by conquest but by the hard, incessant labor of Dutch generations. They created a large part of their land themselves. Their polders are the greatest achievements of the national genius. From the fifteenth down to the twentieth century they have wrested from the water acre after acre of fertile soil with indomitable patience and persistence. And in as many days as it took them centuries to reclaim their land from the water, the Germans took it from them by force of arms. The swastika, emblem of a way of life that is the very negation of all that is essentially Dutch, now blows from spires whose carillons used to sing the songs of a free people into the sky. Will the singing towers of the Netherlands be silenced, or will they be forced to din the Horst Wessel song and Nazi battle hymns into Dutch ears? The people will pretend not to hear them. They will listen to the voice of the bells, no matter what melody it carry, and hear in it the voice of their free past calling out to a free future across the waste of momentary captivity.

July, 1940

A WRY HUMORIST

The German military commander in the Netherlands, Air Corps General Friedrich Christiansen, is a humorist. The *New York Times* treated its readers to his portrait the other day. It is a face that radiates good nature. A benignant smile broadens the mouth, shortens the upper lip, and narrows the eyes to dark slits under bushy eyebrows, all of which gives to his features an expression of amused and quizzical kindliness. But even without a knowledge of his facial traits we could tell that the General is a humorist from the kind of communiqué that he addresses to the Hollanders whom he has come to protect against the wicked English. He recently warned them against any demonstration in favor of Queen Wilhelmina's Government. Listen to the General's delicious irony, "I consider this attitude as a sign that German measures to give safety and peace to the Netherlands have not been understood, or that the people do not want to understand them." Safety and peace! The Dutch people were enjoying both until the early morning of May 10th. There was no need for the

Germans under General Friedrich Christiansen to come and give them. The General knows that just as well as the Hollanders whom he admonishes. But in his playful mood he enjoys the joke of turning the thief into the benefactor. One can see the merry fire-eater chuckling as he talks, "How dare you misunderstand the good intentions of us Germans? You did possess peace, we admit, but it was not a safe peace. For it was menaced by England, and to make it a safe peace we have robbed you of lives and homes and cattle and all that you prized. That is the payment you owed us for the safety and the real peace we have given you. Not to appreciate our protection is ungrateful, and that is why I accuse the Netherland army and population of a disloyal attitude to Germany."

When Holland was not yet invaded, there were among one hundred thousand German residents a great many who, in return for the hospitality of the Dutch people, were plotting with the Nazis against the peace and safety of their hosts. They betrayed the government that gave them protection to the government that bribed them, or threatened them with dire punishment if they refused to turn traitors. That was not an act of disloyalty according to the Nazi code of honor. To serve the Third Reich at the cost of your honor is the highest form of loyalty. But the Dutch who refuse to transfer their loyalty from the Government that gave them peace and safety to the Government that bombed and burnt and massacred them into the peace of dumb cattle and the safety of slaves are, according to that same Nazi code, found guilty of a disloyal attitude.

To any human being who is not German it is obvious that a Hollander's loyalty is due to his own Government and to the Royal House that for a hundred and twenty-five years has ruled the country and shared its destinies. Prince Bernhard of the Netherlands, in a broadcast from London, the other day, told his listeners how the German invaders who expect loyalty from the Dutch people had planned to treat their Government and the Royal House. On the body of a German general who was killed in action a document was found containing two sets of instructions. The first assumed that no resistance would be offered to the German forces, in which case guards should be stationed in front of various specified buildings including the palaces of the Royal family. If, however, the Dutch should be disloyal enough to put up a fight against their German protector, the second instruction should apply. It ordered the capture, on the very first day of the invasion, of the members of the Royal family and of the entire Cabinet, and their immediate transportation by airplane to Berlin, where the prisoners would be dealt with in accordance with the resistance offered. The Nazi code of honor does not respect an enemy who resists attack, but wreaks vengeance on him for fighting back, and the braver the resistance, the harder the punishment.

A clear appreciation what the Nazi code of honor implies is afforded by the noble Count Von Zech Burkersroda, German Minister at The Hague, who, on August 26th, 1939, was received in audience by Her Majesty, Queen Wilhelmina, in the presence of her Minister of Foreign Affairs, and who on that occasion made the following official statement on behalf of his Government: "We are determined, in accordance with the traditional friendly relations between the two countries and in recognition of the well-known independent policy of the Netherlands, to maintain towards the Netherlands an attitude which will not interfere under any circumstances with the inviolability and integrity of the Netherlands and will respect Netherlands territory at any time. We expect, of course, from our side that the Netherlands, in a possible conflict, shall maintain an irreproachable neutrality towards us. That implies above all that Holland shall not suffer any infractions of its neutrality from a third party, but shall resist those with all available means." In other words, if England had invaded Holland, Dutch resistance would have been not only a laudable reaction but, from the German point of view, the fulfilment of an international duty. But when the Third Reich commits the outrage, resistance becomes a crime deserving punishment whose harshness will be commensurate with the fierceness of the defence.

BISMARCK WISER THAN HITLER

Bismarck used to say that Holland would annex herself to Germany. He was a wiser statesman than Herr Hitler. German music, German science, German poetry were popular in Holland before the world war. Dutch scholars studied at German universities and brought not only German methods of teaching back to their Dutch classrooms, but the very jargon in which the pundits of Berlin and Heidelberg and Bonn used to expound their learning. The style of many a learned Dutch scientist is double Dutch, part Dutch part German. Dutch journalists were equally guilty in making a bastard of their mother tongue. In the haste of production they did not take the trouble to search for the true Dutch equivalent of a German idiom; it was so much easier to borrow the phrase of the German original they were translating and leave it at that. And from the schoolbooks and the daily press this bastard Dutch crept into the speech of the educated. Not of the man in the street. He is the stalwart guardian of pure, racy Dutch. But school education has become so thorough in Holland in this twentieth century, that the untutored custodian of the mother tongue is fast becoming a rare specimen. Hence linguistically Holland was in danger of self-annexation. The Nazi outrage may have stemmed this process. Writes Leonard Mosley, "Only on one subject did the Dutch people lose their self-control, and that was the Germans and their traitor accomplices. On Saturday, when we returned to Amsterdam, it was a lynching matter to be caught talking German on the streets." That hatred of the sound of German will survive, after the hot anger that boiled over during the bombings has cooled down to resignation. I notice it, I am sorry to admit, in myself. An irrational anger surges up in me when I hear German spoken on the street, and worse is the sound of my own language being spoken with a German accent. Who would not hate to see a precious heirloom defiled by the grasp of a burglar?

September, 1940

A KIND OF RUTH DRAPER

Dr. Seyss-Inquart, the German Civil Administrator of the Netherlands, has superseded at The Hague the Queen, the Government, and the Parliament. He is all three in one person. His is a kind of Ruth Draper performance. He differs from her in that he shuns rather than seeks an audience. He has informed the Dutch public of his desire that "people notice my presence as little as possible." The wish is doubtless reciprocal. The only spectators whom he is willing to admit to the privilege of seeing him act his threefold role are the Secretaries of the various Ministerial Departments who carry his orders and decrees down the line for ultimate publication among the public. Among these orders are some that cast a revealing light upon the man's character. "I forbid," he ordered, "the ritual slaughtering of cattle in the Netherlands to prevent the torturing of animals." That reminds one of Macaulay's sarcastic remark that the Puritans opposed bearbaiting not because it gave pain to the bear but because it gave pleasure to the spectators. But those who suspect that this order was issued from The Hague not because ritual slaughter gives pain to the animals but because it gives kosher meat to the Jews do the great Austrian a grave injustice. Nazis are no hypocrites. For hypocrites are malefactors who pretend to practice the virtues that are taught by the religion they falsely profess. But the Nazis have repudiated all religion, being worshippers only of *Volk* and *Rasse*, a worship which involves no other commandments than the duty of blind obedience to the Leader. Hence Nazis cannot be hypocrites, there being no moral code that they can break while pretending to observe it. The ritual slaughter decree is an honest attempt to prevent cruelty by a true humani ..., no, that is not the right word ... by a true bestialitarian, who thereby means to serve his *Volk* and *Rasse*.

LOUIS RAEMAEKERS

Holland House has opened an exhibition of cartoons by Louis Raemaekers, the Dutch artist who won international fame during the first World War. He was then in the full vigor of life and gave expression, in bitter and poignant and satirical drawings, to his hatred of German frightfulness in all its ugly manifestations. He is now a young man of over seventy years of age, still a master of his craft, and still capable of visible eloquence. I wish it were possible to inspect this recent work side by side with the drawings of the first World War. That juxtaposition would bring out to advantage the special quality of these later cartoons. They are crisper, more matter-of-fact, less melodramatic than the earlier work. I do not believe that this change is due to the hardening effect of old age on the artist's capacity for indignation and pity. Not his advanced years account for this change, but the general hardening of feeling that is characteristic of the age we live in. Twenty-five years ago, the war atrocities could shock us into outbursts of fiery indignation. But the daily reporting of German frightfulness has made us so familiar with its worst outrages that they have ceased to seem outrageous. Not Raemaekers, but this present age has become callous: and that his latest work, as compared with his earlier, reflects that callousness is proof of his perennial vitality.

December, 1940

DELFT TILES

The city of Delft is famous for many reasons. It is one of the oldest and most picturesque towns of the Netherlands; it offered a residence to Prince William of Orange during the last crucial years of his life, and it was there that the great leader of the Dutch revolt against Spain met his death at the hands of an assassin; it is the birthplace of Hugo Grotius, who thanks to that accident, and also, of course, to his great learning, was given the name of the modern Oracle of Delphi; within its walls Johannes Vermeer painted his marvelous pictures, and Anthony van Leeuwenhoek discovered under the microscope a fauna of tiny creatures of whose existence none of his fellow citizens had any suspicion; and finally it is the home of a ceramic industry that has spread its fame all over the world. Only in the last respect has it usurped an honor that it should justly share with other cities of the Netherlands. Not all the tin-glazed faience that goes by the name of Delft was produced there. Other cities such as Amsterdam, Haarlem, Rotterdam, Gouda had their potteries and faience works. There was probably a larger number of them at Delft than anywhere else, but it is not at all certain that this city excelled the others in the quality of the product. The craft was not a Dutch invention. It was introduced into the Low Countries from Italy in the early sixteenth century. At that early period and for some hundred years afterwards the same shops that turned out the fine ware known as Delft manufactured also tiles for wall decoration. But in the course of the seventeenth century Delft faience became divorced from its commoner sister craft. From then on the makers of faience left the manufacture of cheap earthenware and glazed tiles to the workshops that strove for mass production rather than quality. These catered to the average citizen, the others to the rich, the connoisseurs, and the collectors. Time, however, is an erratic appraiser of values. The common wall tiles, on account of their cheapness, were treated with slight regard in former days. They were not worth saving when a house was demolished. It was a Frenchman, Henri Havard, who in the nineteenth century taught the Dutch the artistic value of these simple tiles; and since the publication of his book they have won an esteem such as was never accorded them by the generations for whom they were made. Their maker were only too glad to see them smashed and thrown on the scrapheap. A seventeenth-century potter at Delft encouraged the vandalism of his customers with a crude rhyme on his sign-board:

> Of making pots and tiles I boast,
> And praise to them who break the most.

Innumerable tiles must have been broken, many more than have survived the breakage. That makes the samples of this typically Dutch art now on view in the library and the lobby room of Holland House such a unique collection. Even the crudest among them are valuable because of their rarity, and the crude ones are rare in this show.

How did it happen that the production of wall tiles became a specialty of the Dutch ceramists? I believe that a happy conjunction of circumstances brought about this development. First of all, the soil of Holland, situated at the mouths of Rhine, Maas, and Scheldt, supplied an abundance of the clay which was the tile maker's raw material. And this river delta was inhabited by an industrious people versed in handicrafts and the art of painting and able to dispose of any surplus output in foreign countries through their widely ramified export trade. And finally the Dutch housewife's craving for cleanliness found in these tiles an easily washable material which gave to her walls a bright and radiating gloss. The Dutch tiles were used in other countries for the same purpose, but only in the homes of the wealthy. There they were a decorative luxury; in Holland they were part of the outfit of the average home. Abroad they were apparently used only for the decoration of the fireplace. Nathaniel Hawthorne gives a description of a chimney mantel so decorated in "Legends of Province House." In the "Old Province House kept by Thomas Waite," the mansion of the old royal governors of Massachusetts, was a bar-room, he tells us, in which apartment the ancient governors probably held their levees with vice-regal pomp, surrounded by the military men, the councillors, the judges, and other officers of the Crown. "The most venerable and ornamental object is a chimney-piece set round with Dutch tiles of blue-figured China, representing scenes from Scripture; and for aught I know, the lady of Pownall or Bernard may have sat beside this fire-place, and told her children the story of each blue tile."

That was indeed an additional attraction that recommended the tiles to Dutch mothers. They were untearable and thumbproof picture books from which the children were taught their first Bible lessons and the rudiments of history and geography. That is how Philip Doddridge, the famous nonconformist divine, learnt the Scripture stories. He told his friend Orton that his education was begun by his mother, who taught him Bible history form the pictures on the Dutch tiles of the chimney. Since he was the youngest of twenty children, the good woman must have run a domestic Bible class by the fireplace for the greater part of her married life.

This useful function of the tiles as teachers of the young stimulated the production of homogeneous sets: natural history sets showing animals, birds, fishes, plants, the twelve months of the year depicting the successive seasonal activities of the farmer from New Year's Day till New Year's Eve, nautical sets that taught the child to distinguish between the different kinds of seafaring craft, sets of city views and famous castles, sets of portraits of members of the House of Orange, mythological sets for the instruction of more advanced pupils, sets of the manifold handicrafts that were being plied in Holland, sets of costume pictures of exotic peoples concerning whom the Dutch seafarers had strange stories to tell when they came home. It was an ethnological wall-picture book of this kind that Longfellow was thinking of when he opened his ode "To a Child" with the following lines:

> Dear child! how radiant on thy mother's knee,
> With merry-making eyes and jocund smiles,
> Thou gazest at the painted tiles,

Whose figures grace,
With many a grotesque form and face,
The ancient chimney of thy nursery!
The lady with the gay macaw,
The dancing girl, the grave bashaw
With bearded lip and chin;
And, leaning idly o'er his gate,
Beneath the imperial fan of state,
The Chinese mandarin.

The biblical sets were, of course, the most popular. They were exported to England in large numbers and graced the fireplace in many an English home. Major André remembered with nostalgia the one in the house of Miss Anna Seward, of Litchfield, England, the lady who, at the news of his tragic death, gave vent to her feelings in a Monody that made her famous. In a letter that he wrote to her from London, on October 19, 1769, he begged her to "be persuaded that I take part in all your pleasures, in the dear hope that ere it be very long your blazing hearth will burn again for me. Pray keep me a place; let the poker, tongs, or shovel represent me; but you have Dutch tiles, which are infinitely better; so let Moses, or Aaron, or Balaam's ass by my representative."

There are not many homes left, either in England or Holland, that can evoke such pleasant memories in the absent. And the few that still existed before the present war broke out have probably been diminished in number by the havoc wrought by Nazi dive-bombers. People do not sit any more in front of an open hearth framed by blue Delft tiles. The picture of our distant friends in the old country that this present age conjures up before our mind's eye is one of a huddled group in a bombproof shelter or in a makeshift shack that replaces, for the time being, the house that was blown up by a German bomb. The scene of the Nativity as it appears on the tile of the New Testament set may be re-enacted in reality this coming Christmas in many places on the Continent and in Great Britain. Only the magnificent Magi, in their gorgeous robes, will not appear in the doorless entrance. If any one darkens the doorstep it is more likely to be a German soldier or an agent of the Gestapo. The little children on their mother's knees will learn of Herod and, not having a tile picture to assist their imagination, create a figure of Herod in the image of a German in military uniform. And the mother will say, "That's what he looks like, that is right. And he wears a funny moustache like Charlie Chaplin. And his hair falls over his forehead. And when he talks he shouts himself hoarse." And when the dive-bombers swoop across the tottering house, the little ones, crouching under table or bed, will whisper to each other: "Herod is angry again."

RECONSTRUCTION

Everyone in Holland seems to be talking about reconstruction. A feverish desire to build anew is stirring all classes of society. Not to restore. There seems to be a unanimous feeling that the Holland that collapsed under the German onslaught must be dedicated to the past. The future calls for a new, regenerated Netherland. The clearest proof that the Dutch people in their captivity do not admit defeat is the nation-wide effort now on foot to plan for this improvement on the past, being sure in their hearts that a better Holland will arise from the ruins of the old.

There was much in that Holland of less than a year ago that deserved destruction and that no one will attempt to revive. I do not refer to slums unfit for human habitation. Those hardly existed at all in the cities of Holland. I am thinking of fences and walls and barriers that kept citizens from citizens and divided them into small groups that were suspicious of each other. The Dutch are stubborn individualists, but their admirable insistence on the right to think for themselves often led them astray. It resulted in the political field in an unwieldy multiplicity of parties. Even the Dutch National Socialists – for they do exist in Holland – could not agree among themselves and split up into rival factions. In that respect they conformed to the nation's tendency towards disintegration, though they are bent on inhibiting most other national tendencies. It was the same in the sphere of religion. The Dutchman's mind works analytically. He sees the little things that divide, and misses the fundamental concepts on which people might agree. Sectarianism is a characteristic feature of life in Holland. There is nothing wrong in that, if it goes along with the tolerance that admits the possibility of other people's forms of worship being equally beautiful and pleasing to God. But that was seldom the case. Each sect believed itself to possess the monopoly of Truth, as if Truth were ever attainable to mortal man. This spirit of selfrighteousness in religious believers caused a cleavage also in the social life of the people. Catholics were not allowed by their clergy to mix on social terms with Protestants, lest mixed marriages, which are frowned upon by the Church, should increase in number; and a similar ban kept orthodox Calvinists from consorting with their agnostic fellow citizens. Mixed tennis clubs of Protestants and Catholics were proscribed by the priests, and for two members of the rival religions to be dancing partners was in the eyes of the clergy an abomination. Thus the shepherds whose task it was to teach the love of one's fellow man in the spirit of Christ taught their flocks to avoid one another and worked systematically for the people's disintegration.

There was the same schism in the sphere of education. The neutral public school, in which the sons and daughters of Protestants, Catholics and Jews were brought together and taught to tolerate each other, was never popular in Holland except among Liberals and Socialists. The majority of the nation insisted on instruction for their children in the religious spirit of the home. The Calvinists had their own Calvinist schools, the Catholics their own parish schools. In the name of the Christian religion the little children were segregated into different camps and imbued not with love but with suspicion of their comrades. Thus the Hollander's individualism showed all too glaringly the defects of its qualities. It had a corroding effect upon national unity. The nation had become a jigsaw puzzle of factions and groups and parties and sects and denominations, each bent on vindicating its right of existence rather than on vindicating the strength of the nation as a whole.

The war has brought a change of mind. The little differences that loomed so large have been reduced to unimportance. Under the fierce glare of burning homes and of searchlights stabbing the darkness of the blackouts, political, social, and theological distinctions have lost their meaning. The will to withstand the evil that has overwhelmed the country generates a desire to stand together, to close their severed ranks, and meet as a united nation the problems facing them, and those that will face them in the days to come. A triumvirate of Dutch patriots addressed to their fellow citizens, late in July, a manifesto inviting them to join in a Netherland Union. "The need of the times," they wrote, "has borne a new task. We call upon you all to join us in assuming that task. We ask you to strive with us for a new Dutch unity, relying on our own strength and on our own Dutch character. What we need first of all is the recognition that the old relationships have changed. We need national collaboration on the widest possible basis, an harmonious reconstruction through the binding together of all labor forces in our people, we need social justice, that work and the joy in work may be given to all, to young and old, to the strong and the weak. We hope to realize these aims in Dutch fashion, respecting the spiritual liberty and the tolerance that are ours by tradition. We intend to work in close contact with the Netherlands authorities and with those of the Power now occupying our country. Those who stand aloof do harm to the Dutch cause. Join our ranks!"

Those are fine words, undoubtedly prompted by noble intentions. But is it possible for a Dutch Christian to work in close contact with the Nazi authorities? Can a reconstructed Holland arise on a foundation that is not cemented by the belief in Christ? It cannot be done, wrote one Dutch Protestant, Dr. J. Eijkman, in a brief but eloquent pamphlet that voiced the thoughts and feelings of tens of thousands of Dutch citizens. He quoted Paul in his first Epistle to the Corinthians: "For other foundation can no man lay than that is laid, which is Jesus Christ." If that is so, then Judas, the betrayer of Christ, must not be allowed to join the work of reconstruction. For the Judas in our midst has made false idols his saviours: the soulless State, Race, Blood, and Soil. "We Dutch Christians," Eijkman declared, "cannot build anew on those foundations, nor join in the work of reconstruction with such Judases as helpers. Our people are forbidden by the German authorities to speak of the House of Orange and of Dutch independence. Teach them then to build upon the Gospel which taught them respect for the dynasty and for their freedom. For as long as we, the people of the Netherlands, form a Christian community, which is determined to build upon no other foundation than that is laid,which is Jesus Christ, then there need be no fear for the unity of the nation. For that unity is being demonstrated every Sunday by the millions who go to church. These millions are willing to build and to rebuild, for the present under the pressure of the occupying Power, and presently, if God so wills, in absolute freedom."

Dr. Eijkman's courageous word found an echo in the people's hearts. And the Nazis made it reverberate throughout the land. For they sent Eijkman to a concentration camp in Germany and thus instilled into his utterance the magic power of a martyr's voice. He will be a leader of his people when he returns to a liberated Holland, and let us hope that he may succeed in teaching those who are one in Christ to forget their dogmatic differences and to build a new national unity upon that one foundation that is laid in the hearts of the over-whelming majority of the Dutch people.

The love of one's neighbor is the fundamental lesson of Christ's teaching. All the Protestant denominations in Holland not only preach it but have begun to practise it in this period of trial. When the German authorities issued some anti-Semitic decrees which barred Jews from appointment to public office and from promotion in their present employments, a public protest was voiced from the pulpits of Protestant churches throughout the land. And also the youth of the country practise it. The universities of Leyden and Delft have been

176

closed by the Nazis because the students rebelled against the dismissal of some Jewish professors for no other reason than that they were Jews. Such bold defiance in the name of Christian love of one's neighbor holds more promise for the future than all praiseworthy efforts to start a premature reconstruction in close contact with the occupying Power. The triumvirate of the Netherland Union, it is true, are not anxious to cooperate with the German authorities. They only accept that cooperation as an unavoidable condition of their being allowed to operate at all. They feel that they must act, even under the handicap of an unwelcome partnership, in order to take the wind out of the sails of the Dutch National Socialist Party, which also aims at unifying the disintegrated nation but only in order to make them fit slaves of a totalitarian state. The Netherland Union wants to rally the people into a self-governing and self-respecting nation; the Nazis hope to turn them into a regiment of will-less serfs. The cry for unification, however, is so loud and so general that the triumvirate fear lest the masses should be lured, for unity's sake, into the trap of totalitarianism, for lack of any better chance of realizing unity. They underestimate, I am sure, the intelligence of the average Hollander and the strength of his love of liberty. They had much better wait until all Hollanders, in their liberated fatherland, can labor for national unity regardless of social station, religious belief, and political conviction. Then Dutch democracy, which the Nazis set out to destroy, will thanks to them come out of the fire of oppression a better and purer democracy.

February, 1941

A GERMAN RICHTFEST

Maastricht is the capital of the Dutch province of Limburg. It is not far from either the Belgian or the German frontier. Its inhabitants are loyal subjects of Queen Wilhelmina, though in temperament and manner of life, they are more closely related to their Belgian neighbors than to their fellow citizens north of the Maas River. On November 22 the Nazis staged here one of those typically German ceremonies that are painfully out of place in foreign surroundings. They have been building a new residence for the Governor who is to rule the province in the name of the Reich Commissioner, Dr. Seyss-Inquart. The latter himself had come down from The Hague to inaugurate the structure. He explained to his audience that the ceremony over which he was presiding was a *Richtfest*, that is a feast, which according to time-honored custom is celebrated at the completion of a building.

Dr. Seyss-Inquart has made a name for himself, not as a master builder, but as a master wrecker. My readers will doubtless remember him as the man who brought about the fall of Schuschnigg and surrendered his native land Austria to Hitler. That was a memorable *Richtfest*. The thousands of suicides that occurred in the weeks that followed the feast and the many victims of Nazi vengeance who were *hingerichtet*, which means executed, turned this feast in celebration of Seyss-Inquart's completion of the *Anschluss* into a *Hinrichtfest*. The news that has since seeped out of Austria reveals a picture of heartrending wreckage. Vienna has become a city without a soul. Its happy, carefree people are shadows of their former selves. The Nazis sit on the top of the wreck and call it the New Order. And Seyss-Inquart has escaped from the accusing spectacle of his handiwork and gladly accepted a fresh wrecker's job in Holland.

He made an unctuous address at the Maastricht *Richtfest*. Money, he told his hearers, is not the most important concept; the most essential one is work. "Labor is the great capital which Nature, or Creation, or God has given us, and therefore, comrades, as I now like to call you, we must begin to think differently; we must turn our thoughts away from money." How pious, and how true! For the money must all be turned into destructive machinery for the *Hinrichtfest* that Hitler hopes to celebrate in Great Britain; so the sooner the Dutch will divert their thoughts from the money that the labor-loving Nazis will steal from them, the better for the quiet of their souls. A young school girl in Holland, in an outspoken letter to a relative of hers in New York, had this to say about this organized looting: "When a child steals it is called mania, when a grown-up steals it is kleptomania, when a country steals it is Germania." But the girl is not old enough to understand that the Nazis are impoverishing the Dutch and other subjugated nations not from ugly greed but from a noble desire to wean their thoughts away from filthy lucre and teach them the value of the great capital that Nature, or Creation, or God has given them.

A GERMAN HINRICHTFEST

Dr. Seyss-Inquart's supply of unction ran freely that day. "This is a fortunate occasion for us to realize our comradeship in labor," he said. "We must seize all such occasions, whenever possible, that those who accomplished something by communal effort may spend joyous hours together when they rest from their labors. He is a poor leader who spends all his time at the council table. The true leader must stand in the midst of human life. He must be able to tell himself,

'I have tried to do what was just and necessary and I shall now read in their eyes whether I have succeeded or whether I must make an even greater effort'." He ought to repeat that noble address standing in the midst of the ruins at Rotterdam, and looking into the eyes of the brave boys whose communal labor erected that impressive monument to the glory of German labor. You and I, dear heroes and fellow workers, he might say, have worked together to make this *Hinrichtfest* possible, you by completing the work of destruction that justifies the celebration of this feast, I by coming away from behind the council table to join you in the joyous hours of rest you have so richly deserved. And then he might turn round to the silent crowd of 72,000 homeless citizens of Rotterdam, invited by the pious leader to attend the feast, and read in their eyes if he had done his task well or ought to do it still better.

What would he read in them? Contempt, loathing, hatred, a flicker of irony, a mocking sneer, and also, to confound him, determination, and hope of deliverance. His reading would convince him that the concerted effort of bombs and bombast has not yet converted the Dutch to the worship of the kind of labor that the Nazis revere above everything. They will not be enlisted as workers for the biggest firm of wreckers in Europe. They do not wish to be counted among the enslaved Herren of the Herrenvolk. They prefer to be the free men they were before Dr. Seyss-Inquart started to preach hypocritical sermons in Holland. They know that, having read in their eyes the evidence of his failure, he will redouble his efforts to bend them to his will. The terror of the Gestapo is being unleashed upon them, leaders of thought and opinion are sent to prisons and concentration camps, harmless citizens are tried and punished for acts that are offences only in the Nazi code of law, the youth of the country is being deported to Germany to join the slave gangs in ammunition factories, and the press and the radio are muzzled and turned into mechanical toys that squeak with the voice of Herr Goebbels.

A DUTCH BOY WHO WAS NOT DUTCH

And what would he see in the eyes of little children who lived through the horror of that orgy of destruction? Children as sensitive as Dirk van der Heide, the twelve-year-old boy who wrote that moving little diary "My Sister and I?"[1] Not fright, but a naive surprise at the cowardice of men who "shoot people who have no guns." The eyes of the horses in the baron's stable looked frightened and wild when

---

[1] Harcourt, Brace & Co.

the baron struck a match. But Dirk's eyes betrayed no fear. They were busy observing everything that happened and recording to his memory all sorts of trifling and irrelevant details which in the retelling create a poignant contrast to the grim background of inhuman warfare. When Heintje Klaes came down into the shelter and told how the parachutist in the baron's garden was killed, Dirk noticed, and made a mental note of it, that Heintje's eyes stuck out like tulip bulbs. "I was really frightened this time," he admitted once when the bombing was going on. But most of the time he kept a level head and made the best of a bad situation. He and his playmates "took turns jumping off the high back steps holding umbrellas and pretending we were parachutists." But the grown-ups would not let them, they said it made them nervous. The boy's very inarticulateness in the most tragic moments of his experience carries terrific force such as no oratory could achieve: "Uncle Pieter came back. He didn't find Mother because she is dead. I can't believe it but Uncle Pieter wouldn't lie. We aren't going to tell Keetje yet. The ambulances are still screaming. I can't sleep or write any more now or anything."

And yet, with all my admiration for this moving and convincing story, I must confess that I do not believe in little Dirk van der Heide. He says things that a Dutch boy of his age could not possibly say. "Keetje and I studied English in school," he tells us at the beginning of his diary. But there are no schools in Holland that teach English to nine and twelve-year-olds. "We were in Belgium," he says on page 10, "when we heard that our country had been forced to surrender to the Nazis," but it is clear from his own story that they never got further south than Flushing, which an American might mistake for Belgian territory but not a Dutch boy so well educated as Dirk van der Heide. It is unlikely, on the other hand, that a Dutch child of his age has any knowledge of the Pilgrim Fathers. "I saw some storks once in Delftshaven, where the English pilgrims stayed before they went to America," is a disturbing, un-Dirkish sentence, which is out of tune with the rest of the book. A school mistress might have added that little touch of instruction for the benefit of American readers. And a Dutch school boy would never speak of The Hague as the capital or *hoofdstad* of Holland. He knows better: the *hoofdstad* is Amsterdam. There is one sentence in the book that is quoted by the translator in the original Dutch words. They are only three in number, but the third of them gives the translator's secret away. "*Dat is gek*", said Father when Uncle Pieter came home with the news that the Germans were massing troops on the Dutch frontier and that Holland was bound to get into the war. Father, of course, was indignant and would not believe his brother's prediction. "You are crazy," he meant to say, and that is the very word that the translator inserted after *gek* between square brackets. However, *dat is gek* means something different. It expresses mild surprise on the part of the speaker. Its English equivalent would be, "that is queer." But queer is certainly not the word that Father, in that moment of tense excitement, would have used. In short, I very much doubt whether I shall ever be able to meet dear little Dirk van der Heide in the flesh. I have a strong suspicion that he lives only in the imagination of the lady who signs herself Mrs. Antoon Deventer and modestly claims no other share in the book than that of a faithful translator. This conclusion does not detract from its value. On the contrary, it is a tribute to the writer who, having lived through that week of horror at Rotterdam, could record her impressions as those of a child with such subtle understanding of the workings of a boy's mind. I hope that, if she ever reads these lines, she will not class me with Seyss-Inquart among the wreckers.

May, 1941

A SHORT STORY

In memoriam
May 10, 1940

Farmer Jansen opened the family Bible and began to read. He read with precision, laying stress on the nouns, and looking now and then at his grown-up daughter with a severe stare that seemed to say, "You had better listen to this for your own good." She had lost respect for the Word of God. The newspapers, and the movies, and modern novels had put pagan ideas into her head. Anna had protested, yesterday, against his reading the story of Elijah's victory over the prophets of Baal. "I won't listen to that, Father," she had said. "You call this Elijah a man of God? He was a cruel savage." And she had left the table with a defiant toss of her head. The boy had said nothing, he was so much younger; but farmer Jansen knew that in his heart he sided with his sister. Still he would not be dictated to by Anna. She would have to hear the sequel of Elijah's story. It wasn't for her to tell him what he should read from the Scriptures. Bible readers shouldn't be choosers. God's word had to be taken whole. He was not sure whether she was paying any attention to the lesson. She never stirred and kept gazing, across the table, at the sunset framed by the open window. "And he said, Go forth, and stand upon the mount before the Lord. And behold, the Lord passed by, and a great and strong wind rent the mountains, and broke in pieces the rocks before the Lord; but the Lord was not in the wind; and after the wind an earthquake; but the Lord was not in the earthquake. And after the earthquake a fire; but the Lord was not in the fire: and after the fire a still small voice." Anna's eyes turned away from the sunset and looked at her father. "That is beautiful," she said. He pretended not to notice her interruption. God's Word was beautiful throughout. She should not presume either to praise or blame it. He read on to the end of the chapter and closed the book. Anna did not speak again.

She could not sleep that night. Spring was in the air. And tomorrow was Fritz's birthday. She had written to him three weeks ago. You never knew nowadays how long a letter would be on its way. He was in the army, but she did not know where. Perhaps in Poland, perhaps in Norway. Hateful to think of him fighting Norwegians. The Germans had no business there. Fritz would admit that, she was sure. As a soldier he had to obey, but he would curse himself for doing it. She knew him too well. He could not harm a soul. Had she not known him from the time when he came to the farm as a little, undernourished boy to be nursed back to health by her mother? They had been playmates then, they had become lovers. For summer after summer he came back to the farm for a few weeks' vacation. He could not forget the Dutch home where his life had been saved. It had become a second home for him. Last year he had surprised her by dropping in unannounced on his birthday. Tomorrow was the tenth of May. Would he come again? Hope and longing kept her awake.

The distant purr of an airplane. There must be more than one. They must be over the house, they sound so near. And lots of them. Going to raid London? They have no right to fly over Holland. What a gruesome errand, going to scatter death on innocent people. Fritz would not do that. He would refuse to drop bombs upon sleeping women and children. Would they shoot him if he did? Gracious God, what was that? Are they dropping bombs on Holland? She jumped out of bed and looked out into the night. The sky was alight with flashes and searchlights, and in their glare she could see balloons dropping slowly down to the ground. They aren't balloons, they are parachutes. "Father!" she screamed, in sudden terror. He was already by her side. "This is war," he said. "Get dressed at once. I am going out to see what I can do. You look after mother and Jan." She did not see him go, she was only aware that he was no longer there. But his words had left her in a state of elation. He had entrusted to her his wife and son. She would not shirk the responsibility. She went downstairs, bolted the door, and lit a fire, for she felt suddenly shivery. Amazing that Jan could sleep on. The noise of the planes overhead was deafening now. Was that a knock at the door? Who could be calling at this time of night? There it is again. "Who's there?" "A friend of yours, Anna. Wish him a happy birthday." "Fritz, darling. O, thank you for coming. I have been longing for you." She was too happy to wonder and ask questions. It was a matter of course for him to come in on the morning of his birthday. She had forgotten the parachutes and the shooting and the searchlights. "Come and sit by the fire, and tell me how you came, my darling boy." "No time, dear. I am not here to celebrate my birthday. I am here on business." "What do you mean, on business? What sort of business?" He shrugged his shoulders nervously, but did not answer. It was then that she noticed his uniform. "Have you joined the Dutch army?" she cried in amazement. "I haven't time to talk. Make us some breakfast. There are six of us. We are in the barn."

He was gone. She felt herself trembling all over. Fear, horror, indignation, disgust, love, were the conflicting sensations that overwhelmed her. She understood: he had come disguised in Dutch uniform to fight her own people. He was betraying the country that had offered him hospitality. But that could not be the Fritz she knew. He was incapable of such treachery. Mechanically she went through the preparations for breakfast, boiled the water, made the coffee, cut the bread, got butter and cheese from the cellar, and carried the tray piled high with all this fare into the barn. There they were fixing up a machine gun. He thanked her abruptly. "Get yourself into the house and stay indoors. And tell the old man and Jan not to budge. It might be dangerous." She looked at him with an expression in which love and scorn were strangely mingled. "Fritz, you are not going to shoot Dutch soldiers? Don't fight my people. They are almost yours." "I'm doing my duty. That's all." "There is no duty in treachery. It's your duty to be loyal." "I *am* loyal, to the Führer. For God's sake, leave me alone. I cannot argue with you now. I'll explain it all tomorrow." She went back to the house, tears streaming down her face. Her invalid mother called out to her from the bedroom. She had heard Fritz' voice, it was no use concealing anything from her. Poor mother, she was so fond of Fritz. His treachery would be a terrible blow to her. While Anna was telling her what she knew, the pale morning suddenly burst aflame. The house shook on its foundations. Bombs seemed to be dropping all around, firing resounded from all sides, a neighbor's farm across the road was burning, shrieks rang out above the turmoil that made the two women shudder. The lull that followed was more terrifying still. "Anna," the old woman whispered hoarsely, "go and see if Jan is all right." The girl went up the stairs to the attic. The boy's bedroom door was open, the bed was empty. Where could he be? She ran downstairs in sudden terrror. The back door was unlatched. Where could he have gone? And father had made her responsible for him! She should have looked after him. Suppose he got killed in the fighting! Father would never forgive her, she would never forgive herself. His blood would be on her head. Through the open bedroom door she heard her mother praying aloud. If only she could pray. That might give her courage. But she could not. The smoke of the burning house came drifting towards her, sparks flew up above the dark pall, the lowing of scared cattle, the rattle of gunfire, the thud of bombs exploding in the distance, shouts of men, shrieks of women and children, turned the scene around her into a hellish chaos. It was impossible to tell where the shooting came from. Was the barn under fire? Would Fritz be alive? Did he deserve to be saved? She shuddered at asking herself that question. She loved him, in spite of all. She could not condemn him to death. She went to the door and tried to get a glimpse of the barn across the smoke. O God, the barn was burning, too. "Fritz," she shrieked. She ran through the smoke towards the burning shed. But before she reached it, the roof came crashing down. She stumbled, blinded and choked by smoke and dust, and lay unconscious where she fell.

When she opened her eyes again, she found herself lying on a mattress in the parlor. Farmer Jansen was sitting by her side in his armchair, anxiously watching her face. She raised her arm and laid her hand on his knee. He patted it gently, but neither spoke a word. Thus they remained, a long, long time, it seemed. At last she found the strength to shape a question: "Where is Fritz?" His face darkened. He said: "Mother is safe; she is asleep." She stared at him, wondering at the strangeness of his answer. There was another long silence. Then he spoke again: "Jan was a brave boy." She waited for more, but he dropped back into silence. "I want to talk to Jan," she said at last. He shook his head slowly. "You will never see him again," he said with a sob in his voice. A cold shudder ran through her body. Hoarsely she whispered: "What happened?" It took him some time to control his emotion. "Jan had heard that traitor knock on the door. He listened to what he told you. He understood. He slipped out of the back door, ran to town and gave the alarm. He showed our soldiers the way to the barn. The scoundrels were done for in no time. But Jan did not come back ... alive." Her hand clutched his knee; she could not utter a word. But he knew what she was thinking. His face hardened, and his voice trembling with pent-up fury he suddenly shouted: "Never you mention that scoundrel's name again. He got what he deserved. And all his cursed race will have to atone for this. An eye for an eye, a tooth for a tooth." She shut her eyes

184

and lay still, wondering at the strange quiet of the house. "How long have I been sick, Father?" "For more than a week. The war is over. Rotterdam is in ruins. The army has surrendered. The Queen and the Government have escaped to London. And Jan is dead." And then, after another long silence, he swore, "God damn them. Our people will never forget this. They will have their revenge. An eye for an eye, a tooth for a tooth." And Anna said faintly, "How then shall we ever have peace?" He did not answer but dropped back into his moody silence. She lay on her back, her eyes closed, listening to the stillness of the house. She touched his knee. "Father!" "What is it, child?" "Father, read me again that story of Elijah hearing the still small voice."

June, 1941

A HERO OF THE SEA

I was walking through Riverside Park in the early morning. Some of our war ships were riding at anchor midstream. They made a fine showing in the light of the rising sun. While I was watching them, not with any knowledge of their efficiency as forces of destruction, but with an artist's eye taking pleasure in their architectural beauty, I heard someone whistle a familiar tune. No one but a Hollander would know that melody. It was a song about a little boy in a blue-and-white checkered blouse turning the wheel in a rope-maker's workshop, and feeling sick all the time with a longing for the sea. Every Dutch child learns to sing it in school and knows the story of that boy, for he became the greatest of Holland's admirals, Michiel Adriaenszoon de Ruyter. I gave the whistler the second stanza and through this musical exchange he and I became acquainted. When we now meet in the park, the tune of Michiel at the wheel is our mutual greeting. It would bring Hollanders together wherever they meet in this wide world.

There are not many Dutch folksongs that keep the memory of the nation's heroes alive. De Ruyter was a man of exceptional stature. He was a son of humble parents, went to sea at an early age, rose through bravery and intelligence to a captain's rank, was transferred from the merchant marine to the navy, and as its commander-in-chief won glory for his country and himself. The funeral procession that conducted him to his grave in the New Church at Amsterdam attracted a crowd of mourners the like of which had never been seen in the Netherlands. A magnificent monument was erected over his tomb and a contemporary biographer published the story of his life in a stately folio volume. Among the great Hollanders of that age De Ruyter was the only one whose greatness was evident to the mass of his contemporaries. And later generations have retold the story of his life into a colorful legend, in which the pranks of his boyhood, the exploits of his sea-roving years, and his victories as admiral of the fleet are touched up with an un-Dutch glamour of romance. Yet the legend that every Dutchman knows does not explain the secret of his greatness. What was it that made him pre-eminent in an age that was by no means poor in naval heroes?

It is easier to pose than to answer that question. He did not prosper through Fortune's favor. On the contrary, he had scorned her advances. At the age of forty-five he had saved enough capital to retire to a quiet existence on land. He said farewell to the sea and started housekeeping with a third wife to give his orphaned children a mother and a home. But soon afterwards war broke out between England and the Dutch Republic, and the States of Zeeland, his native province, offered him the command over their contingent of the federal fleet. He refused, and stood by his refusal until their appeal to his patriotism made him yield. But he yielded reluctantly and on condition that his appointment should be for one voyage only. For more than thirty years he had sailed the seven seas and shared the dangers of that adventurous life with daredevil crews who gloried in the tradition of the Sea Beggars. It was not cowardice that made him hesitate to accept command over the Zeeland squadron. He wavered because he knew that with these gangs of brave but undisciplined individualists a systematic naval war could not be waged. They were good at suddenly descending upon an unsuspecting port, and running away with the plunder. Raiding the enemy's coasts had been their pastime for generations; they had no conception of naval warfare that left the land untouched. And that was the kind of war that De Ruyter would have to wage against the English. For the freedom of the seas was in jeopardy. The Dutch Republic had to safeguard the routes of its overseas trade, and this could not be done by pillaging on land. The British fleet had been unified under the command of military men schooled in the iron discipline of Cromwell's army. There was no centralized authority in the Dutch navy. Local and provincial pride thwarted all attempts at unification. There were five admiralties, each jealous of the others, and none possessing a navy worth the name. In case of war they would requisition armed merchantmen from various shipowners and combine them into a squadron. Thus, in 1640, De Ruyter, for the first time in his sea career, served the States of Zeeland on a ship that the latter had hired from her owner. With three other ships he was sent to the aid of the Portuguese, who had revolted against Spain. It was an ill-fated expedition. De Ruyter returned from it with no ambition to enter the service of the States for good. He bought with his savings the ship Salamander, and carried freight to and from the West Indies and the coast of North Africa until, in 1651, he decided to settle down to domesticity and peace.

But the Republic could not afford to let a man of his proved ability rest on his laurels. The reverses suffered by the Dutch navy in the war with England were due to the deplorable conditions in the fleet which De Ruyter had exposed in his reports to the rulers at The Hague. The States of Holland, impressed by his foresight and intelligent criticism, offered him the vice-admiralcy of Amsterdam. He declined, but was persuaded to reconsider his refusal by no less a man than Jan de Witt, the Grand Pensionary of Holland, and the most powerful figure in the Dutch Republic. That was in 1655. It was the beginning of his ascent to glory. Until then he had been one among a host of daring captains who combined privateering with trading. From 1655 on he was one of a small number of vice-admirals whose task it was to organize and equip a fleet that could maintain the freedom of the seven seas for the farflung sea-borne trade of the Republic. As commander-in-chief of the Admiralty of Amsterdam he was the first among his equals. Backed by the authority of Jan de Witt, he created order out of chaos. He built up a navy that needed not rely any more on armed merchantmen for reinforcement, he saw to it that the new men-of-war were built all of one type so that replacements and repairs could be obtained without delay from the stores and arsenals on land, he supplied the shortage of trained officers by the formation of a professional cadre, and had the fleet on its extended expeditions accompanied by supply ships. In former days the captains were responsible for the victualing of their own ships, and the grafters among them enriched themselves at the expense of their crews, charging the Admiralty for more and better food than they actually bought. De Ruyter insisted on the establishment of an efficient supply and rationing system. Thus the makeshift conglomeration of privateering merchantmen was superseded by a disciplined and firmly organized battle fleet, whose striking power was demonstrated in the second naval war with England. Even when one-third of that fleet was laid up, in 1673, because the crews were needed to help the army stem the onrush of the invading French forces of Louis XIV, De Ruyter was able to defeat the combined naval forces of the French and the British.

The battle of Kijkduin was his last great triumph. The States, in their shortsightedness, were disinclined to appropriate funds for the maintenance of the navy's wartime efficiency after the peace with England had been signed. They needed him again, however, in 1676, to rush to the assistance of Spain against France in the Mediterranean. He objected to sailing with a fleet so inadequately equipped. Had he lost his courage in his old age, one of those pompous merchant rulers had the impudence to ask him. "Where the States will risk their flag, I will risk my life," was his dignified answer. His dead body returned from that expedition and was buried on March 18, 1677, in the New Church at Amsterdam.

Young French noblemen, who served on his ship as volunteers to learn the art of naval warfare, were amazed to see the great Admiral, at the victorious close of the greatest battle he ever fought, seize hold of a broom to sweep the floor of his cabin, and then pay a visit to the hencoop and feed his chickens. De Ruyter possessed an inborn dignity that could not suffer from the indignity of such low tasks. His mariners called him *Bestevaer*, an affectionate equivalent to granddad. He had risen from their midst, but had remained one of them, an unassuming hero without pretensions, never humble or obsequious in dealings with the High and Mighty Lords his masters, but genial with the men who obeyed his commands. That was the secret of his popularity and partly, also, of his successful career. Loving liberty as the highest good, he respected the love of freedom in others. His mariners willingly obeyed his commands because they knew him to be prompted not by pride of authority but by zeal for the common good. The broom with which he swept his cabin clean was also the emblem of his power at sea. He carried it at the mast-head as a token that he meant to sweep the ocean clean of offenders who menaced its freedom. I was reminded of that telling challenge by the spectacle of our modern war craft on the Hudson. The freedom of the seas is again being threatened as it never was before. But free men stand guard on the decks of battleships of free nations as they did in the days of Michiel Adriaenszoon de Ruyter. They will sweep the pirates off the ocean as the Dutch admiral and his men did three centuries ago.

July, 1941

A FRENCH CRITIC OF THE DUTCH

A Frenchman who reads and speaks Dutch is an extremely rare specimen. M. G. H. Bousquet, Professor in the University of Algiers, has paid the Dutch the compliment of learning their difficult language. When he visited schools at Padang, Sumatra, in the Netherlands East Indies, he was invited to address the students in English, Arabic, or Dutch. "I gave them their choice of English or Dutch, and in each case they chose English." He tells this not in order to impress his readers with his polyglotism, but in order to demonstrate the astonishing indifference of the Dutch for their native language. Here was a Dutch school in a Far Eastern island under Dutch rule, and the authorities did not seem to care whether the pupils took any pride in knowing the language of the ruling race. A little later he spoke at a girls' school at Padang Pandjang, in that same district. He addressed them in English, for he found that none of those children knew a word of Dutch.

To a Frenchman such total neglect of the language of the mother country in its overseas possessions is incomprehensible. French colonial policy aims at assimilation. The Frenchman loves to think of France extending her culture, as Rome did in days of yore, over distant regions inhabited by barbarians. Berber, Arab, and Negro must all be turned into Frenchmen able to cut a figure on the Paris boulevards. The melodious beauty of the language, the grace of French manners may well have the power to work that miracle. If the Nazi occupation lasts long enough the German conquerors may all be turned into charming Frenchmen ashamed of shouting "Heil Hitler!" and crying "Vive la France!" instead. M. Bousquet quotes with pride and pleasure the flattery expressed in a letter from an Indo-Chinese fellow citizen: "On landing in France for the first time, I felt as if I were returning to my native land." If a Javanese spoke of his arrival in Holland in this exalted strain, no Dutchman hearing his adulation would either respect or love him for it. The French expect from their subject races a show of eagerness to take their place in the great French family. The Dutch, unemotional realists, expect from them obedience and cooperation. They do not believe that they can turn them into Dutch patriots enamored of Dutch art and literature and architecture. They are not inclined to force upon those Oriental races their own western civilization. M. Bousquet condemns this policy as detrimental to Holland's highest interests. The mother country, in his opinion, should put the stamp of its own civilization upon the life, the speech, the way of thinking of the native peoples. He would like to see all Javanese transformed into tropical Hollanders.

Every Dutchman who takes an interest in the East Indies would do well to read M. Bousquet's provocative book. Its title in the English translation is "A French View of the Netherlands Indies" (Oxford University Press 1940). Its effect on the Dutch reader is that of an unpleasantly cold but invigorating shower bath. It opens his eyes to flaws in the administrative system that he would never detect because he takes that system for granted, and does not question its proved efficacy. The atmosphere of Java was uncongenial to this critical Frenchman. He found the Dutch too much inclined to interfere with the minutest details of native life, to regulate everything, to poke their instructive fingers under Javanese noses, always indeed with the noble intention of bettering the natives' lot, but seldom to their genuine satisfaction. The system suffers from too much painstaking thoroughness. M. Bousquet must grudgingly admit that the Hollanders have made a phenomenal success of their colonial enterprise. But they owe this, he believes, not to the soundness of their administrative ways but to their good luck in having the Javanese for their subjects, the gentlest, and most docile people on earth. But I would ask M. Bousquet, have the Dutch not succeeded equally well with the Madurese, who are a proud and self-assertive race, ever ready to avenge the slightest injury to their keen sense of justice by a stab of the creese? M. Bousquet suspects that the Hollanders' unwillingness to speak Dutch to the natives is due to their wish to keep them ignorant. There are indeed a great many Hollanders in the Indies who are reluctant to have the rank and file of the native population taught to speak Dutch, but not from any selfish reasons. They honestly believe that the native will be a happier creature if he be allowed to develop unestranged from his own environment, like a plant firmly rooted in the soil of its natural habitat.

I wonder how much French the colored members of the great French family acquire in the course of their school education. Sir Walter Raleigh, not the Elizabethan, but the Victorian Oxford scholar, was sceptical about the blessings the Bengalis derived from being taught to copy the rhetoric of Burke. "The effect," he wrote, "is exactly like what may sometimes be seen in the branches of the trees of an Indian forest — the monkeys are behaving in a strange and unnatural manner, a manner that is unintelligible until the cause is discovered: A man has passed that way." I also remember reading an essay by a little Filipino boy trained in American rhetoric and patriotism. It was a panegyric on the cow: "The cow is a noble beast. The cow has four legs, one at each corner. The cow also gives milk. But as for me, give me liberty or give me death." These are the fruits of what might be called imperialistic education. The French are excessively proud, and justly so, of their beautiful and melodious language. How can they endure hearing it broken on the rack of foreign tongues that were shaped by nature for the articulation of quite different sounds?

There is a very sound explanation for the Hollander's neglect of his own language. This nation of traders and navigators has developed, through force of circumstance, a special aptitude for imitating foreign speech. And this aptitude bred pride in such accomplishment, and the desire to show off. The learning of a foreign language is for a Dutch child not a drudgery but an exciting sport. And a Hollander who can speak no other language besides his own passes among his own kind for uneducated. They consider it good form to address the foreigner, if possible, in his own tongue, and derive no little pleasure from being able to do so. When the Dutch first came to Java, they found the Portuguese language spoken there among the Arabs, Chinese, and other Orientals with whom they did their trading. Instead of insisting on the use of Dutch, they adapted their speech to that of their customers and did all their transactions in Portuguese. That was from the merchant's point of view good policy. They came to trade, not to found an empire. An employee of the Dutch East India Company published in 1718 a Portuguese-Dutch dictionary for the benefit of the Dutch who had dealings with "Arabs, Chinese, Orientals, and other pagan nations." In his preface he tells us that in the churches at Batavia God's word was proclaimed in Portuguese. The realistic Hollanders reasoned that there was no sense in teaching the gospel in Dutch, if one wanted to attract to the services Eurasians and Orientals who had no knowledge of that language. Being good, orthodox Calvinists they had the propagation of the gospel closer at heart than the propagation of the Dutch language. M. Bousquet finds this prevalence of Portuguese in the days of the Company clear proof of the Dutchman's indifference for his native tongue. He even denies them a love of country. Their hearts cannot warm to the enthusiasms of patriotism and glory, for they are totally devoid of idealism. Which of the two nations, one might ask M. Bousquet, has shown firmer moral stamina in the present world crisis? And does not moral stamina draw its strength from ideals? The French writer offers himself the best refutation of his absurd charge: His book is dedicated "To the Memory of Joost van Vollenhoven, Governor General of Indo-China and French West Africa. Born in Rotterdam on July 21, 1877, died for France at Parcy-Tigny on July 20, 1918." Was it lack of idealism that brought this native son of Holland to the top of the French colonial service? Was it lack of idealism that made him ask for his discharge so that he might join the colors and fight for his adopted country? He gave his life for it. Might not the memory of that sacrifice have given the writer pause when he was on the point of writing down that sweeping assertion by which a whole nation was condemned for lacking idealism and love of country?

The Letter for July was devoted to a discussion of M. Bousquet's book entitled "A French View of the Netherlands Indies." The reading of it brought back to my mind a conversation that I had with a British-Indian Moslem at Dyocya, in central Java, in the summer of 1925. A Protestant Dutch missionary, Dr. H. Kraemer, had introduced me to this man. The two were good friends, although professionally they were antagonists. For the Moslem was a member of the Ahmediyya, an unorthodox sect of British-Indian Mohammedans who are the only Islamites to organize a mission. They teach a curious doctrine, Dr. Kraemer told me, about the Christian Saviour. Jesus will return to earth at the time set for Him by Allah and proclaim that He had been mistaken and that the true doctrine is to be found in Mohammed's teaching. They also deny that Jesus died on the cross. He was alive when He was taken down, recovered, wandered through Persia to India, and died there. The Ahmediyya know the holy place where He was buried. Dr. Kraemer admired the Dyocya emissary of the Ahmediyya as an honest fanatic, though he found it impossible to argue with him, as all his beliefs were unshakable axioms. "But I like the fellow," he said, "and often go to his house for a chat. I am going there tomorrow. Won't you come along?"

He called for me next day and took me to the Mohammedan quarter. Part of the room in which the Moslem missionary received us was a kind of courtyard, in the centre of which a big tree shot upwards through a hole in the roof. We conversed in English which he spoke with some difficulty. His harelip made it hard for him to articulate clearly. He was extremely courteous, and appeared to have a sense of humor, in spite of his fanatic zeal. When I asked him whether he approved of the doctrine of the Holy War, he emphatically denied the existence of such a doctrine, and said, with a smile and a wink in the direction of Dr. Kraemer, "That's a fiction of Christian missionaries." He boasted of the unalterableness of the Arabic language, which had not changed, he claimed, only added to, its vocabulary since the days of the Prophet. Although I did not know a word of Arabic, I knew enough of the general behaviour of languages to put this down among the man's fixed ideas that had no foundation in fact. He mentioned with pride the names of prominent converts to Islam, amongst others Lord Hadley, and another British nobleman of the Hamilton clan (he pronounced the name with the stress on mil), and boasted of the existence of a large Islamic community of Ahmediyya at Chicago. He wrote the address down for me: 4448 Al Masjid, Wabash Avenue.

"Why had he come to Java?" I asked. His superiors at the Lahore headquarters had sent him to stem the swelling tide of Christianity. "We do not meddle with politics. We only bring a message of love and brotherhood and universal freedom." "Freedom for women too?" I ventured to ask. "Woman," he replied, "must remain subordinate for morality's sake. Her modesty is a more precious treasure than freedom." He strongly disapproved of the Dyocya women who parade their bare breasts in the crowded streets. He made the impression of an honest and kindly man, but devoid of the critical acumen and the scholarly training that are essential in conducting an argument. He presented me with a few copies of the Life of Mirza Ghulam Ahmed, the founder of his sect, when I shook hands with him in parting.

A JAVANESE NOBLEMAN

Dr. Kraemer introduced me to another, this time a self-appointed missionary, a Javanese nobleman who was a crusader for educational reform in line with native tradition. Raden Mas (that was his title) Soewardi Soeryadiningrad called his new type of school *Taman Siswo*, that is Garden of Pupils. I found him in the senior classroom discussing the geography of Belgium. The entrance to the school was through a gate in a white-washed garden wall. Round the garden were the school buildings, if that is not too big a word to describe the simple houses, all in bad repair, on the porches of which the pupils sat at their desks. In the centre of the garden stood Soewardi's house. He greeted me with the courtesy which the Javanese nobleman possesses by nature, and introduced me to his chief assistant, Raden Mas A. Sooijo Poetro, who had studied technology at Delft and spoke fluent Dutch, though not with the flawless accent which Soewardi had mastered. I said to them, "I understand that you favor an education uninfluenced by Western thought?" Sooijo Poetro smiled and handed me half a dozen schoolbooks in Dutch on history, bookkeeping, and Dutch grammar. "These will show you that we are not afraid of Dutch influences. But we lay stronger stress than is done in Dutch schools, on the history, religion, art, and literature of Java; we teach our children *Kawi*, the language of ancient Java; and we arouse in them a love of country by making them proud of the past. We do not accept any Government subsidy in order to retain freedom to do as we think best, but we conform as much as possible to the Government school curriculum, as we prepare our pupils for High School. Of course, the government inspectors do not like our school. They consider our physical equipment inadequate, and we must admit that it does not come up to Government standards. But our funds are limited, and the movement is still in its infancy. That we are able to carry on at all is owing to the idealism of our teachers, who are willing to come to us for one-third or one-fourth of the salary they would earn at a Government school."

Some of the boys were fixing electric wires in the garden trees. "My wife had a baby a week ago," Soewardi explained, "and the school is going to celebrate the event. For the school and the house are one. These boys and girls are all members of my family. There is my house, in the centre of the school rooms, and round the domestic life circles the school life." "Do you give them any religious training?" "We do not. This is a neutral school. But those pupils who ask for it can get it. The Mohammediyya is only too glad to send us an instructor." "And how many pupils are taking it?" "Only twenty-three out of one hundred and forty-three. You see, we are not really Mohammedans. We are Buddhists rather," Soewardi explained. "Has your movement spread beyond Middle Java?" "It has in East Java. But we have had no success in West Java. The Sundanese are so different from us. Anything originating here is for that very reason suspect among them."

I apologized for having detained him so long, but he would not let me go so soon. "Do sit down," said Soewardi. "My wife has prepared a cup of cocoa for us, and according to Javanese etiquette you may not refuse the drink that is offered you." While sipping my cocoa I told them how wrong an idea I had formed of Java from the books I had read. The real Java is quite different even from the pictures one sees of it. They had experienced the same in Europe. "Do you know what surprised us most when we landed in Marseilles? To see white men sweep the streets and carry coal and collect the garbage and perform all kinds of menial tasks that are never done by Europeans in the Indies. That was an eye-opener to us."

A POLICY OF FORBEARANCE

The Ahmediyya is one of many reformist Islamic movements, chief among which is the Mohammediyya, whose exclusive object, it claims, is to spread Moslem culture. M. Bousquet is of opinion that the Dutch Government underestimates the anti-Dutch tendencies of the Moslem movement and exaggerates that of the nationalists, of which *Taman Siswo* is a typical example. Our French critic reminds his Dutch readers of the fact that a government of unbelievers is by its very nature illegal in the eyes of Islam. I believe that this reminder is uncalled for. Dutch officialdom is fully aware of that fact. But the Bureau for Native Affairs at Batavia, from which the Government's policy with regard to Islamic problems emanates, would not agree with him that suppression of such movements would be a safeguard against future trouble. The French scholar wonders why the Dutch allow the Moslems to foster and cultivate their own laws, customs, and traditions, instead of transmitting social institutions from Holland to Java and the other islands. "The superiority of these institutions leaves them indifferent," he says. That shows how little he understands Dutch mentality, and arouses a suspicion that his insight into the native soul is equally faulty. It is not indifference to their own institutions that dictates to them this policy of forbearance. Their native tolerance has taught them respect for that which is sacred to others. They leave intact institutions that the native cherishes, unless their survival should maintain practices that are inhumane from a Western point of view. The same delicate feeling has dictated the Dutch policy with regard to the missions. The Government furnishes no opposition to the spread of Islam, nor is any authorization necessary to preach Islam. But the Christian missionaries must obtain a special license before they can undertake their ministry. Why this lenience towards the Moslems under a Government controlled by a coalition of Christians in the mother country? asks M. Bousquet. For a very good reason. There are regions of the Malay Archipelago where Christianity has gained a permanent foothold: in the Minahassa, North Celebes, on the island of Amboyna, among the Bataks of North Sumatra, and in Java, where some 300,000 natives have embraced the white man's religion. But the fact remains that the large majority of the peoples under Dutch control are Moslems, and that from their point of view Christianity is an alien intruder. The Dutch may dislike and even detest many features of the Mohammedan religion, but they will consistently defend the Moslem's right to believe as he does.

September, 1941

DUTCH SCHOLARS

The Society of Dutch Scholars in North America met this summer, by invitation of Hope College, in Holland, Mich. "In a very important sense there is no such thing as a Dutch scholar and there is no such thing as Dutch scholarship," wrote the editor of the local Holland paper, for "the true scholar is interested in knowledge no matter where it develops, and a scholarship that is merely patriotic, in the chauvinistic sense of that word, is not scholarship at all." And having aired this wisdom, he hastened to express his conviction that the Dutch scholars then meeting in his town would agree with that statement.

Of course they would. The very fact of their teaching the knowledge they acquired in Dutch universities to the students of American institutes of higher learning is sufficient proof that they not only admit but live up to the international character of Science. The good Holland Editor was trying to force an open door. The Society of Dutch Scholars was not formed to propagate a special made-in-Holland brand of science but to unite scholarly Dutchmen who, while sharing with the learned of all other nationalities the scholar's devotion to Science, feel drawn towards each other by their common origin. There are in this country any number of Associations of American Scholars professing a variety of sciences: the engineers, the chemists, the physicists, the philologists, the historians, the medievalists all meet once or oftener a year to fraternize and discuss common problems. That does not make them chauvinistic propagandists for a national Science. Neither do the Dutch scholars, when they meet twice a year, pretend to burn incense to a tribal Muse. They share memories of university life in their home country, affections for the masters under whom they studied, loyalties to customs in force at their Dutch Alma Maters. These alone amply justify their desire for association. But they have a further inducement to seek each other in their Dutch manner of approach to Science. For though Truth and Knowledge are not confined to national limits, there are many ways that lead to the goal, and which particular path is chosen often depends on the searcher's native turn of mind. Science is international, indeed, but the multifarious search for Truth shows national characteristics. In that sense there is reason to speak of Dutch scholarship as distinct from, let us say, the scholarship of France and Germany. It is not mere accident that Holland has not produced philosophers of world-wide fame. For Spinoza, though he was a citizen of the Dutch Republic, was neither physically nor mentally a son of the Dutch race. A Dutch professor of philosophy, whose own reputation never exceeded the national scope, attributed this dearth partly to the Dutchman's nature and partly to educational methods, which aim at a thoroughness that is apt to stifle originality. It would seem that the two causes are only one, since it is not likely that the Hollander could have developed such thoroughness in the training of the young if it were not in his nature to be thorough. Thought cannot take flight into dazzling heights if it is forever concerned about precautions against the danger of being dazzled. Deductive reasoning is an un-Dutch manner of approach. The Hollander likes to build, in the realm of thought, upon solid ground. He relies on the evidence of experiment, and fights shy of all theory that has no other foundation than the hunch of an inspired seer. That must account for the astounding achievements of Dutch scholarship in the field of the exact sciences. Men such as J. H. van 't Hoff, H. A. Lorentz, H. Kamerlingh Onnes, P. Zeeman, J. D. van der Waals, all Nobel Prize winners, penetrated into the depths of nature's secrets and the mysteries of the universe, but their imagination reached that far by the aid of painstaking research in the laboratory. They were like cautious mountain climbers who carefully prepared for their expedition, foreseeing all eventualities and guarding themselves against them, charting their course in advance, and learning from the experience of others who adventured before them and failed. They took no risks but made sure to know all that was knowable before starting in search of the yet unknown. Thus they attained to the summits of present human knowledge and peered into mysteries that revealed greater mysteries. For Science knows no ultimate Thule. Truth is like the magic castle of Arthurian romance which always seems near and yet can never be reached. The Knights Errant of Science are loyal comrades of an international Round Table. But they differ, according to their native character, in the choice of their equipment. The Dutchman does not mount the winged horse of Fancy. He is an unromantic knight who likes his errantry to be proof against erring.

Those who assembled in the lecture room of Hope College Chapel, where the meetings were held, on the morning of Saturday, September 6th, heard Prof. S. Goudsmit, of the University of Michigan, give an account of the achievements of Dutch knights errant who searched for the magic castle in the domain of the exact sciences. Professors are proverbially dull people. I have heard of one who was so very dull that even his colleagues noticed it. But if any one in Holland stayed away from that lecture because of his belief in the legend of professorial dullness, he robbed himself of a most enjoyable hour. For Professor Goudsmit treated us that morning to the most entertaining causerie I ever listened to. He radiated wit and humor, without ever descending to flippancy. He spoke with reverence of the great whose work he surveyed, and gave, incidentally, a striking illustration of the international character of Science. The achievements of famous scientists, he said, become at once the common property of the learned world. The laws they first formulated become the stock in trade of every student in the field, and the knowledge they imparted, not the names that they bore, are remembered by succeeding generations. The composer's symphony, the artist's picture, the writer's novel remain for ever distinct evidences of their genius. The scientist's achievements are merged in the great mass of human knowledge, and the fame they possessed among their contemporaries shrivels to the mere mention of their names in the handbooks of the schools. Among the great

197

of each nation the scholars lead the most unselfish lives. The fruits of their labors enrich, not themselves, but mankind, and their final reward is oblivion.

THE GERMAN ANTHILL

The sluggard is told in Proverbs to study the ants and learn industry from them: "Go to the ant, thou sluggard; consider her ways, and be wise: Which having no guide, overseer, or ruler, provideth her meat in the summer, and gathereth her food in the harvest." The sage who gave this advice was no biologist. He admired the industry of the ants without being able to account for the feverish restlessness of the ant hill. Is it true that they have no guide, overseer, or ruler? The modern observer tells us a different story.

Seven years ago a South African naturalist, Eugène Marais, published in the Afrikaans language a beautiful book on "The Soul of the Ant." The title is misleading, for it becomes clear from the contents of the book that not the ant, but only the ant hill, has a soul. Group soul is the name that Marais gives to this strange phenomenon. He compares the ant hill with the human body. The ants perform within the ant hill exactly the same functions that the white and red blood corpuscles perform in the human anatomy. The queen, who lies imprisoned in her cell, directs from that central position all the activities of the ant hill. If one should dig her out and kill her, the ant hill, deprived of its brain, would perish. The ants have life only through her. They possess neither will nor reasoning power. It is the reasoning power and the will of the queen that drive them on.

The German nation under Hitler has become such an ant hill. Although the German individual has the outward semblance of a thinking, self-willing human being, he is, in fact, nothing more than a blood corpuscle in the gigantic body of the German nation, ever ready to obey the signals from the central brain. Whatsoever that central brain declares to be good and beneficial for the German ant hill is industriously striven for by the entire community, be it the building or repairing of their home, the gathering of food, or the destruction of a neighboring hill and the looting of its stores. The German ant does not ask, "Is it good what I am doing?" He only asks, "Has the Führer commanded it?" If so, it is good. He knows no other morality than obedience to the Führer.

There are, of course, still reasoning, self-willing beings in Germany, who resemble men rather than ants. But those are the outcasts, the

criminals, who do harm to the hill. Shirer tells a story in his Berlin
Diary about a German mother who, having been notified by the German Admiralty that her son had perished with a lost submarine,
advertised in the papers that the boy had fallen for his Führer. But a
week later a British broadcast mentioned his name in a list of German
prisoners of war landed in England. Eight friends called at the
mourning mother's door to tell her the good news in deep secret. But
she, in her slavish ant faith to the Führer, betrayed all eight of them
to the Gestapo as criminal listeners to the British radio. From our
point of view this is a dehumanized woman. But in Hitler's ant hill
she is virtue personified, and the radio listeners deformicized members
of the ant hill.

The Nazis are doing their worst to transform the Dutch nation into
an ant hill. But they are discovering to their mortification that Hollanders have no use for a group soul. They cannot be forced to be
silent in a body. They insist on testifying, if not in words, then in
actions, to their loyalty to the House of Orange. The orange traffic
light that marks the transition from red to green and vice versa is a
signal for every Dutch man and boy to raise his hat in silent tribute to
the Queen. The warning "Jewish Business" is an invitation to Dutch
Aryans to enter and make their purchases there. The movie theatres
that bar Jews are losing their custom. Dutch Nazis are hated and
shunned like the plague by the entire nation. The entire nation, for
they themselves have ceased to belong to it, their treason having
transformed them into fellow ants of the Germans.

DUTCH DEFIANCE

This tenacity of Dutch individualism manifests itself among all sorts
and conditions of men, among all ages, among all denominations.
Count Van Randwijk, burgomaster of Amersfoort, leaves the concert
hall with his wife when Gestapo agents remove Jewish musicians from
the orchestra, and the larger part of the audience follows their
example. An Amsterdam tram conductor, seeing some German
policemen boarding his car, warns his passengers, "Pas op de bocht,
dames en heeren!" (Mind the curve, ladies and gentlemen!), the
word "bocht" having the double meaning of curve and offal. School
boys perform a caricature of the goosestep to the annoyance of the
German soldiers. Minister Colijn, still full of youthful vigor in spite
of his seventy-two years, prefers the honor of detention in a concentration camp to the shame of compliance with German orders. A
minister at The Hague, in defiance of German prohibitions, boldly
prays in the pulpit "for Her Majesty the Queen and the members of

the Royal House, for our legitimate Government in London, and for those who oppress us, if such prayer be pleasing to God." And when the Jewish Professor E. M. Meijers, of the Leyden Law School, is relieved of his functions by order of the German authorities, his colleague Cleveringa takes his place and addresses the Law Faculty and students in words that will forever grace the annals of the University. Having read to his audience the text of the order that barred Dr. Meijers from lecturing in Leyden, Dr. Cleveringa said, "I give you this missive in its naked baldness, and shall not try to qualify it. For my words would be inadequate to express the bitter, painful feelings that this letter has stirred in our hearts. If I had come here only to accentuate that bitterness of mood, I could do no better than to leave you shivering in the icy grip of the silence that would numb us. Neither shall I try to deflect your thoughts to those men from whom this order issued. Their deed qualifies itself. I wish to leave them deep below us, where they cannot be seen from the height on whose top stands the shining figure of him on whose account we are assembled here today. I want to make you realize the greatness of the man whom a usurper has indifferently dismissed from his life's work."

He then proceeded to sketch the importance of Meijers as jurisprudent and as an authority on the history of law, as teacher, as friend and counsellor of his students. "It is this Hollander, this noble and true son of our people, this humane father of his students, this scholar, whom the foreigner now exercising his hostile rule over us has relieved of his functions. I shall try to keep my promise not to give vent to my feelings, though they threaten to burst like boiling lava through every fissure of my being. But in this Faculty dedicated to the study of law and justice one protest must not be left unraised. The Constitution, in accordance with Netherland tradition, declares every Hollander eligible to any office in the grant of the Government, regardless of his religion. Under article 43 of the Regulations of the Hague Convention of 1907 concerning the laws of war on land, the occupying Power is obliged to respect the laws of the country under occupation. It follows then that the removal of Meijers and other Jewish colleagues cannot be regarded otherwise than as a violation of law. We must submit to superior power. But meanwhile we shall wait and trust and hope, and retain in our thoughts and hearts the image and the personality of him whom we continue to regard as the rightful occupant of this place, to which, if God so wills, he shall return."

Those are the words of a true hero. Among that self-styled master race that inhabits Germany not a single German professor, so far as we know, has dared utter a word of protest against the suppression of the freedom of religion and conscience under Hitler. On the contrary, many a German scholar has done his best to slavishly adapt his doctrine and conviction to the philosophy, if it deserves that name, of Nazidom. There are, I am sorry to admit, some Dutch scholars who have equally malleable consciences. But these few turncoats are far outnumbered by those who, for their courage and unbendable conviction, are suffering hardships in prisons and concentration camps. The example of these martyrs for the cause of freedom inspires the nation, and strengthens it in the awareness of being free in spite of German tyranny and terror.

Force and violence cannot enslave people who carry this awareness in their hearts. True freedom is a state of mind independent of outward circumstance. It is not won by the mere release from bondage. The traitors who, prompted by ambition or greed, offer their services to the enemy are the slaves, the free men are the Colijns and the Cleveringas in captivity. For they have remained true to the freedom which the nation has won for itself. Such freedom is the slowly ripened fruit of national self-discipline. A people that has become free by that trying process and has enjoyed the blessings of its hard-won liberty possesses in that experience a source of strength and inspiration which no tyranny can drain. Freedom lives in the Dutch people, and the Dutch people have no life except in freedom. It is an industrious nation, but only if it may work in freedom. For it is a nation of thinking human beings, not of ants who labor without will or conscience.

Go not to the ant, thou sluggard. Go to the man who works and struggles to get free from his bondage in the ant hill, who works and fights for his right to free labor and for his right to be himself.

February, 1942

THE BIRTHDAY OF THE NIGHT WATCH

The Metropolitan Museum has placed on exhibition all the Rembrandt treasures in its possession. The paintings, for which one always had to search in widely scattered places, have all been collected in one oval room, and the drawings and etchings have been rescued from their cardboard prisons in the print-room and are on view in the adjoining rooms to left and right. In this suite of rooms the Master holds open court in majestic grandeur. Is it an accident that this magnificent tribute is paid the artist at the same season in which, exactly three hundred years ago, he put the finishing touches to the Night Watch? A genius should not be honored on the anniversary of his birth or death, which are but common accidents of nature that he shares with all his fellow creatures. He should be honored on the birthday of his masterpiece, the unique manifestation of his genius.

It is a false, but tenacious, legend that Rembrandt was not appreciated by his own age. His contemporaries were often shocked by his bold innovations and wondered what he was driving at. But they did not deny that he was a great and original artist. Samuel van Hoogstraten, one of his fellow painters, wrote of the Night Watch, "This work, whatever faults one may find in it, will outlive, I believe, all its rivals, it being so picturesque in conception, so vibrant with movement, and so powerful, that, in some people's opinion, all other paintings look like playing cards in comparison." The Night Watch was a daring departure from the conventional. There were skilful masters at work in Amsterdam who could paint a group picture of a civic guard arranged round a banquet table or, amid a display of banners and halberds, on the stoop of their assembly hall. But none except Rembrandt knew how to create depth and space around the group, make it live and stir as one, and move forward impetuously out of mysterious darkness into the golden light of day. He was but thirty-six years old when he painted the Night Watch. His earliest dated pictures are of 1627. In the succeeding fifteen years which prepared him for that supreme achievement he must have worked with an intensity of which only the possessed are capable. No genius is born ready-made. The mark of genius is in the gifted man's complete surrender to the inner call, in his stubborn determination to master, no matter at what cost of time and effort, the recalcitrant material out of which he must create his art. Rembrandt never sat with folded hands waiting for the gush of inspiration. He used every moment of his waking hours in training eyes and hands, so as to become a worthy recipient of the divine visitation and capable of rendering the inner experience on canvas.

Rembrandt was a restless explorer of new realms of art, akin in spirit to the Dutch navigators of his age who sailed uncharted seas in search of unknown lands and peoples. He wrestled with the divine spirit that possessed him, as Jacob wrestled with the angel, saying, as Jacob said, "I will not let thee go except thou bless me." But when the blessing had come upon him, as when he painted the Night Watch, he was not satisfied. He never would repeat himself and turn the new discovery into a cliché. Each new triumph urged him on to new conquest. Tradition and conventions set no bounds to his endeavor. He was willing to learn from his predecessors, but only in order to use the knowledge they could give him in fresh experiment and exploration. That pioneering spirit never lagged in him. It was proof against the blows of fate and helped him to triumph over sorrow and disaster. The death of Saskia, the disgrace of bankruptcy, the forced sale of his house and art collection could not break it. These misfortunes made the artist turn away from the glitter of life into the stronghold of his inner self.

In his palmiest days he never sought the company of the rich and the mighty. Houbraken quotes him as saying, "When I want to relax, I seek not honor but freedom." Freedom he found in the company of his fellow painters and among the common people, rather than in the drawing-rooms of Amsterdam. He felt drawn towards the poor and the downtrodden. No other artist has interpreted so movingly on copper and canvas the spirit of Christ. The Saviour speaks in his etchings to the poor in spirit, to them that mourn, to all who hunger and thirst after righteousness. He could not have wrought the miracle of the so-called Hundred Guilder print if he himself had not been warmed and illumined by the healing love that Christ brought to the sick. We know from the testimony of one of Rembrandt's pupils that the master's kindheartedness verged on the extravagant. This personal character sketch by one who had known him intimately is the most human document we possess about Rembrandt. It has come down to us in a roundabout way. A young Danish painter, Bernhard Keihl, a native of Helsingborg, came to Amsterdam in the forties of the seventeenth century, and worked and lived with Rembrandt for a period of eight years. From 1656 until his death in 1687 he resided in Rome. Francesco Baldinucci became acquainted with Monsu Bernardo, as he was called in Italy, and made him tell his recollections of the Dutch master. Keihl's story was included by Baldinucci in his *Cominciamento e progresso dell' arte dell' intagliare in rame*, which was published in 1686. The Danish painter's deep affection for Rembrandt still informs this second-hand account. It is, in my opinion, the most moving tribute paid to the master by one of his contemporaries.

"The singularity of his manner as a painter," Keihl informed Baldinucci, "accorded with his unusual way of living. He was a man of moods, who cared not what people might say of him. His features were ugly and coarse; he always wore dirty and slovenly clothes; and he had a habit, while painting, of wiping his brushes on his back. When he was at work he would not have admitted the mightiest sovereign on earth, but would have kept him waiting outside till he had finished the task in hand. He always attended the public auctions to buy old, discarded costumes if they seemed to him quaint and picturesque, and hung them on the wall in his studio, no matter how dirty they were, among the beautiful things he loved to collect, such as ancient and modern weapons, arrows, halberds, poniards, sabres,

203

knives and various other objects of that sort, and a vast quantity of drawings, engravings of medals, in a word, everything that he thought might be of use to a painter, He was, however, fully worthy of praise for a certain goodness that verged on extravagance, as also for the pride that he took in his profession. When some object was being auctioned that had any reference to art, especially paintings and drawings by great masters, he would make at once so high a bid that no one was willing to outbid him, and he did this, he said, to uphold the dignity of his profession. He was also generous in lending his antiques and curios to fellow painters who needed them in their work."

Thus, in far-away Italy, Rembrandt was affectionately described by a former pupil, years after the latter's apprenticeship to the master. Hendrikje Stoffels had not the gift of words to bear witness to his extravagant goodness. But she had something better to give than eloquence: a lifelong devotion to him and his motherless son. She entered his house, after Saskia had passed away, as his servant; she remained there till her death as his wife and loving mother to young Titus. Rembrandt never married her, so as not to forgo the full possession and usufruct of Saskia's estate, which were to remain his until he should remarry. The consistory severely admonished her to do penance for her sinful life, and barred the good woman from holy communion. If sin there was in Hendrikje, she canceled it by saintlike devotion to her lover and his son. She watched over both with motherly affection. In 1660 she and Titus, then 19 years of age, entered into a partnership for the buying and selling of pictures, engravings, and drawings. Rembrandt was not to have any share in the concern. All the stock-in-trade was theirs, not his, and was, therefore, not subject to seizure by creditors of the artist. "But," continues the contract, "since the partners are badly in need of expert advice, they can think of no one better able to act in that capacity than Rembrandt van Rhijn." Thus Hendrikje and Titus took charge of the master's financial affairs, which he had never cared or troubled to husband with caution. Hardheaded businessmen thought him a fool. The simple peasant girl from Ransdorp who, like the shepherdess in the fairy-tale, married a prince, sensed his visionary wisdom. All that he loved was taken from him; it was his fate to survive even Hendrikje and Titus. One little daughter, Cornelia, the child of Hendrikje, remained. But in those final years of utmost bereavement, he was able to create The Syndics and The Jewish Bride, two of the greatest works that the art of Holland has produced. He rose, phoenix-like, from humiliation and despair to new and powerful achievement.

HATCHETS DAY

Time-servers are a low-grade specimen of humanity. Their name is better than their character. They do not serve the time they live in, they make the time serve them. They are fishermen who make their haul by preference in troubled waters. Self-love, vanity, greed, and cynicism make them the despisable sycophants they are. They are willing to sell themselves to the tyrant and usurper. It is to such men that the Nazi authorities in Holland have to turn for collaboration and aid. The nation as a whole is too firmly entrenched behind its barricades of loyalty to the fatherland and hatred of everything German to be accessible to German blandishments and bribes. The wretches who fall for these are discarded by the nation as refuse and offal. They are relegated to the country's garbage heap which awaits the purifying fire at the hour of liberation. A Dutch journalist in London has aptly called the Nazis ragpickers. For it is on that dump that they rummage for the worthless tools that must serve their ends.

The Dutch people hate these traitors worse than they hate the Germans. And the traitors know it. Their life is made miserable by the open contempt that is shown them by their neighbors and their former friends. They live in dread of a German defeat, which would spell their own doom. For as soon as the forces of occupation are withdrawn from Dutch territory, the pent-up wrath of the people betrayed will burst loose and wreak vengeance on the miscreants. The popular name for that day of reckoning is *Bijltjesdag*, Hatchets Day. Hatchets cannot be bought in Holland for love or money. All the hardware stores have sold out their stock. "Won't a piece of lead-pipe do?" the storekeeper will ask the disappointed customer. That has become a standing joke. But the buyers of hatchets and lead-pipe are in dead earnest. Hollanders who have lived abroad most of their lives find it difficult to believe these stories of Dutch bloodthirstiness. They know their countrymen to be kindhearted, peace-loving people, who go to church on Sundays, take good care of the poor and the aged, and abhor the Old-Testament doctrine of an eye for an eye, a tooth for a tooth. The death penalty was abolished in Holland in the middle of the past century. And now they are being told that each Hollander is anxious to act as executioner on the day of vengeance! Lists of the doomed are circulating, and secret clubs are said to be organizing whose members are sworn to get even with the traitors assigned to them for execution. This revengeful spirit is the crop the Nazis are harvesting in Holland. They have sown terror and will reap massacre. They have transformed a nation of kindly, peaceable Christians into an embittered mass bent on vengeance.

The word *Bijltjesdag* is not a new coinage. In the annals of the Netherlands the fifteenth day of November, 1813, is designated by that name. Holland had been incorporated with the Napoleonic Empire in 1810. French rulers directed the administration of the Netherlands. Heavy taxes were levied by the Emperor. Holland was being drained of her wealth. The strict enforcement of Napoleon's Continental System, which was to bring Great Britain to her knees, was paralyzing Dutch commerce. Unemployment impoverished the working class. But nothing created more bitter resentment than the introduction of military conscription, which forced the youth of the country to enlist in Napoleon's armies. Fifteen thousand Dutch boys marched with the Emperor into Russia, and only a few hundred of them returned to tell the story of their hardships. But in the early days of November, 1813, rumors reached Holland of Napoleon's defeat at Leipzig. On November 14, the French garrison withdrew from Amsterdam to Utrecht by order of the French Governor General Lebrun. That was the signal for a popular uprising on the following day, which has gone down in history as *Bijltjesdag*. But no hatchets were swung at the heads of hated Frenchmen or Gallophile traitors among the Dutch. The day of liberation derives its name from no weapon wielded in the fight for freedom. The men who started the riots were themselves called *Bijltjes*. They were the carpenters employed on the shipyards along the water front of Amsterdam. By a common transfer of meaning they were known by the name that properly belonged to the tool of their trade. They were a rowdy and unruly lot but ardent patriots and supporters of the House of Orange. Headed by a sturdy sea captain, Job May, who was popular among them, the *Bijltjes* proceeded in the evening of November 15 to set fire to the custom-houses, hated symbols of French rapacity. But they were a good-natured crowd out for fun rather than vengeance. They carried no weapons and both Frenchmen and pro-French Hollanders went unmolested. But this sudden outburst scared the French authorities out of their wits. Governor General Lebrun left Amsterdam the next day and fled to Utrecht, and M. De Celles, Prefect of the Department of the Zuiderzee, followed in his track. The *Bijltjes* had done good work, and had done it with self-restraint and moderation. They were tough customers, but even they shared the Dutch people's aversion to cruelty and bloodshed.

The historical *Bijltjesdag* was a harmless operetta revolution; the one that the Dutch people are now looking forward to will be a day of reckoning in dead earnest. I wonder how many among the millions who think and talk about the Hatchets Day that is to be are aware of the original meaning of the name. But whether they know it or not, to them it means not Carpenters' Day, but a day of real hatchets that will fly at the throats of the German bullies and their contemptible helpers among the Dutch. The contrast between 1813 and 1942 is a measure of the hatred that the Germans have engendered in a people that by nature and breeding is gentle of mood. The French were not hated in Holland, only their rule was detested. They behaved correctly and were represented by men of refinement and culture. Charles François Lebrun, the Governor General, was a man of letters by avocation, and prided himself on having translated Homer and Tasso into French. General Molitor, who commanded the seventeenth division with headquarters at Amsterdam, was a humane officer and was generally liked by the Dutch. The Prefect De Celles was unpopular, but the Dutch could not help respecting him for the skill and honesty with which he conducted his administration. These men ruled a recalcitrant and unwilling population with tact and forbearance and acquitted themselves in irreproachable manner of a task that probably was distasteful to them. The Germans, on the other hand, are, as always and everywhere, undermining the authority their military power has established by senseless cruelty and ruthlessness. They possess no tact because they have no fellow feeling. They cannot get out of their own skins and look at themselves with the eyes of the subject people. They know no other means of persuasion than threats, and when threats prove ineffective execution must follow, no matter how cruel and barbarous the punishment. The death penalty is inflicted on perfectly innocent people for acts of charity that the Nazis have proclaimed to be crimes. It is the best and the bravest that come to grief under such a régime. The cowards, the time-servers, the sycophants are its favorites. Each week adds its toll of guiltless victims to the appalling record of German misrule and thus the Nazis, in their stupid arrogance, keep stoking the fire of hatred that is burning underground. Germany is surrounded on all sides by such volcanoes, that will erupt one day and pour their lava torrents of hatred over the German nation.

This clamor for retribution in Holland is causing deep concern to the Netherlands Government in London. Her Majesty's Ministers are dismayed at the prospect of the Queen's returning to her people when their hands are stained with the blood of fellow citizens. They have admonished the nation over the radio to exercise self-restraint and leave to the Law Courts the punishment of those who shall be proved guilty of treason. If the people take that punishment into their own hands, innocent men are bound to suffer with the guilty. There may be some among those deemed traitors by popular suspicion who were prompted to accept office under the Nazis by worthier motives than public opinion ascribes to them. Only the orderly procedure of the Courts can guarantee that punishment is meted out without injustice. The radio listeners in Holland must have grinned at this. For the Nazis and their Dutch hangers-on have been preaching the doctrine that the Code Napoleon, which has been in force in Holland for more than a century, does violence to the Dutch people's Germanic sense of justice and should be replaced by a system that allows their intuitive conception of what is right to express itself in the verdicts of the people's courts. Let us give ear to the impassioned voice of Nordic righteousness, rather than to the cold impartial opinions of learned judges. That is the Nazi slogan, and they have put this conception of jurisdiction into practice both in their own and in other people's countries, with what dire results the world knows all too well. Radio listeners in Holland, who tune in at the risk of their freedom, can hardly be blamed for scoffing at the suggestion that the Nazis shall be given the full benefit of that orderly procedure of law that they themselves despise. Since they pretend to have such faith in the infallibility of the people's impassioned sense of justice, why then should they be spared a dose of their own medicine? That is how the Dutch react to all appeals for moderation, and no one who has not shared their sufferings under the Nazi terror has a right to condemn them for being thus intransigent. The Government need not worry, they will say. Before the Queen and Her Ministers have set foot again on Dutch soil, all will be over. By that time the guilty will have received what they deserve from the people's impassioned sense of justice.

April, 1942

HOLLAND AND RUSSIA

Holland is an ally of Russia, and recognizes in the USSR the most valiant champion of her freedom. The news of Hitler's setbacks on the eastern front kindles the flame of hope in all Dutch hearts. Still, the Netherlands Government in London persists in its pre-war policy of withholding official recognition from the Soviet Republics. There is no Minister Plenipotentiary representing Holland at the Kremlin, nor has an Envoy from Moscow been accredited to the Netherlands Government in London.

The Dutch weekly *Vrij Nederland*, which is published in London, has been vigorously advocating a reversal of this attitude of aloofness. Before the attack of Japan on the East Indies, Holland was able to play the part of a real ally by supplying Russia with products from Sumatra and Java that were essential to her war effort. But now that Holland has lost this means of condoning for her lack of diplomatic courtesy, she finds herself in the unenviable role of a sulking and ungrateful beneficiary who does not, and cannot, offer any benefit in return. That the Dutch Government itself is beginning to see it this way is inferred by the London editor from a congratulatory telegram sent by the Minister of Foreign Affairs to the Russian Ambassador in London on the anniversary of the Red Army. One does not publicly congratulate a man and tell him in the same breath that one does not wish to know him socially. With Hitler's régime, in spite of the blood purge, of pogroms instigated by the Government, of organized massacres in Poland, the Dutch Government maintained diplomatic relations up to the day of the attack on Holland. It has, in the face of that record, small excuse, it would seem, for persisting in its diplomatic disapproval of bolshevism.

The rulers of the Dutch Republic, three hundred years ago, were more realistic in managing their relations with the outside world. The free burghers of Amsterdam and the other cities of Holland did not admire the Muscovite régime that held the entire Russian nation in serfdom. But their abhorrence did not prevent them from exchanging diplomatic courtesies with the tyrant in the Kremlin if these could benefit the commercial interests of Holland. The English and the Dutch were vying with each other for the good graces of the Czar. An English writer of the period, Dr. Samuel Collins, for nine years court physician to Czar Alexei, and author of "The Present State of Russia" (1671), charged that the Dutch carried on a vicious anti-British campaign in Russia by means of scandalous pictures and libelous pamphlets. But they did not put their only, nor their chief, trust in propaganda of that sort. The Dutch merchants had powerful helpers in high places, amongst others in Jan van Sweeden, a Hollander who had organized the postal service in the Czar's domains, and in another countryman called Gerrit Claessen, a descendant, no doubt, of Arent Claessen, who, in the previous century, had been the Emperor's apothecary and a favorite of the Imperial family. And now and then, when difficulties arose, the States General would send a special mission to Moscow that would reinforce the weight of diplomatic argument with a load of magnificent presents.

Such an embassy, headed by Jacob Boreel, sailed on September 18, 1664, from the Texel. In the Ambassador's suite was a young man who had just finished his law studies at Leyden. He was not a member of the mission, but went along at his father's expense to gain experience, to see the world, and perhaps to make personal contacts that might prove profitable to the family fortunes. For Nicolaas Witsen's father and grandfather had carried on, for more than half a century, a lively trade with Muscovy and Persia. The Calvinist merchants of old Amsterdam did not believe in the search of pleasure for its own sake; they approved of the quest only if an increment of profit lent an air of solidity to the pleasure. Young Nicolaas was an earnest, studious boy, on whom the cost of the long journey was not wasted. He collected data about the Tartars and the Kalmuks which he afterwards turned to good account in his famous book on "Noord- en Oost-Tartarije," a description of land and people not based on personal experience but on oral information and the study of books and maps. He kept a diary of his visit to Moscow which is, unfortunately, no longer extant. But an untidy copy of it has been preserved in the Bibliothèque Nationale at Paris. It has never been edited, as far as I know. My knowledge of its contents is derived from a report made on it by Dr. A. Kluyver to the Literary Section of the Royal Academy of Sciences at Amsterdam.

The Dutch Embassy was lodged in the *posolski dvor*, or envoy's palace, where they were practically imprisoned. For they were under the never relaxing surveillance of two *pristafs*, or commissaries, without whose company neither the Ambassador nor any member of his suite were allowed to go out. The *pristafs* would not even permit young Witsen to receive a visitor who had undertaken to teach him Russian. Nor could he get permission from them to inspect the rich collection of maps in the Imperial Library. "Being uneducated themselves," Witsen wrote bitterly, "they will not let any one else study either." They behaved, and had to be treated, as children. They were always begging for presents, and moped and complained when the gifts were not to their liking. Each slandered his colleague behind his back. In short, they lacked all semblance of self-respect and dignity. "Treat them rough," was Witsen's conclusion. "That is the only way to make them behave."

Witsen accompanied the Ambassador to court when he was received in audience. "The Emperor," he wrote, "sat almost in the corner of the room, on a small dais which one mounted by three gilt steps. He wore a caftan and over it a robe with sleeves stiff with gold and jewels. On his feet he wore yellow boots. All his fingers, except the thumb and the middle one, were covered with rings set with diamonds, rubies, and other precious stones. On either side of him stood two young powerful *knyazes* or princes, handsome fellows wearing high caps made of white foxes' skins. Each carried on his shoulder a large sharp hatchet silvered over. They stood still like statues, never moving an eye lid. Their faces were so white that I feel sure they had used paint. His Majesty is very corpulent and fitted closely into his chair. He has a fine face, a white complexion, and grows a big round beard. His hair is brownish black, his hands are coarse, flabby, and fat." After the Ambassador had made his presentation, one of the *knyazes* had to speak in reply. His tongue got caught as in a trap when he came to the name *Staten Generaal*. His frantic efforts to free it started everybody laughing. Even the Emperor, says Witsen, "covered his mouth with his hand to hide his chuckling."

Some time later, on Good Friday, Witsen saw the Czar walk in a procession dressed, in sign of mourning, "in a dirty tunic of liver-colored camlet, his hair disheveled and tied up only with a red ribbon." He was very much impressed by the Emperor's piety and was told by the First Chancellor that the Czar was well read in the Scriptures and loved to discuss biblical problems. He was also interested in modern science and foreign languages, but would not have his children instructed in them for political reasons. One of these was Peter, who was to succeed Alexei and to earn for himself the epithet The Great. His father's anxiety to keep western influences away from him were of no avail. For it was Peter who invited the aid of western science to build up a new Russia. He came to Holland to study ship-building in the year 1697. By that time young Nicolaas Witsen had become one of the most powerful men in Amsterdam. He was a burgomaster of his city and an authority on the history of ship architecture. He had written a voluminous book on the subject and illustrated it with drawings from his own hand. Witsen, therefore, was the very man to act as Czar Peter's adviser when he came to Holland.

At Zaandam, a busy shipbuilding centre, they still show sightseers the little house where Czar Peter lived as a shipwright's apprentice. The fabulously wealthy despot who came to Holland to live and work among ship's carpenters soon became a legendary figure. He was the talk of the country and the hero of various folk tales. One day, the story goes, he called in his workman's clothes at the house of an Amsterdam burgomaster. The servant girl who answered his knock looked in dismay at his dirty boots and ordered him to clean them on the scraper by the door before he entered. The Muscovite despot, amazed at being given orders by a domestic, said, "Do you realize who you are talking to? I am the Czar of Russia." "I don't care who you are. Even if you were God Almighty, I would not let you pass in those dirty boots." This may be pure fiction, but the picture is true to life. It offers a shrill contrast to the observations which the girl's master, as a young traveler in Russia, noted down in his diary. "All Russians are slaves," he wrote, "except the Emperor. Even the nobles at court, the Czar's father-in-law not excepted, call themselves, when addressing the Czar, his slaves." In Holland, on the other hand, no one was subservient. The anonymous Englishman who wrote "The Dutch Drawn to the Life" (1661) told his countrymen that "they are all equal, no way to know Master or Mistress ... Your man (meaning servant) may be saucy, and you must not strike him." The Asiatic despot cannot have admired a social order that permitted a servant girl to bawl him out and would not let him cane an impertinent valet. Nor could the Amsterdam burgomaster admire a despotism that created equality by degrading all subjects into slaves. Still, the two men and the policies they represented could exchange courtesies and maintain diplomatic relations without fear of detriment to either system. Nicolaas Witsen and his fellow burgomasters, while dealing amicably with Czar Peter, never forgot to reject the dogmas and practices of despotism.

May, 1942

A NEW SPRING

"May" is the title of one of the great poems of modern Dutch literature. It appeared in 1889 and immediately gained for the author, Herman Gorter, first place among the poets of his generation. It defies all attempts of the literary historians to label it with some descriptive name from their list of genres. It is not an epic, though its length and form make it look like one. The tone is lyrical, and much of its verse is verbal painting of the beauty that is Holland, the Dutch landscape and all that makes it lovely to the artist's eye, meadows, inland lake and sea shore, birds, flowers, herds of cattle, and the clouds that graze the blue pasture of the sky. In his opening lines the poet claimed, not unjustly, that he struck a new note not heard before in Dutch literature:

> A new spring, and a new, musical note.
> May this song sound as the song of the flute
> I heard one summer day, before nightfall,
> In an old town along the hushed canal.
> 'tWas dark indoors, but outside, the still street
> Gathered-in dusk, and in the sky shone late
> Daylight. A pale and golden glimmer fell
> Across the gables on my window sill.
> Then a boy blew, clear as an organ pipe.
> The notes shook in the evening air, as ripe
> As tender cherries when a breeze begins
> Among the bush its airy wanderings.

He strolled across the bridges, and along
The water's edge, going slow, and scattering song
Like a young bird, and in unconsciousness
Of his own gladness with that evening peace.
And many a tired man, sitting at his ale
And supper, listened as to an ancient tale,
And smiled. A hand that pulled the window to
Paused for a moment as the piper blew.

With this evocation of the peace that descends upon an old Dutch town on a summer evening the poem opens. The average Hollander does not care much for poetry. His memory is better stocked with figures than verses. But that Dutchman must be a flint-hearted fellow who remains insensitive to the poetic vision of his native town that these lines call to mind. It revives for me the Amsterdam of my childhood. The coming of May transformed the old canal on which we lived into a leafy bower under whose arching roof all sounds had a muffled and mysterious ring. People sat at their open windows or on the stoops of their houses and watched the barges float by under the overhanging trees. And then through that tranquil scene would suddenly ring out the liquid note of an ocarina. Its simple music was in perfect harmony with that evening scene. Its serenity is one of the most enduring impressions of my early childhood, and I never read Gorter's opening lines of May without seeing before my mind's eye that beautiful canal of the Fluweelen Burgwal in Amsterdam where I was born. And that vision evokes simultaneously a mental picture of an entire era so strange and unreal that I can hardly believe I myself once lived and moved in it as a child.

Dutch life in the eighties and nineties of the past century was a stagnant existence compared to the restless life to which the present generation is accustomed. The nineties in Holland could not be characterized as gay. Quiet, carefree, unemotional would describe them better. The city dwellers had not yet acquired the commuting habit. Train services were limited and automobiles unknown. One lived in town blissfully ignorant of week-ends. The Saturday was a half-holiday, but otherwise not different from its predecessors. The rich had houses in the country, but lived there only during the summer months.

Town houses were high and dark. Dutch women cared more for unfaded wallpapers and hangings than for the cheer of sunlight in their rooms. Those old houses had a melancholy charm. The merchants who built them in the days of the Dutch Republic used them for living quarters, business office, and warehouse. They stored their stock-in-trade in the attics, two storeys of them, high up under the roof. Each house was still supplied with a pulley for hoisting up the stores. But in my young days the attics were no longer used for storage. By that time the disintegration of the merchant's compact existence had begun. He had his office and warehouse elsewhere, in a part of the town given over to business, and the canals had become a quiet and dignified residential section. Now, fifty years later, few people care to live there any more. The stately patrician mansions have been invaded by business offices, and the grandchildren of their former owners have moved into modern, more cheerful and more comfortable country houses. Office and home, once together under one roof, then divorced and severed by a short walk's distance, are now miles apart, and children grow up in the country in total ignorance of what their father is doing in town during the day.

The middle class was more conservative. The small tradesman still lived over, or at the back of, his store. His limited income did not allow him the luxury of a country home, to which he could retire in summer. Nor could he afford to travel in the holiday season. A short trip into Germany, up the Rhine, was perhaps the one unforgettable event of a lifetime. The middle class was a class of stay-at-homes. Their immobility kept them conservative. They formed the mainstay of the Reformed Churches, the stronghold of Calvinistic orthodoxy. The capitalist class and the class of professional men, unsettled by travel and university studies, had drifted away from the Church and found satisfaction, if no comfort, in a barren agnosticism. They called themselves the Liberals of that age. It was a cautious Liberalism that they confessed, subject to fits of uneasiness and alarm at hearing the slogans of Socialism mentioned. However, in the final decades of the nineteenth century the Liberals still had it all their own way. They had the money, they had the brains, and consequently ruled the country. The proletariat had not yet awakened to a militant discontent, and the pious middle class, conservative to the core, was resigned to living on in the modest way prescribed by the example of past generations.

It is a picture of an era that has no resemblance to the present. It is impossible to think of the Dutch whose lives have been spared by the Nazis as living in an atmosphere of serenity. May will have made her entry as always in gay, joyous mood, but did her gaiety find an echo in the people's hearts? Do boys still stroll at sunset across the bridges and along the water's edge blowing their gladness into the evening air? People do not sit at open windows now or on the stoops in front of their houses. One might be overheard saying things that the Gestapo would punish him for. Besides, one likes to listen to the

214

broadcasts from London and New York; one does not do that with the windows open. A voice from across the sea, that is the music which is sweet to hear. They do not talk politics any more. Liberals and Socialists have had their day. They are all Hollanders, united by their loyalty to the fatherland. In one respect, it is true, their life shows analogy to that of their grandparents. It has become as immobile as was theirs. Home is again the daily anchorage, the only haven where one is safe. One does not travel any more for pleasure. Where could pleasure be found except in free countries? Home is the only place where one can find, not freedom, but the means of hearing freedom's voice. The radio is their only comfort. The voice from London or America is sweeter to hear, on a summer evening, than the notes of the ocarina. They listen in, evening after evening, behind closed windows, in hope of hearing one day the song of a new spring, a new, musical note: Victory! Freedom!

June, 1942

AN ERRING IDEALIST

The Nazis in Holland have found strange bedfellows. The *Knickerbocker Weekly* recently published a list of the members of the *Nederlandsche Cultuurraad*, a Nazi-controlled council that is to shape and revitalize Holland's cultural life with pan-German ideas and concepts. Among them was, to my dismay, H. F. Boot, artist of Haarlem. He was a classmate of mine at Leyden and one of my closest friends. But we drifted apart in later years, owing to a profound difference in our attitudes towards life and society. He came under the spell of Tolstoy's teachings and felt himself called to bring his message to the poor and the downtrodden. He said farewell to Leyden, without completing his studies, and turned to art, refusing any financial support from his parents. They were distressed to see him choose the life of a pauper. His father was District Attorney at Rotterdam, a typical representative of Holland's burgher patriciate, his mother belonged to an aristocratic French family by the name of Saintange de Chasselas. I often dined at her house in Rotterdam, and remember the vivacity of her conversation, her graceful gestures, and the charm and refinement of her home. My friend Henri, in his Tolstoyan mood, scorned the luxuries of that milieu. He preferred to live in a day-laborer's cottage among the groundhogs who were employed in work on the canal that connects Amsterdam with the port of IJmuiden. I went to visit him there. His cottage consisted of one room with a kitchen at the back. He slept in the attic, which was reached by a ladder and closed off from the room below by a trap-door. He rose at daybreak, when his neighbor's wife brought him hot coffee and bread for his breakfast. One Sunday he went to church at Spaarndam and caused an uproar by interrupting the sermon with a fiery protest against the minister's teaching. Disturbing a religious service is a punishable offense and Henri did not escape the penalty. He subsequently moved his scant belongings to Haarlem and established himself in an old house in a narrow street near the Frans Hals Museum. He has lived there for nearly thirty years and has made himself beloved by all the neighborhood. He looks a Christlike figure with his unkempt beard, his sunken eyes, and hollow cheeks, the embodiment of self-abnegation. Women come to him with their domestic troubles, he is called in as peace-maker when there is a brawl among neighbors, and all look upon Mijnheer Boot as a veritable saint. He has been running a private art school and has a great following among Dutch connoisseurs. He is, indeed, an excellent still-life painter and a prominent figure in the little art world of Haarlem.

What is there in Nazism that can attract this Christlike idealist into its fold? Violence and force are abhorrent to his gentle soul. The concept of a master race that believes itself called to rule all peoples cannot appeal to this communist who looks upon all men, irrespective of class, or race, or color, as his brothers. His parents' house on the Kruiskade in Rotterdam was razed to the ground by German stukas. No trace of it is left nor of the entire Kruiskade. Has that outrage, which destroyed a city that must have been dear to his sensitive soul, left no burning scar in his memory? The Nazis have ordered that only those Dutch artists who deserve fame by virtue of their accomplishment will be able to obtain canvas. Was it economic need that forced him to conform? I cannot believe it. He would rather starve than do anything that was against his conscience. Materialistic considerations do not count with him. Besides, he needs so little for his modest wants that even the scantiest rations will suffice for him. And his neighbors would not let him starve. They would take care of their saint. No, knowing Boot as I do, I feel convinced that other motives induced him to accept appointment on the Nazi-controlled *Cultuurraad*. His consent to serve was doubtless for him a consistent application of the Master's lesson that all men are the children of the Father. Not to exclude the Nazis from that all-embracing brother love was the surest proof he could bring of the purity of his faith in Christ. Boot took Christ's counsel of perfection "resist not evil" literally. But in his zeal to turn the left cheek to be smitten, too, he went beyond the Master's intention. For there is a wide gap between non-resistance and collaboration. By attempting to bridge that gap he ceased to be true to Christ's teaching and played false to the fatherland. Christ overthrew the tables of the money changers and cast them out of the temple. Boot sits down at the counsel table with the oppressors of his country.

Henri Boot's case brings to mind that of another artist friend. He was a German by birth, but had come to America as a young boy and had received his education at Franklin and Marshall College. In those early days he hated everything German. He had run away from the cadet school at Salzburg because his generous, high-spirited nature could not endure the drilling and the discipline, nor the hateful prospect of becoming an army officer. He escaped to Bremen, enlisted as a ship's boy on a British freighter, which took him round Cape Horn to the Pacific Coast. He jumped ship at San Francisco, and tried to earn a living as a lumber jack. But a friend of his parents discovered his whereabouts, took charge of him, and sent him to college. There he became an ardent believer in the principles of American democracy. He married a girl from Cincinnati, took out citizenship papers, and gloried in his Americanism. He never did anything halfheartedly. Temperamental and highly emotional, he threw himself with boyish ardor into everything he undertook. He was a popular athletic coach, for a time, in a boys' prep school, he practiced law in Philadelphia, and was a justice of the peace somewhere in the South. But finally he made art his profession, and became a landscape painter. He took his young wife to Switzerland, in 1913, because he wanted to paint glaciers. They never saw America again. At the outbreak of war in the summer of 1914, they took the train for Rotterdam, intending to return to the States on a Holland-America liner. At the German border he took offense at the surly arrogance of a custom house officer, and told him, in his most picturesque German, where to get off. The officer retaliated by confiscating all his crated paintings. They would be sent to Munich, and he might go there and try to get them released with the help of the American consul. So to Munich he went, but the consul's intercession was of no avail. "You had better go to a neutral country and wait there for the release of your pictures," he told him. So he took his wife to Holland and settled at The Hague, where they remained for the duration of the war.

It was there that I met him, and we became fast friends. He felt happy in the free atmosphere of Holland and learnt to speak the language in an amazingly short time. We went on sketching tours together, and talked about art and literature and Germany and America. He longed to go back to the States, the best country in the world, he kept telling me. "That's where you belong. You are cooped up here in an overcrowded little country. There is room in America, there is a future in America for your children." The American Legation began to employ his services. He read the Dutch papers and reported on the editorial comments on the war. He must have done his work well, for he was asked to join the staff of the American Embassy in Berlin when diplomatic relations were resumed after the Armistice. Friends in Berlin persuaded him to sell his American investments and put all he possessed in German industrial stocks. For Germany, they said, was heading for a tremendous industrial boom, and he would be a millionaire in no time. Then the inflation came, and his entire fortune was wiped out.

I went to visit him in 1932 and found him a changed man. Poverty had embittered him. He had become a follower of Hitler and cursed the Jews and the Communists in true Nazi style. America had ceased to be the promised land: it was a wicked stronghold of capitalism, run by Jewish bankers. It was impossible to reason with him. He had been jailed three times for wearing the brownshirt and parading the swastika, which at that time were under the ban of the Bavarian government, and boasted of his martyrdom. He had resumed German citizenship and had but one ambition: to become a Sturmtruppen-führer and serve under Hitler. That ambition was fulfilled when I saw him last, in 1937. He told me with visible pride that he was the oldest Sturmtruppenführer of Germany. He was not in active service, but was employed as a professor of history at the Sturmtruppenführerschule at Bad Tölz, some forty-five miles southeast of Munich. He lived there in a handsome ground floor apartment of one of several Swiss chalets reserved for members of the Faculty. A servant girl, who greeted me with "Heil Hitler," showed me into the drawing-room, which commanded a magnificent view of the Bavarian Alps. My friend's wife came in first, with upraised hand and a solemn "Heil Hitler." I knew that she had never been happy in Germany. She never learnt to speak the language properly, could not get on with German people, and was homesick for America. I mentioned mutual friends of ours in Holland. She shook her head and said, with the intonation of a schoolgirl repeating her lesson, "I do not remember anyone I knew in Holland. I must live in the present. I must create around my husband the atmosphere in which he can perform his noble task." The husband presently came in, clicking his heels, and giving the Hitler salute. He looked smart in his officer's uniform, but seemed dead tired. "You need a vacation," I ventured to suggest. "I can get one for the asking, but there is no one who can replace me." Was he doing such exceptional work? No, he said, it was not the work but his method of teaching that was unique. "German professors are satisfied with pumping knowledge into students' brains. But I do more than just teach, I form their minds and characters, I do not make scholars but men of my students. I learnt that at Franklin and Marshall College. No German can teach my way." I wondered in silence what evidence his pupils had given of the ennobling effect of his American guidance. I wonder still more after two years of German terror and tyranny. Our parting was a cool and, on my side, a sad farewell. Nazism blights whatever it touches. It turns faith into blasphemy, hope into despair, charity into hatred. Even noble characters, even the Christlike, become, through their innocence, enmeshed in its iniquity.

October, 1942

KING MIDAS'S GOLD

On Thursday afternoon, October 8th, New York society assembled in the Duveen Galleries to pay tribute to a group of Dutch middle-class burghers whom the upper ten of the Dutch Republic never admitted into their midst. The sons of a Leyden miller and of a Haarlem linen weaver, with several others of equally humble birth, held open court there and received the homage of New York's élite. The proud patricians who had their portraits done by Hals and Rembrandt are forgotten nonentities. No one knows, and no one cares to know, who were Andries van der Horn and his wife, the burgomaster's daughter Maria Olycan. The dress and strings of pearls in which Hals painted her proclaim their opulence. Three centuries after their death they are worth even more than they ever were alive. Like Midas of the fable they have turned into the gold of which they had such plenty. From investors of wealth they have become investments. King George IV gave Maria Olycan to his kitchen chef in reward of faithful service, and the kitchen chef's grandson made a tidy fortune by selling her to a London art dealer. And now she is on view at the Great Dutch Masters Exhibition, not for her person, or her finery, but for the magic of the linen weaver's son who, God-like, recreated her in more enduring mould than mortal flesh. Time, we say, is the just appraiser of human worth. Actually it is man himself who does the just appraising if he is given sufficient time. In the glare of the mid-day sun it is difficult for him to distinguish tones and values. He is dazzled by the glitter of reflected light and mistakes it for the sun itself. But when the night of oblivion descends upon a passing generation he becomes aware of the greater and the lesser lights he did not notice in

the daytime of its life. Stars of the second magnitude shone upon
Holland in the seventeenth century without leaving a trail of glory.
But since that age has passed into the night, their brilliance has gained
lustre from the surrounding darkness and become apparent to all
the world.

PIETER DE HOOCH

There was Pieter de Hooch, son of a Rotterdam mason and a midwife.
He painted exquisite interiors, which create the impression that his
life was spent among the rich and the well-to-do. But he never earned
enough to buy for himself the kind of house he portrayed with such
feeling and grace. As a young man of twenty-three, when he had
attained the full unfolding of his talent, he could not make a living
with his art and found employment as a footman with a wealthy
gentleman at Delft. His master's name was Justus de la Grange. This
grandee maintained two footmen in his home. One day Pieter de
Hooch's colleague absconded with a number of precious things that
belonged to his employer. He left a small wardrobe behind which was
sold by public auction except a new mantle with silver braid and two
shirts which he had stolen from his fellow footman and were returned
to Pieter de Hooch. If it were not for the documents relating to this
thievish servant, we would have no record about de Hooch at Delft.
He appears in the court minutes not as an artist, but as the victim of
a knave. That was in 1653. Eight years later Mr. De la Grange was
destitute. He had been living in great style and foolishly squandered
his fortune. He had tried to stave off the financial ruin that he apparently foresaw by paying his debts with pictures from his art collection.
In 1655 he shipped to a creditor at Hoorn forty-three paintings including a head by Rembrandt, appraised at twenty guilders, four
canvases by Lievens, two by Van Goyen, together worth no more than
three guilders, a Van Beyeren valued at one hundred guilders, and ten
by his footman Pieter de Hooch. Four of these were appraised at
twenty guilders, two at fifteen, three at ten, and one at six, making a
sum total of 146 guilders. Even if we assume that the guilder in de
Hooch's time had twenty times its present value, these prices are
distressingly low. His picture collection could not save Justus de la
Grange from bankruptcy. It appears from a document of May 10,
1663, a deposition before a Leyden notary, that in March, 1662, he
had sailed with his wife and children to New Netherland, where he
had bought the island of Tinnacincq (Tinicum) west of the South River,
then the name of the Delaware, for the price of six thousand guilders.
We know from another source that he never succeeded in paying the

full purchase price. The famous Journal by Jasper Dankers and Peter Sluyter of their voyage to New York in 1679-1680 tells at length the details of that transaction. Madam Papagoia, the widow of the late Swedish Governor, had sold the island to him and was to receive the sale price in several instalments. He died before the purchase price was fully paid, and De la Grange's widow was condemned to restore the island to Madam Papagoia. Dankers and Sluyter met her son in New York. "Monsieur La Grange," says the Journal, "called upon us, dressed up like a great fop, as he was." If Pieter de Hooch had accompanied his shiftless employer to America, we would know better than we do what a Dutch-American home of the seventeenth century looked like. But he stayed in Delft for several years. In the late sixties he was living in Amsterdam, and that is about all we know about him. The year and the place of his death are a mystery. No contemporary cared to record his passing. There were so many of those skilful painters. There was small news value in one of them dropping the brush. As many another of his brethren he had to wait till the nineteenth century for recognition and fame.

Posterity has not always been thus merciful. There were artists in Holland who enjoyed the esteem of their fellow craftsmen and of whose works no trace can be found today. Dr. A. Bredius, the indefatigable searcher for data about Dutch painters in the notarial archives of Holland, has unearthed twenty documents relating to a marine painter who signed his pictures B. C. K. His name was Barent Cornelisz Kleeneknecht. He must have been a skilful artist, as on one occasion he was called in as an expert to pass on a doubtful Porcellis, together with Jacob van Ruysdael, Willem Kalff, and Allart van Everdingen. The inventory of a large collection of pictures left by Kleeneknecht at his death contained a great many seascapes presumably by himself. What has become of all these? Dr. Bredius never set eyes on a specimen of his art. Another case is that of Govert Jansz, *alias* Mijnheer. He was probably identical with "a certain Govert" mentioned by Van Mander as a skilful disciple of Gerrit Pietersz. Sweelinck. No pictures by Govert Jansz are known to exist, although from seventeenth-century inventories Dr. Bredius had collected forty-eight references to works of this master who, to judge by the prices at which they were then appraised, must have been a man of no common talent.

The market value of pictures in the seventeenth century affords a reliable gauge of the esteem in which artists were held by their contemporaries. The inventories published by Dr. Bredius explode the legend that Rembrandt's genius was not duly recognized. It is true that the Amsterdam burgomasters who paid eleven hundred florins to Jan Lievens for an historical scene in the City Hall, rejected its counterpart by Rembrandt. But this official verdict was given by four grandees too proud and self-reliant to be guided by anything but their personal predilection. Their preference need not represent contemporary taste. A surer test is the opinion of the gentleman dealer Martin Kretzer, who, together with the painter Adam Camerarius, valued the pictures left by the Amsterdam dealer Johannes de Renialme at his death in 1657. They appraised Rembrandt's "Woman Taken in Adultery," now in the National Gallery in London, at fifteen hundred florins, a sum exceeding by nine hundred florins and more the highest prices occurring in the same list after names such as Dou, Van Dyck, Rubens, Claude Lorrain, Titian, Tintoretto. It is clear from these same inventories that Rembrandt's drawings and etchings were eagerly sought after by the collectors. Van de Capelle, the marine painter, who was also a wealthy manufacturer of dyestuffs, owned hundreds of his drawings, and Jan Boursse, a brother of Esaias the artist, possessed a nearly complete set of Rembrandt's etchings.

Johannes Vermeer was also highly valued by his contemporaries. A French courtier, M. de Monconys, who visited Holland in 1665, went to see Vermeer in his studio on August 11, but the artist had nothing to show him. He evidently sold his pictures as soon as they were finished. He did see one, though, at the home of a baker, for which the artist had received six hundred francs. But he did not leave a great fortune at his death in 1675. Painters' incomes rose and fell, as they do now, with the political and economic ups and downs of the times. Holland was, in the seventies, engaged in a life-and-death struggle with France, and when a country is invaded by hostile armies, art is discarded from everyone's thoughts as a superfluous luxury. Vermeer had probably not sold any pictures in the last years of his life, for his widow saw herself forced to pawn three of his works that she treasured, so badly was she in need of ready cash. Do we possess her portrait in The Milkmaid? I like to believe that the artist's wife, who gave his pictures as security for borrowed money, supplies in effigy part of the artistic evidence on which his fame securely rests.

March, 1943

A GREAT POET PASSES

The Netherlands News Agency in London reported a few days ago that Dr. P. C. Boutens died at his home in The Hague on March 14. In him Holland has lost a great poet. He was, in my opinion, the greatest Dutch poet of my own generation. My earliest recollections of him go back to my student days in Leyden. He was at that time teaching Latin and Greek at Noorthey, a boys' prep school a few miles south of Leyden. Several of my classmates had been his pupils, and he often came to Leyden to pay them a visit. He was our elder by only a few years, but we looked up to him, for he was a celebrity and we but raw boys. He had made his début in 1897 with a book of poems that Lodewijk van Deyssel, the leading critic of those days, had found worthy of an introduction from his hand. Van Deyssel was the idol of the generation to which we students belonged, and to be singled out by him as a promising poet was a distinction that commanded respect. And we felt our own insignificance dwindle by being on friendly terms with the young poet who was admired by Van Deyssel. Boutens was not an alumnus of Leyden. He had studied the classics at Utrecht. But it was the bond with these younger Leyden men that he cherished in later years. When he found himself able to live by the work of his pen, he gave up teaching and moved to The Hague. On my summer visits to that pleasant city I often met him at De Witte, the well-known club on the Plein. Every Tuesday he met there with his old Leyden friends at the cocktail hour. He loved conviviality and the pleasures of the table. He was a connoisseur of wines and food, and when I dined with him it went without saying that the choice of the wine should be left to him. His superior knowledge entitled him to that prerogative. A perennial bachelor, he had no cares in the world, except those that were the bitter fruit of his artistic temperament. He could be peevish, caustic, denunciatory, when his sensitive nature was touched to the quick. But he could also be tender and childlike, and when the spirit moved him magnificently eloquent. The last evening I spent in his company was at dinner, one warm summer evening, at Scheveningen. There were four of us. We had a table by the window from where we had an unobstructed view of the beach and the glad, careless sea. Boutens was engaged, at the time, on a translation of the Odyssey. Facing the setting sun he raised his glass and gave us Homer's hero. And then, indifferent to the amazed attention of other diners, or perhaps unconscious of their presence, he began to recite his Dutch hexameters. He had no false modesty. He knew his own worth and assumed that we knew it. Sometimes he would stop and repeat a phrase to draw our attention to a specially felicitous rendering. Few poets read their verse well, but Boutens did. He never spoke the lines in a matter- of-fact tone. His voice became richly modulated as of a priest intoning a prayer. The writing of verse was, indeed, praying to him. He was a deeply religious man, not of the church-going type, but a mystic with a sensitive awareness of the divine. He loved the joys of this life with a wholly unascetic gusto, but the wellspring of his poetry was otherworldliness.

His poetry is an expression of the soul's ever alert awareness of the elusive ebb and flow of beauty's presence. His evocations of the sombre mood, of melancholy, and despair, are but aspects, dark but lustrous, of the joy with which the artist in him responded to beauty's fascinating come-and-go. His early "Verzen" are tinged with sadness and melancholy.

"I can suck melancholy out of a song," says Jacques in "As You Like It." Boutens could sing melancholy into a song. Such melancholy is not dejection; on the contrary, it is an elevation of sadness into the realm of beauty, which is the everlasting home of joy. Boutens was enough of a realist not to fool himself into believing that the many had access to that pleasant home. He did not live in an ivory tower, as he often was accused of doing. The misery of the poor, the greed of the wealthy, the ambition of the powerful, the injustices of the social order, seared his sensitiveness, nor did he try to soothe the pain they caused him by closing his eyes to their stark realism. "Come not, Beauty, ere we are ready to receive thee in our house," he wrote in a hymn "Aan de Schoonheid." Come not

> While we with daily bread, earth's golden food,
> Eat wretchedness and shame. Beauty, stay hence.
> Come not while misery of the multitude
> Is measure of the few men's opulence.
> Come not until our youth has ceased to brood
> On death, and dare affirm life's radiance.

Nor can he have been indifferent to the sufferings of his fatherland and people under the Nazi yoke. For he loved his country passionately and has sung of its beauty in lyrics whose exquisiteness few poets have equaled or surpassed. But he was also a seer who saw beyond the scene on which man's life is cast. Suffering and death were manifestations, no less than beauty and joy, of the divine plan, inscrutable though it be to man's intelligence. He did not presume to explain it. But he did know that there are ways of communion with the divine through which the soul finds truths revealed that are left unspoken in the daily intercourse of man with man:

> Hush, be quiet! Silver-footed
> Strides the stillness through the night
> Greeting earth-bound men, the rooted,
> From the gods above the light.
> Soul to soul leaves much unspoken

224

In the day's redundant din
Which, from spheres beyond our ken,
Clear as star from darkness broken,
Without stain of tongue or token,
God speaks unto men.

I know no better expression of the poet's mission: to speak at the divine prompting what soul to soul leaves unspoken in the day's redundant din. That is what Boutens did for his people. But a small minority thanked and honored him for it. Poetry is not a popular art among the Dutch. But I feel confident that the number of his admirers will grow in the days to come. The tragic experience of the past two years may intensify the latent turn to mysticism that had so marked an upsurge among the Dutch in the late Middle Ages. If that should happen, Boutens' poetry may prove to his countrymen a well of sparkling comfort and invigoration. There is no cause for lament over his passing. He himself has admonished us that tears are only for the dead. But he lives in his poetry.

April, 1943

A DEATHBED AN OBJECT LESSON

Constantijn Huygens is not one of those Dutch celebrities whose fame has spread abroad. The few Americans to whom his name is not unfamiliar probably know him only as the father of Christiaen Huygens, the physicist. But in Holland his memory shines with no reflected glory. Dutchmen remember him for his own sake, as a poet of distinction, as a gifted musician, as an able diplomat, and as a cultured man of the world. He served three Princes of Orange, Frederick Hendrick, Willem II, and Willem III, as private secretary. He was an art connoisseur, and discovered great talent in Rembrandt when the artist was still a beardless boy. It was through his recommendation that Rembrandt received a commission from Prince Frederick Hendrick to paint a crucifixion and a descent from the cross. Huygens was a staunch Calvinist, but there was nothing austere in his orthodoxy. Through his influence organ music, which the zealous among the Reformed had banned from their churches, was reintroduced into the service. Nor did he hesitate to rebuke the ministers of the Church for their artificial and rhetorical manner of preaching. Observe the children talking and learn from them, he told them:

225

Observe the children. There is naked life.
Be not ashamed to imitate their style.
It's God's, who in the young instilled the light
That shines through youth. Yes, do observe the speech
Of the innocents. They know no rhetoric,
Yet take speech seriously, as ye your preaching.
Is one word that they utter ever off tone?
Does their joy mourn, or do their quarrels weep,
So that one hears no difference twixt these two?
Nature won't have it so. Be sure of this:
Less training makes the better orator.

He had not always followed that advice himself. His early poetry is
full of conceits. He loved to parade his ingenuity in coining new-
fangled compounds and twisting the literal sense of words. One
nineteenth century scholar has spent a lifetime annotating the enigmatic poetry of Huygens. Once, on a diplomatic mission in London,
he met the great John Donne, Dean of St. Paul's. Donne's verse made
a deep impression on the young Huygens, and back in Holland he
published a slender volume of nineteen poems by Donne in Dutch
translation including "The Ecstasy." They are brilliant renderings of
the English poet's peculiar diction. But Vondel, Holland's leading
poet, could see no beauty in them, and expressed his disapproval in
some satirical stanzas in which he called Donne's verse caviar for the
epicures:

Now friends, go to, and eat your fill.
Add vinegar and piccalill.
I grudge you not the flavor.
It's not the stuff I savor.

The subleties and intricacies of Donne's style were a challenge to
Huygens's ingenuity, and tempted him to imitate them in Dutch. But
as Huygens grew older, the search for the uncommon and the startling
lost its charm for him. When he addressed his rebuke to the Reformed
ministers he did practice what he preached. He was approaching the
ripe old age of ninety when he wrote, simply and movingly, of his own
birthday:

September is back again and that fourth morn
    Whose sunrise saw me born.
How many a September and fourth day,
    Lord, wilt Thou let me stay?
I ask no respite. I have further gone
    Than man may count upon,

And from my cradle on so many steps, dear God,
  My weary feet have trod
With many a fall and rise, as Thou must know,
  That he who had to go
Through all my joy and sorrow after me
  Would be in a quandary
Which he had better do: go forth or stay.
  Lord, speed me on my way.
My part is played, and all that happens here,
  The laughter and the tear,
Happened to me, and all that shall befall
  Will matter not at all
But be a shadow of things that seem to exist
  And vanish into mist.
Why stay on earth? Why don't I take my leave?
  I wait, Lord, Thy reprieve.
But if one other favor Thou wilt give,
  Then teach me so to leave
That every one who sees me die will pray
  That he may die my way.

I was a high school boy when I read those verses for the first time. The last two lines intrigued me. They sounded as if the poet was looking forward to a deathbed scene that was open to the public. But how could anyone wish to surround himself, in that awful moment, with a crowd of curious onlookers? To me it seemed that so solemn an hour should be shared only with one's very dearest. But I later learned that our ancestors had different feelings on that subject. There are changing fashions even in the manner of dying. When Huygens wrote those lines he actually did think of his death as a public function. It was the custom, in the seventeenth century, to summon not only the nearest relatives but also the neighbors to the bedside of a dying person. The higher the dying man's status in life, the greater the concourse of spectators at his death. In the collected Works of the poet Jacob Cats is a fine engraving by a contemporary artist depicting the scene at the deathbed of Prince Frederick Hendrick. No fewer than twenty-seven people crowd the room, including children and a baby on the nurse's arm. It is not clear from early accounts of such scenes whether the onlookers were called in to console the patient and alleviate his death throes, or to be edified by the manner of his passing. The custom was intended, perhaps, to serve both ends. A minister of the gospel was present, of course, to pray for the sufferer and to read to him the "sieckentroost," the comfort of the sick.

Members of the family also took part in this good work by reading aloud passages from the Scriptures or some devotional tract. But the neighbors were there to learn rather than teach and console. Their presence had, indeed, also a practical purpose. It was a guarantee against any suspicion of foul play. That may have been the origin of the practice to call in the neighbors. But it was no longer felt to be the real reason in the seventeenth century. In that age the public deathbed scene was looked upon as an edifying object lesson. That is why they brought little children to watch the sad spectacle. It was considered good for them to become familiar with the idea of death. To see a man die with fortitude and piety could only fortify them to a resolve to lead as good a life as that which had been dignified by so impressive an end.

The custom was widespread all over Europe and lingered on in many places into the nineteenth century. My old teacher, Dr. Alois Brandl, with whom I studied Old and Middle English at the University of Berlin, once described to me just such a scene, which he remembered having witnessed as a little child. He was a native of Innsbrück in the Tyrol, and there, a hundred years ago, it was still the custom for children to be taken to a deathbed for their moral good. He refers to it in his autobiography, which he published when he was past eighty. "When a neighbor was dying," he wrote, "it was the custom to take the children to his bedside, that he might speak impressively to their malleable hearts from the threshold of the beyond. My mother often took me to such scenes. Death was not hidden from us behind a veil, but presented and utilized as a means of instruction. But one day, when we met a large crowd on the Inn Bridge, swarming around a high, open waggon on which a candidate for the gallows rode together with a priest and the hangman, she pulled me quickly into the nearest church, lest the horror of the execution should coarsen me."

That sudden flight into the church revealed a tenderness of feeling that was new in that age. In the eighteenth century a public execution was not considered an unfit spectacle for children. Millions still believe in the deterrent effect of the death penalty. How then can one blame our ancestors for believing that their children could be held to the straight and narrow path by the awful spectacle of a criminal's end on the scaffold? We are wiser and, perhaps, better than they in that we have ceased to value virtue that is merely the fruit of fear. A life that owes its respectability to the cautious avoidance of punishment is not an edifying example. Fear may be useful in restraining the wicked impulse, it cannot reform it and turn it into its counterpart.

Our age is going to witness the public execution of an international

228

criminal, the most terrible act of retribution that history has to record. The children of this generation will be witnesses of that day of judgment. They will see tyranny atone for attempting to murder liberty. Will that spectacle deter the next generation from shunning the lure of tyrannous power? I doubt it. If the statesmen of this age rely on the deterrent effect of tyranny's punishment for the restraining of wicked ambitions in the future, the post-war world will again be unsafe for democracy and freedom. Military sternness can suppress the symptoms of the disease, it cannot cure the diseased mentality from which they spring. The death of tyranny on the scaffold of military defeat is not enough. Let us rather save the children from witnessing it by directing them into the Church which teaches them the life of Christ. The conduct of a good life is a more efficacious example than the ghastly end of a wicked one. The democracies should pray, with a variant of Huygens' petition, that God grant them to live their free lives in such a manner that those who see them live, even the tyrannously inclined, will wish to live their way.

June-July, 1943

VISIONARY BLINDNESS

The belated appearance of the Letter for June is due to my temporary blindness. I was operated on for cataract and doomed to seven weeks of almost no vision. The operation was a brief and painless experience. Much worse was the corpse-like immobility that was enforced on the patient for the next five days and nights. To lie still on my back in the dark under strict instructions not to turn my head sideways nor to lift it ever so little off the pillow was torture indeed. Yet I never had the sensation of lying in a lightless prison. Though both eyes were covered, I had visions whose beauty made me oblivious of pain and discomfort. They were not dream visions. I was fully awake though not clearly conscious, I believe, of being a hospital patient. I was an effortless traveler through foreign lands. I do not remember, and probably never was aware, how the shift of scene was accomplished. I cannot tell whether the picture I saw imperceptibly faded into the next or was taken away and replaced by another, like still pictures thrown on the screen by slides in a projector. I never saw them fade away, nor was I ever conscious of one materializing out of empty space. I saw each while it was there, that is all I can say. They had no connection with each other. There was an Oriental city climbing a steep mountain slope in dazzling sunlight, a medieval smithy with a huge fireplace and black, mysterious recesses in the walls, a sandy beach in a sheltered bay swarming with bathers, a farmhouse kitchen with a huge, red painted sideboard full of pewter and pottery, a monastery courtyard enclosed by cloisters with a fountain in the centre, a German beer garden with myself sitting at a small round table opposite an elongated El Greco face which stared at my equally dumb stare. There were many others. They were pleasant scenes, most of them. Even the cavernous smithy and the staring El Greco mask had nothing terrifying. When on the morning of the sixth day the cover was taken off the unoperated eye the visions ceased. I could not bring them back by keeping it closed. It seemed as if their sole purpose had been to fill and enliven the black emptiness of utter darkness.

Friends keep asking me how I account for the appearance of these visions. Were they pictures stored in my memory of scenes I visited in the past? I do not know. There was none among them that I remembered ever having seen before. But that, of course, does not prove anything. For we preserve in our subconscious an infinite collection of impressions that our waking mind, incapable of keeping so vast a store on file, has sunk into the depth of oblivion. I am inclined, though, to believe that they were creations of my unconscious wishfulness rather than memories of days that have passed beyond hope and expectation. I cherish a fancy that the scenes I saw were such as I would like, or am destined, to visit and write about and paint in days to come, foreshadowings in the night of experiences that are in store for me in the brightness of the new day.

My thoughts, during that brief period of visual blindness, often turned toward my own people in far-away Holland. Never once, however, did the thought of their sufferings in the Nazi prison dispel the pleasant scenes of my fancy. I could simultaneously think of the former and watch the latter. I saw the Oriental city in the sun while cursing the Nazis for turning my native land into a prison. The thought did not call forth a clear image of the prison; the images of sunlit city, monastery courtyard and bathing beach prevailed. Could it be, I thought afterwards, that even so the imprisoned slaves of the Germans in Holland and the other occupied countries of Europe, who are kept in the dark by censorship and Goebbels' lies, find compensation for their blindness and captivity in visions of a better world to come? The mind of man is a mystery to himself. The Nazis never foresaw that the enslaved peoples, terrorized by the Gestapo and held in check with machine guns, would yet be able, in their helplessness, to defy their power. The mind, in the total darkness of physical bondage, has recourse to mysterious sources of strength. It is like the seed shut off from the light underground which finds in itself the capacity for a rebirth and a new life.

It is impossible for us who are living in safety and freedom to share the visions of a better future that sustain the Dutch people in their misery. The news accounts of Nazi terrorism afford us but a faint conception of their sufferings. We read in our morning papers of hostages murdered by firing squads, of the last remaining Jews of Amsterdam being deported to the Ukraine, of thousands of youths being seized for slave labor in German ammunition plants, of national leaders dying in prisons and concentration camp, of hunger sapping the health of the nation. But the periodic recurrence of these news items, far from heating our indignation to the boiling point, tends to soothe it down to a mere simmer. Repetition dulls our imagination, and each new story of Nazi inhumanity coming out of Holland finds us less capable of picturing and sharing the physical and mental torments of its victims. And being unable to live with them, in agonized thought, through the lightless night of their present hell, we can as little picture to ourselves the mental visions that relieve their darkness. Let us, by all means, devise blueprints for the reconstruction of post-war Holland, but let us do it in all humility and be meekly prepared for a rebuff. For those who have borne and overcome the worst man can suffer, can justly claim that none but themselves can know their needs. Suffering ages more quickly than the swing of the pendulum. Three years and three months have passed by the clock since Holland was invaded. But by the measure of frustrated longing and starved hope the imprisoned slaves of the Nazis have lived ten times three years and three months. They are a generation ahead of us, and wiser, no doubt, than we are by virtue of their martyrdom.

Shall we still know and understand each other, I wonder, when we visit them again after their liberation? Shall we recognize in sunken, sorrow-lined faces the friends who once were of our age? What shall we, painfully conscious of our past and present well-being, find to say to them that will not sound preposterous and banal? What to the workers who risked their lives and lost many of their comrades by sabotage and strike? How shall we confront the boys and girls of high school and college age, nameless heroes of passive resistance, open rebellion, and underground movement? Though young in years, they are old in hours, hours whose every minute was a day of suspense and tense emotion. We may find them to be our elders in experience, in knowledge of evil, in practical wisdom. They will not recognize our conventions. They will not listen to us with any deference. Their hours of intensely lived existence far outnumber our more or less eventful years, and those hours have been burnt into their memory with red-hot irons that left ineradicable scars. We may forget, in the coming years, much of the news stories that we read in the papers, but they will recall, till the end of their days, every incident they witnessed or participated in during the years of Nazi domination. It is these young people who will shape Holland's future. Her new social order will be one of their creation, and it may well be an order that will seem to many of us a dangerous and tragic break with the past. But who can blame them for despising a past that left them a heritage of nothing but suffering? Besides, so much of that past has been destroyed and is lying in unrecognizable ruin that all attempts to build a future in its image will result in a soulless fake.

A couple of decades ago the city hall of Leyden, a noble monument of Dutch renaissance architecture, was burnt to the ground. It was restored in all its former sixteenth-century grandeur. That is to say, its front makes the passerby believe that the old city hall has, phoenix-like, risen from its ashes. But it is a fake front. Behind it is a modern office building that answers the requirements of present-day municipal administration. Our sixteenth-century ancestors did not build that way. They had the courage of their aesthetic convictions. After the Spanish siege of 1574, the people of Leyden replaced their medieval city hall by a new edifice. They did not attempt to restore an antiquity, but created a new structure that was an expression of their late-sixteenth century modernism. This was the building burnt and then restored in our day. It takes a self-confident generation to reject the copy of antique and antiquated beauty for a self-created novelty. The young of Holland, and of all the occupied countries of Europe, do possess that proud reliance on their own power and ability. They have proved themselves to be of heroic mould. They passed through the fiery furnace and came out steeled in body and soul. They deserve to be trusted with responsibility for building anew their country's future.

From London comes the news that the Netherlands Government, together with four other governments in exile, has recognized the French Committee of National Liberation. It is significant that among the four others which took this are Belgium and Luxemburg, close neighbors of France, who are in a better position to gauge French national sentiment than can be done overseas. The fourth is Czecho-slovakia, whose policies are guided by Benes, one of the most astute and far-seeing statesmen of Europe. And the fifth is Yugoslavia, the one nation that has never been wholly subdued but carries on an heroic struggle against mighty odds. The Yugoslavs, hard pressed as they are, would not waste their friendship on an ally they held to be unreliable. The five exiled governments in London do not share the opinion of the government in Washington "that there is no France except for the five per cent outside of the occupied France in Europe." If freedom from enemy occupation of the national territory were the test of a nation's existence, there would be no Holland either, nor would any other nation now living under the German yoke have a claim to national entity. The Netherlands is recognized in London and Washington, and she rightly feels that the recognition she herself enjoys cannot in fairness be withheld by her from France, which has unequivocally repudiated the fake front set up by Pétain and Laval and the rest of the Vichy defeatists and time-servers. The whole of anti-Nazi Europe will stand by the five Governments in exile and declare, both in self-defense and from deep conviction, that there is a France, as there is a Czechoslovakia, a Yugoslavia, a Greece, a Poland, a Norway, a Luxemburg, a Belgium, a Holland.

August-September, 1943

LIBERTY, I NEVER DESPAIR OF YOU

The thirty-first of August is Queen Wilhelmina's birthday. It will be commemorated, wherever Hollanders gather together, in a mood of mingled sadness and pride, sadness over the continued plight of their countrymen under the Nazi yoke, pride at the unyielding courage with which the Dutch nation keeps up its resistance to the barbarous usurper. Such courage commands even deeper respect than the courage of the soldier who, in the excitement of the battle, hurls himself into mortal danger without giving a thought to his precious life. The courage of the people under Nazi occupation is not the reckless bravery of emotion but the daring of determined will which derives from strength of character. We in America do not know all that has happened in Holland since the invasion. Yet we know enough to help us form a mental picture of the atrocities that the Nazis resort to in order to terrorize the people into slavish submission. The murder of hostages is one of these. The Nazis could not have hit upon a more effective means of stiffening the nation's will to resistance. For the slaughter of innocents raises its victims to a new and more vital life, in which they are more dangerous to the tyrants than they ever were before their deaths. For now they live, beyond the reach of their executioners, in the hearts of all their countrymen and fan there the fire of resistance. Injustice always revenges itself on its perpetrators. For the wrongs inflicted upon their victims sow seeds from which new power of resistance springs. Said Walt Whitman:

"Not a grave of the murder'd for freedom but grows seed for
    freedom, in its turn to bear seed.
Which the winds carry afar and re-sow, and the rains and the snows
    nourish.
Not a disembodied spirit can the weapons of tyrants let loose,
But it stalks invisibly over the earth, whispering, counseling, caution-
    ing.
Liberty, let others despair of you – I never despair of you."

Those who died for freedom are the living. They are the guardians of
the nation's independence, they are the avengers who will call the
executioners to account. It is their voice that, from beyond the grave,
salutes Her Majesty on this her day. It is their voice that calls to her:
"Your people are with you, and are waiting, strong in the knowledge
that their cause is just, for the day that shall reunite you with your
nation."

November, 1943

TO OUR FRIENDS IN HOLLAND

When the days begin to shorten my thoughts turn to Holland more
readily than at other seasons of the year. There is a sweet melancholy
in the ebbing away of the light while the day's work is still in progress,
and for some mysterious reason the contrast of the concentrated light
of the lamp on the desk to the spreading dusk outside reminds me of
late fall afternoons in my native city Amsterdam. It is, perhaps,
because Amsterdam seems in retrospect most beautiful to me in its
autumn mood. But there is also the thought, in the back of my mind,
of approaching winter and the hardships it will bring for every man,
woman, and child in the occupied territory. I want to turn this
November Letter into a message of good cheer to all of them. It
will reach them, I am sure, by some way or other, in spite of Gestapo
and censorship. They say that bad news has wings. If that is so, these
are not winged words. They are content to travel slowly. Their good
intention will not suffer in transmission, whereas bad news is apt to
grow worse by tardy delivery. My message cannot spoil, for it is
not news, either good or bad. It is merely the expression of thoughts
that must occur to many Hollanders who are separated from their friends
and dear ones in the fatherland. If there be something new in them, it
is due to the unprecedented happenings of the days we live in and not
to any spark of originality or inventiveness in the writer's mind. I do
not mean to speak my own mind, but would like to send to the Dutch
at home an impersonal message expressive of the feelings that all

234

Hollanders in America must share when they think of their country-men in their present plight.

Friends in Holland, the comradeship that binds us to you was never stronger than now, in spite of three thousand miles of u-boat-infested ocean that keep us apart. We have shared with you, for three and a half years, the horrors of war, the dread of the Gestapo, the scorn for German insolence and arrogance, the indignation at the cool-blooded murder of hostages, the despair at parting with fathers, sons, and brothers deported as slaves to Germany, the hunger that is slowly starving the nation. You will probably smile at the thought that we have "shared" these woes with you. But imagination can create out of news reports a mental reality more horrible even than its original, and pain actually suffered is often more easily borne than pain imag-ined. Worse than to know the worst is to wonder whether you know it. And we are not buoyed up with the thought by which you are sustained that in the coming hour of relief you will feel exalted by your triumph over suffering and despair. We shall have nothing to be proud and exultant about, for we have lived a physically comfort-able existence that was plagued by few and only minor privations. You will be the heroes of this nightmarish period, and your endurance will be praised in books of history and illumine the memory of future generations.

The hour of your liberation is approaching. Mussolini's fall made Hitler shake in his shoes. His Germans would say, "If the Duce is so easily overthrown, what about our own Fuehrer?" That's why he was so anxious to have the sawdust Caesar kidnapped and set up again in all his former stuffed-shirt glory. He could not let the mighty dictator of Fascism drop out of sight like a beaten dog. That would be tantamount to admitting that his own rule might be shaky. Had he not boasted that the third Reich he had founded would last for a thousand years? Within two years of that boast his armies all along the Russian front are performing elastic retreats according to plan – the Russians' plan of course – and German cities are crumbling – according to Anglo-Saxon plan – under thunderstrokes from the sky. Hitler, planless and dumbstricken among the ruins – have you noticed how seldom he treats his followers nowadays to his orations? – suddenly saw his dear comrade in crime thrown off the Axis seesaw and his own prestige flopping down with a bang while his partner's empty seat stuck high up in the air for all the world to see that it was vacant. That would not do. He had to get the fellow back again and hoisted into his seat at the end of the seesaw. But the figure had been pricked, all the sawdust had run out, and the empty puppet, slumping down on the plank, offered no counterweight to his seesaw playmate.

It was not even impressive enough to act as a scarecrow. An unbalanced Hitler, meanwhile, sat in the mud with no one to give him a lift.

There are other signs of his approaching doom. He has made Himmler his Minister of the Interior. No ruler would turn the Home Office over to his chief executioner unless he had given up all hope of keeping his subjects in check by other than terroristic means. The master race that thought to rule the world with the fear of the Gestapo is now itself being ruled by that fear. The boastful masters are now the hangman's slaves. But Hitler would never have enslaved them to Himmler if he himself were not the slave of fear. He fears his sheepish Germans whom he has duped and lied to and bullied and sent to the Russian shambles, and who now are beginning to ask questions. "If ever a single bomb is dropped on German soil, my name is Mayer," Goering once told the master race in the usual boastful Nazi style. The German people do call him Herr Mayer now. And there is that fellow liar of Herr Mayer, yell-in-the-mike Goebbels, who has been doing Hitler's lying with a versatility worthy of a less mendacious cause. The day after the heaviest bombardment Berlin had suffered so far, he went to inspect a badly damaged spot. He clambered on top of a heap of rubble and began to address the ominously silent crowd. They listened sullenly for a moment, and then some one began to intone the formula that he has taught the millions of Germany to parrot and repeat on all occasions: "Wir danken dem Fuehrer, wir danken dem Fuehrer." The one voice soon swelled to a storm of voices, a threatening thunder of sarcastic gratitude. And Goebbels, scared to death, took to his heels. No wonder Himmler is needed. For the terror that the people's discontent creates the Nazis have no remedy except worse terror.

And see what the satellites of Germany are up to. Like scared rats they are anxious to leave the sinking ship. Finland is begging Sweden to act as mediator between her and Russia. Hungary, Rumania, and Bulgaria would like to sneak away from under the German shield that has ceased to shield them. And the neutrals? Sweden will no longer allow the passage of German courier planes transporting military personnel and refuses to sell the Nazis chlorine, which is used in making poison gases. Portugal allows Great Britain the use of the Azores as a naval base. Turkey releases the crew of a United States bomber which crashed in Turkish waters after raiding the Ploesti oil fields in Rumania. Switzerland orders the dissolution of pro-Nazi groups and suppresses their newspapers. In the Argentine four members of the Ramirez Cabinet resign by way of protest against the pro-Axis policy they consistently supported thus far. The neutrals are evidently satisfied that Germany has not sufficient strength left to retaliate. The fear of Hitler is on the wane.

We may be sure, then, that the nearby future will bring Hitler's overthrow and freedom to the nations that German Nazidom was to rule for a thousand years. We Hollanders in America shall be ready to come to your aid with all that you may call for, food and clothes, money for the rebuilding of your cities, books for the restocking of your libraries. But we shall not force any advice upon you. We know that you have been debating and planning for the reconstruction of society and government and realize too well that you know better than we what is needed and what the people expect from the future. Whatever changes you may decide upon, they will no doubt be changes for the better. Your own historian, Jan Romein, has convincingly illustrated the theory that progress never follows a straight line but is apt to branch off in other directions. The attainment of a certain degree of excellence makes for inertia. The work that is done so well goes on, as it were, automatically. There is no need and no urge for improvement. But somewhere else, in a more backward region, similar work is started in emulation, and the vigor and inventiveness that the freshness of a new enterprise always inspires steer the industry into new channels where it evolves an excellence far beyond the now sluggish perfection of its long established rival. Thus Amsterdam, in the days of the Republic the centre of international finance, had to cede its eminence to London with the rise of the industrial revolution in the early nineteenth century. Holland's commercial capitalism had developed too far in its own special way to be able to adapt itself to the new conditions created by the machine age. London could do it, because it could start, as it were, from scratch. There is food for comfort in that picture of historical development. After-war Holland has ample opportunity of branching out in new and untried enterprises. Those cities that have been most cruelly victimized by German vandalism and have to start afresh when they begin the work of reconstruction, may find some advantage in not having to pay regard to anything good which is old and established but which might prove an obstacle to the rise of something better. Where destruction has been thorough, as it was in Rotterdam, the chances for the development of the nearly perfect are the greatest. The same applies to social and political institutions. Those that have totally perished in the orgy of demolition will have left room for new and original creation. It is better to build from the ground up than to rebuild a ruin. And Holland has the brains that can make the country a model of wisely balanced democracy, and the artistic talent that can create a new architecture that is in harmony with the landscape and a true expression of the national character. We in America are sure that a greater Holland will arise, a Holland purified and steeled in the fiery furnace of the war for new endeavor, and greater freedom and prosperity for all.

January, 1944

A LAYMAN'S NEW YEAR SERMON

When the twelve strokes of the clock have ushered in the new year we have a feeling that we have made a definite break with the past. We are like travelers who, for fifty-two weary weeks, have struggled on, falling and getting to our feet again, until at last we have reached the top of the pass in the mountain range that separates the new year from the old. We turn our backs towards the land of our past trials, and peer hopefully into the distance of the unknown landscape that opens up before our view.

New Year was celebrated in Europe on March 25, until in the year 1582 the pagan date to which Luther objected was adopted throughout the European continent. But it makes no difference whether we break with the past on a day in December, January, or March. A new year begins whenever a man renews himself. But no one feels the need of self-renewal who is satisfied with himself. The self-satisfied never stand on top of the mountain pass with their backs turned towards the valley of their trials. They imagine that they have not known any trials, that they have got that far not with falling and struggling back to their feet, but solely through their own strength and genius.

A Hindu sage of the past century, Sri Ramakrishna, told a parable that illustrates the folly of the self-satisfied. The disciple of a guru, a religious teacher, had so strong a faith in the infinite power of his master that he walked across the river while pronouncing the guru's name. The latter, seeing this miracle, said to himself: "If there is such a power in my name alone, I must be great and omnipotent indeed." The next day he tried to cross the river on foot himself, repeating aloud, I, I, I. But as soon as he stepped upon the water, he sank and was drowned. Faith, concludes Sri Ramakrishna, can work wonders, but arrogance and egoism are a man's destruction.

Who does not recognize in the pride of that guru a counterpart of Hitler's arrogance? For the past twelve years he has greeted himself, and had himself greeted, with "Heil, heil, heil." He believes that in him the German nation is personified, that he is identical with it, and that his master race, as it arrogantly calls itself, can rule, and consequently must rule, over all the peoples of the globe. He knows no higher power, because he believes himself to be the highest. He need

238

not chase a scapegoat into the wilderness, because he does not commit any errors, sins, or iniquities. All that he does cannot be otherwise than good. The Führer is always right. He is above morality and the law.

But now the Germans, embodied in their Hitler, stand in the mountain pass and stare, frightened and aghast, at the prospect of the new year that opens up before them. What do they see? Their proud armies that they thought invincible defeated on the battlefields and driven out of the occupied countries, their German homeland occupied in its turn by the armies of the United Nations, its cities laid in ashes, its man power doomed to forced labor in the lands the Nazi troops have ravaged, their criminal leaders tried before an international court of justice, the very name of German an abomination among all peoples of the globe. It is a nightmarish vision such as the prophet Isaiah saw and described in haunting words to the people of Israel. There is bitter irony in that comparison. The pride and wickedness of the modern master race that despises the Jews and has done its brutal best to extirpate them have their exact counterpart in the arrogance and iniquities of the ancient Hebrews that were castigated by Isaiah. "Jerusalem is ruined, and Judah is fallen: because their tongue and their doings are against the Lord, to provoke the eyes of his glory. The show of their countenance doth witness against them. And they declare their sin as Sodom, they hide it not. Woe unto their soul: for they have rewarded evil unto themselves."

"They declare their sin as Sodom, they hide it not." Indeed, Hitler does not make a secret of the depth of his depravity. He and his henchmen loudly proclaim the evil schemes by which the master race must be exalted and all others subdued to helots and slaves. They boast of their wickedness and see in their daring to defy all moral laws an evidence of German genius. They do not honor the commandment, "Love they neighbor as thyself." The Nazi creed is, "Love thyself and hate all others." But hate is a poor conqueror. Hate never wins a following, it can only enforce slavish submission. And the slaves are ever ready to seize the first chance that offers for self-release. They will never recognize the master race as their master. They want recognition of the equality of all peoples, and of the equality, within the national compass, of all citizens regardless of race, color, creed.

Another figure stands in the mountain pass scanning the future, a noble woman, who, immune to arrogance, is conscious of greater inner strength than the self-deified Führer of the master race can boast of. Queen Wilhelmina also personifies her people, and that people's strength is manifest in the unity that common suffering and common resistance to evil have created among them. Whatever sins they may have committed in the past year are as nothing compared to the virtue of their brotherliness in helping each other endure the trials of their bondage. If there is need for them to send a scapegoat into the wilderness of the old year, it will carry a light burden. And the prospect that greets them at the top of the pass is bright and promising. It fills them with joy. For they enter into the land of the new year as a united nation in which the invidious inequalities of the past have been effaced. Said the Queen in her Christmas message broadcast to Holland: "The more I learn from reports reaching me by many channels about what these times have wrought in you, the more I share your joy over it. Your unity and firmness, your great brotherly love and mutual assistance, your fellowship which has removed many partitions and made you understand each other, all this is proof to you and to me that God himself is active in our hearts in order to bring out in us all that which will enable us to build a better future."

Indeed, a better future will dawn, not only for Holland but for all the world, if social partitions are removed and fellowship supersedes old hatreds. Millions of the master race, millions of the subjected peoples and of the armies of the liberators, have fallen in battle. They have joined the great democracy of death in which all men are equal. The bloodshed and the heart-rending misery that is being suffered all over the world can never be justified in the judgment of history unless that democracy of the dead be given its counterpart on earth in the unity and equality of the living.

March, 1944

HENDRIK WILLEM VAN LOON

Hendrik Willem van Loon, the great popularizer of all that is knowable, has passed into the great unknown. He always knew much about more things than most of us, and found pleasure in generously sharing his knowledge with everybody. Now, in the possession of perfect knowledge, he is beyond our reach. If any regret can mar his present state of blessedness, it must be caused by his inability to tell us the Story of God and His Angels.

Van Loon was an exceptional case of a Hollander who won nation-wide fame in America. Edward Bok was another. Their rarity is not due to a lack of outstanding talent among the Dutch in this country. The average immigrant from Holland does not adjust himself unreservedly to his new environment, and cannot, in consequence, bring his native gifts to full fruition. The American melting pot has produced

240

a nervous, excitable, romantic type of people fond of novelty and sensation. Newcomers from Holland are out of their element among them. The Dutchman is an unromantic specimen of humanity. He is a sceptical realist with a good amount of critical common sense and a strong aversion to publicity and self-advertisement. It is no mere accident, I believe, that the two Hollanders who have achieved national fame in the United States were so little representative of the nation they sprung from. Bok hit upon the right title for his autobiography. Thorough Americanization was the secret of his success. The immigrant who remains to some extent the alien he was cannot make his mark in this country. In adopting America he must give himself wholeheartedly to the American nation. That is what Van Loon did without stint or reserve. He spoke as an American to Americans and always found the catching phrase because he himself had been caught by the spell of America.

I well remember my amazement on meeting this un-Dutch Hollander for the first time. It was in The Mad Hatter, a little tea room in a basement on Fourth Street, west of Washington Square, where Miss Helen Criswell, generally known as Jimmy, sold tea, coffee, and ice cream from five o'clock in the afternoon until midnight. It was Van Loon's evening hangout in the winter of 1919, and owed its popularity among the literary highbrows of that era to the entertainment he supplied. I had never seen his like in Holland. He seemed entirely free from all the inhibitions that turn life for many a Dutchman into a painful straightjacket. He gave a generous and unabashed exhibition of his many talents, told funny stories, sang songs in various languages, showed card tricks, drew pictures on the wall, and did caricatures of the visitors. People came to the Mad Hatter to see and hear Van Loon. He entertained in the front part of the small cellar space, while Jimmy was busy with kettles, pans, and crockery in the kitchen at the back. She had been a teacher of German in a girls' high school, but the war had expelled German and Miss Criswell from the classroom, and she was then making a much better income by catering, for seven evening hours, to the admirers of Hendrik Willem van Loon.

I came in early, one night, and found him sitting alone. "Come home with me, I have to tell you something," he said. "It's just around the corner." He took me to an apartment on Barrow Street, poured out two highballs, raised his glass, and said, "Well, I've done it." "Done what?" "Married Jimmy." "Here's luck to you both," I said, and drank their healths in prohibition Scotch. He showed me lots of quick drawings he had done for a book he was writing, "The Story of Mankind," that was to make him famous almost overnight. At the time of our first meeting he was finding life hard sledding. His wife had divorced him, he was sharing with an artist friend a one-room apartment in 16th Street, west of Fifth Avenue, and writing advertising for a Dutch concern that was on the verge of bankruptcy. With Jimmy's entrance into his life the tide began to turn. She kept him from scattering his boundless energy, made him concentrate on work that was worth while, did his typing, read his proofs, and looked after the practical details of everyday existence with which his mind could not be bothered. For twenty-five happy years, except for a brief tragicomical interlude, she performed with admirable dignity the self-effacing task of helpmate to her famous husband.

At the time of his death Hendrik Willem was writing the story of the first twenty-one years of his life. "A Report to St. Peter" was to be its title. Why did he think it necessary to inform the heavenly gatekeeper about that particular period? Had the experiences and impressions of those early years determined the kind of man he was, and did he think that those who wanted to understand him should know him in his childhood and youth? He seldom spoke to me of his beginnings in Holland, but the little he did tell seemed to hint at unhappiness at home. There was an undercurrent of sadness and melancholy in his conversation. He was not at heart a happy man, I believe, and the playful humor, the nonsense, and the buffoonery that colored his talk sometimes struck me as a form of ironical self-pity. He liked to tell his friends that he was a sadly misunderstood man, and there was, perhaps, more truth in the complaint than the friends were ready to believe. If angels exist and people his present abode, he must feel that he has come home. For he always was on the side of the angels. He loved his fellow men, and had a tender heart for the victims of social injustice, the poor, and the downtrodden. He championed unpopular causes, with utter disregard of his own interest. When his best-sellers had brought him opulence, he gave generously to less fortunate brethren of the writing craft, and his home in Old Greenwich stood ever open to all who appealed to him for advice, encouragement, and help. How he managed to write answers to all the letters he received is a mystery to me. Those that I treasure in my files were all written in longhand, that nervous scrawl of his that I found hard to decipher. If his correspondence ever appears in print, it will probably fill as many volumes as that of his beloved Erasmus.

"When Hendrik Willem van Loon writes history," John Chamberlain once said of him in a *Times* book review, "you can be certain of getting both plenty of history and plenty of Van Loon." *R. V. R.*, his so-called life of Rembrandt, introduced Hendrik Willem to the reading public discoursing in seventeenth-century disguise on all sorts of subjects under the sun. I wonder how many American readers laid down *R. V. R.* in the pleasant belief that they had learnt a lot about Rembrandt? It requires some knowledge of both Rembrandt and Van Loon to see through the author's device. He gave it away to those readers who can read Dutch and his illegible handwriting. For on page 164 he published a page from the fictitious manuscript of which *R. V. R.* is supposed to be a translation. It was omitted, I don't know why, from the de luxe edition published by the Heritage Press. "This book is not genuine," the final paragraph runs, "and I tell you this in advance. It is pure fiction from beginning to end. The diary from which this is supposed to be a page does not exist, or rather it exists only in my brains. And for that very reason it is much more genuine than it would be if it really existed. Much more so! It was the only way in which I could say what I had to tell."

Here, I think, is the explanation of Van Loon's popularity. When he wrote history, he did not produce the dead bones of scholarship but a recreation of the past from his imaginative brain. University professors – pedants he called them – would carp at inaccuracies, and accuse him of distorting facts. But the faulty, distorted picture his invention produced, freak though it might be from the scholar's point of view, was a vivid, amusing, and genuine reproduction of the one that was alive within himself. This jocose historian was not a prophet in his native country. The scholar who amuses his audience is not taken seriously among the Dutch. They had no confidence in the knowledge he imparted because he offered it in a playful, waggish spirit. Dullness among them is the badge of true learning. There was a time when their lack of appreciation embittered him. But it was not in his nature to harbor grudges. His love for the country of his birth was proof against Dutch coolness and misunderstanding. Holland had in him her most eloquent spokesman in America after she herself had been gagged by Nazi tyranny. He championed her cause before countless listeners and readers, he heartened the people in the occupied homeland with his broadcasts over Station WRUL. Uncle Hank has repaid the injustice they did Hendrik Willem with good-nature and magnanimity. Holland may well be proud of having inspired such tenacity of love in one who had so completely identified himself with America. There was no contradiction between his Americanism and his Dutchness. Wholehearted surrender to his adopted country and undying affection for the scenes of his childhood were both expressions of a deep sincerity which he tried, self-consciously perhaps, to conceal under a surface show of cynicism and clownery. That sincerity was the essence of Hendrik Willem, and when he said that the story of R. V. R., because of its sole existence in his brain, was so much the more genuine, he spoke in earnest and truthfully. That sincerity made him the passionate hater of the arch-liar Hitler and of Nazism, which is mendacity parading as a political philosophy. He was unfortunately taken before he had witnessed its downfall. But from his vantage point of perfect knowledge and understanding he will be able to foresee that consummation and the return of freedom to the country of his birth.

April, 1944

OF HIGH SCHOOLS AND HIGHER SCHOOLS

The Dutch have an unpresumptuous word for university. They call it *Hoogeschool*, that is high school. Holland's equivalent of the American high school is called *Hoogere Burgerschool*, Higher Citizens' School. The positive takes precedence over the comparative degree. The latter is an equivocator. It appraises value in terms of other values. It does not look straight at the person or thing it must appraise, but hems and haws and, looking askance at something else, avoids the issue by drawing attention to the difference between the two. It is true that the laws of the Netherlands call the instruction imparted within the walls of the university *Hooger Onderwijs* (Higher Education) with that same noncommittal comparative, as if the legislature were reluctant to guarantee positively the high standard of all its teaching. But the university itself as an institution of learning is above any doubts as to its worth. It stands upon a height that none can assail. It has proved its eminence for more than three centuries, and needs no superlative to proclaim it. Holland's supreme court is simply called *Hooge Raad* (High Council). In the same way the positive asserts, with dignified restraint, the supremacy of the university over all other educational institutions.

Chauvinism and nationalistic exclusiveness do not belong on the campus. The university is a nursery of science, which is not a single country's private domain but belongs to the world. The universities of Holland have always lived up to that self-evident truth. Leyden showed itself receptive to foreign thought at the very outset of its teaching career. It was a French refugee, the Huguenot theologian Guillaume Feugueray, who, in the early summer of 1575, was charged with the task of drawing up a programme of studies for the newly founded university, and the school did its best to attract the greatest scholars of the age, regardless of their nationality. Its portrait gallery of former members of the Senate includes the effigies of Scaliger and Salmasius, and in our own time the Dane Brede Kristensen, the Englishman Kirsopp Lake, the Austrian Paul Ehrenfest, the German Albert Einstein taught at Leyden, the Frenchman Gustave Cohen and the Swiss Otto Lanz at Amsterdam. Dutch scholarship did not recognize political frontiers. After the first world war, which severed the ties that united men of science all over the world, Dutch scholars did their best to heal that lamentable breach. I remember Dr. Ernest Cohen telling me of a meeting at his house for the reëstablishment of international relations among scientists. He was Professor of Chemistry at Utrecht and had invited a group of his colleagues from the former belligerent countries that were then trying at Versailles to restore peace among themselves. He was in a quandary as to which language he should propose as a vehicle of discussion in the multilingual gathering. But he was spared the invidious task of making a choice. Just when he was ready to start the proceedings he was called out of the room for a telephone call. The speaker at the other end of the line was somewhat long-winded, and when Dr. Cohen reëntered his study he found his guests in animated conversation. And to his surprise the language they had chosen to converse in was German. "That made me hopeful," Cohen said, "that the restoration of peace would prove less difficult than I feared it would be."

He lived to see the shattering of his hopes in May, 1940. He lived to see his Jewish colleagues expelled from the universities of Holland, not for any incompetence that could be charged to them, but for their descent from the race that gave us the Bible and the exalted example of Jesus Christ. I never thought of Cohen as a Jew. He was a Hollander, and a great scholar, and it never occurred to any Dutchman to speak contemptuously of his brilliant research as "Jewish chemistry." But the Nazis have discovered that science taught by Jews is science of a low order. They claim that by purging the universities of Holland of Jewish scholars they have restored to them the right to call themselves *Hooge Scholen*, schools that rank high indeed.

They rank, indeed, higher than ever in the appraisal of the world. But not for the reason that the Nazis allege. They are honored at home and abroad for the courage of professors and students in protesting against that anti-Semitic outrage. The true function of a university is the vindication of quality. It must raise its voice in defense of what is right and wise and true against the powers of darkness which, for their selfish ends, would trample on justice, stifle wisdom, and distort the truth. The undistorted truth is that Holland has been intellectually enriched by the wisdom of her Jewish scholars. Ernest Renan said of the Spinoza house at Rijnsburg that from it, perhaps, God had been seen at closest range.

LOOK UPON THAT PICTURE AND ON THIS

History, it is said, repeats itself. But it arranges its repetitions in such a way as to throw the variations into relief. When you place the picture of the earlier event side by side with its seeming duplicate, it is not their similarity that strikes you most but the differences that disturb the likeness. Holland under Hitler is often compared with Holland under Napoleon. For three years, from 1810 to 1813, the Dutch were not a nation but an alien minority within the French empire. Dutch freedom was lost as it was again in 1940, and the yearning for liberty and for the return of the House of Orange were just as strong then as they are now. But the differences are far more striking and significant. Hitler's rule has bred in every Dutch patriot's heart a fierce hatred of all things German. There was no hatred of France and all that France stood for in Napoleon's days. The withdrawal of the French administration after the Emperor's defeat at Leipzig was not accompanied by revengeful bloodshed. The collaborators of that period were not traitors in the eyes of their compatriots. They were looked upon as adherents of a political party which was unpopular, to be sure, with the rank and file of the electorate, but did not bear the stigma of treason. The anti-French majority thought them misguided but had no desire to see them hanged or shot as criminals. There was no underground organization of resistance. Justice and tact informed the French administration. It is only by their opposites that secret defiance is fostered among the oppressed. The underground movement of today thrives on German injustice and brute force.

It is not exclusively due, though, to the terroristic methods of the Nazis that the comparison between the Hollanders' feelings towards their enemy of then and now turns out so much more favorable to the French. The events that preceded the French occupation were so many steps by which the Dutch people were gradually led into submission under the French yoke. They were shell-shocked into a daze by the suddenness of the German invasion. In 1940 Holland was treacherously pounced upon and conquered by overwhelming odds. In 1810 the French army that entered Holland did not come to conquer the country by warfare but to occupy it peacefully. For that occupation was merely the unblushing proclamation of a long accomplished fact made acceptable to the Dutch people by a clever pretense of Napoleon. Since 1795 Holland had been a dependency of revolutionary France. The Dutch themselves, or, to be more exact, the revolutionary anti-Orangist party, had welcomed the soldiers of the revolution as harbingers of fraternity, equality and liberty. The volcanic eruption that had its centre in Paris shook the entire continent, and the Dutch Republic, long tottering on its foundations, collapsed in the general earthquake. A new, revolutionary commonwealth arose upon its ruins, the Batavian Republic so-called. But events moved fast in those days of violent turmoil. The Patriots, as the Dutch revolutionaries called themselves, were still feverishly at work to get their new political home in working order when Napoleon, who had meanwhile risen to power in France, decided to make his brother Louis King of Holland. The Patriots were not asked for their consent. They were simply ordered to accept the new form of government. If they refused, Napoleon warned them, the Batavian Republic would be annexed. They bowed to the inevitable and accepted the foreigner from Corsica as their king.

Their compliance won them only a brief stay of the final execution. An autonomous Holland was incompatible with the Emperor's continental system by which he hoped to starve Great Britain into surrender. The Dutch seaports were so many loopholes through which supplies from the Continent could reach English harbors. King Louis was too lenient with his Dutch subjects. He was accused by his imperial brother of courting popularity by failing to enforce the law against trade with England and conniving at the lucrative smuggling trade of the Hollanders. In 1809 the English effected a landing on the Dutch island of Walcheren, and although this commando raid finally miscarried, it had brought unwelcome proof that Napoleon's continental fortress was less impregnable than he would have the world believe. He seized upon the incident as a pretext for his brother's removal. King Louis was summoned to Paris and forced to sign a treaty by which he ceded all the land south of the Maas, promised strict prohibition of all commerce with England, accepted customs inspection by imperial appointees, and submitted to occupation of the river mouths by an army corps of eighteen thousand men. But when Marshal Oudinot, Duke of Reggio, the commander of these troops, received orders from Napoleon to occupy Amsterdam, which Louis had made his capital, the latter resigned and left his kingdom, and Holland was incorporated with the Empire. A proclamation to that effect appeared in the *Moniteur* of July 10, 1810.

Hitler's invasion of Holland in May, 1940, was, therefore, not a case of history repeating itself. Oudinot's march upon Amsterdam was not a treacherous surprise attack but a military consolidation of Napoleon's political hold upon Holland, a hold that King Louis' humane and beneficent rule had made acceptable to the Dutch. And Oudinot performed his mission with great tact and moderation.

Several months after his departure from Holland the city council of Amsterdam sent a deputation to Paris to present him with a costly sword in token of their own and their fellow citizens' gratitude. It might be argued that his tribute was not so much a testimony of their sincere esteem for the marshal as proof of their abject subservience to Napoleon. The magistrates were hoping, perhaps, that by honoring his general they could curry favor with the Emperor. But that uncharitable construction is denuded of much of its convincing force by the subsequent action of the Prince of Orange. When Holland, in 1813, had been liberated from French domination and the Prince had returned into his own as King William I of the Netherlands, he sent to the Duke of Reggio the highest military decoration within his grant. The testimonial that accompanied the presentation was couched in the following terms: "The illustrious House of Orange, on re-entering the fatherland, knows how to appreciate your Excellency's moderation. The noble disinterestedness you constantly showed when you possessed unlimited powers inspires in the Dutch people an admiration which is shared by the king. He wishes to present you with a token of his esteem by conferring upon you a decoration on which your brilliant exploits will shed a fresh lustre." This was uncommon praise indeed. For it came from the monarch who had regained the fatherland which only a few years before had been occupied with military might by the man he thus honored. Is there among all Hitler's proud generals one humane, chivalrous soul who deserves the thanks of the people over whom he wields unlimited power? If there be, it is not Friedrich Christiansen, the military commander in Holland. No Dutch order shall ever decorate the chest of this arrogant tyrant. If he is ever caught alive, the only order that awaits him will be to face the firing squad and meet, as a convicted criminal, the same kind of death to which he doomed hundreds of brave patriots and innocent hostages. He may have time yet to send many more young heroes to their graves. The fear of D-day coming to Holland may drive him on to ever more acts of cruelty. But his victims will find comfort in the knowledge that, although they die defenceless, they fall as fighters in the war of liberation that began its course on the beaches of Normandy.

The closer one looks at the French and the German picture, the greater the differences appear. The Dutch people's first reaction to the governmental innovations introduced by the French was to loathe and thwart them as much as they could. But they gradually came round to admitting that the smoothly running machinery imported from Paris was a vast improvement on the Dutch Republic's complicated mechanism, which was chronically out of order. And finally, when, after their liberation, they were free to discard it, they retained it in

248

its entirety. For they could not deny that under it justice was administered without favoritism or graft, that taxes were evenly imposed and were less of a burden than in former days, and that the police system was severe but impartial. Under Hitler's new order, on the other hand, corruption is rampant, justice a ghastly farce, taxation organized loot, the police system terrorism. The Dutch freely admit their indebtedness to the Napoleonic administration. But Hitler's new order will leave no imprint on the government and the institutions of free Holland.

November, 1944

A PEEP HOLE

Four months have elapsed since the appearance of the previous letter. Serious eye trouble was the cause of the writer's default. A hospital bed in a darkened room is not a suitable place for literary composition. And for several weeks after the patient had been discharged he was allowed no more vision than a little pin hole in a dark glass could give to the one eye that was left to him. When he could read again he came across a short story by Dorothy Canfield that made him realize the full extent of his good fortune. It tells of a carload of Frenchmen, all prisoners of war, who, packed like cattle, have been traveling for days they know not whither. They have a hopeful suspicion that they are being returned to France, but they only get a glimpse of the sky overhead, which gives them no clue to their whereabouts. Then one day, when the train has come to an agonizingly long halt, one of the men discovers a knot hole in the side wall of the box-car. There is discipline among them, not enforced by the German guards, but imposed by a born leader among themselves, to whom they give willing obedience. Each waits impatiently for his turn to take a peep at the outside world, and the line files past again and again for the repeated joy of looking out. For what they see is a corner of France, old men and women and children, unmistakably French, strolling alongside the stalled train. The story touched me deeply. Those poor fellows were grateful to have that one peep-hole in common. And I had mine all to myself!

And yet, profoundly grateful though I am for my rescue from darkness and for the blessing of normal vision, I must confess that I would gladly put on again the dark glass if through its pin hole I could get a glimpse of some corner of my native land: pasture with grazing cattle, children in wooden shoes clambering to the top of the dike, a farmhouse in its cluster of trees, windmills and church spires in the far distance, and above that peaceful scene the slow procession of the clouds. Supposing the pin hole possessed the magic power of conjuring up a vision of Holland, would there be any peaceful scene to look at? The eye would probably see the pasture land flooded, the cattle drowned, the farmhouse abandoned, the dike a scene of battle, the windmills transformed into pillboxes, the church spires ghostly skeletons. The news and the pictures that come from Holland tell a heart-rending tale of devastation. The pleasant town of Breskens, at the mouth of the Schelde, is a homeless waste of rubble, to judge from a photo in *Knickerbocker Weekly*. Flushing, on the south tip of Walcheren, met a similar fate. A ferryboat used to ply between the two places. It seems a ghastly farce to start that shuttle running again from ghost to ghost. The isle of Walcheren, one of the beauty spots of Holland, has been torn apart into five tiny islands, the five high sections that the invading sea could not submerge. Fighting on that inundated terrain must tax the ingenuity, courage, and endurance of the troops to the utmost. British and Canadians have performed a brilliant exploit in wresting those sea fortresses from the Nazis. With the mouth of the Schelde in Allied hands, supplies will reach the armies now fighting on German soil in ever-increasing quantities. Napoleon called Antwerp the pistol aimed at the heart of England. It is now being turned into an arsenal whose arms are aimed at the heart of the Third Reich.

The watery nature of western Holland retards the process of liberation. The dikes serve as ramparts to the defenders. Each polder within its protective dike is a natural stronghold. But as soon as the enemy's forces have been overwhelmed, the island fortress becomes their trap. There is no escape for them except in death or surrender. It is not sufficiently clear from the dispatches about the fighting in this region how large a part the Dutch people are taking in clearing their country of enemy troops. The national forces of resistance, we know, have valiantly gone into action. The railroad workers went on strike as soon as the Allied armies entered the Netherlands, and neither threats nor the promise of doubled wages induced them to go back to work. But all sections of the nation, no doubt, are doing their part. At the very first news of the occupation by the Allies of Eindhoven and Maastricht the underground movement is sure to have risen. One should not take the term underground in its literal sense. There is no lower level beneath the Lowlands by the North Sea. Nor are there dense forests and mountain caves where guerrillas can hide and lie in ambush. The forces of national resistance had to operate in the open, because the entire country lies open to the sky. They found security and shelter under the cover of impassive faces. The underground that was their field of operation was safe from invasion by the Gestapo. For the secret police could not pry into their hearts. They make up a civilian militia of more than a quarter of a million, a formidable army of silent, unarmed soldiers whose armor is absolute trust in each other. The discipline maintained among them emanates from a common determination to free their country at whatever cost of suffering and sacrifice. Their clandestine papers, which number more than a dozen, are the sole organs of public opinion. The muzzled journals which the Germans approve have no following. The forbidden press flourishes in spite of all attempts of the Gestapo to stamp it out. Its writers have turned their pens into weapons that the Nazis cannot match in kind, and many wield them courageously at the price of their lives.

January, 1945

THE MASSACRE OF THE INNOCENTS

The Kunsthistorisches Museum at Vienna possesses a sixteenth century winter scene by Peter Brueghel the Elder that has a poignant actuality in the present winter of man's history. Modern critics do not take it for an original. Brueghel, they say, was a better draughtsman and colorist than the artist proves himself in this picture. Their scepticism loses some of its force in view of the fact that Carel van Mander, some thirty years after Brueghel's death, described this panel in his rhymed "Foundation of the Noble Art of Painting" and added the information in the margin, "This piece is now, I believe, the property of the Emperor Rudolphus." It is, of course, possible that his imperial majesty was fooled by a not too honest art dealer. Or if he knew that the picture was a studio copy by one of Brueghel's pupils, he may have bought it, nevertheless, because of its dramatic subject matter. The scene is the main street of a Dutch village deep under the snow. There are houses to right and left and the center of the background is occupied by a large farmhouse round which the street winds out of sight. Above the roofs the village church towers in the distance. It is a picturesque composition that could be used without any change for a stage set. The actors are Spanish soldiers and Dutch villagers. In the middle of the stage a troop of mounted lancers have halted in close formation and form a dark, ominous blot upon the white landscape. A number of them have dismounted and are breaking the house doors with axes and poles, others have succeeded in forcing an entrance and are dragging little children out of hiding to kill them before the eyes of the horror-stricken parents.

One little boy is being slain in front of the threatening mass of immobile horsemen, while the mother on her knees in the snow appeals to
heaven with upraised hands. The picture may not be genuine, but it
certainly was Brueghel who composed its original. Its dramatic power
is irresistible. You cannot look at this massacre of the innocents
without hating those soldiers who are committing this cold-blooded
butchery. The Christmas-white village looks all the more lovely for
the very contrast of its serenity with the outrage that it is made to
suffer. The naked trees that stretch their helpless branches to the
sky, the snow that hushes the shrieks of those poor people express the
mercy of nature in this spectacle of man's inhumanity to man.

It was this picture that suggested to Maurice Maeterlinck the
subject of a short story entitled "Le Massacre des Innocents."
An English version by Mrs. Edith Wingate Rinder was published,
more than thirty years ago, in the short-lived English monthly
The Dome. "*Cet humble petit conte est la première chose de moi qui ait été
imprimée,*" the author wrote to his translator. He had chosen for his
literary debut a medieval theme that was widely popular in the Low
Countries. The little children of Bethlehem were the first martyrs of
the Christian Church, and their saintliness was enhanced by their
unique merit in having died as substitutes for the child Jesus. The
little martyrs were a haunting reality to the devout of all ages, and
their memory was celebrated on December 28 in every town and
village of western Europe. And not only on that date. The week day
on which the twenty-eight day of December happened to fall was
accounted an unlucky day all through the ensuing year. It was dangerous to undertake any work of importance on a Monday, let us say,
if the previous twenty-eighth of December had been a Monday. That
taboo was slow in dying. It survived in England into the eighteenth
century. Joseph Addison, discussing in *The Spectator* of March 8, 1710,
some superstitious customs still prevalent among middle class
Englishmen, said he had once been a dinner guest in a family of his
acquaintance, where he listened to a curious conversation. A little
boy at the lower end of the table told his mother "that he was to go
into join-hand (meaning cursive handwriting) on Thursday." "Thursday, says she. No child, if it please God, you shall not begin upon
Childermas day: tell your writing master that Friday will be soon
enough." Addison hearing this wondered "that anybody would
establish it as a rule to lose a day in every week."

There are many Bethlehems now in Europe where the people are
mourning their little ones slain by the wrath of Herod Hitler. The
town of Heusden in Holland is one of them. The Nazis ordered the
women and children to take shelter in the cellar of the town hall and

then blew up the bell tower, which buried them under its débris. In the Belgian hamlet of Pafenondroy, in the area that was freed by our armies and then retaken by the Germans, soldiers of Hitler's élite troops wreaked vengeance in cold blood upon the innocent villagers, not sparing even the smallest babe at its mother's breast. The burnt countryside, the abandoned farms, the demolished churches are transitory reminders of German fury. The people's industry will soon build anew upon the ruins and obliterate all traces of destruction. But the German nation's lasting shame is written on the tombstones over the graves of little children. The anniversaries of the massacres of Lidice, Pafenondroy, Heusden, and many another modern Bethlehem will be observed by generation after generation. They will be days of ill omen, marked in the calendars with a token of man's curse, days on which no labor is begun that requires the worker's full devotion and effort. For no one's heart can be in any work on such a day. All thoughts will turn to that scene of horror that cannot be blotted from men's memories. If any mother has survived the sight of her murdered child, she well may curse the very week day that was stained forever by the crime. Who would blame her – not Joseph Addison, I am sure – for establishing it as a rule to lose that day in every week.

April, 1945

PIET MONDRIAAN

Mondriaan's neo-plasticism cannot be understood without a knowledge of the theories and tendencies of his predecessors: Van Gogh, Jan Toorop, Willem van Konijnenburg, and the cubists. Van Gogh was the first rebel against the impressionist school. He preached through his practice the artist's emancipation from the tyranny of nature. The painting, he felt, was to be a unity built up out of purely spiritual elements, but that ideal could not be attained unless the artist's ego autonomously – that is to say, independently of external reality – was fully conscious of himself as a cosmos. He showed the way towards a new manner of artistic creation in which the artist does not passively accept the phenomena of reality, but grasps them and transforms them into a new reality expressive of his own uniqueness. But Van Gogh was emotionally too much enamoured of reality to free himself from what he felt to be its shackles. Color and light were still the predominant elements in his paintings. All objects were drowned, as it were, in their ebb and flow. That is why Van Gogh was at his best, perhaps, in his reed pen drawings. In these the line was his only means of expression. Here the linear value of forms alone sufficed to create the pictorial unity.

After Van Gogh came Jan Toorop who, more consistently than he, employed the line as the basic element of his art. But it still served expressionist aims such as color and line did in Van Gogh's work. Linear rhythms make a visual music in such pictures as "The Three Brides," "The Garden of Woes," and "Songs of this Age", which symbolize the disintegration of the material world and the chaotic collapse of European beliefs and philosophies. The lines in these pictures form a tanglewood whose purpose seems to be the ornamental filling of space rather than the expression of abstract thought. Only in his latest works, such as the murals in the church at Oosterbeek, did he subdue the emotionality of his linear design and bind it to geometric control, which lends them a monumental grandeur that is lacking in his earlier works.

Greater consistency was achieved by Van Konijnenburg. To him the rhythm of the linear design was the basic element of art. Visual fidelity to nature counted for little. In geometric proportions lay the mystery of all harmony and beauty. He became the chief exponent in Holland of dynamic symmetry. In his drawings and paintings the line is free from all arbitrary bending and capricious movement. For the regular, mathematical figures and the forms derived therefrom are in all arts, he said, the substructure of the creator's handiwork. A work of art that does not present matter in mathematical configuration, in which alone matter can be sublimated, is aesthetically incomplete. Hence in the picture the mathematical figures that form the groundwork must clearly come to view, and may not be obscured in the process of painting. A naturalistic semblance in the picture reveals a lack of sensitiveness in the painter to the component parts: the matter, the color, and the mathematical figure. Perspective is admissible only as a means of emphasizing proportions and rhythms, in other words as part of the mathematical design; to use perspective for the deceptive representation of reality, of space in the atmospheric sense, is tantamount to a conjuror's trick unworthy of the self-respecting artist.

This concept of art as a skill of applied geometry brings it into close contact with architecture. "Pictorial creation," wrote Van Konijnenburg, "in the form of an independent picture, must always become manifest in union with architecture and be encompassed by it." The painter must be the subordinate collaborator of the builder who conceives the whole of which the painting is a part. Even the urge to satisfy aesthetic cravings should not come into play. Artistic creation must be purged of all striving for artistic effect. "A truly monumental work of art does not give expression to any emotional state of mind.

The emotional element is accidental, the loose end as against the compactness or unity of the inner being."

Piet Mondriaan shared this belief. It was, in fact, the gospel of his art. Subdue the subjective in your work, he told his fellow artists. If it were possible to eliminate it altogether, art would be the triumphant expression of pure reality. By pure reality he meant the unchanging constant which is veiled to us by time and by our ever changing subjective vision. The expression of this pure reality is attained through "dynamic movement in equilibrium." Our subjective vision throws us off balance; it is the cause of all that is tragic in this world. We cannot free ourselves, it is true, from everyday experience. The tragedy of life is inescapable. But we can free our vision. Mondriaan claimed that his neo-plastic art can teach us to see the pure reality behind the veil. And because it can do this, it is the art of the future. For art is art, in his opinion, only in so far as it represents life in its unchangeable aspect, as pure vitality. But in order to do this the artist must reduce natural forms and colors to the verge of annihilation. They must be divested of all particular expression so as to free them for their aesthetic function of creating the dynamic equilibrium that is revealed in the universe.

Mondriaan's neo-plastic art, therefore, is the culmination of an historic process that tends to eliminate all non-essentials. He banned the curve from his later compositions. The straight line was his only means of expression, and even that means was restricted in its scope by his refusal to admit any diagonals. Only horizontals and verticals, he claimed, could help us to liberate art – and life into the bargain – from the obstacles that thwart our vision of the universal aspect of life. The tools of the artist, no less than the forms of expression, were simplified and reduced to a minimum by neo-plasticism. An advertising board, a T-square, a pencil and brush, three colors, red, yellow, and blue, make up the needed equipment. Do not imagine that it is easy to draw horizontal and vertical lines on a white background. It takes no end of thought to create out of these an harmonious whole, thought – and a tape measure. Furnished with these even a blind man can be a neo-plastic creator. Lucas de Heere, a Dutch poet and painter of the sixteenth century, wrote a poem in praise of Jan van Eyck's "Adoration of the Lamb" – which, by the way, was a proto-plastic attempt to represent the eternal aspect of life – and in it he listed the four mental requisites for every artist: Patience, Memory, Intellect, Genius. Neo-plasticism has successfully eliminated three of these. It needs the intellect for the thought that it takes to distribute the lines into an harmonious whole. But genius, with its emotional subjectivity, would be a troublemaker in the serenity of the studio where the universal aspect of life is objectively rendered. And why should Patience be needed in that unruffled atmosphere where the irritating sensations of our everyday world do not intrude? And Memory can be dispensed with because neo-plastic art does not represent natural objects. Mondriaan, it is true, gave names to some of his creations, such as "Broadway Boogie-Woogie," "Ocean," "Ocean and Pier," but these titles are only a sop to the unintelligent layman. You can change them around at will, call the ocean boogie-woogie and vice versa; the testimony of the pictures themselves cannot refute you. In this pure art that transcends the value of subjective memory the artist's creation is a nameless sublimity; and since it has no name, you can give it any name you please. But to label it with a title is to impair its transcendental purity. A name connects it with this tragic, imperfect, subjective world of which Mondriaan's art is meant to be the denial.

The master has not completely cut loose from it though. His art is still attached to the workaday world by the materials that went to its creation. The one and only work in which he almost reached absolute perfection is, unfortunately, not included in the show. It was, perhaps, kept out of this retrospective exhibition because it is so obviously a foreboding of neo-plasticism's future. It is that masterpiece called "White on White," in which he had the courage and the consistency to carry his aesthetic theory to its ultimate conclusion by establishing the universal aspect of life in a square of pure white on a somewhat larger square of pure white. He stopped on the brink of the absolute. Who shall say why he hesitated to take the final step? What kept him from revealing, at last, the universal aspect in a square of pure white upon a square of pure white of equal dimensions? If he had done that, the neo-plastic process of elimination would have been consummated by the blessed translation of art into Nirvana.

May, 1945

FREEDOM REGAINED

Holland is free again! It is impossible for us who have not shared their bondage to fully realize what liberation means for the peoples whose countries endured German tyranny for five long years. In May, 1940, Adolf Hitler proclaimed that the Netherlands had been reunited with the Reich in the great New Order that was to last a thousand years! One feels inclined to laugh at the ludicrous discrepancy between the millennium of his boast and the half decade of his performance. But for the Dutch and the other European nations that were enslaved by Hitler's hordes their bondage was not a short interruption of their independent nationhood. Every hour of those five years must have seemed to them endless torture, and their deliverance a rescue from the eternal terrors of hell into the bright sunshine of heaven. When daily life is lived in constant anticipation of something dreadful to happen, the minutes creep by at a snail's pace. Suspense is a mocking mirror in which the moment looks grotesquely swollen. It disfigures every thought that it reflects. Three months after the invasion a friend of mine wrote me from Leyden that a hundred years had passed since the tenth of May. People aged quickly in those years that were centuries. The young became middle-aged under the impact of hard, incredibly cruel experience, and children were grown up before they had known youth.

Fear was the women's daily bread, fear lest their husbands and sons be arrested and executed as hostages, or sent to concentration camps, or deported to Germany for slave labor. The thud of a hobnailed boot in front of the house, a hard knock on the door, the screech of an auto siren outside might mean the coming of the Gestapo. Fear also of sickness due to the lack of proper and sufficient food, of clothing, and of cover at night. For the Nazis made a regular business of requisitioning wearing apparel and blankets. At The Hague, during the final months of the occupation, a quarter of all the children went barefoot, and the others wore little wooden boards that were fastened to their feet with strings. All wore torn rags, and many had no underclothing. In rural areas the people fared better than in the larger cities. The peasantry living in isolation never lost the art of helping themselves. The townspeople, spoiled by all the comforts and mechanical gadgets that make modern life pleasant, were helpless without them.

But they were helpless only for a time. When German ruthlessness and greed had looted the country with systematic thoroughness, and life had been stripped of all amenities and comforts, the people learnt to manage with the bare essentials. And in that way they found a new freedom. Necessity is the mother of invention, and inventing is creating, and creating is a source of inner satisfaction. For it gives the maker a proud sense of self-sufficiency and independence. It makes him free. The Germans never got so much pleasure from the wealth they had looted as did the Dutch out of the various devices by which they made up for the loss. Their free press was taken from them, and the Nazis thought that without it the people of Holland could easily be turned into dupes of Goebbels's propaganda. But soon in all parts of the country surreptitiously printed papers took over the task of the muzzled press. Those were read more eagerly than the established dailies had been read in the days when the printed word was still free. They were written with greater force and eloquence because the writers wrote from deep conviction, in passionate earnestness. They wrote from a necessity of saying what they said, not from a necessity of filling the columns of their papers. And the knowledge that they wrote at the risk of their lives made the work they did all the more precious. The sense of potential martyrdom ennobled their underground labors to the dignity of sacrifice.

Faith is the substance of things hoped for, the evidence of things not seen. The peoples of Europe have borne abundant testimony to the truth of those words during the five years of their affliction. They did not lose faith in a providence that could so mercilessly try them. On the contrary, their faith in God was strengthened by the ordeal. An Oriental story tells of a village priest who asked his neighbor for the loan of a large copper kettle. He returned it a few days later, together with a tiny kettle, a miniature replica of the one he had borrowed. "What about this?" asked the neighbor. "That is yours, too. While your kettle was in my house it gave birth to a baby." The neighbor accepted it with thanks. Some weeks later the priest borrowed the kettle again, but this time he did not return it. The neighbor went to claim it. "I am sorry," said the priest, "while your kettle was here it got sick and died," The neighbor flew into a rage, but the priest said, "If you are willing to believe that a kettle can give birth to a little one, you must also believe that it can die." Thus it is with our belief in God. I have heard people say, "I cannot reconcile my conception of a just and merciful deity with this orgy of cruelty and injustice." But it is a worthless faith that is willing, in days of peace and prosperity, to thank providence for its blessings but refuses to believe in God's mercy before the spectacle of such misery as the Germans have let loose over Europe. That was not the prevailing mood in Holland. There was no rebellion against the teachings of the churches. On the contrary, the churches were sought by ever increasing multitudes for the consolation they gave to the afflicted and the mourning. The people, in all humility, accepted the mystery of their suffering as an ordeal divinely willed.

IN MEMORIAM
FRANKLIN DELANO ROOSEVELT

President Roosevelt has passed from the great democracy of which he was the chosen spokesman to the greater democracy of the dead. Untold millions all over the world were stricken with grief at the news of his sudden passing. In the annals of history there is no other case of a man who by his death brought tears to so many eyes that never beheld him in the flesh. President Roosevelt was a legendary hero to the masses of the five continents. His American critics have no conception of the intensity of the worship that was given him abroad. He was to the common man of every foreign land the embodiment of American freedom and democracy, an ideal whose counterpart they hoped and prayed might one day emerge from their own native midst. When the Nazis spread abroad the silly story of the Roosevelts' Jewish origin, they did not realize that the lie cast no discredit upon the President but added distinction to the race from which they alleged he had sprung. Dutch-Americans are proud of the distinction Roosevelt's origin from Holland lends to their group; and the Netherland-America Foundation was never more greatly honored than when the President accepted honorary membership proffered to him in a letter Mr. Thomas J. Watson addressed to him on March 7, 1944. "This action on your part," the President wrote, "brings back happy memories of the days when I helped to organize the original body."

It was Mr. Edward Bok who persuaded Mr. Roosevelt at the outset to join its Board of Directors and accept the Vice-Presidency. That was not long after the elections of 1920 in which Mr. Roosevelt had been the running mate of the Democrats' Presidential candidate, Mr. James M. Cox. The Board had many a meeting either in Mr. Roosevelt's downtown office or at his private residence in 65th Street just west of Park Avenue. When Mr. Bok could not be present Mr. Roosevelt presided. He could not have given more serious attention to the matter in hand if weighty affairs of state had been at issue. When the business was over he never appeared to be in a hurry to dismiss us. He always had time to spare for a friendly chat. On one such occasion I described to him an old sketch-book I had once picked up at The Hague full of drawings by the Dutch-American marine painter Albertus van Beest, and I told him of my intention of going to New Bedford to collect material for a biography of the artist. For it was there that he had worked a good part of the time he had lived in America. Mr. Roosevelt wanted to see the book and, being a lover of ships, found so much pleasure in the sketches that he became as keenly interested as I was in the story of Van Beest's New Bedford years. He gave me a letter of introduction to an aunt of his in New Bedford, and with her aid I collected much information about the painter, who was much better remembered there, I found, than he was in his native country. It was a long time before I had an opportunity of giving Mr. Roosevelt a report of my visit to the old whaling town. For he had been stricken meanwhile by the paralysis that was supposed, at the time, to have frustrated all his hopes of a great career. I remember with how heavy a heart I went to call on him when at last I could be admitted. I expected to find him broken in health and in spirit. But there he was, undaunted as ever, his crippled body drawing vigor from his inner strength. After his election to the Governorship I witnessed an incident one day that was symbolic of that heroic resurgence from defeat. It happened at an annual dinner of the Holland Society. The entire gathering rose when the Governor was conducted to his seat by two adjutants. They left him standing, supported by his hands upon the table, and smilingly acknowledging the applause. Suddenly he collapsed and disappeared from sight. The guests stood petrified, their clapping hands stilled in the frost of suspense. The two adjutants ran back to the centre of the dais; they raised the Governor up on his feet; and with the same gallant smile he stood bowing his thanks for the thundering ovation that greeted his reappearance. The awful news of his sudden removal from the world's scene has stunned mankind. But his unconquerable spirit will rise from the defeat of death and be an inspiration to Americans and foreigners alike, among history's unforgotten men one of the greatest.

July, 1945

THE VIRTUE OF ILLEGALITY

The last quarter of the nineteenth century produced a rank crop in Holland of shady companies that sought to stimulate emigration to the United States. The promotors were usually not prompted by an excessive love of their fellow men. They did not boost the golden opportunities that the Far West offered from a Christian desire to help the victims of economic ills and over-population to a better lot in the New World. As agents of real estate speculators and translatlantic steamship lines they drummed up buyers of land and steerage passengers. Whether the land was worth the money paid for it was no concern of theirs, nor did they care to make sure that the treatment on board was decent. Their responsibilities were limited to supplying the human material that the Far West needed and the steamship lines were anxious to transport. Misrepresentation was an essential part of the game. The innocents who swallowed the bait paid for their credulity with terrible hardships, often with death. And yet, the false prophets who fully deserved their curses unwittingly foretold the future correctly. Many of their dupes survive in prosperous offspring. The second and third generations, now scattered throughout the Far West, and glorying in their American citizenship, have forgotten the story of their grandparents' disillusion and sufferings. Or if they remember, they will think of their hardships as the initial price that had to be paid for the wellbeing that is theirs. One Dutch promoter wrote in the early seventies, "The Netherlanders who will settle in California have the certainty that their posterity is destined to have a glorious future as citizens of a powerful commonwealth when the old fatherland will have lost its freedom or perished perhaps in one of the many great wars with which Europe's future is pregnant."

Five years ago it seemed as if that forecast had come true. Thousands who were living in Holland under the Nazi yoke must have wished they had emigrated in time to the free United States. But the majority of the Dutch did better. Instead of regretting their failure to emigrate they did their utmost to make the German occupation of Holland a failure. Thanks to the underground forces of resistance the fatherland, though involved in the greatest war that ever ravaged Europe, proved that it was imperishable. The nation had saved itself before it was liberated by the Allied armies. These lifted the yoke off the neck of a nation that under the load had saved its self-respect. And he who respects himself knows no despair. I am struck by the expressions of confidence and determination in the letters from Holland I have begun to receive. "We are still alive," writes my youngest brother, "and full of courage to start life anew." A friend at The Hague, who was editor during the occupation of an underground paper, writes me that he is planning to continue it as a fortnightly issue. Remarkable energy in a man of over seventy who for the last eight weeks before the liberation had to subsist, he tells me, on no more than a small daily ration of dry bread. During the bombardment of the Bezuidenhout quarter on March 3rd, all the windowpanes and most of the doors, walls, and ceilings of his house were broken, and it took him a month to make it habitable again with the assistance of his three sons. They had to do most of the work themselves, for outside help was not available. That was hard labor for undernourished bodies. But he survived it and is now starting not only his own life anew but that of a periodical into the bargain.

We have been kept informed of life in Holland under German rule, but much of that information, even when it seemed reliable, lacked the convincing quality that private letters derive from the recipient's close acquaintance with the writers and the scenes they refer to. I had read about people starving at The Hague, but when I am told by a friend, prominent journalist and former member of parliament, that for eight weeks his daily food was a handful of dry bread, my mental picture of the hunger plague, until then out of focus, acquires sharpness and precision. I knew that Amsterdam was a city without gas and electricity and telephone service, without transportation facilities, without all the comforts and amenities that we have come to take for granted. But that general concept of privation becomes a graphic, clear-cut picture that my eyes can see, when I read my brother's description of how he, with his wife and daughter, survived in those terrible final months. They baked their own bread on a stove in the living room, which they kept burning at excessive expense. Four bushels of anthracite cost about $140. The black market kept them warm and alive, but a fortune went into the purchase of food and fuel. Another brother was locked up in the concentration camp at Amersfoort for having offered shelter to a Jew. It is a measure of the viciousness of the Nazi system of government that under it an act of Christian charity was punishable as a felony. Knaves occupied the seats of authority and good Christians starved in prisons and torture camps. For Nazi law was such a wicked perversion of justice that none could live up to his Christian faith except by ceasing to be law-abiding. Hence, illegality lost its opprobrium. To do the illegal was thwarting the Germans, and therefore justifiable and patriotic. To join the illegal forces of resistance was serving the fatherland.

With the return of the Queen to The Hague illegality got its reward. But in achieving its aim it ceased to exist, or, to be more exact, lost its reason for existence. The laws it had justifiably broken left the country with the Nazis. Leaders of the resistance forces are among the ministers in the new Government, because the daring with which they organized illegality under the Nazis is a guarantee of their loyal enforcement of the nation-made law of the land. Five of them faced torture and death in concentration camps, where Nazi brutality must have proved to their satisfaction that the breaking of the law under such a regime was the only true course.

Seven of the sixteen members of the new Cabinet of Ministers were born in this century. It is not often that youth predominates in a Netherlands government. Before the war statesmanship was considered the exclusive attribute of old age. It was not safe to entrust a portfolio to a man in his forties. He might do reckless things in youthful ardor. Don't trust him with responsibility till the blood begins to creep in his veins. The nation learnt to its pain what kind of security is won by pusillanimous reliance on safe old age. The elder statesman Jonkheer De Geer was a member of the Netherlands government in exile. He was a fainthearted waverer, broke his given word to Her Majesty, and turned disloyal to his country. His disgrace was an object lesson that did not pass unheeded. Youth now stands at the helm. The majority of the ministers are under fifty, and one of them, S. L. Mansholt, Minister of Food Supply, Agriculture, and Fisheries, is only thirty-six years of age. Though young in years, he is old in days of experience. He is an agricultural expert by profession, has worked

262

on plantations in the East Indies, and made his knowledge useful, after his return to Holland, in the administration of the newly reclaimed Wieringermeer Polder. During the occupation he did dangerous underground work in supplying food to concentration camp victims and to the starved in the hunger provinces in the west of the country. Such men can be trusted to face the difficulties that will confront the Dutch government in the coming months with alertness and intrepidity. They will have courage to break new ground, and vision to lead the nation along untried paths. They are leaders of emigrants from the ravaged past into an uncharted future, even braver than those who crossed the ocean to build a new life in California. For rather than let the old fatherland lose its freedom and perish, they risked the perilous crossing from the rule of law to illegality in order to save the fatherland from slavery and death.

November, 1945

DIVIDED ALLEGIANCE

All loyal American citizens of German descent – and they constitute a large majority among German Americans – have good reason for loathing the Nazis and all their works. The cloud of suspicion that Nazi duplicity has raised casts a shadow even upon immigrants of non-German stock. Hitler has supplied the Rankins and Bilbos in our midst with a pretext for denouncing all aliens, forgetful of the fact that they themselves are descendants of aliens. In order to represent them as unreliable citizens they call them people with a divided allegiance. They seem to assume that every foreigner comes to America with only a limited and unalterable allotment of loyalty, which he has now to divide into two halves. But love of country and loyalty cannot be weighed and measured and sliced like loaves of bread. Primitive peoples think they can. When a Javanese child is sick and crying with pain the father will take a stick and beat his wife. The Dutch missionary who told me this could not understand why he did. Not out of viciousness, he realized, for when he tried to intervene the mother remonstrated; she was evidently perfectly willing to be beaten. The missionary had this strange behavior explained to him by a colleague from New Zealand who came to visit him on his way back to England. When a Maori boy, he said, has fallen out of a tree and hurt himself, the father will break a branch off the tree and beat everybody around with it. Pain to them is something concrete that you can distribute, and by dividing it among nine bystanders, the boy's pain is supposed to be reduced to one-tenth of its vehemence. In the same way the Javanese mother, by taking a beating, relieved her child of half its pain. But love of country cannot be divided that way, one-half for the native land, the other for the land of one's adoption. Love is an emotional asset of variable strength and content. As Shelley says in *Epipsychidion*:

> True love in this differs from gold and clay
> That to divide is not to take away.
> Love is like understanding that grows bright
> Gazing on many truths.

That is equally true of love of country. Both the land of the immigrant's birth and his adopted one may receive from him a larger measure of devotion than he was able to render to his native country before he left it. I can testify of myself, at any rate, that Holland is dearer to me now than it ever was; yet that does not prevent me from loving America with a wholehearted and steadfast loyalty. When the immigrant joins the singing of "My country, 'tis of thee, Sweet land of Liberty, Of thee I sing," he does not sing it with less fervor because it never was the country of his fathers' pride. It is the country of his own pride, and he has reason to be proud that it is his country, for he made it his by his own free choice.

The Dutch immigrant, though, who sets foot on Manhattan for the first time comes to an island that actually was the pride of his seventeenth-century forebears. It is an un-Dutch scene that confronts him, this petrified forest of towering skyscrapers. For in Holland everything is on a modest scale. We like littleness because it suggests to us neatness, finish, beauty. Dutch speech uses a profusion of diminutives, especially when we want to give expression to our inner well-being. It was before the war our way of saying that all was well with the world. Hence New York, when first seen from the Bay by the immigrant from Holland, may terrify him by its size. But his terror soon subsides. For he finds in this giant city something precious that is thoroughly Dutch, which is, in fact, an inheritance of New York's Dutch past; I mean the city's broadminded tolerance. New Yorkers do not scoff at recent immigrants with a twofold allegiance. Even those whose American past goes back to New Netherland days do not forget that their earliest ancestor was himself an alien to this country. I had the privilege, the other day, of being the guest of the Holland Society. There I sat among descendants of Peter Stuyvesant's contemporaries and felt at home among them. They even honored the newcomer from the land of their own distant origin by presenting him with the Society's gold medal which is annually awarded to an American they consider worthy of the distinction. To me the medal was a symbol of that twofold love of country of which I spoke. It has two sides facing opposite directions. But who would say that these two are divided? They are joined within an unbreakable rim that holds them as one. The reverse is not separate from the medal, it is part of the medal, and the medal is part of its reverse. Neither exists without the other. In the same way, in the immigrant the two loves for the native and for the adopted country are not separate and conflicting affections, they are two facets of one emotion. I treasure the Holland Society medal as the American I have become and as the Hollander I shall remain at heart.

January, 1946

FORGIVENESS

In every language ancient wisdom lies embedded of which the speakers are seldom aware. We use words and phrases in which the experience of the distant past has been crystallized; but we use them so mechanically in everyday intercourse that we fail to realize the beauty and the effectiveness of those thought crystals. Only the linguist whose business it is to study speech collects and treasures them and often wonders whether the language is not wiser than its speakers. The Dutch word for war is *oorlog*, an ancient Germanic compound, which the etymologists have not been able to explain satisfactorily. Its original meaning was, most likely, dissolution, decomposition; it certainly never expressed our primitive ancestors' glorification of war. The Dutch language also knows the word *war*, but it has there the exclusive sense of confusion. Politicians and flag-waving patriots may shout from platforms and palace balconies that war is a glorious exploit and that it is beautiful to die for the fatherland, but the language, which voices ancient experience, knows that war is identical with confusion and condemns it implicitly. The phrase *in de war* is used in Dutch as a euphemism for crazy. War is confusion worse confounded and a world at war is, indeed, a world gone mad.

The war is over, but the world is still madly confused. Which is tantamount to saying that the war is still on. The new year inherits nothing but confusion from its predecessor, and confusion is strife. We need only glance at the headlines on the front page of our morning paper to realize that the world, under this so-called peace it has newly won, is living in a warlike upheaval. Hatred is rife everywhere. The memory of German and Japanese outrages is like a frost in men's hearts that will not let forgiveness grow. According to an estimate of the Director of the Central Bureau of Statistics at The Hague two hundred

265

thousand Hollanders perished as a result of the war; that is twenty out of one thousand inhabitants. One cannot write off such a heavy loss of precious lives in a relenting mood. The new year is not yet the time for forgiving and forgetting.

Yet forgiveness is a Christian virtue which true followers of Christ must cultivate. The noblest answer to Hitler's gospel of hate can be found in the Epistle of Paul to the Romans: "Avenge not yourselves, but rather give place unto wrath: for it is written, Vengeance is mine, I will repay, saith the Lord. Therefore, if thine enemy hunger, feed him; if he thirst, give him drink; for in so doing thou shalt heap coals of fire on his head. Be not overcome of evil, but overcome evil with good." That is, indeed, a counsel of perfection which it is hard for even a devout Christian to turn into practice. The churches in the Netherlands do not expect their members to live up to its letter. The utmost they demand from them is the negative virtue of abstaining from vengeance. In a joint pulpit message which was read in all Dutch churches on October 28th of last year the Catholic hierarchy and the ministry of the Protestant denominations addressed an earnest appeal to office holders and congregations that they should "impress upon all that the prestige of our people stands or falls with the answer to the question whether in the Netherlands action is according to justice or according to vengeance and hatred. This applies especially to the treatment accorded to political prisoners. It would be a national disgrace if after five years of struggle against violations of the law and of suffering under the most cruel practices of German barbarism a similar spirit should infect our people. The churches, therefore, will support the Government in opposing unjust and arbitrary treatment of these prisoners. They call upon the Dutch people to prove themselves immune to the contagion of German depravity and aware of the truth that the strict maintenance of right implies the exercise of the mercy of Christ."

This admonition comes with special force and persuasiveness from the leaders of the churches, for they never wavered, during the German occupation, in their steadfast resolve not to submit to the dictates of iniquity. They had the courage to protest, again and again, when Nazi orders violated all concepts of decency and Christian charity, and many a priest and minister paid with his life for following Christ rather than Hitler. To cite only one instance out of many: Early in September, 1941, Nazism was denounced in a pastoral letter signed by the five bishops in protest against German interference with Catholic trade unions. The Workers Union had been ordered by the Nazis to affiliate with the National Socialist Party, and since the Church took the stand that membership in that party automatically excluded Cath-

266

olics from the sacraments of the Church, the clergy could not remain silent when so arbitrary a measure confronted Catholic workers with the choice between loss of livelihood or excommunication. "Openly and loudly we raise our voice," the bishops wrote," against the injustice done to these tens of thousands by robbing them of their social status. We protest against the moral constraint and the attempt to force upon them a conception of life conflicting with their religious convictions."

The men who, at the danger of their lives, dared vindicate the rights of their flocks have thereby won the right to warn them against the evils of vengeance. None more so than Archbishop Jan de Jongh, the head of the Catholic Church in the Netherlands. He was fined a few times by the Nazis, but they never dared imprison him. Intrepidity and determination are expressed in the lines of his face. Most Dutch Catholics belong to the southern provinces of Brabant and Limburg, but Monsignor De Jongh is of Frisian ancestry. His father was the local baker of the village of Nes, on the island of Ameland, in the far north of Holland, a windswept and sea-menaced strip of land where nature's inclemency breeds a hardy race. The people of Friesland are proverbially obstinate. *Koppige Friezen*, headstrong Frisians, they are called by their Dutch countrymen. The Nazis found, to their annoyance, that the Frisian Archbishop did not deviate from the type. They did him an inestimable service. For by their persecution they helped him, unintentionally, to rise to impressive stature in the eyes of his countrymen, both Catholics and Protestants, a revered embodiment of the people's will to live their own lives in freedom of conscience. Monsignor De Jongh is also a scholar of distinction and the author of a Handbook of Church History in four volumes, which had reached a third edition before the German invasion. His outstanding merits recently won him just reward when he was one of the thirty-two prelates who were named by Pope Pius XII to become members of the Sacred College of Cardinals.

February, 1946

OF TIME AND THE HOURS

My watch has caught the general contagion and gone on strike, after having served me faithfully during the past ten years. I wonder what moved it to stop moving. Perhaps I made the mistake of taking its motion for granted, instead of making sure that it would continue to move by tender care for its health. Now it makes me atone for my neglect. For watches are no mere mechanisms. They are individuals that react to human treatment like animate creatures. The watchmaker from whom I bought it at The Hague gave me strict instructions how it should be treated. "Remember, Sir," he said, "a watch likes to be wound up in the morning. Never do it at night." "What difference does it make?" I asked. "It's better for her health. A wrist watch is a sensitive creature. Your hand is never still. You shake it, wave it, throw it up, drop it down, bang it on the table. You think she does not feel that? Every violent motion you make gives her a nervous shock. But at night she is quiet; then she can rest as you do. That's why you must load her with new energy before the day's work begins, not when it is over. You must not excite her when she is tired." A few days later I happened to meet on the train the Dutch novelist Louis Couperus. He took the seat opposite mine, leaned his cane very gently against the window with the handle turned outward, and, patting it, said, "Look at the scenery and enjoy yourself." And then to me, "I see you are laughing. You take me for a fool, I suppose. I would be a fool if I denied that the things I live with have souls. I know they have. I love them, every one of them, my watch most of all. She talks to me and tells me the time. She is wiser than I." He took it out and looked at it with annoyance. "You naughty little girl, why did you stop? I wound you last night, I am sure. Go and hide yourself in shame." And with a jerk of pretended disgust he threw it into the corner of the cushioned seat by the opposite window.

A stopped watch gives one, indeed, a sense of being disappointed in a trusted companion. I feel the loss more in New York than I would if I were in Holland. For I have discovered that public clocks are rare in this time-ridden metropolis. I never had noticed that before. In Holland every church tower lifts its dial high above the roofs of the houses that are huddled at its foot. But church towers are inconspicuous in New York. They themselves have joined the huddle at the base of a skyscraper. The crowds of time-obsessed workers scurry through a city that parades its ignorance of time. No eyes look up towards the communal town clock, they all look down at millions of wrists. Who says we are a standardized nation? Each American lives by his own time.

The individual time-piece has made us minute-conscious. Before the invention of watches the tower clock made the townspeople aware of the quarter hours at best. They measured time by the stroke of the church clock. The Hollander's equivalent for "punctually at five" is klokslag vijf, that is, five by the stroke of the clock. The phrase has outlived the communal reliance on the public time-keeper. In my young days Dutch homes were filled with clocks that kept up a steady competition with the public one in the tower. Each room had its mantlepiece, and the centre of each mantlepiece was occupied by a *pendule*. There were many rooms in my father's house, and as many *pendules*. Every Monday, about noon, a watchmaker's assistant called to regulate them. The employment of this weekly inspector was prompted, I suspect, by Dutch love of orderliness. It was untidy to have twelve clocks in the same house tell twelve different times. Accurate knowledge of the right time was less essential than their agreement. I have forgotten the watchman's name. We children called him The Giraffe. He was lank and tall, and balanced a head far too small for the length of his body, on a precariously thin neck. He always tiptoed around with self-effacing deference, as if he were afraid lest his feet should be suspected of wanting to vie with his ticking wards. He lifted the glass dome off the empire *pendule* with tender solicitude, and curved his long neck down to wind the clock and set it right. He was not tall enough to reach the cuckoo clock in the hall. I still remember gazing up in big-eyed wonder at The Giraffe bravely balancing his fragile frame on the stepladder, and making the little bird appear and call cuckoo, cuckoo, for my entertainment. He and his like do not go around any more to create temporal harmony in tidy Dutch homes. The *pendule* has ceased to be an essential adjunct of the mantlepiece. A change of taste in interior decorating and, perhaps, the popularity of the wrist watch have ousted the Giraffes from their domestic stamping grounds.

Our age, which has put a high price on every minute of time on the air, cannot help being painfully minute-conscious. Our medieval forebears were conscious only of the hours, but they were so with a vengeance. They reckoned with two different kinds of hours. The hours of the clock, which are our sole concern, were not half so important, in their estimation, as were the planetary hours. Each of these was one twelfth of the periods between sunrise and sunset and sunset and sunrise. Another name for them was "unequal hours," because their duration grew and decreased with the lengthening and shortening of the days. Only twice a year, at the equinoxes, were the planetary hours identical with the hours of the clock. They were called planetary hours because each was supposed to be ruled by one of the seven planets. Two abbots, called Emo and Menko, of the abbey of Wittewierum in the Dutch province of Groningen, wrote in the thirteenth century a chronicle of their monastery, in which, among other things, they discussed at length the influence of the planets on the hours that were assigned to them. On Monday the first hour of the twenty-four that make up a full day belonged to the moon, the six that followed to the other planets. The eighth again was ruled by the moon, as well as the fifteenth and the twenty-second. Each planet revolved around the earth within a sphere of its own, the moon in the one nearest to the earth, Saturn in the outermost sphere. If we start from the latter, the order of the seven spheres was: Saturn, Jupiter, Mars, Sun, Venus, Mercury, Moon. So the second hour of Monday belonged to Saturn, the third to Jupiter, the fourth to Mars, the fifth to the Sun, the sixth to Venus, the seventh to Mercury, and the eighth again to the Moon. Since the twenty-second, as we saw, was also ruled by the Moon, the twenty-third was again Saturn's, the twenty-fourth Jupiter's, and the twenty-fifth, which was the first hour of the new day, was ruled by Mars. And for that reason the day that follows Monday is Mars's day, *mardi* as the French call it. The second, ninth, sixteenth, and twenty-third hours of Mars's day were ruled by the sun, the twenty-fourth by Venus, the twenty-fifth, which begins another day, belonged to Mercury, hence Mars's day is followed by Mercury's, called *mercredi* in French. In other words, the sequence of the days within the week is determined by the order of the planets. Each twenty-second hour was ruled by the planet that presided over the first hour of the same day, and the first hour of the next belonged to the next but two in the order of the planets. In Dutch and English the names of heathen gods have taken the place of four from the Roman pantheon. The Teuton Tiw ousted Mars, Wodan Mercury, Thor Jupiter, and Freya Venus. But the sequence was not changed. By compulsion of the planets Freya's day still follows Thor's, Thor's Wodan's, Wodan's Tiw's. Our weekly round remains nominally a circuit through a pagan planetarium.

It was important for our medieval ancestors to possess this knowledge, for since the planets influenced all human affairs, and the phenomena of nature besides, one had to choose carefully the planet and the hour for every important enterprise. The planets did not always conform to the expectations of the trusting. In the Wittewierum chronicle occurs an account of a terrible deluge that swept away a large strip of the coast. Strange to say, remarks the annalist, the second, ninth, and sixteenth hours of that fatal Tuesday, January 16, 1219, were perfectly quiet, although ruled by the moon, which is supposed to cause sudden commotion of the sea. But the hours in between were those of the raging tempest. However, the pious author had no difficulty in explaining the strange phenomenon: "The sea had forgotten its own law, that with God's consent it might rage the more cruelly against the unsuspecting mortals." We modern mortals are no less unsuspecting victims of destiny. But the disaster that has overtaken our generation is not due to nature forgetting her own law, but to our own forgetfulness. While watching the puny minutes crawl around our wrists, we have become oblivious of the timeless revolution of the stars.

March, 1946

THE ALARMIST PRESS

The daily press is by compulsion of its function a chronic alarmist. It gathers and makes the most of all that is abnormal. It cannot help doing so, for only the abnormal is news. A man who murders his wife or a woman who kills her husband will set the reporters busy. They will not waste time on describing the peace of a happy home. There are millions of such homes and very few murderous consorts in America, yet the headlines would lead one to believe that domestic strife is more common than domestic harmony. The exceptional is the fare on which our dailies feed. Hence they create in the minds of the reading public a distorted picture of society which must alarm all people of good will. Thus it happens that foreigners know only the worst of us, because the worst is worth writing about. In the same way we are given a very deceptive idea of conditions abroad. We construct from uncommon happenings that are reported an imaginative picture that is supposed to represent the common life. From the exceptions we deduct the rule, and by that rule we presume to judge our fellow men in foreign lands.

What do Americans know of Java? They knew nothing of it before the island was invaded by the Japs. Few, even now, can find it on the map, but many will tell you that its people hate the Dutch, and that being so, they must have good reason for hating them. Stories of murderous attacks on Dutch internees in concentration camps have appeared in our press. They were true, no doubt, but they were apt to create the entirely false belief that the Hollanders had not a single friend among the Javanese. The truth is that those outrages were the work of youthful hooligans, whose terrorism is abhorred by every decent, peace-loving islander. And men and women of the latter kind can be counted by the millions, whereas the terrorists are comparatively few in numbers. But the headline reader infers from the atrocity stories that all Java is hostile to the Dutch, and that of course the Dutch themselves are to blame for the predicament in which they find themselves.

Recently a story came from Java that does not fit into the newspaper picture of a strife-torn land where it is not safe for white men to live. On January 21st the little chapel of the Tjikini hospital at Batavia was the scene of a simple, yet impressive ceremony. Those who were present had not come to attend a religious service. The occasion was an academic function. The university of Batavia was re-opened there with brief addresses by its President and the Director of Education. They called it a *Nood-universiteit*, a word that is hard to translate. Emergency university does not fully cover its meaning. It is, to be sure, a makeshift institution that has to help out in an emergency. But *nood* means distress, and the name was chosen, no doubt, to imply that this emergency school must serve a country in distress. Public order has been disturbed, abnormal conditions prevail in the capital, the beautiful buildings in which the university was housed before the Japanese invasion have been damaged or claimed for other uses, and valuable books and laboratory equipment have been looted or destroyed. Under those circumstances the university that arises from its ashes is bound to be a makeshift. It will have to do its teaching without the tools that higher education needs. It is like a mediaeval university before the invention of printing, when lectures were the student's only source of knowledge, unless he were rich enough to buy the professor's writings in manuscript. Yet the dearth of study material and physical equipment did not deter the authorities from re-opening the doors of the academy. Its chief asset is the learning of the Faculty members, and most, if not all, of these have apparently survived the rigors of the concentration camp. They realize that the distress resulting from war and revolution must be fought with means that only science can provide. The economic needs of the island are pressing. Industrial plants and harbor facilities have been damaged or destroyed, the food supply is dwindling, the people's morale is at a low ebb, school education at a standstill. There is stagnation in every field of human endeavor, and unless the island's youth be given intellectual guidance, the present distress may turn into nation-wide disaster. The university makes no distinction between Indonesians, Chinese, Arabs, and Europeans. Its doors are open to all, and its teaching aims at building a brotherhood of scholars on the foundation of disinterested love for knowledge and for the common fatherland which that knowledge must serve in the days ahead.

Scholarly research has infinite patience. It does not seek immediate reward. The publicity that the daily press gives to the sensational is not coveted by the scholars who pursue their quiet, unobtrusive tasks in study and laboratory. If their labors have value, they will ultimately win recognition for their share in increasing the sum of human knowledge. Many eminent scholars and scientists have gone to the Indies not to exploit the islands' resources for their own enrichment, but for the enrichment of mankind. What these men have accomplished for the Indies will be gratefully remembered by the Indonesians themselves when the rampant nationalism that animates them today has been sobered by the misery that the present upheaval will carry in its wake. The record of scientific achievement in the Indies is now available to American readers in a splendid volume compiled and edited by two Dutch scholars, Dr. Pieter Honig and Dr. Frans Verdoorn. This work, entitled "Science and Scientists in the Netherlands Indies," contains original articles prepared especially for publication in this volume, reprints of others that have appeared elsewhere, travel accounts by explorers of earlier days, and an imposing list of scientific institutions, societies, and scholars to be found in Indonesia at the time of the Japanese invasion. In nearly five hundred pages the editors unfold a fascinating story of research that began three centuries ago. For even under the sway of the grasping East India Company research was practised by a few and fostered by enlightened managers of the Company.

The story of the life and work of George Everhard Rumphius, a saga of Job-like resignation to misfortune and heroic achievement, proves that commercialism may go hand in hand with scientific interest. This faithful servant of the Company, which employed him for half a century, devoted all his spare time to collecting and describing the flora, the fauna, and the minerals of the island of Amboina, a work of such accuracy and intelligent observation that today it is almost as new and important as when it was published two centuries ago. In 1670 he went totally blind, but the Company supplied him with helpers who wrote down what he dictated and drew the pictures he could no longer design himself. Four years later he lost his wife and daughter in an earthquake. But the measure of his trials was not yet full. In a fire that laid the entire Dutch section of the town of Amboina in ashes his books and collections were destroyed. The manuscript of his principal work "Het Amboinsche Kruidboek" was saved by a miracle. The Governor General Camphuys sent him an able draughtsman with whose aid and that of his own son, Rumphius repaired the damage in a few years. In 1690 the first six books of his masterpiece were sent to Holland, but the ship that carried them was sunk by the French and the manuscript was sealed forever in Davy Jones's locker. Fortunately, Rumphius had a wise and cautious patron in the Governor General at Batavia. Before entrusting the precious manuscript to the risks of the sea voyage, Camphuys had copied it with his own hand. The history of the Dutch East India Company is not throughout a record of rapacity and heartless greed. Men rose to the top in its service who were far better than the Company's reputation. This head manager of a proud and powerful corporation copying his learned underling's manuscript, lest it should perish in transmission, is a memorable figure in colonial history.

May, 1946

SPECKSNYDERS

I recently read, for the third time, the haunting story of Moby Dick. There are long passages in it that bore and irritate, but one always comes back to it drawn by its powerful magic. As Masefield said, "In that wild, beautiful romance Melville seems to have spoken the very secret of the sea, and to have drawn into his tale all the sadness, all the wild joy of many waters." I would enjoy it better without the chapters that display the author's learning. But even in these I sometimes find intriguing matter. The thirty-third bears the curious title of "The Specksynder." That is meant to be Dutch. Melville was aware of the origin and meaning of this strange word, but not knowing any Dutch he misspelt it. "The command of a whaleship," he wrote, "was not wholly lodged in the person now called the captain, but was divided between him and an officer called the Specksynder. Literally this word means Fat-cutter; usage, however, in time made it equivalent to Chief Harpooneer." The correct spelling, of course is specksnyder. Melville must have miscopied the word from an old book, for in his time it was no longer used, at least not in that form. "In the British Greenland Fishery," he explained, "under the corrupted title of Specksioneer, this old Dutch official is still retained." This queer spelling reflects a change in pronunciation less radical than would seem at first sight. Dutch *specksnyder* was in former days, and is still locally, pronounced *speksneer*, and the only corruption that the title suffered in its transfer from Dutch speech to the mouths of British whalers was the substitution of *sh* for *s*. For the English spelling is clearly an attempt to reproduce the pronunciation *spekshneer*. In Murray and Bradley's "New English Dictionary" the word is duly listed and its etymology correctly explained. Among the quotations there given is one from Kipling's "Seven Seas": "Up spake the soul of a gray Gothavn 'speckshioner." The apostrophe shows that he mistook the harpooner's title for an abridged form of "inspectioner." You can't blame a poet for not being an etymologist. But his error is shared, strange to say, by the compilers of Webster's "New International Dictionary." These assign *specksioneer* to its proper place in the alphabetical order, and add the information that it is a whaling term meaning "inspectioneer." That does not give much help to an inquisitive student. So he looks up "inspectioneer" and there learns from Webster that it is a name for "the chief harpooner." Kipling is in good linguistic company. The Dutch blubber cutter's elevation to the rank of inspectioneer as suggested by the poet has been sanctioned by the authority of Webster's great dictionary. But linguistic "inspectioneers" who take the trouble of comparing Murray and Bradley's account of the word with that of Webster must wonder why the latter ignored or refused to follow the New English Dictionary's lead.

That British and American whalers gave a Dutch title to the chief harpooner is proof of the prominent part that Hollanders formerly took in these fisheries. The Dutch and English were competitors in the field in the early seventeenth century. The British Muscovy Company began to hunt whales around Spitsbergen in 1611, and the Dutch soon followed in their track. The British were determined, however, not to tolerate any rivals in this region. King James I had presented the Muscovy Company with a monopoly that left no room for competition and empowered it to use armed force against all who attempted to infringe its rights. In 1613 the English appeared with seven ships off the coast of Spitsbergen, attacked all foreign interlopers, and drove them off their hunting ground. The shipowners in Holland then clubbed together and obtained from the States General a monopoly for the North Company. British hostility was not their sole inducement to consolidation. That is clear from the wording of the charter, which mentions as an additional motive "the preservation of the trade, which otherwise was in peril of being destroyed by confusion." Competition among themselves was as harmful to their interests as was the rivalry of the Muscovy Company. The North Company succeeded in overcoming both. In "A History of the Whale Fisheries" by J. T. Jenkins one chapter is entitled "The Dutch Whalers Predominant (1623-1750)." The learned author, who was Superintendent of the Lancashire and Western Sea Fisheries, states that "at the end of the seventeenth and the commencement of the eighteenth centuries English whaling was practically extinguished, yet the Dutch, in the ten years, 1699-1708, equipped one thousand six hundred and fifty-two ships, which caught eight thousand five hundred and thirty-seven whales, the produce of which sold for over twenty-six million florins, of which four and three-quarter millions was clear gain."

The island of Spitsbergen was the headquarters of the Dutch whalers during their seasonal sojourn in the Arctic. They had built an establishment there which they called Smeerenburg, that is Blubber Town. Each city in the Netherlands that was a participant in the venture of the North Company had its own plant there, the technical name for which was *tent*. There is a detailed account of the life and the activities of the whalers at Smeerenburg in Zorgdrager's classic history of the "Flourishing Rise of the Ancient and Contemporary Greenland Fishery," which was published at Amsterdam in 1720. The heyday of Smeerenburg was in the early thirties of the seventeenth century, when the place was annually visited by over a thousand whalers, not counting the many camp followers. The ships from Holland brought up double crews; those of skill, courage, and experience were assigned to the sloops that went out to kill the whale and tow them to the cookeries on shore; the others remained on land and were employed in cutting up the blubber, boiling down the oil, filling up the casks, and loading them on to the ships. In 1720, when Zorgdrager's book appeared, the town was in a state of decay. The foundations and ruins of eight or ten oil coppers and those of the warehouses were the dead remains of a once flourishing community. A party of British explorers who landed there in 1799 found little left except the scattered brick-work of a cookery furnace.

August-September, 1946

A NATIONAL PASTIME

Before the war Holland was to me a holiday playground. It has ceased to be that. The visitor from America cannot help feeling somewhat embarrassed with his leisure and his supply of dollars while moving among people who are impoverished and hard at work to regain their lost prosperity. They are apt to deny that they are. If one were to believe their own appraisal of the present situation in the Netherlands, the country is in a sorry state, not so much because it is poor but because the people are lazy. Every Dutchman will tell you that the nation is afflicted with mental fatigue and an abnormal aversion to any kind of work. The testimony of my eyes belied that self-criticism. "Have you not rebuilt your railway system in one year and are not the trains running on schedule?" I asked. They could not deny that, but this was an exceptional achievement. "And what about the polders that were flooded by the Nazis? Have the dikes not been restored and the water drained off?" That also was true, they admitted; but dire necessity forced them to that effort. It did not disprove their contention that the nation as a whole was tired and loath to work. And I was warned not to mistake the public's willingness to spend money lavishly in restaurants and theaters for a symptom of returning prosperity. They squandered it because they had no confidence in the future of the guilder. "Why should they save? They can get more for their money now than they are likely to get later on. Besides," my spokesmen complained, "the Government leaves them nothing to save; it taxes the people's earnings away to pay salaries to a monstrously overgrown bureaucracy." One hears, indeed, such grievances galore in all parts of the country, but a visitor who knows the Dutch will take them a grain of salt. The word with for beefing in Dutch is *kankeren*, a verb derived from the Dutch name for cancer. But the Hollander's *kankering* is not an epidemic disease that gnaws at the body politic; it is rather a national pastime with which the people play irritation and annoyance out of their system.

The *kankering* that is going on among Dutchmen is also in part the result of their lack of perspective. They have been looking at themselves and their own affairs for several years during which comparison with conditions abroad was made impossible. Even now they know little of life beyond their borders. For the daily journals, owing to the paper scarcity, are limited to four small pages that leave but scanty space for a discussion of world affairs, and though the radio can again be listened to with impunity, not many can enjoy that new freedom because the Nazis have stolen every receiving set they could lay their hands on. New sets cannot be bought yet, hence only the fortunate few who succeeded in hiding theirs from the Gestapo can tune in on the news from foreign capitals. Everything that happens at home looms, in consequence, unpleasantly large to their mental shortsightedness. They will notice blemishes that are hardly apparent to the visitor freshly arrived from America and see them magnified into serious defects. The stranger has the advantage of distance which merges all shortcomings in the attractive perspective of the whole. His vision, of course, is not accurate either. Living in fairly comfortable hotels he is unaware of the privations and hardships that are being suffered in private homes. Many common necessities of life are still extremely scarce. Coffee is an expensive luxury, sugar is meted out in tiny quantities, rice is unobtainable, butter and cheese, the country's own products, are withheld from home consumption and exported in exchange for foreign currencies. The ration booklet is the Dutch housewife's breviary and her daily beadroll the counting of her coupons. The show in many a shop window is a make-believe, a false front for an empty store. And as long as this dearth continues, the black market will continue to do business. There is no remedy for that evil except an unlimited supply.

This epidemic myopia has made the Dutch people egocentric. Having lived for five dreary years in the Nazi prison camp in strict isolation from the rest of the world, they have become accustomed to imagining the world as persistently concerned with them and their sufferings as they themselves are. It amazed and pained them to be told that the New York papers do not report much news from Holland. "That explains," they would say, "why public opinion in America is so unfair to Holland in the matter of Indonesia. If Americans were better informed about us and knew how well and conscientiously we have ruled the Indies, their editorial writers would not acclaim Sukarno and denounce the Dutch as a nation of oppressors and ex-tortionists. Such hostility to Holland can result only from ignorance." I did my best to explain that such press comments as were unfavorable to the Dutch cause were not inspired by hostile feelings. They were not anti-Dutch, I said, but anti-colonial. "Don't forget," I told my Dutch friends, "that Americans have grown up with the story of the Boston tea party and the War of Independence. They are a nation that won its way to freedom from colonial dependence, and it is only natural that they feel sympathy for another people that wants to do the same." To that the objection was made that the analogy was faulty; the Hollanders did not treat the Indies as colonies. "Has not the Queen promised them an autonomous place within the Nether-lands commonwealth as co-equal partners of Holland, Surinam, and Curaçao? The American critics ignore that promise or perhaps have never heard of it. Our own Government, no doubt, is to blame for that. Its information service is no good." That was the chief grievance of my *kankering* Dutch friends. The Americans misjudged them, they believed, because the Netherlands Government had failed to supply the United States with the right information. It was an irrational grievance for which there was no remedy in reasoned argument. They knew that they were misrepresented in the American press, and their own Government was to blame for that. Were they in the habit of reading American papers? No, they were not. How then did they know? "Our papers print extracts from American newspaper stories. Here is one. It says that Queen Wilhelmina enriches herself with the proceeds from the pawnshops in Java. No wonder we have a bad press in America if our Government lets such libelous statements go un-contradicted." "Would you have the Government stoop to taking notice of such scurrility? Much wiser to ignore it. The Dutch correspondent who repeated that story for consumption at home as a sample of American press comment on Holland was misleading his countrymen. For he created among them the impression that one irresponsible scandal monger in Washington is a typical representative of the American newspaper guild, which he is not. And he committed the worse error of giving wide publicity to a libelous story that in America is forgotten the day after it is published. Stop complaining about America's being misinformed about Holland; you are yourselves no better informed about America. If you were you would not demand that the Government contradict the sensational nonsense of a cheap columnist. The type of reader who swallows that for truth is of that low order on whom all efforts at enlightenment would be wasted. No one else believes it; not even the writer himself. He invents because he thinks that fiction is stranger than truth. American newspapers consume a lot of pulp. To read every column of the morning issue would take a man's whole day. Experience has taught him what to skip, and he skips more than he reads. A journalist who has little information and less conscience tries to capture the attention of this skip-and-ignore-the-rest type of reader by making up cock-and-bull stories. The American public is wise enough to laugh and forget them, much wiser than the indignant Dutch reporter who hawks them around as prize samples of American journalism."

Seldom did a day pass on which some such argument did not arise in the course of conversation. I travelled around a good deal and every-where I found the people keenly interested in America, but lacking in the most elementary knowledge of the country, its people, and its history. Many were anxious to emigrate, a desire that was not limited to the young. At Goes, a small town on the island of Zuid-Beveland, in the province of Zeeland, I visited a lady of my age whom I have known for a long time. She told me she would like to settle in the Middle West, and she for one knew the difficulties that such a change would involve. For she visited this country ten years ago and stayed for three months with relatives in Grand Rapids, Michigan. I met her at the dock in Hoboken, and showed her the sights of New York before I put her on the train. She was herself a sight for New Yorkers to gaze at. For she had come in her national costume, the large lace cap like a spread of wings, the gold antenna-like ornaments at the temples, the richly embroidered velvet bodice and the layers of skirts that give solidity to the figure. She did not speak a word of English, but that handicap did not disconcert her. The exotic dress and the handsome face in its frame of lace wings invited attention and assistance. People everywhere were kind to her and helped her on. She came back, three months later, with excited stories about her stay in

Michigan. She had been feted by her relatives, had won the first prize at a costume ball, and had received and declined a proposal of marriage. She has never ceased talking about that journey, the one great experience of her life. I went to see her in her tiny house at Goes, which supplies her with more space though than can be found in many a New York apartment. It was large enough, at any rate, for twelve Canadian soldiers to be billeted there. She did not mind having them, she liked to mother them and also to practice her English. "If only I had dollars I would move to Grand Rapids," she told me. "You should not transplant old trees," I said tactlessly. "A Zeeland woman is not old at seventy," was her proud reply. These Zeeland people are indeed a magnificent and sturdy race. They have passed through a terrific ordeal, especially the farmers on the isle of Walcheren. But they are tilling their ravaged land again and harvesting a sickly crop from silted soil, in the confident hope that both will improve with the passage of time. It takes courage to plough and sow and toil for a harvest that one knows in advance will be unrewarding. A people capable of such determination cannot be suffering from fatigue. That common complaint, I believe, springs from their awareness of the discrepancy between the labor supply and the gigantic task of reconstruction that faces them. But whatever discouragement that sense of inadequacy may cause, they express it in words only, they deny it in action.

October, 1946

A POPULAR FALLACY

It is a popular fallacy that dead men tell no tales. Most of our mystery stories are based on the assumption that they do. The murdered man's body supplies the clue as a rule. Our ancestors, who coined the proverb, did not give it credence themselves. For it was a common superstition among them that when a murderer approached the corpse of his victim it began to bleed again from its wounds. That often happens in medieval thrillers. It was the evidence by which Siegfried's dead body proved Hagen his slayer in the German *Nibelungenlied*. And what would we know about prehistoric man without his telltale bones? We listened the other day to Dr. Ralph von Koenigswald when he addressed members and guests of the Southeast Asia Institute at its fifth annual dinner. Until that evening I thought that the *Pithecanthropus Erectus* of Java was, by his bony self-confession, the earliest specimen of humankind. But the speaker revealed that behind the Java man, in a still more distant past, older and taller ape men have arisen from their perennial concealment to tell tales of a still remoter past, tall tales about men of gigantic stature, *Meganthropus* and *Gigantopithecus*. Man grows in size as retrogressive research traces him back to his origins. Giants appear to have been our forebears, and each new type developed in the course of evolution was more concise than its predecessor. If we could see the complete sequence coming down in the flesh along the trail of time, the farthest towering with head and shoulders above the one in front of him, we would recognize in them the originals of the ogres and giants that haunt our fairy tales. In these the memory of mankind may have preserved its recollection of their existence. They need not be creatures of man's imagination, but may be realistic pictures of the last stray monsters of a perishing race from which their diminished offspring once fled in terror.

Some ten years ago, when Dr. von Koenigswald's finds were reported in a brief message from Java, a metropolitan daily sent a reporter to Princeton to interview Professor E. G. Conklin and obtain from him more detailed information about the forgotten man of pre-history. The account of this visit quoted the Princeton biologist as having said that the original discovery of the Java ape man was made by two boys. If that is true, they had deserved a better reward than inglorious anonymity. For there is great merit in having shown the way to this cemetery of fossil man, which, to quote Sir Arthur Keith, "has proved to be rich beyond any other in every respect, rich in actual numbers and in types which preserve details of the sequence of humanity that has flitted across the time stage of Java these millions of years past." But Professor Conklin had given due credit where credit was due. He had not carelessly referred to a couple of nameless boys, but had mentioned as the discoverer the Dutch scientist Dubois, whose name, as he pronounced it, sounded like *dooboys*. The reporter cannot be blamed for his mistake. It is just the kind of discovery inquisitive boys might stumble on in their search for adventure. Eugene Dubois, who pronounced his name the French way, published the first news of his epoch-making find in 1894. All that he possessed to go by at that time was a skull cap, a third upper molar, and a femur. He thought that they belonged to a manlike transition form between ape and man, in other words that he had found the missing link. But in his opinion this ape man was really a man ape, more like a gigantic gibbon than a human being. In the half century that elapsed between that first publication and his death, which occurred on December 16, 1940, many new remains of early man were brought to light, which forced the biologists to drastic modifications of his conclusions. But nothing can detract from his lasting merit in having been the first to whom the dead man of the Middle Pleistocene told a tale of human life that existed some half a million years ago.

When we listen to the palaeontologist who measures life by hundreds of thousands of years, the two milleniums that have passed over Java since the light of history dawned upon the island seem to dwindle into a short span of time. And three hundred years of Dutch rule appear as but a fleeting episode by comparison. It is good for one's sense of proportion to see them related to the distant past. What is happening in Java now is a catastrophic upheaval in the eyes of those whose political, economic, or social destinies are closely involved. They cannot measure its real import, just as little as the sailor on the stormswept deck can measure the height of the waves that threaten to overwhelm him. It must be hard, indeed, for the Dutch in the East Indies who are seeing the fruits of their life's work thrown into the discard or destroyed, to view the present turmoil in relation to past events and to possible developments in the future. To them this is the end of all their hopes. What they hoped for and actually considered possible was a restoration of conditions such as existed before the Japanese invasion. But the clock cannot be set back, not even in the proverbially static Orient. The Far East has ceased to be static. A return to the past is impossible. The long ebb of submissiveness is over, the tide of self-assertion is rising. I met Hollanders, last summer, who could not understand what is happening. "The Javanese," they said, "are a gentle, docile people; we Hollanders who lived among them were never in danger, although we were not allowed to carry arms. They liked us, in fact, and were satisfied with Dutch rule." They could account for the Indonesian uprising only as a Japanese plot. "If the Japs had not been given time to foment this revolt when they saw that the island was lost to themselves, Java would again be the peaceful paradise it used to be."

SHAHRIR

That, of course, is self-delusion. Japanese intrigue is, no doubt, a contributing cause of the Indonesian uprising, but the time-bomb planted by the defeated invader could not have wrought havoc over so wide an area if inflammable matter had not spread all over Java. I have just been reading the diary kept by Sutan Shahrir during the years of his exile, first at Upper Digoel in New Guinea, and subsequently in Banda Neira. It was published in Holland in 1946 under the title *Indonesische Overpeinzingen* (Indonesian Meditations). The author uses the pen name Shahrazad, but it is common knowledge in Holland that his real name is Shahrir. It is a most illuminating book.

282

It has filled me with a profound admiration for his farsighted wisdom, his richly informed mind, and his noble tolerance. This man whom the government in Batavia imprisoned and exiled as a dangerous revolutionary was able, in the third year of his banishment, to write about Holland with real affection. "I am not a Hollandophile," he set down in his diary, "although I know that through my training I am a semi-Hollander. But I retain beautiful memories of that little country that is so much hated by most of us here. I have always loved it, perhaps because it has occupied so large a place in my mental make-up through the hundreds of boys' books and novels and my entire intellectual nourishment. Little was strange to me when I first came to Holland, and the beginning of my stay there was a continuous recognizing. Afterwards I felt at home there; I never was homesick." This admission is the more remarkable because he cares little for that particular part of Indonesia where he was born. Shahrir is not a Javanese but comes from Menangkabau in the Padang Highlands, in central Sumatra. "In spite of the beauty of its natural scenery I could never become attached to Menangkabau...Java, on the other hand, has become dear to me, middle Java, in the long run, more than west Java. I am fond also of Banda (the island in the Moluccas to which he was banished). I love the Bandanese even more than I do the inhabitants of Holland, although I have a sharp eye for their faults and defects, but I can never be happy in this island, not as happy as I could be in Holland or elsewhere in the world where no colonial relations corrupt life."

Not hatred then of Holland but hatred of colonial rule has made him a leader of the Indonesian Republic. He sees in its proclamation the inescapable outcome of forces that have been at work in Java since the beginning of this century. Nine years ago he wrote: "Great social changes have taken place, and time has leveled contrasts. There is much less show of self-importance among the rulers than there was some fifteen years ago, and also more self-confidence among the Indonesians. The abnormality of such a colonial form of society, which has its principal cause in those psychical relationships, is gradually disappearing, neither through the ethical policy of the Dutch rulers, nor through the conscious determination of the ruled, but through the automatic process of penetration by the modern production apparatus to which society is adapting itself." His chief grievance against the Dutch is not that they presumed to rule Indonesia; but that they did not use the power they wielded for the westernization of the islands so as to make them an integral part of the modern world. "Of one thing I am certain," he wrote in 1936, "this colonial government and the colonizing Dutch will regret one day that they never followed a grand-scale policy of far perspectives adapted to the changed structure of the modern world ... This shortsightedness due to lack of imaginative vision and courage is bound to prove their undoing." Reading this diary I could not help wishing that the rulers at Batavia, instead of sending Shahrir into exile, had taken him into their counsels. He is wiser than most of them.

January, 1947

LOSS OF PRIVACY

New Year's Eve in Holland as I remember it was a quiet and dignified celebration. We went to church after dinner and spent the rest of the evening at home talking or reading or playing games while awaiting the twelve strokes of the clock that would usher in the New Year. Oysters were the special treat on that occasion. They were brought in at half past eleven, and we would drink each other's health and happiness with a glass of pale ale. In other homes the fare and the libation might be different, but the character of the feast did not differ much; it was an intimate meeting of the family circle around the supper table. We did not foregather at riotous parties in hotel dining rooms and restaurants. The closing of the year was felt to be a solemn moment that called for withdrawal within the intimacy of the home. Hollanders are not a vocal people; even among themselves they are reserved and reticent. That is why they like to be *en famille* on New Year's Eve. Members of the same household can indulge the luxury of silent intimacy; they can think the same thoughts without the need of uttering them. In many a home that was bereaved in the past year the names of the dear ones may not have been mentioned, but that does not mean that the dead were forgotten. Shared remembrance can dispense with words. I can recall one New Year's Eve when the stillness was to me more meaningful than anything that could have been said.

Christmas and New Year's Eve must have been a trying season, this time, to millions of Hollanders. For on this one occasion when every Dutchman craves privacy and seclusion few families could be among themselves. The destruction of so many dwellings during the war has created a housing emergency that the Government has tried to solve by drastic and arbitrary measures. No one who has room to spare in his house may continue to enjoy the luxury of space. There is a Government Housing Bureau that has made a careful survey of all available accommodation; a householder who is found in possession of a drawing room and a spare bedroom is forced by the Bureau to cede

284

them to a homeless family. Domestic architecture in Holland never reckoned with the possibility of part occupancy. Most Dutch houses are built on the same plan. If you know your way inside one, you know it in most of the others. After passing through the front door you enter a hallway at whose far end is the door to the kitchen. The hallway is more spacious near the front door than in the rear, for in the middle its width is partly taken up by the staircase. Adjoining the hall, either on the right or the left, is a suite of rooms of which one faces the street, the other the garden at the back. The latter, being next to the kitchen, is the dining room, the other the drawing-room, which in some families is used exclusively for the reception of visitors. It is now occupied in many a home by strangers. The two rooms can be shut off from one another by means of sliding doors, but these do not constitute a sound-proof partition. The fear of being overheard and letting the next-room neighbors in on your secrets and your quarrels applies a curb to the natural flow of conversation. The one kitchen must do for the two families. They will, of course, arrange their mealtimes in such a way that the two housewives need not use it simultaneously. But even alternate occupancy will be a constant source of friction. I had to listen to many outbursts of exasperated housewives. "The mess she leaves in the sink after 'washing up' as she calls it. And she never puts things back in their proper places. I can never find them when they are needed. And the noise in the kitchen when she is cooking! We can't hear ourselves talk in the room next door for the clatter she makes." Another grumbled – not unjustly I thought – because she was forced to take in a couple who had collaborated with the Germans during the occupation. They had both been imprisoned after the liberation of Holland and their house had been occupied by loyal citizens who had lost their own in an air raid. They were brought to trial, the tribunal acquitted them, and the Government which had given them room and board in jail now had to find them shelter elsewhere. "So I have to make room for these traitors and put up with their insolence. We thought we were free again when the Nazis went; but there is little freedom left in liberated Holland." The rehabilitation of her tenants by the tribunal did not soften her feelings towards them. They remained traitors to her, and how could she share her home with them and live at peace?

Such people have indeed reason to start the new year with the wish, "May we recover the freedom to use our home as we please." "My home is my castle" is a sentiment that the Hollander shares with the Briton though he does not profess it in proverb form. In rural districts the farmer gives it ostensible expression by drawing in the little bridge that gives him access to the main road. His individualism craves isolation, and on his ditch-framed island farmstead he feels as proudly alone as did the medieval knight behind his castle moat. Even in the crowded cities Dutch builders have devised a means of communal living that saves the illusion of separateness. Though two or three families be housed under one roof, each has its own front door and its own staircase. This architectural contrivance makes it possible for each tenant to move around on his own premises without ever meeting his next-door neighbors. The tenants even scorn a common parking place for their bicycles. These are hoisted up and suspended from the hallway ceiling by an ingenious contraption. I always wonder what would happen to the visitor waiting on the doormat if the tackle overhead gave way. Dwelling on top of a steep staircase has of course its drawbacks, but these are outweighed by the pleasures of privacy. Besides, the tenants have developed certain practices and devices that make repeated climbing of steps unnecessary. Dutch housewives do not go to market. The errand boys of the butcher, the baker, the grocer, the fishmonger call for orders, unless these are given by telephone, and deliver them later in the day. They need not, and are not expected, to run up three or four flights of steps. They announce themselves by yelling up the stairway and deposit their wares in a basket attached to a cord by which the housewife pulls it up along the banisters. Callers shout their names and errands towards the upper regions, and, if welcome, are told by a downward shout to shut the door and come up. In one-family homes of the more stylish type this vocal check-up is negotiated through a barred little window in the front door, which offers at the same time opportunity for an ocular scrutiny of the visitor. People who love their privacy so intensely as not to tolerate the sharing of a common hall and stairway must suffer terribly under a system that calls for meek acceptance of its intrusion as a civic duty.

A peculiar feature of Dutch domestic architecture is the smallness of the front door. Even the magnificent Royal Palace at Amsterdam, in former days the City Hall, has an unimpressive entrance out of all proportion to the massive pile to which it admits. A foreign visitor who was aware of the Hollander's jealous love of privacy once maliciously suggested to me that the small door signified to the outside world: stay away, we don't admit Tom, Dick and Harry. There is perhaps a streak of truth in the malice. The Dutch do not go in for open-house hospitality. They do not care for crowded cocktail parties such as we are supposed to enjoy in New York. They like to listen and be listened to at a social gathering, and relish both pleasures better while seated in comfortable chairs. Big receptions are held only for very special occasions; the favorite form of entertainment is a

286

gathering of some ten or a dozen friends at which you can converse without the painful need of pretending that you hear what is being said. Hollanders do not like to extend a feigned welcome to guests whom they barely know. But they do not mind, strange to say, admitting the gazes of perfect strangers into the privacy of their homes. At night they do not draw the curtains but offer passersby a free view of the family circle assembled round the table at which the lady of the house presides over the tea tray. A foreigner who wants to make a study of Dutch home life can get a good first impression by going for a walk through the darkened streets on a summer night. He will pass many a genre picture that will arrest his attention. I cannot explain this anomaly in Dutch behaviour. Perhaps it is the Hollander's way of saying, "The small door and its barred window do not mean that I am secretive. I have nothing to conceal, look in, you are welcome to the view."

David Anderson of the *New York Times* cabled from The Hague on New Year's Eve that two million people – that is twenty-two per cent of the population – want to leave Holland for good and seek better fortune elsewhere. He attributes this desire for mass migration to fear of a Russian war. That, of course, is too simple an explanation. There is, indeed, fear of Russia, especially among Catholics and Protestant conservatives. But it is only one, and I believe a minor one, among many causes of the prevailing restlessness. The disordered state of Europe, the uncertain economic future, the slow progress of reconstruction due to lack of materials, the monotony of the daily fare, the memory of better days that makes the present seem drab and unbearable, all these contribute to the longing for change. But I should not wonder if the chief cause of the general *wanderlust* were the people's feeling that their homes are no longer their own. When love of home is weakened, people are easily uprooted. Their homes having ceased to be their castles, they start building castles in Spain.

A DUTCH-AMERICAN NOVEL

In view of the large number of American citizens of Dutch origin it is surprising that the literature of their migrations is so scanty. Many a family could tell a story that a novelist might turn to good account. But few have attempted to write such a family saga. David Cornel De Jong has done it successfully in *Belly Fulla Straw*. Another attractive tale of life in a Dutch-American settlement is "The Bells of Helmus" by Cobie de Lespinasse, who is the wife of an Oregon dentist. In spite of her husband's French name, he too is a descendant of Dutch settlers. In the seventies of the past century a Dr. A. F. de Lespinasse, a graduate of the university of Utrecht, began to give pre-medical courses at Orange City, Iowa, as a preliminary to the establishment of a medical school which he hoped to build out into a university. That was five years after the settlement was started. Nothing came of his ambitious dream, but the fact that he dared dream it proves him to have been a man of courage and vision. The Dutch dentist in far-away Oregon, who bears the same initials as the Orange City doctor, is doubtless a grandson of this Iowa pioneer. He and his fellow settlers were evidently a determined group of men. When they arrived in 1870, political life in Sioux County centred in Calliope, a town twenty-three miles distant from their own place of settlement. They soon succeeded in getting one of their men, Jelle Pelmulder, elected to the office of clerk of the District Court, and another, Tjeerd Heemstra, obtained a seat on the Board of Supervisors of Sioux County. Graft and mismanagement were rife at Calliope. The men in power there floated loans in the name of the County, but used the money for private business ventures. The Dutch newcomers, not being used to that kind of corruption, put up more candidates in the Fall elections of 1871, and succeeded in returning three Orangists to the Board of Supervisors. But only one of these was seated, the two others, on some cooked-up pretext, were refused admission when they presented themselves at Calliope. Then the settlement at Orange City decided to take the law into their own hands. One hundred and fifty men drove in sleighs to Calliope, invaded the court house, seized the safe containing the records, and returned in triumph with their booty. In the fall elections of 1872 the Dutch carried the field, and the forcible transfer of the county seat to Orange City was belatedly legalized by a majority vote.

The settlers of Helmus made their town the county seat by a similar raid. The boy hero of the story proudly recounts the episode to his girl friend: "Yes sir! Stole all the papers in the middle of the night and brought them right here and we've been the county seat ever since." The raiders did not imitate the men of Orange City; they were no doubt identical with them. The name Helmus is a transparent disguise: the settlement, the author explains, was named for Wilhelmus, Prince of Orange, the national hero of the Netherlands, the same whose memory is honored in the name of Orange City; and the picture that the author paints of Helmus half a century ago is a picture of Orange City as it was at the turn of the century. It is not an idyllic retrospect. The scope of social life in that small prairie town is dwarfed by the immensity of the physical scene surrounding it. Petty jealousies, intolerance, gossip, backbiting poison life in that rural community. The settlers are Calvinists, but they do not agree among themselves on the creed they confess. Some belong to the Dutch Reformed Church, others to the Christian Reformed, which is a more orthodox offshoot of the former. There is no love lost between the two congregations. The Dutch Reformed have a bell in their church tower and are immensely proud of its resounding voice; the Christian Reformed are unchristianly jealous of their heterodox fellow Calvinists and rejoice when, one day, the bell-proud church is struck by lightning and the bell with its steeple comes down with what sounds to them as a clang of anguish. There is one man in Helmus who hates the bell more even than do the Christian Reformed, but he hates it for a nobler reason; he hates it not because it belongs to another church than his own, for he has no church, but because it is a cause of communal discord, which according to him is an epidemic disease in Helmus. People there are dying of the bell, like little Katie. "All she needs," he says, "is love and understanding and all she hears is the bell and the dissension it is causing, for when it calls, her mother goes to the Dutch Reformed Church and her father to the other." He knows what he is talking about; he can diagnose Katie's trouble, for he is the physician of Helmus. Dr. Hendricks is an outspoken agnostic unable to share the faith and hope of his Calvinist patients but infinitely richer than they in the third of the Pauline trinity, in charity, which is the greatest of the three. He finally leaves the settlement when slander of which he is made the butt makes life among these pious folk unbearable. He starts a new practice on the West coast and is followed by others who feel as he the need of a freer life untrammeled by hairsplitting dogmas. Cobie de Lespinasse and her husband came after in their track and found a home in Hubbard, Oregon, where they have ministered for thirty-seven years to the needs of their fellow citizens in the Christian spirit in which Dr. Hendricks practiced in Helmus.

May, 1947

GULIAN VERPLANCK

The Century Club in New York celebrated its hundredth anniversary on the evening of Saturday, April 26th. The party was for members only and I do not intend to satisfy the curiosity of outsiders with an account of what happened on that memorable occasion. But a retrospect to the Club's beginning is not out of place in the Monthly Letter since its first president was Gulian Crommelin Verplanck, whose middle and last names mark him as a man of pure Dutch stock. Crommelin was the name of his grandmother. Gulian's grandfather Samuel was betrothed, at the age of seven, to a Dutch cousin over in Holland, the daughter of an Amsterdam banker, and when he was grown up he was sent to Europe to do the tour of the continent and, incidentally, marry Miss Judith Crommelin and bring his bride home. Gulian's mother was Elizabeth Johnson, granddaughter of Samuel Johnson, the first President of Columbia College, and daughter of Samuel Johnson, its second President. She died when Gulian was three years old. He was brought up by his two grandmothers, the Dutch lady from Amsterdam and the widow of Columbia's second President. He must have been a child of an angelic nature, for he managed to keep the peace between his two guardians. He was also a precocious child, for he was not yet fifteen years of age when he took his B. A. at his grandfather's College.

Thus far there is nothing characteristically Dutch in the story of his career. But in 1811 the rebellious Dutchman in him suddenly asserted himself. He appeared that year in the new role of leader of a Commencement riot which desecrated the sanctity of Trinity Church. Part of the exercises was a political debate between some of the students. One of them, Stevenson, had been told by Dr. Wilson, a member of the Faculty, that he should delete from his prepared manuscript a sentence that seemed offensive to the College authorities. But Stevenson, once upon the platform, defied his professors and boldly spoke the dangerous words, "Representatives ought to act according to the sentiments of their constituents." He was punished for this heinous offence by being refused his degree. Hugh Maxwell, an alumnus, took the student's part and, jumping on to the platform, addressed the audience in his defence. Verplanck supported him and proposed a vote of thanks to Mr. Maxwell "for his zealous and honorable defence of an injured man." This was greeted with three cheers from the graduating class and three groans for the provost. The police were brought in and the Commencement came to an end in great disorder. Stevenson, Maxwell, and Verplanck were brought to trial before the Mayor's Court and heard themselves described, in Mayor De Witt Clinton's charge to the jury, as perpetrators of "the most disgraceful, the most unprecedented, the most unjustifiable, and the most outrageous disturbance that had ever come to the knowledge of the Court." The jury was duly impressed and fined the defendants $200 each.

The verdict rankled in Verplanck's mind and caused him to change his political affiliation. He was a Federalist by family tradition and founded in 1808, together with Isaac Sebring and Richard Varick, the Washington Benevolent Society to perpetuate Federalism; but the perpetuity of his own membership proved as shaky as party platforms after an election, for ten years later he joined the anti-Clintonians or

Bucktails, the nickname given by De Witt Clinton to the members of the Tammany Society. He opposed Clinton not only in the open politically, but also poetically under an assumed name. "Letters of Abimelech Coody, Ladies' Shoemaker" were Verplanck's satirical revenge on the Mayor of New York. He had the satisfaction of receiving printed proof that his enemy smarted under the rhymed attack. For he was given first place among the literary worthies of New York whom Clinton attacked in "An account of Abimelech Coody and other celebrated writers of New York, in a letter from a traveler to his friend in South Carolina." In this pamphlet Clinton stated sneeringly that the Ladies' shoemaker "had finally settled down into a magazine writer for money, and that he had become the head of a political sect called the Coodies, of a hybrid nature, composed of the combined spawn of federalism and jacobinism ... neither fish nor flesh." His personal appearance was described by his enemy as squat and clumsy reminding one "of the figure called by children Humpty Dumpty on the wall."

In 1821 we see Verplanck in an entirely new role for which his career thus far does not seem to have prepared him: that of professor in the General Theological Seminary of the Episcopal Church. In this new capacity he wrote "Essays on the Nature and Uses of the Various Evidences of Revealed Religion." He used a novel approach, rejecting the a priori method and basing his reasoning on legal principles of evidence, which he applied to revelation. This book, it seems, brought revealing evidence that Verplanck was not of the right scholastic timber, for it is probably no mere coincidence that its appearance in print was promptly followed by his disappearance from the Seminary Faculty. He proved more successful as a legislator in the House of Representatives, to which he was elected in 1824, largely because of his opposition to the high tariff. He was chiefly instrumental, in 1831, in obtaining a law improving the copyrights of authors; it gave additional security to writers and artists by lengthening the term of legal protection from 28 to 48 years. In recognition of this achievement he was tendered a dinner by the literati of New York, the expense of which was defrayed by a generous bookseller called Elam Bliss. On this occasion Verplanck delivered an address on "The Law of Literary Property."

In 1837 he was elected to the State Senate, which at that time was still a Court for the Correction of Errors. During the four years that he sat in this court he delivered seventy-one opinions. Chief Justice Charles P. Daly, in the obituary of Verplanck that he read to his fellow Centurians, said that it was "a matter of astonishment that a man who had never sat before in a court of justice, who never argued or tried a case for a client in a court in his life, should take a commanding position in the highest judicial tribunal of the State. In fact, he was the controlling power, for whenever the Chancellor differed from him, he invariably carried the Court, and the weight that was attached to his opinions may be inferred from the fact that during the four years that he served, it was only in three instances that his vote was recorded with the judges in the minority."

Once in his life, in 1825, he ventured to publish an essay on a legal topic: "The Doctrine of Contracts," in which he maintained that the transaction between buyer and seller should be one of perfect frankness. He termed the Latin maxim *Caveat Emptor* not only a selfish but a knavish and immoral rule of conduct. Verplanck had been induced to write it by the want of commercial morality in that period of wild speculation and fluctuations in value which preceded the panic of 1825. William Cullen Bryant says in his discourse on Verplanck that he had heard jurists object to this essay on the ground that "if its doctrine were to prevail, it would greatly multiply the number of lawsuits." But it is hard to see why lawyers should object to it on that account.

After his retirement from the Senate he spent most of his remaining life on the family estate at Fishkill. There he employed his leisure in preparing for the press a three-volume edition of Shakespeare's plays, which appeared in 1847 with woodcut illustrations by H. W. Hewet. It was in that same year that he helped to found the Century Association. The club was not prophetically christened with an eye to its hundredth anniversary; the name was suggested by the number of one hundred gentlemen engaged or interested in Letters and the Fine Arts who were invited to join in forming the Association. Forty-two accepted and became Founders, forty-six others joined during the year. There was no President in its early days. The members met during the first two years in rooms that the Club occupied at No. 495 Broadway, and at each gathering one of them was "called to the chair." This custom prevailed until 1857, when the office of President was created and Gulian Verplanck elected to the place of honor. He filled it until 1864. He seems to have been a successful orator and possessed the kind of eloquence that begets eloquence in others. For when he had died in 1870, his fellow Centurians met in the Century rooms in East Fifteenth Street and listened to a lengthy sketch of his life by Chief Justice Charles P. Daly and briefer obituaries by four other members.

I have read all these speeches but in none did I find an answer to the question to what outstanding merit Verplanck owed his election to the presidency of the club. The Centurians did not honor him, I am sure, as the exponent of "The Nature and Uses of the Various Evidences of Revealed Religion," nor as the author of "The Doctrine of Contracts," nor even as the editor of Shakespeare. But William Cullen Bryant has left us a glimpse of the man that explains the affection he inspired in his fellow Centurians. Verplanck one evening attended a dinner party of members of the bar at Delmonico's, then in William Street. One by one the guests left, until Verplanck and one other lawyer remained. The two rose at last to go home. The lawyer lived on Brooklyn Heights, Verplanck uptown. Instead of parting from his fellow guest, Verplanck walked on with him to Fulton Ferry, and crossed the river with him. As he declined the other's invitation to go home with him and spend the night at his house, the lawyer stayed on the wharf until the ferry should leave again for Manhattan. The night editor of the *Courier and Enquirer* came on board to go to his work, and the Brooklyn attorney introduced him to Verplanck. He afterwards learnt that Verplanck had gone with him to the editorial office and had stayed there till broad daylight, talking, reading, and ruminating. We have a special name in Dutch for these boon companions who cannot tear themselves away from pleasant company. They are called *plakkers* in Holland. As a typically Dutch *plakker* Gulian Verplanck must have been popular among his fellows. I feel sure that Bryant has drawn the best likeness we possess of the first President of the Century.

June-July, 1947

THE PAY SAY

There is a very dull and ugly street in Amsterdam which the name plate proclaims to be the Pieter Corneliszoon Hooftstraat, but which all Amsterdammers are accustomed to call the P. C., pronounced Pay Say. I was taken there as a little boy to have my portrait painted by Wally Moes, who had her studio in that dismal thoroughfare. There was no beauty in the Pay Say that could attract an artist, but it was close to the Rijksmuseum, and that may have reconciled her to living on Sinister Street. I had no idea what the name stood for. Pay Say meant to me a cheerless row of similar houses built of a dull-colored brick that drained the narrow street of all light. It was not until I was taught at school the history of Dutch literature that I learnt the meaning of the name. P. C. Hooft was a great poet, the greatest of the early seventeenth century, who had loved the light of the sun and observed with an artist's eye the wonderful things that it did to the land and the water of the Dutch landscape. The city fathers under whose administration the street was laid out and named for the poet

293

had probably never read a single line of his sunlit verse. They had at any rate a strange conception of how a great artist should be honored by his native city.

The only way to honor a poet is to read him and know him. But that is not the Dutch way, I regret to confess. They honor him at centenaries of his birth or death and leave him unread in the intervals. F. A. Stoett's two-volume edition of Hooft's collected verse is not a treasured possession in every home along the Pay Say, I dare take an oath on that. Not one in ten families that live there is likely to own a copy. And very few residents of the street that mishonors his memory will be able to recite one of his lyrics. I am told that the Dutch have mended their unpoetic ways; that love of poetry and the reading of it are common now among all classes; and that the city fathers of the present day would hear angry protests from their constituents if they committed an outrage such as was done three quarters of a century ago to the name of P. C. Hooft. I hope that is true and that this year's commemoration of Hooft's death in 1647 was not one of those committee-run affairs sponsored by all the big-wigs in government, commerce, and finance, but a spontaneous homage by genuine lovers of the poet. But I shall not believe it until I hear that a popular one-dollar edition of Hooft's collected verse has seen the light and is being sold in tens of thousands of copies.

The Hoofts belonged to those Amsterdam families that had come to the fore after the surrender of the city to the forces of the Prince of Orange. During the early years of the revolt Amsterdam was pro-Spanish; the ruling class saw greater safety for their commercial interests in loyal adherence to the king of Spain, whom they also regarded as the protector of their Catholic faith. The Calvinists were dangerous radicals to them, a menace to law and order and old-established institutions. Hence when these radicals gained control of Amsterdam, a social upheaval took place in which the old Catholic families were ousted from power and replaced by supporters of the Reformed religion. Hooft's father was a leader among the rebels and when they were firmly in the saddle he took a prominent part in the city government. Having fought under Prince William for freedom of conscience, he was not willing to deny it to his Catholic fellow citizens. His tolerance was not shared by the Calvinists and for that reason he never joined their Dutch Reformed Church. Such independence of mind was rare in those days, and only a man of his moral stamina could be a noncomformist and yet retain the lasting respect and confidence of the citizenry. He was not of Amsterdam stock nor of patrician birth, yet in spite of those handicaps he rose to first place among the Amsterdam patriciate. His father was a skipper and shipowner of Zaandam, the centre of Holland's shipbuilding industry; his mother was a farmer's daughter. Of this Zaandam skipper the story goes that one day, in 1572, he sailed into the Danish Sound surrounded by seven other ships all belonging to him and each under command of his seven sons. The king of Denmark, having heard of this family squadron, invited this patriarch of the sea and his offspring to dinner at Elsinore.

Strength of character, independence of mind, and great moral courage were the traits that the poet inherited from his forebears. There is no trace in them of the poetic strain that was to run its course in him. In the portrait that Van Mierevelt painted of Pieter Corneliszoon he looks a man of aristocratic features. He belonged to an upstart family, but nothing in his appearance belies the patrician. He had risen far above his grandfather's status. Prince Maurice of Nassau had made him Sheriff of Muiden and Het Gooi, a town and district south of Amsterdam. That office required his residence in the castle of Muiden, a medieval structure on the shore of the Zuiderzee, and he acted the role of Lord of the Manor with the dignity of a born nobleman.

His courtly manners were in part, no doubt, an acquisition from abroad. The son of burgomaster Hooft must have possessed innate refinement, but the breeding he had inherited was enhanced during a protracted residence in Italy. He left Holland in his seventeenth year and returned three years later a cosmopolitan gentleman rich in accomplishments that few of his like possessed in Amsterdam. He became acquainted in Florence with the poetry of Petrarch and was the first in Holland not merely to write sonnets but to write sonnets that can vie in beauty with those of his Italian model. He had read Tasso's "Aminta" and Guarini's "Il Pastor Fido" and tried his hand, with less success, at pastoral drama in his native Dutch. The passionate ardor of his Amsterdam love lyrics seems an afterglow of the Mediterranean sun. The Italian journey made him conscious of his poetic power. But with all his love and admiration of Italy he never stooped to aping everything Italian. He remained a true son of the stock from which he came and a loyal citizen of the Republic for whose freedom his father had been willing to risk martyrdom.

He erected later in life a magnificent monument to the memory of his people's fight for freedom in a history of the first twenty years of the reign of King Philip II. It is not a mere chronicle of events, but a dramatic account of their causes and effects by a student of human affairs who had trained his mind to weigh and judge without bias or prejudice. By modeling his style on that of Tacitus he succeeded in taming the undisciplined and prolix prose then in vogue into a terse and unambiguous utterance. It is the first history in the Dutch language that is at the same time a great work of art.

August-September, 1947

TWO KINDS OF EMIGRATION

The town of Holland, Mich., celebrated in the third week of August the centennial of its founding. The settlers were orthodox Calvinists who had seceded from the Dutch Reformed Church of the Netherlands because it had swerved, they charged, from the true doctrine of Calvin. They were forbidden, in the reign of King William I, to hold conventicles and thrown into prison if they were found to disregard the ban on their meetings. They hoped to find in America unshackled freedom for their religious observances. But by the time they left Holland that freedom was already theirs. Under the reign of Queen Wilhelmina's grandfather, King William II, who came to the throne in 1840, all persecution ceased. Yet the urge to emigrate persisted and gained additional force from the prevailing economic need. A potato blight destroyed the food that was the rural population's principal means of subsistence. Hunger and poverty added a persuasive argument to the longing for change that their sufferings for religion's sake had aroused. And so in the late forties the trek to the New World began that was to settle a new Holland in the Middle West of America.

The newcomers intended to remain Dutchmen. That was clear from the name they gave to their settlement. It was not by way of a sentimental farewell to the native land that they called it Holland. They proclaimed by that choice that they meant to perpetuate the old country in the new, not only their Dutch Church, but also their Dutch language, their Dutch schools and their Dutch way of living. For a long time the Dutch of Michigan stuck to that purpose of the founders. Still, each succeeding generation, in spite of the native tenacity, gave way more and more to the leveling forces of the American environment. Externally, the town of Holland has nothing characteristically Dutch any more. A visitor arriving fresh from Holland will not feel at home among its domestic architecture. And though he can speak his own language there and be understood by most residents, Holland has ceased to be a Dutch enclave within the territory of the United States. It is to all intents and purposes an American township. Mr. Willard Wichers, the active propagandist of cultural relations between the Netherlands and the Dutch-Americans

of the Middle West, once told me that when he was in high school –
which must have been some twenty years ago – the children of Dutch-
American homes were ashamed of their origin. They felt insulted when
you called them Dutch. That is different now. It is now considered a
distinction to be of Dutch ancestry. I suppose that this change of
feeling is due to the total Americanization of the Dutch community.
As long as the people of Holland were still part aliens, their children,
anxious as all children are to conform, were looked upon to their
chagrin as outsiders by their American classmates. But now that even
the grown-ups behave as Americans and entire Holland is proud of its
Americanism, no stigma attaches any longer to a citizen of Holland's
Dutchness. On the contrary, it is now deemed an honor to be related
to one of the early founders, and the entire community, regardless of
erstwhile nationality, takes pride in the town's Dutch origin.

Group migrations from the Netherlands such as Van Raalte's colony
inaugurated are possible only when the group is held together by the
cement of a common faith. There are Roman Catholic and Calvinist
settlements of Dutch immigrants in the United States, but I never
heard of any that were founded by Dutch agnostics. These prefer to
come alone and would not choose to settle in Holland, Mich. Its
Dutch origin would have no attraction for them. Dutchmen feel a
common bond in the faith that they share, they find no means of
cohesion in their common Dutchness.

Recent immigrants to France gave a striking illustration of this
binding force in religious faith. The French Government is encourag-
ing immigration of Dutch farmers but does not want group settlements that would plant alien colonies among the native population. It
offers therefore attractive inducements to those newcomers from
Holland who are not averse to being absorbed in the French community. But a number of orthodox Calvinist farmers insisted on settling on
French soil as a group and were content to accept land of inferior
quality in return for the Government's permission to stay together.
Unyielding land is a continuous headache for a farmer, yet these men
chose the headache they could suffer together rather than the economic
well-being that was to be enjoyed alone. They have not done so badly
after all. They are settled in the northeast of France, in the valley of
the Yonne, a tributary of the Seine, and some of them have large
tracts of land under cultivation. A year ago they had reached a state of
prosperity in which they could seriously discuss plans for the appointment of a Dutch Reformed minister and the establishment of a
school of their own.

It does not follow, though, that the individual Hollander cares little
for his country and his people. The men who volunteered to settle in

France were asked why they did not go to America or Canada, and the answer of all of them was that France was preferable because it was nearer home. They were anxious to keep in personal touch with their relatives and friends by flying back once in a while to the old nest. For most of the first settlers in Michigan that pleasant prospect was cut off for good. They took leave forever from all that they cherished to begin a life of hardship in an unknown wilderness. Emigration in those days was not a concern of the Government. The authorities at The Hague assumed no responsibility for the future lot of the quitters. If they wanted to forsake their country, they had to pay the penalty of the venture. The Dutch public took much the same attitude. It was either indifferent or critical. E. J. Potgieter, the editor of De Gids, the leading literary monthly, deplored Van Raalte's decision to lead his flock to America. Holland, according to him, was able to secure employment to all her workers; the economic crisis was only a temporary decline that was not symptomatic of the nation's general state of health. If there were citizens, nevertheless, who wanted to seek a livelihood elsewhere, they should emigrate to the East Indies and give the Dutch colonies the benefit of their energy rather than a foreign country. Emigration to America meant a costly loss to the fatherland and was, consequently, unpatriotic. The Government, therefore, was fully justified in washing its hands of these disloyal citizens.

The Netherlands Government's attitude towards emigration nowadays is the very reverse of that in Potgieter's time. Now would-be quitters are patted on the back and are told that they do the country a service by leaving. Loyalties are relative values. In a land that suffers from over-population the worker who turns his back to it deserves well of the fatherland. Emigration under those conditions becomes an act of patriotism, and the Government speeds the patriots on their way with its grateful blessings. And not with blessings only. It cares for them in their land of exile, and sees to it that none comes to grief. The men who volunteer for settlement in France receive all the help and instruction they need to make their venture a success. The Dutch Government has rented Méridon castle in the valley of the Chevreuse and turned it into a clearing-house for immigrant farm boys from Holland. A correspondent of Neerlandia, the organ of the General Netherlands League, gave an interesting account, half a year ago, of his visit to the castle. Here they find a provisional home where in attractive surroundings they can overcome their initial nostalgia and can learn what they need to know for the new life that awaits them. A former governess of Princess Juliana heads the establishment with the aid of a staff of some thirty assistants. The boys attend courses in the agricultural methods of France, in knowledge of the soil, in French manners and customs, and, of course, in the French language. After half a year they are set to work with a Dutch or French farmer in the neighborhood of Méridon, so that they can keep in touch with their instructors and turn to them, in case of need, for help and advice. And after the completion of their practical training they can rent a farm and start work on their own.

Van Raalte's Holland of 1847 was a different kind of training school. The Netherlands Government, a century ago, never thought of sending agricultural experts ahead to instruct his followers on the spot in the ways of American husbandry. They had to rely exclusively on the experience they had acquired at home and on their common sense. When these did not suffice, they learnt in the hard school of adversity. That proved a more expensive way of training than the schooling at Méridon. For adversity's lessons were paid for with the lives of many of the students. But those who survived were steeled by the ordeal and bred a race of sturdy, self-reliant Americans. Their descendants of 1947 would have less reason to be proud of the founders if Van Raalte's enterprise had been a case of de luxe immigration à la Méridon castle.

October, 1947

A GREAT PUBLISHER

Lange Voorhout is the name of the most beautiful thoroughfare at The Hague. Its shaded walks have been the pride of the citizens for more than three hundred years. In the early seventeenth century the poet Constantijn Huygens wrote a long poem in praise of *Batava Tempe*, this Netherlands counterpart of the idyllic vale of Tempe in ancient Thessaly. The preposterous comparison suited the baroque taste of the age to which Huygens belonged, an age that liked to imagine itself a modern reincarnation of classical antiquity. Delphi lived anew in the Dutch town of Delft and Hugo Grotius, who was born there, was the latter-day Delphic oracle, Leyden was the Dutch Athens, rural Holland a modern Arcady and its milkmaids Arcadian wood and water nymphs. The vale of Tempe was not out of place in this Hellenic travesty. The burghers, though flattered by the playful fancy of the poets, had the good taste and common sense not to follow their lead in their domestic architecture. The mansions they built for themselves along the Lange Voorhout were not Grecian temples but honest-to-goodness burgher homes which harmonized with the actual environment. Only the wealthy patricians could afford to live there. The architecture that lined the street in Huygens's day has not survived, except for the ancient *Kloosterkerk* or Minster, which dates of course from pre-Reformation days. All the burgher homes are of a later period, the majority of the eighteenth century. They are private homes no longer. Four decades ago they were still occupied by patrician families; but nearly all of them have since been invaded by government or private business. The erstwhile drawingrooms of the great are now buzzing with the ticktack of typewriters, a doorkeeper guards the noisy and untidy lobby through which formerly an impeccable butler moved with soundless treat, and the shabby façade makes shameless admission that the house behind it has come down in life. The most palatial of all, though, still puts up a respectable front. It has reason to, for it still serves a respectable purpose. It houses the collection, rich in rare books and precious manuscripts, of the Royal Library. And on the opposite side a modern building, whose style does not clash with its old-time surroundings, is also a home, or rather a hostel, for books, which enter it not to stay there but to pass through. Here is the publishing house and bookstore of Martinus Nijhoff, a mecca of rare book collectors from all over the world. The aristocracy of birth has fled the *Lange Voorhout*; the aristocracy of the mind has entrenched itself there in two of its most impressive buildings. Once the favorite haunt of the *beau monde*, it now attracts the men-of-letters. *Batava Tempe* has become a shrine of the learned.

The firm of Martinus Nijhoff has been in the publishing and bookselling business for more than two centuries. Its original home was at Arnhem, in the province of Gelderland. But on January 1, 1853, Mr. Martinus Nijhoff established himself at The Hague. Under him and his son Wouter, a worthy father's worthier son, both the publishing house and the rare book trade acquired international reputation. It was a daring move on Wouter's part to transfer the business, in 1910, from its modest quarters in a quiet, narrow side street of The Hague to the aristocratic sphere of the *Lange Voorhout*. Old fogeys shook their heads over this presumptuous invasion by vulgar commerce into the precincts of the privileged class. One of these left-overs of a bygone age, a high government dignitary, was heard to complain that Mr. Wouter Nijhoff was not submissive enough for a tradesman. The remark reached the unsubmissive bookdealer, and he chuckled with glee. To him the man's grievance was an implied homage. Wouter Nijhoff was much more than a mere tradesman. He scorned to act the obedient servant to any man, but as a publisher he was willing to be the servant of scholarship and science and promote them by publications that often brought him financial loss instead of profit. He was a scholar himself and the author of books in the field of bibliography that won him international fame. In *L'Art typographique dans les Pays-Bas pendant les années 1500 à 1540*, he reproduced in facsimile the typographic characters, publishers' imprints, woodcuts, and other ornaments employed by the printers during that period. And while this monumental work was in progress, he prepared with the assistance of Miss M. E. Kronenberg a Netherlands Bibliography for those same forty years, an invaluable sourcebook for all students of early sixteenth century history and literature.

Nijhoff's choice of that particular period of typography was prompted by his interest in the evolution of the book. The output of Dutch incunabula, the printed books of the fifteenth century, had been catalogued and described before Nijhoff's day by Holtrop and Campbell. Those earliest books were specimens of handicraft, the products of an individual typesetter's loving care. In the next century the growing demand for books, especially devotional ones, stimulated by the rise of heretical sects, affected the methods of bookmaking. The quantity produced was increased and the tempo of the labor involved accelerated. Typography, in consequence, changed from a handicraft to mass production. Incunabula are somewhat amphibious creatures; they partake of the nature of the medieval manuscripts in that the typesetter's painstaking labor still resembles the laborious penmanship of the scribe; but since the typesetting copyist could multiply his copy mechanically, the book he produced resembled more closely the printed book that the sixteenth century produced in large quantities. The output of the first four decades of that century marked the gradual transition from the medieval incunabulum to the modern book and for that reason Wouter Nijhoff's historical instinct was attracted to that particular phase of its evolution. He had a passionate love of books, or rather of the book in the abstract, the book as a repository of knowledge, a noble tool of science, and the research of the historians. In 1926 he issued a complete list of all the publications of his firm; his preface to this book closed with these words: "To participate or to initiate important editions in the fields of science and art is a noble passion, but as all passions often dangerous. I acknowledge with a deep sense of gratitude the support I received from various sides, especially from the other departments of my firm, which enabled our publishing house to make decisions that were not always primarily dictated by financial considerations." He was a prince among Dutch publishers, the latest upholder of a great tradition which goes back to the sixteenth century. Christopher Plantijn, of Antwerp, was its first outstanding representative. The house in which he lived under the same roof with his printing office, his publishing business, and his bookstore is now a museum that no foreign sightseer in Antwerp should fail to visit. Nijhoff kept his private residence separate from the firm's quarters and the printing of the books he published was done elsewhere. Otherwise the modern publisher had much in common with his sixteenth century forerunner. Both were scholars and deeply conscious of the important role they played in their day and age as promoters of learning and distributors of knowledge. The bookdealer's store was a meeting place of the lettered, and the publisher's office a sanctum to which even the great were proud to be admitted.

Wouter Nijhoff's office did not look like one. It was a scholar's study, a spacious workroom that impressed each caller with the exquisite taste of its owner. Nijhoff always sat behind the large desk near the left window, from where he overlooked the *Lange Voorhout*. For thirty-seven years he occupied that place. Next door was the Admiralty, and the Minister of Marine, no doubt, enjoyed the same view from his desk by the front window. But Ministers of Marine come and go in rapid succession. Mone can ever have felt part of the scene framed by the window. But to Nijhoff the *Lange Voorhout* must have seemed a projection of his business, the park belonging to his mansion, which customers and callers approached by the drive under its waving trees.

It was often my privilege to cross the threshold of his study. Duty and pleasure combined to make me call on Wouter Nijhoff as soon as I had arrived at The Hague. He was one of the prime movers in establishing the Dutch chair that I have occupied at Columbia since the year 1919, and from the outset he acted as secretary of the Committee in Holland that administers the funds from which part of the incumbent's salary is defrayed. He had "discovered" America, as he used to say, in 1901. Before that year he had no business dealings with this Continent; but after the turn of the century the firm entered upon the American book market and rapidly expanded its custom in this country. There cannot be many book collectors in the United States who are unfamiliar with the scholarly catalogues of books on special subjects that the firm sends out at regular intervals. The latest I received was No. 673, listing works on Roman and Ancient Foreign Law. A notice was inserted informing the American customers that this catalogue was being mailed to them one month before it would be distributed in Europe. "It has happened that the greater part of items ordered by American libraries had been sold when the orders arrived. I made this arrangement in order to avoid disappointments in the future."

This communication in the first person was signed Martinus Nijhoff. It was the firm that was addressing its clients, not Martinus, who died in 1894. In January of this year Wouter followed his father in death. His nephew and namesake, Wouter Nijhoff, Jr., has succeeded to the desk by the window overlooking the *Lange Voorhout*. Wouter Sr. must have died proud and happy in the knowledge that Martinus Nijhoff would carry on.

November, 1947

A SEPTUAGENARIAN'S RECOLLECTIONS

When I was young and thought of life as an unending adventure, I looked up with profound respect to those aged people who had lived threescore years and ten. But now that I have reached that goal myself, my respect for septuagenarians is gone. No man can look up to his contemporaries. Besides, the traveler through life, having climbed that far, realizes in looking back on the distance covered that the journey was not the steep ascent that it seemed at the outset. To the child the seventieth milestone appears to mark a mountain top; it is but a hillside token to the man who has come to rest there. And the road by which he reached it seems less long in retrospect than he imagined it to be at the start. To the young old age is a far-off region to which they never give a thought in connexion with themselves, to the old youth is a near-by neighborhood which they left only a short while ago. Man's life shrinks in retrospect, and the weakening sight of his memory is so focused that it sees more clearly the distant than the recent past. The scenes of childhood are vividly remembered and friends and acquaintances of half a century ago are still alive in the old man's farsighted recollection.

These thoughts have flitted through my mind off and on ever since the ninth of October. In the afternoon of that day I came home with a medal that Mr. Pieter Grimm, on behalf of the Netherland-America Foundation, had presented to me at a luncheon in the Union Club. I hope that I succeeded, on the spur of the moment, in choosing appropriate words wherewith to thank our President for the honor he conferred upon me. It was a distinction that I deeply appreciate. The legend on the medal states that it was given me "for eminent service in the fields of Netherland-America friendship." I did not grasp the full meaning of those words until I was home and tried to determine what kind of service I had rendered to that good cause. I have lectured and written articles and books on Dutch history, art, and literature, and made contacts with Americans in various walks of life in order to spread knowledge, on a modest scale, about Holland and her people. It vexed me to discover that the names of many places where I had

303

lectured and of many people whom I had met or corresponded with had slipped my mind. My visual memory recalled some of the places and the faces, but I could not give them a local habitation and a name. But when my thoughts take me back to the days before my arrival in America I find no difficulty in reconstructing the past.

It was a past whose remembered image offers a striking contrast to the present. Amsterdam, where I was born and grew up, was a very small place compared to New York. It was just beginning to outgrow the limits that it had reached by the end of the eighteenth century. One could easily walk its circumference between sunrise and sunset. There was not a street or alley within that limited space with which I was not familiar; I knew every nook and corner of Amsterdam. My father was a physician with an extensive practice. On holidays he often took me with him in his carriage when he went on his morning round of professional calls; my chief delight was to sit, on warm summer days, on the box seat next to the driver. Thus I got to know Amsterdam from north to south and east to west, for my father had his patients in all parts of the city. It was a city of many moods. Under a sunlit sky it sparkled with the reflections of barges and house tops and elm trees in the water of its winding canals; when the sky was overcast it had a melancholy charm; when a heavy snow fall muffled all sounds it gave me a sense of eeriness and mystery. There was a painter in those days at Amsterdam who made the old city in all these moods live on canvas, a very great artist, the greatest, to my mind, of his generation. I just received this morning an illustrated catalogue of a memorial exhibition of his work that is on view in Holland during the months of October and November. "Breitner and Amsterdam," it is justly entitled. Though Geo Breitner (1857-1923) lived and painted in many places, it was in Amsterdam that he did his greatest work. He made the city his very own by glorifying it on canvas and making his fellow citizens see beauties in those different moods that they had never seen before. The citizens of Amsterdam are not too fond of rainy days. They get too many of them in the course of a year. They will hasten home through the muddy streets without suspecting that they pass anything deserving their admiring attention. But Breitner taught them otherwise. He saw beauty in a rain-splashed city square aglitter with the reflections of street lamps in the puddles, the shining skins of cab and streetcar horses, and the white bonnets and aprons of servant girls. Or he showed them, more amazing still, that builders digging the foundations for a new housing development on the outskirts of the city were unconscious creators of beauty to the exploring artist. Or he made them look at a wharf in the snow, a muddle of boats and beams and logs and ramshackle sheds against a background of weather-beaten gables and red-tiled roofs, and they saw that there was beauty in that chaos. Amsterdam was painted in the seventeenth century by Job Berckheyde and Jan van der Heyden, but their views of the city, however masterly in execution, are dull and lifeless in comparison with those of Geo Breitner. The older artists painted the picturesque architecture; their pictures look like stage sets at the raising of the curtain before the action of the play has begun. But Breitner painted the city in action, its pulsating life, not the architectural framework of the play. His Amsterdam is animate with the labor of its people, with the gusts of the west wind, the pelting of the rain, the drift of winter snow. The reproductions in my Breitner catalogue are evocations of the Amsterdam I remember so clearly that I know it better than present-day New York.

Other memories crowd upon me: of vacations spent in my grandmother's house in Zutfen, a rambling eighteenth century structure built over much older cellars that must have belonged to some medieval monastery; of hikes through the *Achterhoek*, the region east of Zutfen that is dotted with picturesque old villages; of bicycle trips across the *Veluwe*, a wide expanse of heath and wood that is the summer play ground of many Dutch city dwellers; of visits to the North Sea shore, the beaches of Zandvoort, Noordwijk, and Scheveningen; of my student years in Leyden and the friendships then formed whose ties have not been slackened by years of separation; of hikes, with all our luggage in a rucksack, through the Harz, the Black Forest, or the Ardennes; and of Berlin where I spent a year of study under Alois Brandl and Andreas Heusler; of an unforgettable summer in Oxford, where I had gone to do some research in the Bodleian Library, and where I met my future wife; and finally of seventeen years spent at The Hague in bringing up a family and teaching at the municipal gymnasium and the university of Leyden.

Such fond remembrance, to which I plead guilty, of persons, places and incidents of the past should not be taken to imply that the septuagenarian has lost all interest in his American present. Far from it. But it is only natural that the traveler, resting for a moment by the milestone on the hillside, should take pleasure in viewing the far distance and finding it undimmed by the mist of time. It gives him a sense of being still close to youth, of being only seventy years young.

December, 1947

OF TURKEYS

In the middle of the sixteenth century a printer at Antwerp published a series of engravings after drawings by Pieter Brueghel the Elder depicting in allegory the Seven Deadly Sins. The personification of each sin is accompanied by some creature from the animal kingdom supposed to show the symptoms of the vice in its instinctive behavior. A turkey cock is the attribute of Envy. I leave it for naturalists to explain why this particular fowl was chosen from among the vast variety of nature's fauna as an emblem of jealousy. Brueghel in making the choice cannot have followed a set tradition. For the turkey was then a recent discovery. A contemporary of the artist wrote in the year 1578, "The Calcutta cock became known during my lifetime; when I was young people paid a farthing to go and see one." Specimens were on view at fairs and kermises, and townspeople and country folk gaped at them in wonder as we used to do at the giant panda at the late World's Fair. Poultrymen will doubtless be able to tell whether Brueghel's envious fowl is one of the Mexican or the North-American variety. The chances are that it is a specimen of the Mexican breed. For the first on view in Europe must have been brought there from Central America. That may be inferred from its name in the languages of the old continent. The same error that led the European invaders of the western hemisphere to call its aborigines Indians gave rise to the belief that the turkey was an Indian bird. It was impossible for stay-at-homes in France and the Netherlands to distinguish between the East and the West Indies. They thought of them as one exotic domain which had of course its western and eastern boundaries. The showmen at the country fairs cannot have been anxious to clear up that confusion. The farther away the bird's habitat, the greater its attraction for the sightseers. A bird from fabulous India was a sight so rare that everyone would gladly pay a farthing to look at it. Hence the cock from the Indies in the western hemisphere was readily believed to have come from Asia; and thus it became known in France by the name of *coq d'Inde* or *dindon* and in the Netherlands by that of *kalkoetsche* or *kalkoensche haan* (Calcutta cock), which was in course of time shortened to *kalkoen*, pronounced *kolkoon* with the accent on the final syllable. The English knew a Turkey cock before they became acquainted with the American one. That was the African bird which they now call Guinea fowl. It was probably imported from some Mediteranean region under the domination of the Turks or of potentates mistaken for Turks; later on, when the Portuguese brought it in from the west coast of Africa, it came to be known as Guinea fowl and its original name was erroneously transferred to the American variety with which it was wrongly identified. The bird can plume itself on the honor of having been claimed, in name at least, by two continents; but it belongs in fact to America alone.

The turkey has remained a sort of exotic bird in Holland. It did

not like the damp climate and the humid soil. The Dutch, in consequence, never learnt to include turkey meat in their Christmas bill
of fare. The traditional Christmas dish of the Netherlands is goose.
But even that is an exceptional treat. To confess the truth, the Dutch
do not celebrate the feast of the Nativity with eating and drinking.
Christmas day is a holiday which is spent in church in the forenoon and
quietly at home after the midday meal. It was different three generations ago. J. ter Gouw, who published his book "De Volksvermaken"
(Popular Pastimes) in 1871, says that as soon as St. Nicholas Eve was
past the Christmas geese appeared. Shiploads of them were brought
to the quay at Amsterdam and on Christmas Eve every pub and pot-
house sought to attract customers by raffling an especially fat one
which had dangled for days from a nail in the door post. Ter Gouw
also knew the custom of baking a special wheat loaf at Christmas that
was shaped like the shank of a large animal and bore the strange name
of *duivekater* (devil's cat). The Dutch folklorist G. J. Boekenoogen
saw in the baking of these loaves an ancient pagan custom and supposed that the *duivekater* was an image of the wild boar which was
sacred to the sun god. Suspicion of its heathen origin may have
discredited the shank-shaped loaf. It was at any rate on its way out
in Ter Gouw's day. "At present," he grumbled, "they advertise
German *Weihnachtswecke* in the newspapers, along with the German
Christmas trees." He heartily disliked both alien intruders, and it
would seem that his dislike was shared by the majority of his countrymen. The *Wecke* have never been nationalized and the tree has not
won general favor. It serves to enliven an occasional Christmas party
for children, but it never became an indispensable decoration of the
home. That is doubtless due to the competition of St. Nicholas Eve,
on the fifth of December, which is Holland's counterpart of England's
boxing day. The season for the giving of presents is long over when
Christmas arrives; and in the homes where the German tree is set
up it does not gather any parcels under its spreading branches. In
short, the Dutch Christmas is no occasion for fun and merriment.
It is a season of rest and relaxation for grown-ups, it has nothing
exciting to offer to the little ones who are the natural playmates of
the Holy Child.

This austerity suits the Calvinist temper. The ministers of the
Dutch Reformed Church always frowned upon customs that were
suspected of being survivals of the heathen past; feasting and banquet-
ing and merrymaking were desecrations, in their eyes, of the night of
the Nativity, and the faithful were accordingly discouraged from
participating in such unseemly frolics. The Church of Rome has been
more tolerant towards such relics of a bygone age. In the Catholic

provinces of the Netherlands ancient beliefs and practices still prevail that lend poetry to the lives of the country folk. The peasants in Flanders like to believe that their beasts and their bees share in the adoration of the Christ child. The bees, they tell their children, hum carols in the Christmas night; the horses pray aloud; and the sheep bend their knees in devotion. At Moelingen, in Belgian Limburg, the rooster calls "The Child Jesus is born." "Moo, moo? (Where, where?)" asks the pigeon, and the lamb replies, "In Bethlehem." In other parts of Limburg the peasants put the fodder out in the open so as to have it blessed in the Christmas night. The ashes of the yule log on the hearth are strewn upon the fields, because they are believed to have the magic power of warding off evil and giving fertility. For the yule log is a symbol of the sacrificial fire which betokened the new life that was to be imparted to nature by the returning heat of the sun.

January, 1948

VAN MEEGEREN

On November 13th of last year Hans van Meegeren was sentenced to one year in prison on charges of fraudulently signing the names of great masters to pictures that were confessedly his own. Seven weeks later, on New Year's Eve, he succumbed in an Amsterdam hospital to a heart ailment. No wonder he died of a broken heart. He had buried his face in his hands and wept when the District Attorney denounced him for having swerved from the path of righteousness and expressed his insulting and wholly uncalled-for assumption that the defendant, after having served his term in prison, was not likely to return to society a better man. He was a better man than most in so far as he excelled in the art that he had made his profession. When his painting of Christ at Emmaus was unveiled at the Boymans Museum in Rotterdam in the presence of the city authorities and a dense crowd of invited guests, a hush fell upon the gathering and then the emotion of the spectators found relief in murmurs and gasps and exclamations. Van Meegeren himself was there to watch Vermeer's vicarious triumph, an amused but also embittered witness. Amused at the folly of the experts who had been duped so completely that, were he to claim his authorship of this masterpiece, their pretence to special knowledge would drop off them and leave them exposed in naked ignorance; embittered by the conviction that, if the picture were exhibited as a Van Meegeren, no crowd of city magistrates and connoisseurs and lovers of art would gather round it with gasps and murmurs of admiration. His own signature on the picture would have deflated its value. The Museum had paid half a million guilders for the unsuspected forgery; it would not have cared to purchase it for one hundredth of that amount if it had been offered for sale as a Van Meegeren. From a legal point of view his condemnation to a year in prison may have been just and unavoidable; but the stigma of that sentence attaches not to his memory but to the snobbery of the fashionable world which buys names when it pretends to buy pictures and buys those names as an investment while pretending to honor art. Van Meegeren has deserved well of his ungrateful fatherland, for he enriched it with a painting that even the experts whom he exposed cannot deny to be a masterpiece since they proclaimed it a Vermeer; and he proved to everybody's satisfaction that the infallibility of the self-styled "art experts" is a myth. The public prosecutor argued that Van Meegeren's forgery was an insult to art. It was nothing of the kind. It was, on the contrary, a vindication of art. For he brought proof that art is being insulted by many who, while posing as its patrons, traffic in paintings as they traffic in stocks and bonds, for the purpose of self-enrichment. His Christ at Emmaus, which the experts declared to be the greatest achievement of the Delft master, is still the same picture. Will the city of Rotterdam accord it the same place of honor that it occupied as Vermeer's masterpiece? It would be an insult to art to answer that question in the negative. For that would be tantamount to an admission that art is not a thing of beauty but a mere commodity of trade.

The art expert who does not create but only judges is a product of the modern tendency to theorize about art. He came to the fore in the eighteenth century and has gained in importance and self-assurance in inverse ratio to the decline of art production. It would seem as if the growing preoccupation with the essence of the beautiful tends to stifle man's ability to create it. Reasoning interferes with creation and the artist who is too self-consciously aware of how he ought to paint is robbed of the creative impulse. The early masters went through a severe schooling. Apprenticed to a master craftsman they learnt in the studio, by the sheer force of routine, all the mysteries of his technique. But once possessed of these they felt them to be second nature; their painting ceased to be a conscious effort and became the spontaneous expression of their talent. Neither Vermeer nor Rembrandt could have defined their concepts of the beautiful, nor could they have explained why they painted as they did and not otherwise. Armed in the hard school of experience with an unfailing technique, they could dispense with barren theory and be satisfied with just painting. Van Meegeren's Vermeer technique was a late acquisition that never became an integrated part of his artistic self. It was an assumed pose, which he could painstakingly maintain for a time with an admirable gift for impersonation. He never was a Vermeer, he only acted one with undeniable talent. That became evident when, under arrest, he was challenged to produce another Vermeer. The Vermeer manner was so little ingrained in him that it eluded him when he was forced to work under the supervision of indifferent strangers. No expert was needed to determine that the picture he then produced was clumsy of composition and a poor piece of painting. But the experts, if they were worth their salt, should have been able to detect the pose in Christ at Emmaus.

February, 1948

OF CHURCH ORGANS

Among the treats of my childhood was an occasional excursion from Amsterdam where we lived to the nearby city of Haarlem. My mother was fond of music and liked to attend the organ recitals that were given there on Thursday afternoons in the Great Church on the market place. I loved to go with her, not so much for the sake of the music, I must admit, as for the pleasure of the train journey and the sight of unfamiliar scenes. The church itself was not the least of these. The lofty Gothic nave always impressed me; it seemed to dwarf the crowd of music lovers who flocked to these concerts. We went in through a small side door, a most undignified way, I thought, of entering so magnificent a building. It made you feel like sneaking in. As soon as the door had closed behind us the noise and clamor of the market place was hushed. The stillness that suddenly immersed us made you catch your breath; its solemnity was heightened by the spectacle of the mute multitude that was waiting in silence for the concert to begin. Those recitals attracted hearers from all over the country, for the organist was a great musician and the organ was said to be one of the finest in existence.

In my young days I believed in its excellence without questioning. But with the passage of the years credulity gave way to scepticism. Was it really the wonderful instrument it is boasted to be, I began to ask? How can anyone tell? One would have to travel all over Europe to test the most famous organs and compare them with the one in Haarlem. And where is the man who has done that? The negative answer was implied in the question: nowhere of course. But I recently discovered that I was mistaken; there actually is such a man. He is Albert Schweitzer, the famous Alsatian who gave up a brilliant career in the fields of music, philosophy, biblical scholarship, and letters to labor as a mission doctor at Lambaréné in French West Africa. During my Christmas vacation I read the story of his life by George Seaver, who as an assistant native commissioner of northern Rhodesia became acquainted with Schweitzer and his work. The third chapter of this biography is devoted to Schweitzer as one of the world's great organists and an expert on organs and organ building. I was reminded of the recitals in Haarlem when I read his appraisal of Dutch organs. He considers the organ of St. Sulpice in Paris as the finest creation that he knows, and next to it that of Notre Dame. But Holland, in his opinion, "is the country where there is most appreciation of the value and beauty of old organs. Dutch organists have conscientiously refrained from sacrificing magnificence of tone to securing the abolition of technical defects." Schweitzer knows what he is talking about, for he is both organist and organ builder and has no less intimate a knowledge of organ construction than he has, as a doctor, of the human anatomy. Several years ago, during one of his visits to Holland, he was invited to preach on Christmas Day in the ancient St. Walburg Church at Zutfen, in the province of Gelderland. He arrived five days earlier, but nothing was seen of him during the day time until Christmas Eve. He had spent all his hours in the organ loft "covered with grime and sweat, cleaning the pipes and the accumulated deposit of years." Pierre van Paassen, who was his fellow guest on that occasion, witnessed the amazement of the congregation on Christmas morning as they listened to the prelude. "Is that our old organ?" they clearly asked with wondering eyes. The memories of his organ recitals in Holland are evidently dear to Schweitzer. In the guesthouse at Günzbach, his native village, which he had built for the accommodation of the many admirers who come to visit him when he spends a vacation there, the staircase is lined with photographs of famous old organs on which he has played in Holland.

How old are these organs? That of St. Sulpice which is rated so highly by Schweitzer was not completed until 1862. Are the organs of Holland much older? The building of them was a medieval handicraft that had several skilled practitioners in the Netherlands. Jan van Eyck painted a sample of their work on one of the panels of his Adoration of the Lamb at Ghent. The Church of St. Martin at Groningen had an organ installed in 1479 which, according to unverified tradition, was the handiwork of the humanist Rudolf Agricola. The foremost organ builder of the Netherlands in the early sixteenth century appears to have been Jan van Koevelen at Amsterdam. When the parish church at Franeker in Friesland needed a new organ the priest and church wardens concluded with Van Koevelen a contract dated October 5, 1528, by which the latter bound himself to make "a

new six feet wide organ of a new construction with three pairs of
bellows and two keyboards, the front pipes to be made of fine English
tin." The document specifies at length every detail Van Koevelen
undertook to supply; the technical terms that he used may be intelligible to a modern organist and builder, but to a layman such as myself
they convey little meaning. This much, however, is clear from its
context that on the order's being completed and duly installed in the
Franeker church Van Koevelen would be entitled to the sum of five
hundred guilders to be paid in five yearly instalments of one hundred
each. The organ was delivered within a year of the date of the contract, and Van Koevelen received his final payment on March 1st,
1534. He must have done a solid piece of work, for it did good service for nearly two centuries. A new one took its place in 1719,
which was apparently inferior to Van Koevelen's handiwork for it
had to make way for a fourth in 1842.

It is somewhat of a miracle that the technique of organ building
developed in the Middle Ages has survived in the Netherlands until
our day. For it was threatened with annihilation in the late sixteenth
century. The Calvinists, who had seized the medieval churches,
denuded them of everything that had been their chief glory; stained-
glass windows, statuary, paintings, organ music, and choir singing
were banned as the trappings of popery. For more than half a century
the congregations sang the psalms without any instrumental accompaniment. As the singers possessed more religious zeal than voice
control, the acoustic effect of their psalmody was an insult to the
Deity they meant to praise and implore. Each was eager to be heard
above his neighbors, and in trying to outshout each other the pious
created a cacophony reminiscent of Bedlam rather than Paradise. The
poet Constantyn Huygens, who was also an accomplished musician
and composer, was so outraged by this profanation of the sacred service that he launched a campaign for the restoration of organ music.
The consistory of Leyden was the first to heed the rising tide of
protest. It reintroduced the music of the organ into the religious
services in the hope that its effect would be "to edify and to stimulate
devotion." The Church of St. Martin in Groningen also thought better
of it and ceded to Rudolf Agricola's organ a part in the service. The
stadtholder, Prince Frederik Hendrik, accompanied by Constantyn
Huygens, who was his private secretary, worshipped there in November 1640 and both were so deeply impressed by the music that the
Prince promised to erect an organ in his court chapel at The Hague
and Huygens decided to come out in the open with a printed plea in
defence of the organ despite the certain opposition of the Dutch
Reformed ministers. The pamphlet appeared in 1641 under the title

"Use and Misuse of the organ in the churches of the United Netherlands." The ministerial counterblast was less formidable than Huygens had expected. His booklet met with more acclaim than vituperation. Even the synod of the Dutch Reformed Church expressed its approval of his plea for the organ, and during the next decades one church after the other followed the example of the Leyden consistory. In 1578 the synod had passed a resolution demanding the demolition of the organs in the Netherlands churches. How did it happen that any were left to be played when the synodal ostracism was lifted?

The secular rulers of the Dutch cities are to be thanked for that. In the Dutch Republic the medieval church buildings had become the property of the municipalities, and the burgomasters backed up by the majority of the town councillors not only forbade the destruction of the city's organs but ordered them to be used for the delectation of music lovers among the community. The organists were appointed and salaried by the magistrates, and accordingly took their orders from them. And they employed them as purveyors of secular music in the church buildings to which all who liked to listen were welcome regardless of creed. The Leyden burgomasters told their organist Cornelis Schuyt in his instruction of the year 1593 that his organ recitals were intended for the recreation and the enjoyment of the burghers and for weaning them away from taverns and taprooms. We owe it to this worldly use of the city-owned organs that they survived demolition at the hands of the Calvinist fanatics. It is strange that Huygens condemned in his pamphlet "the frivolous evening recitals" as profanations of the sacred houses of God. His orthodoxy, after all, was stronger than his love of music.

May, 1954

THE GOSPEL OF SIGNIFICS

We are living in a hectic era, which leaves a writer no time for the careful weighing of words. We sling them onto paper nowadays. There is danger in this hasty, slovenly word manipulation. Communion between citizens is obscured by the vagueness and instability of meaning, and if speakers of a common language are apt to misunderstand each other, the chances of confusion are all the greater in the intercourse with speakers of another tongue. I remember an incident, a harmless one fortunately, that happened years ago in the office of the Foundation, which at that time was located on Madison Avenue near Fortieth Street. Miss Ethel Ingram, who was our secretary, was listening to a distinguished visitor from Holland. "What do you know

313

about that!" she exclaimed by way of expressing her keen interest in what he was telling her. He looked offended and said, in a tone of stern rebuke, "Young lady, I do know. You should not question my authority. It is my business to know." I had to explain to him that her exclamation was not an expression of incredulity. Word meanings are elusive and offense is often taken where none is intended, the speaker having used an expression that the hearer understood differently. If this were more widely realized, there would be less bitterness and strife in the world.

The insufficiency of language and people's unawareness of it was a much debated subject half a century ago among a group of Dutch writers and scientists who saw their chief spokesman in Frederik van Eeden, a leading figure of the literary movement that revolutionized Dutch literature in the eighties and nineties of the past century. He spread the gospel of Significs as he called his study of word meaning not only among his compatriots but also abroad. He brought it to America and lectured on April 2nd, 1902, to a large audience of students of Kansas University. "I dare say this is probably the first lecture on this subject ever held on Significs," he wrote to his English correspondent, Lady Victoria Welby. She too was painfully aware of the pitfalls of misunderstanding that endanger verbal intercourse among men, and she welcomed Van Eeden as an ally in the cause of Significs when they met in August, 1892, at an international conference on Experimental Psychology in London. She liked the address he delivered there and invited him to spend a few days at her country seat, Denton Manor, near Lincoln. That visit was the beginning of a lasting friendship of which the letters they exchanged form an eloquent and distressing record. Distressing I found it because it proves that these two thinkers who strove so valiantly for the elimination of ambiguity in language were themselves unable to understand each other. In 1908, after sixteen years of correspondence, Van Eeden wrote: "You never will understand me, because you have always lived the life of an English aristocrat, and I first that of a middleclass bourgeois and then of a sort of social outcast." That was an unintentional confession that the science of Significs was not the cure-all he and she believed it to be. So many other elements come into play where people fail to grasp each other's meaning; differences in social background, in religion, in national preconceptions, in school education, and many others. Van Eeden had a reformer's tendency to lecture his noble correspondent. He reproached her, most unjustly, with leading a life of aristocratic luxury and idleness, he ridiculed her devotion to Queen Victoria, wounded her feelings by speaking contemptuously of the old lady, and inveighed indignantly against the

314

perfidy of England when Lady Welby's country was at war with the Boers in South Africa. The wonder is that his outspokenness never shattered their friendship; it was shielded against harm by her truly noble forbearance. She recognized the nobility of mind in her Dutch friend and was willing to overlook the many rude manifestations of his friendship. The letters were published recently in the Transactions of the Frederik van Eeden Society at Amsterdam, but in this reader's opinion they are less of a tribute to him than they are to Lady Victoria Welby. She was the more convincing exponent of their common message because she actually practiced what she preached. On June 7 he wrote to her, "Name me an Empire in history which suppressed a little republic, and is not now cursed for it. Be it the Persian Empire, the Austrian Empire, the Napoleonic Empire, the Russian Empire, or the Roman Empire. And it is my view also that to compel pious men who worshipped only God, to worship a 'most Gracious Imperial Majesty' is about the most terrible blasphemy and offense to God ever committed by man or nation." That was indeed the common view in Holland at the time of the South-African war and the Dutch had good reason for feeling that way, but there was no reason for Van Eeden to write in this vein to the friend whom he knew to be closely attached to Queen Victoria. In the letter she wrote him in reply she said, "Others wonder that I should tolerate your letters. But the really grievous thing is that you should tolerate them yourself. I never feel a shadow of blame for you or those like you; only for those who have knowingly sown so evil a crop of malignant lies that even a generous heart like yours falls victim to their poison ... May you soon find the 'deeps of deliverance'[1] from this; may there soon be born the new life of that new world which you are striving to realize. For that, your practical devotion to the Ideal of Brotherhood of which your federation is a symbol, you know how much I honor you." Van Eeden did know it well. When the news of her death reached him, he wrote in his diary on the first day of April, 1912: "I have lost the treasure that was almost my dearest in the world, my spiritual mother."

February, 1955

OF CHURCH BELLS

Last year a simple, yet impressive, ceremony took place at the University of Leyden. Two bells for the tower of the academy building were consecrated for their high calling by the rite of baptism. Their high

[1] An allusion to the title of the English translation of one of his novels.

315

calling in a two-fold sense, for it will be the calling of the larger one to call the hours from its high perch, the half hours will be called by its smaller partner. The crowd that had assembled to watch the christening of LIBERTAS and SCIENTIA was attracted to the scene not so much by a desire to see the initiates as by the memory of the lost pair they replaced. During the days of the Hitler terror the bells whose voices had proclaimed the hours and called the students to classes and lecture rooms were silenced by order of the Nazi rulers. They were requisitioned, with many other tower bells throughout the land, to be turned into cannon. The Leyden authorities did not rest until the two were somehow replaced, but the best they could devise for a substitute was a pair of iron kettles, which feebly and unmusically recalled to the Leyden people the mighty and resonant voices of their predecessors. Still even the larger one of these humble makeshifts was honored with an inscription in Dutch:

> Though feeble my voice, yet listen to me
> When I strike the hour of liberty.

The Nazis were still in power when these kettle voices began to be heard. They left them undisturbed. Perhaps they were not aware that the kettle, high in its dark tower, expressed the yearnings that stirred in the hearts of students and burghers. The brave kettle has since been lowered from its high beam, but not in the esteem of Faculty and student body. It will be given a place of honor in the historical collection of the university.

Ever since tower bells were tolled in the Netherlands they were endowed by popular sentiment with an individual life. Their call was to the citizens the voice of a spirit who watched over the town and its burghers. That is why many were given names that expressed the people's sense of the life spark inherent in those metal voices. Roland hung in the belfry at Ghent and himself proclaimed his name and his function in the inscription that encircled him: "My name is Roland, my ringing warns of fire, my tolling of tempest in Flanders land." I do not believe the Leyden bells were thus christened. I was enrolled as a student in 1895 and studied there until 1900, but I never in all that time heard them referred to by name. They had hung there long enough, though, to acquire one. They were the work of Pierre Hemony, the younger of two brothers who were famous in the Dutch Republic and far and wide beyond its borders in the middle of the seventeenth century. I was familiar with their name long before I knew that they had been master bell founders. There was a street in Amsterdam, my native city, that was named for them, not an attractive street in an unattractive neighborhood, one of those trite reale state developments that sprang up on the outskirts of the beautiful old city in the second half of the nineteenth century. It was a poor monument to the men whose name it bore. The municipal authorities in those days did not pay much attention to the fitness of their nomenclature. The names they selected from the nation's hall of fame served merely as identity labels; they were not meant as badges of distinction for the godfathers. Hence the aspect of those streets is seldom a reflection of the godfathers' greatness. There is a district of Amsterdam where all the streets have been named for masters of Holland's school of painting, an unpicturesque, depressing scene of flat monotony. Close by is the Rijksmuseum, the national picture gallery. Within its walls Rembrandt's contemporaries testify with their paintings to the greatness of their art, outside a soulless architecture seems to deny them any greatness. Hence it never occurred to me, when I was a little boy, that the name Hemony affixed to the nameplate of an ugly street, might belong to a Netherlands immortal. Not until much later, when I became interested in the country's history, did I discover the identity of its bearers.

The brothers had come to the Netherlands from Lorraine, where François Hemony was born in 1609 and Pierre ten years later. During the Thirty Years' War they found employment as casters of ordnance in Germany, but the unsettled conditions east of the Rhine soon induced them to seek security in the Dutch Republic. They first made their home in the town of Zutfen in the province of Gelderland. They received a commission from the magistracy to supply the new tower that was being erected over the Wine House – which was Zutfen's name for its town hall – with a carillon of nineteen bells. Two expert musicians were called in to test the workmanship and declared the carillon to be "not merely good but excelling in tone and resonance the carillons of other towns in the vicinity." That initial success spread the fame of the Hemonys throughout the Dutch Republic. Amsterdam offered François generous terms if he would settle there, and later on Pierre followed him thither as his brother, being swamped with commissions, needed his expert assistance. The secret of their success was in accurate tuning, which they never left to even the most skilful among their helpers. They were not unconcsious of their eminence among the bell-founding craft and, modest artists though they were, signed every bell that left their workshop. It was a signature that no one ever read in the inaccessible height to which the bells were hoisted. *Sit Nomen Domini benedictum. Petrus Hemony me fecit. Amstelodami Ao Domi 1669* (Blessed be the name of the Lord. Pierre Hemony made me at Amsterdam in the year of the Lord 1669) ran the inscription on the bell of the town hall at Stirling, Scotland, but it was not until two hundred years later, when the bell had to be recast, that his name was discovered. Yet both he and François left another mark of their authorship that to the connoisseur and expert musician is unmistakable in the bell's purity of tone.

Carillon music is a specialty of the Netherlands. I do not think that its popularity is due to the activity of the Hemonys. There was tower music in the Low Countries before their time. It is more likely that the Dutch people's pleasure and pride in their singing towers attracted them by the promise of employment in their highly specialized skill. After their death the bell-founders' craft began to decline and in the nineteenth century it became totally extinct. The present generation has witnessed a revival. Bell founders are active again in the provinces of Groningen and North-Brabant and are producing carillons that can bear comparison with those of their illustrious predecessors of three centuries ago. When Queen Juliana visited the United States in the spring of 1952 she announced her nation's intention to present to this country a carillon of forty-nine bells as a token of the Dutch people's gratitude for generous aid during the trying years of the late war and its aftermath. No more typically Dutch tribute could have been devised. It is a gift to which all groups and classes of the nation have contributed: farmers, sailors, fishermen, miners, nurserymen, tradespeople, merchants, bankers, journalists, artists, scholars, civil servants, teachers, school children. The inscriptions on the bells are an indelible record of all these groups of donors, and when their music is sent out upon the air the residents of Washington, D. C., will hear the voice of a grateful nation singing its thanks to the American nation's capital.

September, 1955

OF CATACOMBS AND BENTVEUGHELS

A sojourn in Rome is not complete without a visit to the catacombs. I completed mine in the summer of last year with an excursion to the catacomb of San Callisto. I had my misgivings on entering, for my eyesight is not too good in the dark; but a young aviator from the States who was in our party kindly offered to guide and support me on our progress through the dim and narrow corridors and up and down sparsely lighted steps. We were conducted through the subterranean maze by a white-bearded monk whose jocund face and well-fed corpulence looked out of place in these sombre haunts of the dead. But so did we, a crowd of Americans in bright summer outfit chattering cheerfully in nasal accents unlike the melodious Latin that must have been intoned there at early-Christian burial rites. The guide's English had no nasal quality; he spoke it fluently but one could tell that he was not born to the language. It sounded to me like faintly disguised Dutch idiom, and my impression proved correct: he was a Netherlander from Maastricht. In the course of our conversation I asked him whether he knew that the catacomb of Domitilla was discovered by a Dutch resident of Rome in the late sixteenth century. He had never heard of it and probably thought that I was talking through my hat, though he was too polite to confess his disbelief. Since it is not likely that any of my American readers are any better informed than the Maastricht monk, it might interest them to hear the story of the Roman Dutchman.

He was a young apothecary from Delft called Hendrik de Raeff, and settled in Rome around the year 1590. He must have been expert in his profession, for by 1603 he had become the owner of a flourishing dispensary in the *Vicolo del Pavone*, or Peacock Alley, close to the public hospital of the Holy Ghost, round which the principal physicians were established. It was shortly after his arrival in the Eternal City, in the year 1591, that he made his discovery. When two years later Antonio Bosio, who has justly been called the Columbus of the subterranean world, explored the catacomb of Domitilla, De Raeff had made three or four descents into it in the company of several of his compatriots. Such visits under De Raeff's guidance were popular entertainment for Dutch travelers during the following years of that same decade, and of each descent the party left a record on the plastered walls of the cubicles of the dead. They picknicked not in the sunlit fields outside but in the gloomy darkness among the graves. *Pransi sumus*, we had lunch here, they wrote once in a while on the plastered wall of a crypt, and here and there they left a drawing of a couple of sturdy rummers accompanied by the legend *tibi-mihi*, the formula they used in drinking each other's health. But it was at the same time, I have no doubt, a macabre allusion to the medieval inscription on so many tombstones: *hodie mihi, cras tibi*, today my turn, tomorrow yours.

I claim no credit for the discovery of these facts. That goes to Dr. G. J. Hoogewerff[1], former Director of the Netherlands Historical Institute in Rome and author of a history of the association that held the artists from Holland and Flanders together in seventeenth century Rome. Their group was known as the *Bent*, that is the band, and its members were called *Bentveughels*, or band birds. They were mostly young men in their early twenties. Ignorance of the Italian language

1 *De Bentveughels* door Dr. G. J. Hoogewerff. The Hague: Martinus Nijhoff, 1952.

and of the Italian way of life was a handicap that they could overcome only by solidarity. They sought each other and lived as much as they could among compatriots. The home of apothecary De Raeff was always open to them. He married in 1603 the daughter of Frans van den Kasteele, an Italianized painter from Antwerp who was regarded by the artists of Rome as one of theirs. But he did not shun the acquaintance of the young painters from his native land and often consorted with them at his son-in-law's home. After his marriage De Raeff ceased to give parties in the catacomb of Domitilla. The shop where he dispensed remedies that were to save the sick from burial was after all a more congenial meeting ground.

The *Bent* was not a formally constituted organization. It was never planned but a spontaneous growth. The need for companionship in an alien community brought the members together, but their cohesion was never verbally established in written by-laws, as far as we know. It is therefore impossible to tie its genesis to a definite date. It came into being, it seems, in the year 1623 and when in the following decade the need arose for concerted action in defense of the freedom of their craft, the *Bent* became a recognized organization with which the Italian authorities had to reckon. The menace to their freedom came from the *Academia Romania di San Luca*. This had been founded in 1577, but it was not until the end of the sixteenth century that its privileged status became an impediment to artists from abroad. By a papal decree of 1593 it was given authority over both Italian and foreign artists in Rome. None was allowed to practice his profession there unless he had paid an alms to the patron saint of their craft on the festival of Saint Luke. The *Bentveughels* refused to pay the levy and calmly continued to paint and sell their work. The Academy proved powerless in the face of this collective opposition and gradually desisted from exerting further pressure on the recalcitrants from the Netherlands.

The Academy, under papal protection, was a stronghold of conventional art. It abhorred as almost sacrilegious the terrible realism of Caravaggio. But it was Caravaggio who attracted the Hollanders and Flemings. Realists themselves, they joined the rebellion against the Academy. That made them doubly despised by the Academicians. One of these, Giambattista Passeri, condemned Pieter van Laer from Haarlem, whose *Bent* name was Bamboccio, for his "boorish and folk scenes of low-life orgies which give so much pleasure to plebeians but little to the minds of those who are actuated by noble principles." Van Laer's pictures were indeed popular, so much so that his admirers made him godfather of the genre of which he was considered the outstanding master. *Bambocciate*, as they were called, were much sought after, not only by plebeians but by titled collectors and cardinals as well. They won their case against the critics by the undeniable talent and technical skill of the painters. The Academy itself gave them finally its blessing and put the stamp of respectability upon at least one of Pieter van Laer's followers by hanging a low-life scene painted by Michiel Sweerts in its Council Room. There it is still on view three hundred years later, a telling trophy of Dutch realism over the Academy's cult of the conventional.

Admission to the *Bent* was a matter of course. Few artists stayed out of it, and none of these because he was blackballed. He remained outside by free choice. Anthony van Dyck was in Rome in the year of its genesis, but he was not among its early members. He probably thought himself too good for the companionship of his rowdy brethren of the brush. There is indeed plenty of evidence in the court records that these young artists were intemperate topers and ready fighters. Several got themselves into serious scrapes with the Roman police. The induction of a newcomer was always an occasion of a big carouse. They called it a baptism, for it was at this feast that the novice was given his nickname. There was no Bentveughel without one; Dr. Hoogewerff gives a long list of them. It is a strange assortment of vocables: Hector, Magician, Beerfly, Lantern, Gladiator, Gold Sceptre, Ape, Winter, Horizon, Adonis, Kettle Drum, Sandbag, Oak Tree, Goldfinch, Tortoise, and some seventy odd others. The ceremony was an impressive one and calculated to overawe the boy to be initiated. He was led into a dark room which the artists had ingeniously turned into a temple-like sanctum. Here, high upon a throne, sat the artist who was to perform the baptismal ceremony. This so-called priest instructed the greenhorn in the rules of the painting craft and the customs of the *Bent*. When the youth had promised faithfully to adhere to these, the "priest" baptized him with wine and crowned him with a laurel wreath.

The ceremony was concluded with a banquet to be paid for by the new member. At dawn, when the dinner was over, the boon companions went in solemn procession to a deserted little church outside the Porta Pia where the final libations were drunk and what remained of the wine was poured out in front of a massive sarcophagus which was commonly but erroneously known by the name of Bacchus's Tomb. The authorities of Church and State took offence at such mockery of the sacrament and in the early 18th century forbade the dawn procession and all nocturnal revelry. Dutch art of that period was in decline. The painters from the Netherlands had relinquished the bold realism of their predecessors and lacked the strength and originality to resist the influence of Italian art. The *Bent* had degraded into a feeble reflection of the Academy and ingloriously sank into oblivion.

AN UNPOPULAR CHIEF OF POLICE

The traffic congestion in the streets of Amsterdam is an insoluble problem. It was already a problem, though not insoluble, as long ago as the middle of the seventeenth century. The wealthy merchant who built himself a country home in the newly reclaimed polder land needed a carriage and pair to carry him and his family back and forth between town house and country house, and as the rich increased in numbers the private carriages became such a nuisance that the magistracy passed an ordinance forbidding the use of them on the city streets. That was not such a drastic measure as it would be today. Amsterdam, three hundred years ago, was a small town that could easily be circled on foot in an afternoon, and no one needed a vehicle to reach his destination within the circumference of the city walls. The wealthy merchants could stable their carriage and pair outside the gate; it would do them no harm to walk a short part of the way to their farm in the country. Yet, since they had a carriage they wanted to use it from door to door, so the city fathers, amenable to the protests and also, probably, because being carriage owners themselves they felt inconvenienced by their own ordinance, conceded that a private vehicle might proceed unhindered provided the driver took the shortest route from door to city gate and vice versa. Proof that the driver did was hard to bring and the ordinance, to the annoyance of pedestrians, was never enforced. If in those easy-going days horse-drawn transportation caused congestion in the city streets, it is no wonder that in modern Amsterdam, with one million inhabitants, the public thoroughfares are chronically stopped up to the choking point.

It is not only the cars on the move that cause trouble. There is much grumbling among motorists about the lack of parking facilities. The space between the trees that line the canals has to be utilized for the purpose. All day long it is filled by automobiles. They stand there with the front wheel on the water's edge. To me, an inexperienced driver more afraid of a car at the wheel than in front of the wheels, it seems a perilous exploit to bring the car to a standstill just as it has reached the point where it might drop off. It actually happens sometimes that the driver loses his nerve and plunges into the canal. That is a treat to passing pedestrians and cyclists. In no time the scene of the accident is swarming with onlookers who get in the way of the rescue squad. They are dispersed by police but find a vantage point for their curiosity on top of the arched bridge nearby. Curiosity is infectious, the crowd of onlookers attracts others, and soon the bridge is filled with people on tiptoes who crane their necks in hope of getting a glimpse of what is going on, and the traffic across the bridge is seriously slowed up by congestion.

Auto drivers are not the chief obstructionists nor do they cause the greatest danger. Accidents happen every day, yet not the chauffeurs but the cyclists are the chief offenders. These aggravate the traffic jam which, even without them, would be bad enough. Practically everybody moves on wheels through Amsterdam; even babies and little children too young to pedal, for these ride in baskets in front or back of their pedaling parent. At the rush hours, between eight and nine in the morning, at noon, and from five to six, the bikes invade the streets in serried ranks. They swerve inaudibly around corners and frighten the poor pedestrian out of his wits. For this two-footed animal is not yet totally extinct. Owing to his scarcity, however, the travelers on wheels give little thought to him and proceed at inconsiderate speed. For there is no speed limit in Amsterdam; it used to be on the statute books, but the authorities abolished it on the naive assumption that by abstaining from speed control they would put drivers and riders on their honor and encourage them to practice self-restraint. Riders too, for the cyclists are now able to compete with the drivers of cars thanks to a simple device that changes the bike into an engined monster. The Dutch call it *bromfiets*, that is buzz bike. Buzz bike are the greatest menace of the city streets. They are the special favorites of middle-aged women who find pedaling a tiring chore. The buzz bike carries them along without any physical effort on their part. But it carries them along with such ease that they lose awareness of the rate at which they are traveling, and in an emergency they are apt to lose control of the wheel. Yet, nothing daunted, all middle-aged Amsterdam buzzes and turns the city into a swarming bee hive.

Swarming bees are dangerous when interfered with. Amsterdam's Chief of Police discovered that last year. He was attacked with the barbs of their angry criticism, most unjustly, for the poor man had nothing worse in mind than a plan to speed up their swarm. A police commissioner is seldom popular in any city. Few people know him personally. He is an autocrat behind the scenes, a dark power whose very invisibility inspires awe and respect but never affection. He is not popular in Amsterdam, a city whose people have the spirit of rebellion in their blood. To resist the orders of authority has always been a pleasant sport to them, and when they see good reason to complain of what they consider to be an ill-advised police action, the Chief becomes the butt of gusty criticism. He gave them cause for it some time ago by a letter he addressed to the Burgomaster and Aldermen in which he outlined a plan designed to loosen the traffic tie-up. Reduce the number of Amsterdam's waterways, he proposed. By filling up some of the canals and cutting down the trees that line them we shall create streets three times their present width, through which the stream of traffic will be able to flow unimpeded. Vandalism! shouted an outraged public. The Amsterdam papers were bombarded with letters of indignant protest. The writers did not want relief from traffic congestion at the price of their city's most beautiful feature. They would fight and struggle through the ever denser crowds rather than lose some of their tree-shaded canals that are the pride of Amsterdam.

Among the canals that the Police Commissioner had marked for reclamation is one that is especially dear to all Amsterdam burghers. It is that part of *The Singel* along which florists and gardeners are accustomed to exhibit their wares. It has been the central flower market as long as I can remember and I am sure it had been there a long time before, as a little child, I first set wide-open eyes on its mass of colors. Here the barges lie moored along the quays, their decks presenting a gorgeous display of the flowers that are in season, and this wealth of color spills over onto the street between the trees, where blooms in red earthenware pots are neatly arranged for the inspection of passing customers. They leave no room for the parking of cars, a rare instance of utility giving way to beauty. The police chief, being in the service of utility, performs only his duty in wanting to accelerate locomotion at the cost of beauty. Being a Hollander, he is probably just as fond of flowers as all his compatriots. The market, he probably reasons, may just as well be held elsewhere; its removal to another spot does not involve the loss of beauty. If he does, he is mistaken. The beauty of that part of *The Singel* is not only in the setting of the flower show alongside and on the water of the shaded canal, it is partly also in its tradition, in its having been there since ever so long ago. The utilitarian policeman cannot allow sentiment to deflect him from the course that he knows to be the most useful one, but sentiment, he discovered, is an irrational opponent that cannot be reasoned with. Its self-righteousness is an armour that the sharpest to-the-point arguments cannot pierce. I am conscious of this irrational stubbornness in myself. If I were still a resident of Amsterdam and had a say in the matter, I would join the ranks of the Police Commissioner's indignant critics, and write a letter to the papers in defence of my native city's aquatic beauty. I was born on one of the oldest canals, which proclaims in its name its medieval origin. *Oudezijdsvoorburgwal* it is called, which is best translated with Old Side Inner Moat. It must have been part of the medieval town's fortifications long before it was enlarged, in the early seventeenth century, with the New Side so-called, consisting of a ring of semi-circular canals on the west bank of the Amstel river. My earliest memories of Amsterdam are visions of that ancient *Burgwal* in the different seasons of the year, of joy at seeing the young foliage leap forth in spring and design a mosaic of sunlight and shadow on the dark surface of the water, of bronze twilight on summer evenings when the *Burgwal* looked melancholy under its trees, of winter days when frost immobilized the barges and gave the burghers unwonted mobility on skates, of the mysterious hush after a snow fall that muffled all sounds in the street. Those are unforgettable impressions, and the thought that such beauty is doomed to effacement and oblivion casts a pall over my bright recollection of childhood happiness. But we must resign ourselves to the sacrifice that is demanded from us by what we call progress, which wills that populations grow, that room be made for ever larger numbers, and that the millions get out of each other's way by moving faster and ever faster. The beauty that our slow, deliberate ancestors created is an obstacle to progress, and the next generation, even though it be aware of its spell, will be forced to despoil it unless it be content to stagnate. I thank my good fortune that I shall not live to be a witness of the sacrilege.

April, 1956

THE ZAAN

My father's grandfather was schoolmaster in Zaandijk, a small industrial town on the bank of the Zaan, a river north of Amsterdam. The schoolmaster's son moved away from his birthplace and settled in a village near Rotterdam. But my father, being related through his mother to several Zaandijk families, always kept up the connection. He often visited his mother's people and sometimes took me, his eldest son, along. I must confess that I accompanied him on those excursions with mixed feelings. The boat trip across the broad expanse of the IJ was enjoyable, but the calls that we paid to various relatives were to me more a pain than a pleasure, in spite of the cookies to which I was treated everywhere. I felt ill at ease among people who spoke Dutch so differently from the way I was accustomed to. At that time the old Zaanland dialect, it is true, was no longer in general use; the educated were adapting, either deliberately or unconsciously, their manner of speech to the model set by the better classes of Amsterdam. But there was one feature of that speech that no Zaanlander could ever get rid of, a peculiar singsong intonation. I was greeted with "Wel, Adriaaa-an, hoe gaat 'et met jou-ou?" (literally, Well, Adrian, how goes it with you?), the *a* and the *ou* being drawn out to excessive length, while the voice rose from low to high pitch towards the end of the question. This way of greeting for some mysterious reason always embarassed me. It was perhaps the protracted insistence on the vowel in my name that made me feel painfully conspicuous.

One home among the many that we used to visit stands out in my memory with special distinctness. It had a large living-room – it seemed at least large to me, who was so small – and it was full of furniture which my father said was very old, more than a hundred years, and very precious. I was too young to appreciate its antiquity and have an eye for its beauty. But the thing that fascinated me in that room was a painting the like of which I had never seen elsewhere. It showed a view of the Zaan and a cluster of houses on its left bank with a church rising out above the housetops, and in its tower was a dial plate that was not painted on. It was a real dial of white porcelain and tiny hands on this miniature tower clock actually indicated the time of day. My fingers itched to pull the picture a little away from the wall so that I could get a peep at the mechanism that must be hidden behind the panel. But I was too shy to satisfy my curiosity. It must have been an ingenious contrivance, for it set in motion not only the hands of the clock but also the arms of a windmill on the right bank of the river. It was the first motion picture I had ever seen, and it gave me a bigger thrill than is felt by my grandchildren in front of the television screen. The pleasure of a treat grows less at each repetition, but since I saw my moving picture only three or four times a year its fascination never grew stale.

Zaandijk is not the only town on the Zaan river. Coming from Amsterdam one arrives at Zaandam, then further north follows Koog, then Zaandijk, and finally Wormerveer. A stranger will not be able to tell where the territory of one ends and that of its neighbor begins; the four towns stretch an unbroken chain of dwellings along the west bank of the river and seem to the casual sightseer to form a homogeneous community. In the days of which I retain a visual memory green was the predominant color of Main Street. Wood was then the common building material and it was painted in various shades of green. The facades alone had a covering of brick. Domestic architecture along the Zaan provided each house with two front doors, one of which was never opened except when there was a death in the house. On the day of the funeral it was unlocked to let the coffin be carried out.

Folklorists believe that the death door, as it was called, owes its origin to a belief of our pre-Christian ancestors that the spirit of the deceased always wants to return to its old home but that it can never reach it by any other way than the one by which it left. Finding the door locked through which he passed on the way out, the ghostly visitor will be prevented from entering and haunting the house. It is not a convincing story, but I cannot refute it by suggesting a better one. No Zaanlander knows why his house must have a death door, he only knows that age-old custom prescribes it. I should not wonder if the present generation no longer respects the prescription. The death door, as everything else that was quaint and a typical mark of the Zaanland, has had its day.

The relatives whom we used to visit in the eighties and nineties of the past century never repaid our calls. The people along the Zaan river liked to keep to themselves; they formed a closed community with its own peculiar customs and traditions. Only one cousin of my father's ever crossed our threshold, and his visits were not social calls. He shared with my father the trusteeship of a demented uncle's estate, and once a quarter he came to discuss details of administration. Nearly every Zaanlander was commonly known by a nickname, and cousin Honig's was Lange Jan (Tall John). We little children looked up at his towering height in awe and amazement. He never took any notice of us while he sat at our luncheon table munching away in embarrassing absent-mindedness. He probably did not speak to us because he did not know how to. Those sophisticated city children, I suspect, made him feel ill at ease. He was always dressed in black and carried a large, limp bag of a baize-like material which he brought with him into the room and put down between his feet. I always wondered what was in it but never dared ask him; I never had any conversation with Lange Jan. He must have regarded Amsterdam as a place where one had to be on one's guard and Zaandijk as his only safe anchorage.

Lange Jan's type and the era he typified are gone forever. Yet the spirit that animated them and made these river dwellers the chief industrialists of Holland before steam and electricity replaced the wind has not been locked out by any death door. The Zaanland industries are humming as before and the leaders of those which through adverse circumstances began to decline refused to bow in defeat: they started anew elsewhere, even, if needs be, far away across the Atlantic Ocean. I recently visited New Orleans and found there a member of the prominent Laan family, the principal rice millers of Zaanland, established near the source of supply, the rice-growing regions of Louisiana. He settled there, with a wife and six children, nine years

327

ago when chaotic trade conditions resulting from the late war imperilled the continuance of his business in Holland. It was this pleasant meeting with an enterprising immigrant from the Zaanland that called these boyhood memories to mind.

July, 1956

AFRIKAANS

It is a curious fact that the most difficult languages are spoken by peoples that have no literature. Basque and the Algonquin languages of North America are mental puzzles to the student, whereas the study of English does not cause the learner many headaches. Otto Jespersen, the great Danish philologist, saw in the simplicity of English morphology a mark of the British nation's superior culture. It is indeed a rare accomplishment to have developed a mechanism for the expression of the most complicated thought that is itself so little complicated. It seems doubtful, though, whether there is a causal connection between culture and uninflected speech. If there were, the Dutch of South Africa should be reckoned among the most highly civilized people on earth. Their language, which they call Afrikaans, surpasses English in austerity of structure. Still, English influence had no part in its development. The speech of the Dutch colonists at the Cape of Good Hope had evolved its present uninflected state nearly a century before any Briton set foot on South-African soil. They could hardly be called cultured at that time, and did not possess a literature of their own. How then must we account for the uncomplicated structure of their language, which is no less capable than English of expressing complicated thought?

The speech of the early settlers had no anchorage in a literary standard. They were a mixed race, Frenchmen, Germans, Scandinavians having settled among them and adopted the Dutch language under compulsion of the Dutch East India Company. The Dutch that these foreigners spoke was a language shorn of all features that were not essential to mutual understanding. Irregularities were smoothed out, the definite article reduced to one indeclinable form, the verbal conjugation leveled under one single stem serving for all persons and tenses; in short, Cape Dutch was reduced to the common denominator of the various forms of broken Dutch that were spoken by uneducated Frenchmen, Germans, Scandinavians, and Netherlanders.

The Hottentots and the black slaves imported from West Africa, Madagascar, and the Malay Archipelago, who spoke a mixture of Malay and Portuguese, the *lingua franca* in use throughout the territory of the Dutch East India Company, added to this process of detrition; for the children, left largely to their care, must have imitated their broken prattle. They did, no doubt, their best when grown up to drop a manner of speech which, because it belonged to the slaves, was undignified for whites; but some of its traits, especially the modulation of the sentence, were so little part of the speaker's consciousness that they never could be shaken off.

The metamorphosis of Holland Dutch to Afrikaans was accomplished in less than a century. The first settlement at the Cape dates from 1652 and already the fourth generation of colonists spoke Afrikaans. The development is very similar to the rapid change of Old into Middle English. The symptoms of detrition were apparent in Northumbrian before the Norse and Norman invasions, but the subsequent intermixture of Scandinavian, Anglosaxon, and Norman French accelerated the tendency toward leveling and simplification. The dialectal varieties of standard Dutch that the early settlers brought along bore the seeds of most of the changes that became characteristic of Afrikaans, but the rapid growth of these seeds was due to their falling in the soil of an isolated and linguistically mixed society. The course of development was predestined by tendencies inherent in both Old English and Holland Dutch; its tempo, on the other hand, was set by external conditions of a social nature.

The analogy between Afrikaans and Middle English may be carried yet farther. The former's destinies in the nineteenth century are a striking repetition of what happened to English speech under the Plantagenets. William the Conqueror and his nobility governed England as French rulers. French became the language of the court, the higher clergy, the law courts, and of Parliament. In 1345 the chronicles of London were still written in French. When in 1348 the university and the town of Oxford concluded a treaty concerning the assay of weights and measures, the language employed by the contracting parties was French. It is doubtful whether Edward III, the king who led his English archers on to victory over the French, possessed a ready command of English. The speech that had been King Alfred's had become the despised idiom of the common folk. But the One Hundred Years' War with France aroused the nationalistic spirit that was to regain recognition and respect for the native tongue. On October 13, 1363, Parliament, for the first time, was opened with an English speech by Henry Green, Chief Justice of England, and the same Parliament forbade the use of French in the law courts. Towards the end of the thirteenth century Robert of Gloucester wrote, "Unless a man knows French, he is held in small esteem, but lowly folk hold on to English," but half a century later Trevisa stated that "gentlemen nowadays have ceased to teach French to their children." Thus the vernacular began to reassert its rights at a time when the war with France stirred the nation into action.

Afrikaans in the nineteenth century was very much in the same predicament as English was in the thirteenth. The Cape Colony had become British in 1806, and British policy aimed at complete anglicisation of the colonists. Scottish divines were imported to serve as ministers in the Dutch Reformed Church, government schools were established in which instruction was exclusively in English, preferment in government service was open only to English speaking citizens, and Afrikanders were made to feel the disgrace that attached to their native speech. English ruled supreme as French did in England about the year 1300. The Boer's despised idiom was relegated to the farm, and even there they spoke it shamefacedly in the presence of the Dutch schoolmaster and the Dutch *dominee*. For the language problem in South Africa was more complicated than it ever was in medieval England. What little power of resistance the Dutch idiom of the veld could muster against the danger of extinction by the steam roller force of the world language was still further weakened by the rivalry it met from the side of Holland Dutch.

The ministers of the Dutch Reformed Church, either natives of Holland or South African alumni of Dutch universities, and the schoolmasters imported from Holland in great numbers held the Afrikaans language in equally low esteem as did the English. They considered it unfit for use in either church or school and would allow no other form of Dutch there than the mother tongue, the standard speech of the Netherlands. Hence, the Dutch Reformed Church gave, unintentionally, indirect support to the English language by teaching the Boers disrespect for their own idiom. It was not a language that one could write. Only Holland Dutch and English were fit to be used for the expression of one's thoughts on paper. When in the seventies of the past century a group of young men at Paarl, in the western Cape Province, started the publication of a periodical in Afrikaans, the new venture met with fierce opposition from the side of their own people. These felt self-conscious and embarrassed at the sight of that homely idiom presuming to parade in black on white like English and Holland Dutch.

Hence, when the Afrikander was unable or unwilling to write English, he had to express himself in Holland Dutch. "Our written language," wrote a leader of the movement for the rehabilitation of Afrikaans, "differs so much from our speech that it seems a foreign language to the large majority of our people." The conservatives did not deny that Afrikaans speech and Dutch writing were like strangers to each other, but they did not approve of the logical solution, which was to write Afrikaans instead of Dutch. They recommended by way of compromise the free use of Afrikaans words and idioms, expressive of the life and customs of the veld, provided that they were dressed up in the grammatical forms of the parent language.

But then the South African War broke out, and just as in Chaucer's England the war with France aroused the English people to a pride in their native speech, the *Taal*, as Afrikaans was then called, became to the Boers the symbol of their Afrikaanderism. At the peace of Vereeniging the two Boer Republics signed away their freedom, but they had won in the ordeal of war something equally precious that could not be taken from them: a new sense of their own worth, a pride in their Boer inheritance, a jealous love of their spiritual independence. And the language was the shibboleth of this new-born nationalism. Its claim to recognition could no longer be denied. In 1914 Afrikaans was admitted as a vehicle of instruction in elementary schools by decisions of the Provincial Councils in the Cape Province, the Orange Free State, and Transvaal; in 1925 it was recognized, along with English and Holland Dutch, as one of the official languages of the Union; and even the Dutch Reformed Church admitted Afrikaans into its services and authorized a Bible translation into the language which it once rejected as unworthy of being spoken from the pulpit. And now it need not share with Holland Dutch the honor of being an official language of the Union; it is *the* other official language since Holland Dutch has been discarded and ousted from its privileged position. To the Afrikanders of today the language of the Netherlands is a foreign tongue that one learns to read in school for its literature but that no one needs to speak or write.

I know from my own experience when traveling in South Africa that a Hollander can understand the deliberate utterance of an Afrikaans speaker. I found it hard, indeed, to follow a conversation among Afrikanders, but that was because the clipped forms in which the Dutch words have survived obscured for me their identity in the rapid flow of animated discussion. Yet Afrikaans is pure Dutch all the same. It is surprising that out of the melting pot of languages which society at the Cape must have been in the latter half of the seventeenth century Afrikaans has emerged in such undefiled condition. Its vocabulary is predominantly Dutch. It has, indeed, loanwords from Malay-Portuguese, which, however, do not number more than one hundred and twenty, and English, of course, has added its quota. But Afrikaans is not a medley of tongues. It is a homogeneous language which is uniformly spoken through the length and breadth of the Union of South Africa.

THE MILLER'S SON

The chief event at Amsterdam this summer was an exhibition of a hundred paintings by Rembrandt in commemoration of his birth three hundred and fifty years ago. His father, a well-to-do Leiden miller, was aware that his fifth child had something uncommon that distinguished him from his older brothers. These were trained for a handicraft, but Rembrandt was sent to the Latin School and, in his fourteenth year, enrolled as a student in the university. But the boy knew better what he was destined for: preferring painting to the study of the classics, he said farewell to the lecture-room and entered the studio of Jacob van Swanenburgh. The pupil soon excelled the master. He left Leiden for Amsterdam and studied for a time under a better artist, Pieter Lastman. But Lastman could not teach him much, and after half a year he returned to his native city and, together with his friend Jan Lievens, set up a studio and took in pupils.

There was a picture at Amsterdam that Rembrandt painted in the late twenties of this simple Leiden workshop. The room is bare of all decoration. Nothing except a palette hangs on the white-washed wall, and in the left-hand corner stands a rickety table with some crockery on it. The only other piece of furniture is an easel. A young artist, a boy in his early teens, stands in front of it, a palette and a bundle of brushes in his left hand, and a very thin brush in his right. He has stepped backward to look from a distance at the effect of his latest touches. The panel on the easel turns its back to the beholder, so we cannot tell what the child is working at, otherwise we might be able to guess at his identity. Perhaps it is Gerard Dou, who in his fourteenth year was apprenticed to Rembrandt. That assumption is strengthened by the thin brush the boy is using, for Dou inclined to paint with miniature finesse; he learnt from Rembrandt to contrast light and dark, but in his brushwork he went his own, almost finicky, way, entirely different from Rembrandt's. A striking feature of this picture is the odd manner in which the boy artist is dressed. He wears not a painter's smock but some sort of costly dressing gown. The little fellow probably borrowed it from the master; for it is much too wide for him and hangs down on his feet; it does not cover, it envelops him. The wide-brimmed hat is also too large for his small head. I should not wonder if Rembrandt, who was still a boy himself, had taken an impish delight in thus accoutring his little pupil and painting him in the queer outfit for the fun of it.

It must have been in that simple workshop that Constantijn Huygens, the private secretary of the Prince of Orange, came to see

Rembrandt and Lievens and inspect their work. They were still beardless boys, he wrote in his account of that visit, but their fame was no longer a local vogue, it had reached The Hague and aroused the great secretary's curiosity. The young artists must have been impressed by the honor he paid to their talent, but no more impressed than Huygens was by what he saw. In ornate Latin he gave expression to his amazed admiration. "I want to single out," he wrote, "as an example of all Rembrandt's works, the picture of the remorseful Judas returning the pieces of silver to the High Priest. Confront it with all the art of Italy and with everything impressive and admirable that has survived from earliest antiquity; the gesture of despair with which Judas returns the blood money, not to mention so many admirable features on this one canvas, is a match to any attractive work of art that former ages have produced." Rembrandt would soon surpass himself in greater pictures, but the extravagance of the diplomat's praise for this early work is eloquent testimony to the wonder his precocity aroused among the connoisseurs. The picture was on view at Amsterdam, and even there, where it was surrounded by the noblest creations of his maturity, it lost nothing of the dramatic effectiveness that so captivated Huygens.

There was among these one hundred paintings not one of the many portraits he did of his mother. That seemed to me a flaw in the otherwise perfect collection. The woman who gave life to his genius should not have been left out. She may be represented in a dressed-up disguise in a panel that, on account of that travesty, passes as a presentation of the Prophetess Anna; but the artist's deep affection for his mother is not apparent in this panel. Little is known of the home in the Weddesteeg where he was born and grew up except what he tells us in his etchings and paintings, and these are unmistakable expressions of his devotion. At her knee he listened to her reading of the Scripture, and when he grew up he loved to paint her bending an aging face over the Book and holding on to it with wrinkled hands. It was probably the only book she knew and Rembrandt's frequent treatment of his favorite Bible stories must every time have been a tender communion with the dear one in whose voice he had first heard them told as a child. She came from peasant stock, but there was nothing boorish in her face. It had dignity and distinction. One of Rembrandt's portraits of her was acquired, three years before her death, by King Charles I and now hangs in Windsor Castle, where it passes for a portrait of the Countess of Desmond. A German critic has discovered a certain harshness in her features. I cannot see it. What he calls harshness is but the rigidity of a face in which the years have etched their story of toil and hardship. In an etching of 1628 the straight, thin line of the mouth expresses strength and determination, but the slight upward curve at either end of the upper lip softens the severity and lights up the face with the glimmer of a smile. There is a pensive look in her downcast eyes; she may have been thinking during the pose of the future that awaited her young son already famous.

It was not a future of social eminence such as Anthony van Dyck and Peter Lely, both natives of the Netherlands, attained in England. Rembrandt knighted is unthinkable. He would have scorned the honor, though in his youth he was not averse to painting himself in shining armour. When an admirer who was concerned for Rembrandt's reputation expressed regret that he consorted with low-born people, his retort was, "When I want to relax I seek freedom, not honor." He was a proud, not an arrogant man, and proud only in devotion to his art. At a public auction he bid six hundred florins for a collection of prints by Lucas van Leyden, and when a friend called him a fool for paying that much for what he could have got for one tenth that price, he said, "I did it to uphold the honor of my art." He never kowtowed to the great and did not try to associate with them. The wealthy patricians, with the sole exception of Burgomaster Jan Six, never realized that an intimate friendship with Rembrandt would have done them honor. They employed him as a craftsman, they did not treat him as a social equal. The artist did not care. He felt drawn towards the weak and the humble. Christ comforting the sick, the Holy Family in a simple home or resting on the flight to Egypt were subjects that he loved to paint. The Amsterdam exhibition included a picture of Anna and Mary sitting by the Christ child's cradle while Joseph is at work in a dark corner under the staircase. A hidden light placed on the floor throws Anna's shadow upon the wall, and Mary, who is reading to her from a large book, is seen in silhouette against the brilliance of the invisible lamp. It is a moving scene of great tenderness and peace, to me one of the most appealing in the exhibition. Thus he must have remembered in nostalgic retrospect the warm intimacy of his parental home.

The abiding impression that I carried away from the Rijksmuseum was amazement at the diversity of Rembrandt's oeuvre. We think of him first and foremost as the painter of soul-searching portraits; but there was nothing in the world around him that his brush did not re-create on panel and canvas: Landscapes, either realistic or imaginative, still-lifes to which he added movement by painting some human figure in the background, biblical scenes for which the Jewish quarter where he chose to live supplied the types, stories from Greek mythology, which are his least successful compositions. But he amazes also

334

by the diversity of his technique. Never satisfied with his latest achievement he tried to do differently and better next time. He was a restless explorer of untrodden tracks, a tireless seeker of pictorial effects never before attained, a heretic unafraid of the charge that he sinned against convention and tradition. In retort to a critic's reproof that he painted in a queer manner he said, "I am a painter, not a dyer." His unshakable faith in himself is fully justified by the Rijksmuseum exhibition. Here the miller's son from Leiden, this prince of painters, held court among the majestic splendor of his works to receive the homage of admiring multitudes.

January, 1957

A VONDEL MEMORIAL IN NEW YORK

One Hundred and Seventy-one East Eighty-third Street is a small, unpretentious apartment house that has nothing of interest to write home about, and there would be no reason to refer to it in a Foundation Letter if it were not for the name that stands out in big letters on the lintel over the front door. It caught my eye one day in the early twenties when New York was still a new city to me and I loved to wander and explore. The name was Vondel. That intrigued me, for why should the great Dutch poet who lived in the seventeenth century and is hardly known in America have stood godfather to a house on Manhattan Island? A man on the stoop whom I took to be the janitor shrugged his shoulders when I asked him for information. He did not know what Vondel meant and he did not care and no one else around the house could enlighten me any better. It was by mere accident that I solved the riddle. At a dinner meeting of the Authors Club I met one day in 1927 Mr. Samuel Henry Wandell, the author of a life of Aaron Burr. He had read my biography of Vondel, he told me. "I was interested in it," he said, "because of a tradition in our family that the Wandells are descended from your famous poet. I don't believe in it myself, but I have a cousin who is convinced that Wandell is a corruption of Vondel, and in honor of his supposed ancestor he has called an apartment house he owns for him." "The house on East Eighty-third Street?" I asked. "That's where it is." I happened to pass there the other day and found it still standing and the Vondel name still in evidence over the door. It is a slight memorial to the poet; it will not add lustre to his name, few residents of East Eighty-third Street will be able to identify Vondel, and none, I am sure, will go to the Public Library to read his "Lucifer," the only tragedy of his that can be read in English translation. Even Mr.

335

Wandell who christened the house never read one line of his poetry. He did not mean to honor his genius, he meant to honor himself as the bearer of his illustrious name.

A GREAT EYE DOCTOR

Another great Hollander, whom the average New Yorker is just as unlikely to know by name, has a memorial in this city that is much more impressive than the name on Mr. Wandell's apartment house. I had occasion the other day to go and consult Dr. Raymond Pfeiffer, Professor of Clinical Ophthalmology, at the Medical Centre's Eye Hospital. His waiting room is always crowded, and that morning it was a long time before I was called away by the doctor's nurse. But I did not mind waiting, for I found something there that riveted my attention. It was a beautiful scroll resembling in execution medieval royal deeds and muniments. Handsomely framed, it made an attractive wall decoration. The text was in Dutch, which was not immediately clear to me, for the script was of the ornate type that is meant to be decorative rather than legible. I found it to be a rhetorical tribute to Frans Cornelis Donders, which was presented to him on his retirement from the chair of ophthalmology at Utrecht in 1887 and signed by some fifty Dutch citizens prominent in various walks of life. How did that document come into Dr. Pfeiffer's possession? I asked him when at last I was admitted into his consultation room. He smiled and said it was not the only one, he had a large collection of similar ornamental testimonials to Donders. When he studied in Germany he was the guest for a time of Dr. Paul Krais, whose wife was a granddaughter of Donders. When she discovered that her visitor was keenly interested in the treasures she had inherited from her grandfather, she let him take the entire collection with him to America. "Come in one afternoon," Dr. Pfeiffer said, "and I will show you what she gave me." I did not wait long to make an appointment, for my curiosity was aroused. It was amply rewarded. A small room in the Presbyterian Eye Hospital has been set aside as a Donders museum. There was a glass-enclosed showcase full of letters addressed to Donders by great scientists of a century ago: Sir James Paget, Sir William Bowman, Herman von Helmholtz, Rudolf Virchow, and many others. There were copies of the first editions of his books, and six volumes of diaries written in the years 1881-1886 on cheap-looking notebooks of English manufacture, the T. J. and J. Smith's Small Scribbling Diary and Almanack. There was a book case full of testimonials and scrolls presented to Donders by learned societies and universities of almost every country in Europe and

336

portfolios crammed with a mass of correspondence that may contain precious data for the historian of nineteenth century medical research. I could not help wondering why Frau Krais, if she did not care to keep her grandfather's papers, did not present them to the university of Utrecht, where he taught for forty years and established an eye clinic that attracted patients from all over the world. But I had to admit that she entrusted them to the custody of an admirer who takes care of them with reverent piety. Dr. Pfeiffer wrote for the "Bulletin" of the New York Academy of Medicine of October, 1936, an account of Donders' life and work, in which he gave expression to the admiration bordering on worship that the Hollander's achievement has evoked in him. "Donders," he wrote, "stands out as the greatest Hollander of medical science: great first as physiologist, then as ophthalmologist. It is as ophthalmologist that his name will go down in history among the immortals. His great work, the elucidation of the anomalies of refraction and accommodation, a contribution to physiologic optics, stands today as a classic and the authority on refraction. As a man there is perhaps in the whole history of medicine no character more noble, no personality more attractive, no savant more deserving of the adjectives 'great' and 'good' than Donders."

Donders was born in Tilburg, an industrial town in the Netherlands province of North Brabant. He was the youngest child of a Catholic middle-class couple who in the small community where they lived were admired, but probably not envied, for their parenthood of no fewer than eight daughters. When the ninth child was in the offing the family must have prayed for a break in the sequence. When it actually came, the little boy was doubtless welcomed with great rejoicing. The parents' joy would have been a hundredfold greater if they could have known that their tiny Frans Cornelis was destined to become one of the greatest and most famous Hollanders of his generation. He showed at an early age the symptoms of an original and perceptive mind. At the village school of Duizel, a hamlet not far from Tilburg, the master found him an embarassing pupil, for the boy proved to be his better in knowledge and intellect. Since there was little he could teach him, he had him appointed his assistant, a twelve-year old youngster who earned his "tuition" by giving it to his fellow pupils. His mother, who lost her husband shortly after the boy's birth, destined her Benjamin for the priesthood. She sent him, when he was thirteen years old, to the Latin school at Boxmeer, but his inquisitive mind and his insatiable thirst for knowledge deflected him from his theological curriculum. He chose the study of medicine instead. In his doctoral dissertation, written, as was customary in those days, in Latin and orally defended in Latin before the medical faculty of Leyden university, he gave an accurate description of spinal meningitis, which was notable, says Dr. Pfeiffer, "for its precision, the completeness of the clinical observations, and the thoroughness of the autopsy examinations." In 1847 he was appointed professor in the medical faculty of Utrecht university, where, during the first years of his tenure, he taught six different subjects, amongst others physiological optics. He taught this so well that he was urged to devote himself to practical ophthalmology. After further studies in London and Paris he began to practice as an oculist in Utrecht in his thirty-third year. Necessity made him a consultant, for he needed additional income to eke out the meagre salary he received as professor. The young doctor's financial need redounded to the lasting benefit of his fellow men. Numerous original papers established his fame as one of the great eye doctors of Europe, and in 1864 he brought out his masterpiece, which was first printed in English under the title "On the Anomalies of Accommodation and Refraction of the Eye." It is one of the ophthalmological works which, according to Harry Friedenwald, writing in the *Archives of Ophthalmology*, "deserve to be called classic in the sense that its value is enduring." People suffering from eye trouble came to Utrecht for relief from all parts of Europe, and the fame of the Donders clinic attracted physicians and medical students of many nationalities, including several from the United States. When he reached his seventieth year, which is the age at which university professors in the Netherlands are forced to retire, delegations from medical societies and universities in foreign countries came to Utrecht to do him honor, and liberal gifts from admiring donors established the Donders Fund, which was to be used as he should designate for the advancement of medical science in Holland. The beautiful scrolls in Dr. Pfeiffer's collection were presented to him on that occasion.

"In 1858," says Dr. Pfeiffer, "Donders wrote two epoch-making papers on the use and selection of spectacles." When the eye doctor nowadays tests the eyes of his patient and finds out, by constant shifting and changing of glasses, which particular kind of spectacles are needed, he uses a system devised by Donders a hundred years ago. Not dark glasses such as are now the fashion among the ladies. The hot summer of 1955 and the stark glare of the relentless sun made dark glasses popular, but since they remain popular in winter it is clear that the majority of women have no other reason for wearing them than the wish to follow the fashion set by Greta Garbo. They remain attached to the nose in all kinds of weather and under all kinds of lighting. You see them worn when it rains and under clouded skies, in the gloom of the subway, in dimly lighted bars and restaurants. Dr.

Pfeiffer assured me that the medical profession does not approve of them as fit for indiscriminate use. If you give in to a weakness you are apt to increase the weakness. If the sun is kept away from perfectly healthy eyes they will become less able to endure the sun's brilliance and cease to be perfect. The light of the body is the eye, and Donders, who made it his life's work to strengthen and brighten the body's light, would have frowned on a fashion that darkens it. Said Goethe:

> Wär nicht das Auge sonnenhaft,
> Wie könnten wir das Licht erblicken?

The eye is sunlike; if that were not so, how should we be able to perceive the light? Why then screen off the light, why divorce the body's sun from the sun of the world?

April, 1957

THE SYMBOLIC CANDLE

Whenever I happen to be in London I go to the National Gallery chiefly for one purpose: to see Jan van Eyck's picture of the Arnolfini couple. It is an early specimen of the genre piece in which the Netherlands School excels and it is, surprisingly, the very best of its kind, not surpassed even by the greatest masters such as Johannes Vermeer and Pieter de Hoogh, who were at work more than two centuries after Van Eyck. The artist has given expression here to deeper and sincerer reverence than informs his altar pieces where madonnas are enthroned in costly robes that with their splendor distract the attention from her face and the faces of attending saints and donors. Here no exuberance of color, no display of glittering wealth; the artist's joy in rendering magnificence is here subdued. There is beauty too in this burgher home, but it is restrained by an atmosphere of quiet devotion, which made a stronger appeal to Van Eyck's feelings than all the lustre and brilliancy of church and court. This simple domestic scene inspired him to the supreme achievement of his career.

It is not absolutely certain that it is the home of Arnolfini, the immigrant from Lucca in Italy who was a prominent merchant at Bruges. In an inventory compiled in 1516 of the art treasures owned by Margaret of Austria, Regent of the Netherlands for her nephew King Charles v of Spain, is mentioned "ung grant tableau qu'on appelle Hernoul le fin, avec sa femme dedens une chambre ... Fait du painctre Johannes." It was James Weale who in 1861 suggested that Hernoul le fin was a corruption of Arnolfini, and this ingenious conjecture seemed so convincing that it has been generally accepted. Yet ground for doubt remains. The Dutch, in the late Middle Ages, did not use to refer to a man by his family name; his baptismal name was used followed sometimes by a characteristic nickname that served to distinguish him from his namesakes. Van Eyck himself was called Master Johannes, by which name he appears in the inventory of 1516; and Albrecht Dürer, who visited the Netherlands in 1520-1521, calls him in the diary of that journey "Meister Johannes." In Carel van Mander's "Schilderboeck," which was published in 1604 and reprinted in 1618, the Index lists the painters in alphabetical order according to their given names, hence the brothers Van Eyck have parted company, Hubrecht appearing under the letter H and Johannes under J. It would seem more likely, therefore, that this man was some Arnout (the Dutch equivalent of Hernoul) nicknamed De Fijne, that is the rich or the eminent one, a burgher of Bruges. He does not look like an Italian, he is more of a Flemish type; and his wife has many likenesses among the ladies portrayed by Flemish artists of the fifteenth century. They were evidently intimate friends of the painter, for one sees in the convex mirror on the wall in the background a reflection of him entering the room; it must be he, for under the mirror he painted the inscription *Johannes de Eyck fuit hic*, Jan van Eyck was here. In this case, it is true, he broke with the custom of preferring the given to the family name; but this was a solemn occasion, as is proved by the use of Latin; the signature in full was ceremonial because the full name was never used in daily intercourse.

What was this solemn occasion: A wedding ceremony, according to Panofsky, who devotes a lengthy discussion to the picture in his brilliant history of "Early Netherlandish Painting." The lone candle that is burning in the chandelier above the couple is to him convincing proof of the correctness of that assumption. "A burning candle," he writes, "symbol of the all-seeing Christ, not only was, and often is, required for the ceremony of taking an oath in general but also had a special reference to matrimony: the 'marriage candle' (*Brautkerze*) was either carried to church before the bridal procession, or ceremoniously given to the bride by the groom, or, as is here the case, lit in the home of the newlyweds." Since this is a Flemish scene, the author should have given us the Dutch name of the "marriage candle"; that there is a name for it in English and German does not prove that Van Eyck and his countrymen lit a *bruutkeerse* at a wedding. I doubt whether the Germans and the English did, for Grimm's "Deutsches Wörterbuch" does not list the word *Brautkerze*, nor is there a flicker of a "marriage candle" in the great "New English Dictionary." In my opinion the little candle is a symbol of the new life that is coming into the world. The wife of Hernoul le Fin is in an advanced stage of pregnancy. Many women in those early days died in childbed, and this wealthy burgher of Bruges had his friend Johannes paint a likeness of himself and her that would visibly perpetuate their union if its reality were to be destroyed by death. Hernoul le Fin has lit the tiny candle in his chandelier devoutly praying that the child may live and that all the sockets may be gradually filled with flickering symbols of its life. Candles still flicker symbolically on birthday cakes. If we light only one, it is blown out in token of the life year that is past; if we light as many candles as the number of years the celebrant has lived, we repeat in one blow the extinguishing action of all previous celebrations. Thus by the bedside of a dying man a candle was kept burning which, at the moment he gave up the ghost, was snuffed out. One can see this very distinctly in an engraving after Pieter Brueghel the Elder representing the death of the Virgin Mary. The solemn gesture with which Hernoul raises his right hand towards the light above him apparently accompanies his inward prayer that the child may live.

I have additional reason for my disbelief in Panofsky's wedding theory. Weddings were the concern of the entire neighborhood. People living in the same bailiwick were organized in neighborhood guilds and took part in all events that affected the family of one of the members. Weddings, christenings, burials were communal ceremonies. The neighborhood had a right to be feasted at a wedding, and a well-to-do couple who failed to wine and dine the guild would begin their married life as social outcasts. Jan van Eyck was not in this room as a wedding guest; it is more likely that he came in response to the couple's request to stand godfather at their baby's christening; and the candle that he lit in his picture was his way of saying: "I will watch over this new life and be a guiding light to it in the years to come."

The candle was not exclusively a religious symbol. It signified also the irresistible passage of time and its irrevocability. At public auctions of real estate it was customary for the auctioneer to light a candle after he had finished reading the conditions of sale. That candle was the centre of attention, for everyone in the audience knew that its final flicker would mark the end of the sale. The person who made the last bid before that decisive moment was the purchaser of the lot. This was not solely a Netherlandish practice, it was in vogue all over Europe. Among the French, most conservative of nations, auctions by the candle are still in force. I came across an instance of it in a short story "For Sale at Auction" that appeared in the November

5th issue of *The New Yorker*. And shortly afterwards I found another reference to *vente à la chandelle* in a highly entertaining account of a wine auction at Beaune contributed by Clementine Paddleford to the *Herald-Tribune*. "To keep bidders in suspense," she wrote, "to create excitement and accelerate sales, the bids were decided *à la chandelle*. Bids on a lot of wine last only as long as the taper burns. Eyes of hundreds of buyers concentrated on the auctioneer and the lighted candle. The flame flicked out; the last bidder won." A similar scene of excitement and suspense is described by Samuel Pepys in his Diary under the date of November 5th, 1660: "To our office, where we met all, for the sale of two ships by an inch of candle (the first time that ever I saw any of this kind), where I observed how they do invite one another, and at last how they all do cry, and we have much to do to tell who did cry last." And in an entry of two years later, September 3rd, 1662, he wrote of a similar auction: "Pleasant to see how backward men are at first to bid; and yet when the candle is going out, how they bawl and dispute afterwards who bids the most first. And here I observed one man cunninger than the rest that was sure to bid the last man, and to carry it; and inquiring the reason, he told me that just as the flame goes out the smoke descends, which is a thing I never observed before, and by that he do know the instant when to bid last, which is very pretty."

June, 1957

HAROLD DE WOLF FULLER

The death of Harold de Wolf Fuller on May 2nd at Smithtown, Long Island, dissolves a friendship that had bound me to him for more than half a century. We used to run the Netherland-America Foundation together in the days preceding the presidency of Mr. Peter Grimm, but that partnership did not create the bond between us, it was the result of our friendship. We met in 1903, when Fuller was studying at Leyden under Gerrit Kalff, Professor of Netherland literature. I had been a pupil of Kalff at the gymnasium in Amsterdam and remained closely attached to my former master. It was he who brought Fuller and me together. He invited us to his home, which stood in the shadow of the ancient church of St. Peter, and there, in the professor's booklined study, our friendship took root. Harold, after that, often came to visit me in my bachelor's quarters at The Hague and discussed with me the questions that baffled him in the literary study on which he was engaged. I am writing this away from books that might refresh my memory, but I believe I can state the nature of the problem on which he was working for his doctoral dissertation. An obscure Dutch dramatist produced in the early seventeenth century a tragedy of Romeo and Juliet, not a translation of Shakespeare's play but, as Harold believed and hoped to prove, of an earlier draft of it that is no longer extant in English. He had no difficulty in reading seventeenth century Dutch and acquired, in the course of his year in Holland, a ready command of the spoken language. That enabled him to participate wholeheartedly in the joys of the students' life at Leyden. He was not a supercilious critic of their boyish antics but loved to share them, and many years later, in the early forties, when the Hollanders in New York who were Leyden alumni organized a dinner at which an equal number of members of the Harvard Club were their guests, Fuller, though an alumnus of Harvard, chose to attend as one of the Leyden hosts.

When Fuller was back in the States he became an instructor in English and Comparative Literature at his Alma Mater and offered a course there to students who wanted to study Dutch. In 1909 he sent me, as evidence of his continued interest in that language, a booklet containing his metrical version in English of the early legend of Beatrice, the run-away nun who, forsaken by her faithless lover, returns to her convent and finds that she has never been missed; the Virgin Mary had, in her guise, performed her duties as sacristan to reward her for dutifully praying her daily Ave Marias. After that I lost track of him. We ceased to correspond, and it was only by a fortunate coincidence that I was given a chance to renew our friendship. One day I bought, at a bookstall in the open-air market at The Hague, a vellum-bound folio sketchbook full of pencil drawings and water colors of ships and scenes of seafaring life. The artist had signed his name on the inside cover: A. van Beest 1843. I had never heard of this marine painter and found that no one else had at The Hague, not even the Directors of museums and art galleries. I discovered a brief biography of Van Beest by a French art critic who had known him personally. From this I learnt that in 1845, when Van Beest was twenty-five years old, he absconded in disguise to America, had there rehabilitated himself, and had died, honored as a great artist, in St. Luke's hospital at New York in 1860. I sent a query to *The Nation*, which, I was told by my American correspondent, Carlton Brown, was the periodical most likely to be read by people interested in matters of art. Together with the copy containing my request for information about the painter's life in America I received a letter from the Editor, who signed himself, to my pleased surprise, "Harold de Wolf Fuller." He had joined *The Nation*, he wrote, in 1911, and asked me to send him, now and then, correspondence from The Hague that might be

343

of interest to American readers; and when the war broke out in 1914 so much happened that I could report on that I became a regular correspondent of *The Nation* at The Hague. Fuller was an appreciative editor and often wrote me courteous notes in praise of what I sent him. In 1918 he wrote me that he and Oswald Garrison Villard, the owner of *The Nation*, did no longer see eye to eye in regard to the war. He had handed in his resignation and was planning to start a new weekly in conjunction with Fabian Franklin, former editor of the New York *Evening Post*. "Come over and join us as an Associate Editor," he wrote, "I shall let you know in course of time when we launch our new venture." Early in February 1919 he sent me a cable: "Be here April 15." By that time, my wife and I had made up our minds and decided to emigrate. The United States offered a better future for our four children than over-populated Holland, and their mother, a native of Yorkshire, felt attracted by the prospect of living again in an English-speaking community, though she had mastered the Dutch language to perfection. We were still young and faced the removal to a faraway and unknown country as an exciting adventure.

The two years I was an associate editor on the staff of *The Weekly Review* were among the happiest of my life. Harold was an ideal chief, courteous, considerate, never ill-tempered. The Tuesday mornings were always hectic, for at noon all copy had to be ready for the printer, and we all sat bent over our desks writing comments, in nervous haste, on the latest news in the morning papers. Fuller alone was always calm. I admired his composure all the more because I knew he was faced with financial difficulties. The paper did not pay for itself, it had to rely on financial backing by wealthy donors. I never knew who they were; Fuller and Franklin never discussed with the staff the provenance of their resources. I only knew that they fluctuated; there were times when the outlook seemed bright, and then again we heard that there were hard times ahead. After three years of a precarious existence *The Weekly Review* gave up the struggle; Fuller realized that his paper was unable to compete with the Sunday editions of the metropolitan dailies.

He soon found new employment for which, by inclination and training, he would seem to be eminently fitted. He was appointed Professor of Journalism at New York University. But the teaching of journalism was not to his liking, he craved the practice of it. To edit a paper was his ambttion, and he succeeded in persuading the Chancellor to let him start a weekly, under the University's auspices. That again, however, proved a short-lived venture, and since he had resigned his professorship to become an editor, he was again without a job. Not for long, though. The firm of John Price Jones enlisted his services in fund-raising campaigns, and subsequently I was fortunate in persuading him to assume the Directorship of the Netherland-America Foundation. He knew and loved Holland, he could read Dutch, possessed administrative qualities that were badly needed in our amateurishly run office, and he had experience in the technique of fund raising which proved an invaluable asset to us. He obtained a handsome subsidy from Mr. Thomas J. Watson and subsequently his consent to act as President of the Foundation. Fuller moved the office to Stuyvesant Square, where the Dutch past of New York, he claimed, though it was lost to the eye, made itself felt in ways that he himself was at a loss to define. It was, in any case, a quiet quarter of the city that had retained an early nineteenth century atmosphere in which his gentle nature felt at home. It irked him that the official address of his office was East 17th Street; the Post Office refused to recognize the existence of Stuyvesant Square. It was through his endeavors that the old Dutch Governor, who had his Bowerie on or near that spot, came back into his own. He did not rest until the Park Commissioner gave his consent to the erection, in the centre of the square, of the statue by Mrs. Vanderbilt Whitney that had stood in front of the Netherlands Pavilion at the New York World Fair. It was a happy day for him when it was unveiled in the presence of city dignitaries and representatives of the Netherlands government.

When what we used to call Holland House was inaugurated the office was moved thither. That had its advantages, for we were there under the same roof with the Consulate General and the Netherlands Library of Information. The Foundation could make use of part of the latter's quarters for lectures, receptions, and social gatherings. At those functions Fuller was in his element. He knew most of the members of the Foundation personally and possessed the ideal host's gift of remembering their names. When the war was over the Foundation drifted into the doldrums. Fuller, disheartened, obtained from Mr. Watson an appointment on the staff of *THINK* and gave what energy old age and failing health left him to his editorial task. His final years were a sad anti-climax. His mind began to fail, Mrs. Fuller, who had been his life companion for over forty years, was taken from him, and he ended his days in a nursing home at Smithtown, Long Island. There he lived in a room bare of all but the indispensable furniture; books, which used to be the daily sustenance of his mind, were not in evidence. It was a depressing visit, my last one, that I paid him there. I feel thankful to know that from his second childhood he has risen to the maturity of the ageless.

A DUTCH BIOLOGIST

A few miles south of Taos, New Mexico, on the road to Santa Fe, stands the Sage Brush Inn, a popular hostel built in a fantastic style that is evidently meant to emulate the beautiful Spanish architecture of former days. It had a good restaurant in the early forties, which was capably run by two young women who had grown tired of teaching school and had turned, for a novelty, to the catering business. I attended a memorable dinner party there ten or twelve years ago. Our host was Mr. Jan van Houten, a western mining magnate and a prominent figure in those parts. He was not a resident of Taos but of Denver, Colorado, whither he had moved some years before from Raton, New Mexico. Van, as he was affectionately called by his many friends, had come from Holland at an early age and carved unaided a highly successful career for himself in the "Land of Enchantment." Economic necessity did not compel him to leave his native country. It must have been love of adventure or, perhaps, recalcitrance to the authority of a domineering father that induced him to turn his back on the comforts of a well-to-do home. Old Mr. Sam van Houten played a conspicuous part in Dutch politics around the turn of the century. He died in 1930 in his ninety-third year, but the obituaries that appeared in the papers did not remind the readers of a long-forgotten celebrity. He had taken good care that his countrymen should not forget him after he had withdrawn from active participation in public life. Until he was ninety years old he published at irregular intervals Political Letters, which were widely read for the originality of the writer's ideas and for the force with which they were expressed. He was a pioneer but not a leader. The electorate, half a century ago, was too conservative to care for his progressivism. He sowed radical ideas in an unreceptive soil; yet thanks to his long life he had the satisfaction of seeing several of them enacted into law when he had become an inactive observer of the political turmoil.

The son in New Mexico was not a politician, though he had the mettle and the sagacity to follow in his father's steps. He chose to enter business and prospered beyond his own expectation. I do not remember what was the occasion for the party he gave at the Sage Brush Inn; it may have been in celebration of his seventieth birthday. Opposite me at the dinner table sat an English-born artist from New Hope, Pennsylvania, Mr. Harry Leith Ross. A few months earlier I had seen an exhibition of his water colors at the Ferargil Galleries in New York, and I was glad of this opportunity to tell him how much I admired them. That started a lively conversation between us across the table. He had heard that I was an amateur painter and inquired what I specialized in. "Portraits," I said. "Then life need not have a single dull moment for you; a training in the painting of portraits makes one observant of human faces." I agreed and said, "Even a subway ride in New York is to me not the distressing experience most people find it; I enjoy the opportunity to study potential models all around me." When he smiled at that I felt encouraged to make a personal remark. "I have been studying your face," I said, "and it struck me that you resemble Van in the shape of your nose and chin." "Well," he said, "that is not surprising; I am the son of his sister." And then, with a twinkle in his eye, he said, "You remind me of another Hollander whom I met a few years ago. My wife and I went to Europe on a ship of the Holland-American Line. We shared our table in the dining room with a Dutch couple who were most uncongenial company. We did our best to engage them into conversation, but they answered merely with yes or no. The man especially annoyed me. He often stared at me and studied my face and then he would shake his head as if he meant to say, 'I give up.' But at the Captain's dinner the general spirit of good-fellowship thawed his icy silence. He suddenly addressed me and said: 'You are a Scot, aren't you?' I admitted that I was. 'I can't understand it. I have studied your face and came to the conclusion that you must be a Van Houten. You have the Van Houten nose and chin.' You should have seen his face when he heard that I actually was a Van Houten, he was so happy that he had not been mistaken. He was a biologist, he told me and was the director of a genealogical research centre at Leyden. I wish I could remember his name." "I think I can tell you"; I said, "it must have been Van Bemmelen." "Right you are, that was it!"

Johan Frans van Bemmelen was not the unsocial, taciturn man that Harry Leith Ross believed him to be. I had known him well forty years earlier, when we were colleagues at The Hague gymnasium. He was nearly twenty years my senior, and far richer in knowledge and experience; he had studied in Leyden, in Jena, in Heidelberg, and at the Zoological Station at Naples, had traveled in Indonesia, and was the author of an impressive list of publications on zoology and paleontology. But he was never condescending to his much younger colleague. I found him affable and very modest about the results of his research. His pupils were fond of him, not only because he was a first-rate teacher, but also for his artistic talent. Slides were not used in the classroom in those days, and motion pictures, of course, were unknown. But he himself supplied the illustrations to his lessons. The children watched with fascinated attention the motion of his hand across the blackboard as he designed in white chalk the

347

shapes of skulls and skeletons and prehistorical animals. That was creative motion more entrancing than the ready-made motion we nowadays watch on the screen. He did not remain my colleague long. Five years after I made his acquaintance he was called away to the university of Groningen, which appointed him professor of zoology. He taught there until his seventieth year, the age for retirement. The leisure that long service had won him gave him time at last to pursue his special hobby: the study of heredity. He assumed the directorate of a Bio-genealogical Institute at Leyden, where he collected data concerning the persistence of characteristic traits, both physical and mental, that run and spread through succeeding generations of families.

During his visit to the United States, from which he returned on the same ship with Harry Leith Ross, he came to see me at Columbia University. Heredity was the main topic of his conversation, but he never bored me, he talked about it in a most entertaining way. With amusing anecdotes he illustrated his contentions. He was firmly convinced, and based his conviction on the famous theory of Mendel, that two persons who show a striking likeness to one another must have a common ancestor. His memory was stocked with stories that tended to confirm it. I remember one that he told with great pride and pleasure. He had to attend one day an international conference of biologists in Venice. Its president, a personal friend of his, wrote Van Bemmelen that he was too busy to go to the station to welcome him, but he would delegate one of his colleagues to meet him at the train. He gave him no description of the man, and Van Bemmelen was wondering how they would find each other; but to his surprise he was greeted with much warmth, as he stepped down on the platform, by an Italian whom he had never seen in his life. "How could you tell that I was Van Bemmelen?" he asked. "That was easy," the other answered; "I was told to look for a man who looked like Pietro Mascagni, and you were the only traveler who did." That was a blow to Van Bemmelen's pet theory. He could not believe that he shared a distant ancestor with Mascagni. However, when he was back in Holland he started to investigate the history of his family as far back as he could trace it; and he actually discovered that they were related. A French artist, a Huguenot, escaped to Holland after the revocation of the Edict of Nantes in 1685, and settled with his family in Middelburg. He had two daughters, one of whom became the wife of an Italian and Mascagni was a descendant of that couple; the other married a Hollander and figures among the ancestors of the Van Bemmelens. Such discovery of unsuspected relatives on the strength of similar facial traits does not always result in pleased surprise. Last year an imposter in Vienna impersonated Mr. Eduard van Beinum, the conductor of the

Amsterdam Concertgebouw orchestra. His double lived in great style as befits a famous maestro. Among his many victims was a lady to whom he owed, when he absconded, four thousand florins for the rent of an apartment. The Dutch conductor proved by an act of generosity that he had nothing in common with the crook except his looks. He paid the poor lady's bill in full and presented her with a free ticket to one of his concerts. Van Bemmelen would have said, those looks they had in common meant a great deal, they proved a distant relationship, descendance from a joint ancestor. And the imposter might say, "There you are, he accepts family responsibility for my misdeeds."

Physical likeness, of course, is more readily observed than the resemblance between mental traits. Everybody knows, to be sure, that musical and artistic talents are apt to recur in a family's successive generations, but the similarity between less conspicuous endowments of the mind such as reveal themselves in an aptitude for a special kind of work or in the choice of some definite avocation remains mostly unnoticed. Those who observe it usually ascribe it to the influence of education or of family tradition. But Van Bemmelen, though not denying that these two are contributory agents, was convinced that heredity is the determining factor in the choice of a career. Look at my own family, he used to say. All the male ancestors of his children in four consecutive generations devoted themselves to educational pursuits. His great-grandfather, though destined by his guardians to become a hydraulic engineer, chose to be a schoolmaster and wrote books on pedagogy; this man's son studied philology and was head-master of a Latin school before he was thirty years old. His two sons, early orphaned as was their father before them, again chose a teaching career, although no parent could influence their preference. Van Bemmelen's great-grandfather had a brother in whose descendants the didactic strain cropped up repeatedly. He had a grandson who was active in commerce and insurance, but this man's three daughters founded a boarding school for girls which gained great reputation throughout the country, and the girls' brothers, who like their father followed other pursuits than education, each had a daughter who made teaching her profession. Van Bemmelen lived and died firmly convinced that the didactic propensity in his cognates was an heredi-tary characteristic more powerful than outside persuasion and family tradition.

HONORING A SEXAGENARIAN

Shortly after my arrival in America – I had just started my lectures at Columbia University – a young Hollander walked into my office and introduced himself as Jef Last. I was glad to see him, for I felt a little homesick for my native country, and he made a favorable impression on me with his ready smile and his open face. He did not ask for any help or any favor, he just wanted to make my acquaintance as we were countrymen in a strange land. He had studied Chinese at the university of Leyden, and had come to New York to continue his studies at the Department of Far Eastern languages of Columbia. He often came to our apartment after that first visit, and sometimes went hiking with me along the trails between Tuxedo and Bear Mountain. One day he came in and said he was dropping his study of Chinese. The instruction at Columbia did not advance him beyond the point he had reached at Leyden, he was wasting his time and his money here. Was he going back to Holland? I asked him. No, he had thought of something better to do. He was interested in American labor conditions, and was going to earn a living as a factory hand. "Are you looking around for a job?" "No, I have one, at the Otis plant in Yonkers, where they make elevators. Fascinating work, and I like the fellows that I work with." He had, of course, joined the Union, and took an active part in the meetings of the workers. I do not remember how long he stayed, but I do know that it was not for long. His restless nature drove him to fresh adventures and experiences. He worked in the mines, he went to sea as a common sailor, found employment in the Dutch silk industry, was a schoolteacher for a time, took up journalism, published verse, and finally became a successful novelist. All his books had a socialist slant, for having been a factory hand himself, he had a strong fellow feeling for the working class and for the sailors whose hard life he had shared on the sea. When the civil war broke out in Spain a generous impulse to rush to the support of the oppressed drove him to join the revolutionary troops and as captain of the Republic's milicias he fought against Franco until the collapse of the resistance.

I was reminded of Jef Last the other day when I received a circular appealing for contributions to a fund that is needed to stage an impressive celebration of his sixtieth birthday. They make a great fuss in Holland about a man reaching that not so very venerable age. It is an old tradition, though. In my young days more people used to die in their sixty-third year than at any other age. That was at any rate the popular belief, and people received congratulations when they had safely arrived beyond that perilous point. It may be that honoring a man at sixty had its origin in this superstition about the fatal year that was approaching. Let us honor him now while he is still hale and hearty, three years from now he may be dead. Or the practice may arise from the medieval conviction that a man at sixty is entering upon his dotage. That is the end of him as a rational being, let us do him homage while he is still in his senses. A Dutchman's foolish remark is countered with the scornful or good-humored question, "Are you sixty?" meaning "Have you lost your mind?" Modern hygiene has lengthened the human life span far beyond its length in the Middle Ages, but in this popular saying the Hollander still measures the duration of life by medieval standards. Whatever the reason for paying special honor to a man on his sixtieth birthday, I think it is a good custom. We should not wait till he is dead and cannot hear the eulogies that are pronounced over his bier. He will soon be forgotten when he is in his grave, let him know now that we think of him while he is still alive.

That must have been the thought which prompted the signers of the circular to try and rally the friends of Jef Last to a celebration in his honor. Americans do not know him and probably never heard of him, and I would not use the pages of the Foundation Letter to pay tribute to this aging stranger if it were not for the illuminating light the appeal sheds upon a characteristic trait of the Dutch nation. If Jef Last, the Socialist reformer and erstwhile fighter in the armies of the Spanish revolutionaries, were an American citizen, he would be blacklisted in this country by patriotic societies, hounded from public platforms, and called a commie and a fellow traveler by the columnists who used to applaud Mc Carthy's witch hunt. In Holland a group of respectable citizens from various walks of life, not only from the ranks of Labor, join hands to form a human wreath with which to crown him. University professors, journalists, editors, schoolteachers, artists, actors, authors, department heads of Government ministries, and a titled dowager whose father was once Minister of Foreign Affairs, have signed the appeal without fear of being denounced as fellow travelers by association. Tolerant respect of opposing opinions is an ancient tradition in the Netherlands. It was the spirit of Erasmus that prevailed in the days of the Dutch Republic. Although Calvinist orthodoxy triumphed at the Synod of Dordrecht, the merchant rulers refused to support the hotheads among the preachers who wanted them to suppress heretical sects. Huizinga, the late historian of Leyden university, makes the interesting observation that in the villages around Leyden and Alkmaar, the cities that had been the centres of Holland's struggle for freedom, the population has remained predominantly Catholic, so little did the Calvinists themselves care for the conversion of the erring. Coercion was never resorted to. The government of the Dutch Republic was, as Jan de Witt defined it, a government of persuasion. Liberty trained the Dutch in the art of urbane debate. Sir William Temple, who was the British envoy at The Hague when Jan de Witt, as Pensionary of Holland, was the most powerful man in the Republic, wrote in his memoirs: "It is hardly to be imagined how all the violence and sharpness which accompanies the differences of religion in other countries seems to be appeased or softened by the general freedom which all men enjoy, either by allowance or by connivance; nor how faction and ambition are thereby disabled to colour their interested and seditious designs with the pretences of religion, which has cost the Christian world so much blood for these last hundred and fifty years. The Dutch argue without interest or anger; they differ without enmity or scorn, and they agree without confederacy," by which he evidently meant collusion. That is a picture of Dutch tolerance and moderation which is still true as applied to the popular mood of the present day. According to the law of the land Jef Last, by enlisting in a foreign army, risked the loss of his Netherlands citizenship. He was not deprived of it on his return from Spain. He is still an honored citizen of the land of his birth as his many admirers proved at the ceremony staged on his sixtieth birthday.

A WITTY SCHOOLMASTER

Last January Rotterdam honored a native son on the centenary of his death. That was, to my way of thinking, more than one hundred years too late. But the city had a good excuse for its neglect in the past: the man whom it honored never reached his sixtieth birthday. When he died on January 27th, 1858, his fiftieth was in the offing. He lived in London, where he was headmaster of a boys' school, a better school than its contemporary Dotheboys Hall. He was an unusual headmaster in that he abhorred corporal punishment, which Mr. Squeers considered the moral salvation of the boys and a daily enjoyment to himself. When his predecessor handed him the cane as the symbol of his authority, he laid it quietly aside. Some parents were pleased with this humane regime and called on purpose to tell him so. But there were others who did not approve. One mother called to ask how it was that her son's welfare was no longer attended to; repeatedly these last weeks, she said, she had examined the boy's back and found no welts on it. That was evidence of neglect she would not stand for. He was, indeed, a unique kind of headmaster in Dickens's England, and the explanation of his singularity was his foreign birth. He bore the typically Dutch name of Gerrit van de Linde. He had studied at Leyden, not too seriously, it would seem, for nine years after his enrollment he had attained no higher degree than Candidate of Theology. He gave up his theological studies and decided to emigrate to South Africa via London. He never got further than London. Friends in Holland had supplied him with letters of introduction to persons of quality who supplied him with funds with which he took over the boarding school that he ran successfully until his death. Being a Hollander, he practised in his school that tolerance and forbearance that Sir William Temple admired in the Dutch of the seventeenth century. There was something brutal in the corporal punishment that was the common practice in boys-schools throughout England. Three hundred years earlier Erasmus had already condemned it in no uncertain terms: "Reward industry and good behavior," he wrote, "and refrain from bodily chastisement. The master who canes his boys is more fit to be a hangman." Van de Linde adhered to that precept. Jacob van Lennep, a Dutch author, who knew him well and sometimes visited him in London, reported, on his return from one of these visits, that former students retained a deep respect and affection for their old headmaster and often called at the school to shake hands with him.

It was probably not only his humaneness that made him popular with the boys. We do not know how he taught, but we do know that he did not take his learning and the teaching of it too seriously. He found relaxation in writing humorous verse in Dutch which was published in Holland. He acted wisely, perhaps, in making his flippancy inaccessible to English readers; it might have given his school a bad name. He poked fun in his rhymes at the romantic poets, and wrote absurd doggerel about Geography, Roman and Natural History, the very subjects which he taught in all seriousness in the classroom. He found probably a relief and escape from the boredom of teaching in composing these humorous nonsense rhymes. He found his models for this kind of versification in the pages of Punch and in the Ingoldsby Legends. Its spirit is English, yet when his queer sallies in verse were published in book form by his friend Van Lennep, "*Gedichten van den Schoolmeester*" (Poems by the Schoolmaster) met with applause from an amused and grateful public. Old fogies might frown at such undignified stuff written in common, plebeian language, but the book won a secure place in the hearts of Holland's reading public. The Schoolmaster who never taught anywhere but in England is best remembered in his native country as "De Schoolmeester" who wrote funny poetry.

WHAT GERMANS THOUGHT OF HOLLAND

Travelers who come home from abroad and publish their impressions
of foreign lands and nations seldom reveal as much about them as
they do about themselves. In their preference for special features of
the countries they visited, in their judgments on the great masterpieces of art, in their prejudices and their fault-finding with uncommon customs, in their sneers at the foreigner's unintelligible speech,
they paint their own portraits. I have been reading an anthology of
opinions by Germans on Holland and the Dutch collected by Dr.
Claus Victor Bock, a professor of German at an English university[1],
and I learnt more from it what sort of visitors they were than what
sort of country they visited. Few among them have anything original
to say, not even great original minds. Bismarck was in Amsterdam
in 1853, when he was thirty-eight years old, and wrote his wife a
description of what he saw there: "As I walked with a long clay pipe
in my mouth and looked through the forest of masts across the canals
at the chimneys in the background, all the old Dutch ghost stories of
my childhood came to mind, of Dolph Heylinger and Rip Van Winkle
and the Flying Dutchman." It is revealing to know that the Iron
Chancellor-to-be, before he had hardened into iron, walked through
the streets of Amsterdam in so mellow a mood that he remembered
fairy tales of his infancy, but it is disappointing that he said little else
that is worth quoting. The great Schliemann of Trojan fame spent
five years of his life as an impecunious office boy at Amsterdam, from
December 1841 till 1846, but the long passage that Dr. Bock quotes
from his Autobiography does not contain a single hint that he was
impressed by its beauty nor a passing reference to his contacts with
the people. He was too much absorbed in himself to pay attention to
either. All he cares to tell is how he suffered shipwreck on the coast
of the isle of Texel, how he found work in an Amsterdam business
office, how little they paid him, and why they refused to promote him.
He neglected his work, he admits, studying languages. He taught
himself Dutch, Spanish, Portuguese and Italian, and his memory, he
boasts, was so well trained that in only six weeks he mastered each so
completely that he could speak and write them fluently! He then
tried to tackle Russian, but being unable to find a teacher he memo-
rized a Russian translation of Fénelon's "Télémaque" and recited it
to a poor Jew totally ignorant of Russian, who charged him four
guilders a week for listening two hours each evening to his unintel-

[1] *Deutsche Erfahren Holland.* The Hague: L. J. C. Boucher.

ligible declamations. He claims that he did learn Russian in this manner, and armed with this precious knowledge he found his way to St. Petersburg, where he prospered and amassed the fortune that enabled him to excavate the ruins of Troy. That story is indeed startling evidence of Schliemann's linguistic ability, but the great man's absorption in himself prevented him, apparently, from looking around in Amsterdam and studying the Dutch in addition to their language.

Friedrich Freiligrath, the poet, was also employed for four years in a commercial house at Amsterdam. He lived on a picturesque canal in the oldest part of the city, which might have stirred his impressionable mind to poetic effusions. Dr. Bock's anthology does contain one poem that he wrote there, a farewell to a friend whom he saw off in the harbor; but it has nothing specifically Dutch; it might have been written in Hamburg, or Bremen, or London. In the third year of his residence in Holland his longing for the mountains and forests of his homeland found vent in a nostalgic outburst in which he curses "this plebeian churchwarden-pipe land." Four years later, though, when he was living in Cologne, he wrote to a German friend in Amsterdam: "In retrospect everything is pleasant, even the misery one has endured; I feel more and more that Holland, despite many a sad, lonesome hour I spent there, has grown dear to me." Travel impressions are creations of the observer's momentary state of mind, the foreign scene, chameleon-like, taking on the coloring of his mood.

There is a distinct difference in the tone of these comments before and after 1870. The eighteenth and early nineteenth century visitors were inclined to admire and praise what they saw in Holland. They had inherited from previous generations a profound respect for the Dutchman's excessive wealth. "Der steinreiche Holländer" was a proverbial phrase reflecting the sense of awe and envy that the phenomenal prosperity of the Dutch Republic inspired in seventeenth century Germans. German boys in those days came to Holland in great numbers to look for employment in merchants' offices or to enlist on board Eastindiamen in hope of amassing a fortune in Java. Students from German universities came to Leyden assured of finding there a richer assortment of books than was available in their own college town. Albrecht von Haller, a native of Bern in Switzerland, who went to Leyden to study medicine under the famous Hermannus Boerhaave, was amazed at the abundance of reading matter he found there. "Nowhere else in the world," he wrote, "do so many people make a living out of books. Whole streets are lined with bookstores and printing offices. Everyone wants to collect a library, and often when Boerhaave in his morning lecture has praised a certain book, it is everywhere bought up in the afternoon at twice the original price. Many Hollanders pride themselves on possessing everything in various languages and sciences, and often a single man buys more books than all his posterity will ever read." There were many book-owners, though, who read omnivorously and were acquainted with the contemporary literature of England, Germany, and France. Sophie von la Roche, the grandmother of Clemens and Bettina Brentano, made in the *trekschuit* (the horsedrawn canal barge) the acquaintance of a Dutch Mennonite who amazed her by discoursing over their tea in perfect German on the merit of Wieland, Klopstock, and Goethe.

After the Franco-Prussian war the German's attitude toward Holland and the Dutch changed. The ascendancy of Prussia and her dominant role in the new German empire of the Hohenzollerns made the Prussians swell-headed. They laughed at the Dutch and made their language the butt of their ridicule. A. W. Schlegel was still disposed to believe that this contempt was a foolish prejudice. To his friend Heine he wrote in 1791 : "It interests me to solve the question whether the commonness that we Germans inseparably connect with our concept of the Dutch language is really something essential or only a semblance due to its similarity to Low German." But Von Treitschke, who was an outspoken admirer of Holland's great past, but despised her in her decline, admitted that the Dutch language made a comical impression on him. Pan-German propaganda, which became rife after 1870, represented the Hollanders as unlawfully occupying the mouth of the Rhine, which was the German's river, and they might only be left in undisturbed possession of it if they consented to join the great German nation and become part of their Empire. As long as they refused, and they did refuse emphatically, to annex themselves, they were treated by the Pan-Germans with contempt and vituperation. These did not heed the wise warning of Von Treitschke, who wrote in 1870: "If we should ever enter into Holland as conquerors, we should hardly kindle another eighty years' war, but we should obtain a nation of disloyal, rebellious allies. Who would desire such an unreliable acquisition?" The Nazis did, and they found, to their discomfiture, that Von Treitschke was a wiser prophet than their charlatan Leader. Dutch culture has its roots in the culture of France, and neither Nazi terror nor German protestations of monkey love for the little sister nation in the Rhine delta were able to eradicate the wide-spread ramifications of French influence from the depth of the soil from which the social and culture life of the Netherlands has drawn its nourishment ever since the Middle Ages.

Once in a while an individual German conceived a warm affection for Holland and gave expression to it in writings that won him popularity among the Dutch. Hoffmann von Fallersleben (1798-1874) was one of them. He was a rare combination of scholar and poet and went to Holland to study the country's medieval literature, which even in the Netherlands attracted few scholars and admirers. The results of his research among the neglected manuscript material he discovered in Dutch libraries were published in the twelve volumes of his "Horae Belgicae," a monumental achievement of a pioneer in this field of study. Hoffmann got to know the language so intimately that he wrote ballads in medieval Dutch which the poet Bilderdijk, a connoisseur of early Dutch literature, mistook for genuinely ancient compositions. At Bilderdijk's Leyden home he was an ever welcome visitor, which proves him to have been a very engaging individual. For Bilderdijk, a sickly misanthrope and not an amiable character at any time, was known to hate the Germans and never to be at a loss for words to express his loathing for the *Moffen* as he called them contemptuously. Bilderdijk, besides being the leading poet of Holland at the time, was much admired among his compatriots for the vast knowledge on all sorts of subjects that he had amassed in half a century of sedentary life among his books. One wonders how a man so learned and so solidly grounded in the elements of philosophy could be obsessed with so foolish a hatred for an entire nation. Even a philosopher feels the need, perhaps, of an occasional escapade into unwisdom. The late Count Hermann Keyserling, who is supposed to have been a philosopher, reciprocated Bilderdijk's Germanophobia (a century later) with an equally irrational contempt for the Dutch. He knew one area in Europe, he wrote, "Whose culture was the culture of the ugly." The absurdity of such a statement is its own refutation. A German contemporary of his, the poet Stefan George, held the very opposite opinion. "I love this country," he wrote of Holland, "it has the good fortune to possess spiritual nobility."

December, 1961

FAREWELL

This slight publication has in the course of the years dwindled from a monthly to a quarterly sheet. The cause of this emaciation was not the writer's incapacity to supply the needed nutriment, but the necessity, I suppose, to economize on the Foundation's expenses. It had the unfortunate effect of forcing him to turn his attention from current events to the stilled life of the past. The week's happenings observed in flight make an ephemeral record; what happens the week after obliterates, as a rule, its authenticity. The Letters in manuscript were kept in cold storage until the office decided to select one of them for publication not always in the order in which they were written. Sometimes they were a year old when they appeared in print. Those looked to the writer like dead bodies brought up from the morgue. It was better, then, to look beyond recent mortality at a more distant past, even at prehistoric times of which archaeologists are the historians. I must confess that excavation is not a subject in which I am especially interested. The past that I have known myself has fascination for me, and since I have marked my passage through time with eight crosses I have stored in my memory many impressions that have for me historical value. The scene of my childhood becomes dearer to me the farther it recedes into the distance. With an old man's nostalgia I like to recall those early days and tell about them in this final letter. It must serve the twofold purpose of a farewell to my native land and a farewell to my readers.

It was a solid old house in which I was born. It stood on the side of an Amsterdam canal that bore the name of Old Side Borough Moat. It was surrounded by equally old houses and darkened by huge old elm trees that overarched the water of the canal. I grew up among old things. When I had learnt to walk and was taken by my nurse for strolls in the neighborhood, I discovered a dark old archway lined on one side by deep, dark niches where old Jews offered old books for sale to the passers-by. The name of the archway was Old Men's Almshouse Gate, though it no longer admitted to the Almshouse. The old men had been removed to another shelter and the city, perhaps in order to relieve the depressing prevalence of mouldy old age, had made the Almshouse the headquarters of its University. The students who swarmed in and out of the building were the only evidence of youth in the area. Its age left an indelible impression on my mind. The boisterous young students could not dispel it. They were a daylight disturbance; at sunset the old borough moat wrapped itself up in its cloak of darkness and became its old, somber self. Growing up in its dimness I felt old before I went to school.

The house was a gloomy place. Its location was useful to my father who was a physician and wanted to live close to the city hospital where he taught obstetrics and attended to his patients. But as a place for living it had many drawbacks. Most houses along the canals of Amsterdam had a garden at the back, but ours had not.

Opposite our house, across the Old Side Borough Moat, stood an old building that dated from the early seventeenth century, the city *Lommerd*, a municipal institution that lent money upon pawns at a moderate interest. I was told that the great poet Vondel, when he was an old and poverty-stricken man, had served there as a clerk, keeping a record of the pawns in the *Lommerd* ledger. The house looked to me like a prison, and I felt sorry for the old man who was locked up there for ten years. Half a century later I was to write in English a biography of Vondel and when I reached the period of his life that he spent within the walls of the old pawnshop I was proud of my native city in being able to record that the burgomasters, in accepting the eighty-year-old clerk's resignation, let him retain his full salary for the few years that he was likely yet to live. When I grew up I became aware of the architectural beauty of the old *Lommerd*, but in my boyhood I found it a depressingly gloomy structure, and the sight of the poor who entered it with sad faces and the pawns of their destitution under their arms confirmed my suspicion of its sinister purpose. I was wrong, of course. Its aim was a blessing to the poor who were saved by it from falling into the clutches of usurious pawnbrokers. These were in the Middle Ages Italian bankers from Lombardy. The memory of those early moneylenders survives in the name of Amsterdam's municipal pawnshop, for *Lommerd* is Lombard.

When my parents moved away from that neighbourhood to a house with garden on the more dignified *Prinsegracht* I took with me a melancholy disposition, a reflection no doubt of the gloom in that quarter where everything was ancient and dark. When I was nine years old my portrait was painted by Wally Moes. The picture shows a pale, pensive lad in whom I find it difficult to recognize my youthful self. My parents, though, were pleased with it and told me it was an excellent likeness. Our new home was close to the *Rijksmuseum*, which was opened with great ceremony in 1885. The paintings that the city owned were removed into the new State building from the Trippen-huis on the *Kloveniersburgwal*, originally a private home of the patrician family Trip, but then, as still today, occupied by the Royal Society of Sciences. In that dignified mansion Rembrandt's Nightwatch was seen at its best in the light that fell in from aside through the high windows. After its removal to the *Rijksmuseum* it had to be lighted artificially, not by the kind of light in which it was painted. Nor is the building the kind of home that is characteristic of Amsterdam's architecture in Rembrandt's age. It is a neo-Gothic cathedral fit for the sumptuous art of Jan van Eyck and his followers but out of harmony with the paintings of the seventeenth century. Anyhow, it is a beautiful and impressive edifice. Its nearness to our home was a blessing to me. I spent all my free Saturday afternoons there, for I had no opportunity to relax in any kind of sport. There were no tennis courts yet in Amsterdam. Football was played on the empty land at the back of the *Rijksmuseum*, but that was the sport of common roughnecks with whom I was not allowed to consort. The only playgrounds that were open to the young of the city were its streets and squares and, in winter when frost had immobilized all shipping, the ice in the canals. Yet youthful delinquency was not a problem for the city police. The young were either more subdued or better behaved than they are today. My sport was to go to the *Rijksmuseum* and compose my own catalogue of the pictures. It was of course a very amateurish performance. I had no conception of a card index, but wrote the names of the painters and data about their lives in an old copybook that my grandfather had owned but never used, giving to each half a page of space and listing underneath the paintings by which the artist was represented in the Museum. It was impossible, of course, to maintain alphabetical order in that way, and when the book was half full I gave it up in despair. But while it lasted it gave me hours of intense pleasure and excitement, and I taught myself a great deal about Dutch art.

My father's practice grew rapidly during our years on the Prinsegracht. His carriage stood at the door every morning at half past eight to take him on his round of visits in various parts of Amsterdam. On holidays I might go with him sitting on the box seat next to the driver. Those were unforgettable expeditions. Father had his patients among Protestants, Catholics, and Jews, and his calls took him to sections of the city that I would never have seen otherwise. The Jewish quarter was the most fascinating. Its streets were crowded on summer days, children playing among pedlars' pushcarts, venders shouting their wares, old people sitting on the house stoops squabbling and gesticulating. But even the patrician canals were alive with commotion and noise in the early morning. I wish I had records of the street cries that I was familiar with in my youth. The fisherwomen from Zandvoort hawked their shrimps yelling *As beerze binne de gerneele* (the shrimps are big as bass), drawling out the *ee* to excessive length and suddenly raising the pitch of their voice as they reached the final syllable. There was the old fellow who sold *oblies* (stressed on the second syllable), a kind of crisp pastry that looked like rolled-up dry pancakes. His call started with a deep long drawn-out *ooooo* followed by a high-pitched *blie*. On dark November nights we heard the pathetic cry of poor children offering *ramanas* for sale, a kind of black radish which, thinly sliced and put between two pieces of bread made a tasty sandwich. The quaver with which they trilled their *a's* gave me a depressing sense of the poverty that drove them out into the dark streets to earn a scanty profit with their radishes. More engaging was the sight of the small drove of she-asses that we met in the morning on our way to school. Their owner milked them on the stoop of the house where an anaemic patient needed their milk fresh from the udder.

When I pay a final visit to Amsterdam I shall find it a different city from the one I knew. There will be no Jewish quarter, for the Nazis have decimated its population in concentration camps and gas chambers. There will be no street cries, for the hawkers cannot make themselves heard above the infernal noise of motor trucks, auto horns, and scooters. No donkeys will trot along the canals, for the doctors no longer believe in the efficacy of the ass's milk diet. Only the old houses will still be there and the paintings of the old masters in the *Rijksmuseum*. That last visit will bring home to me how far I am left behind by the living present. I realize that I have no right to comment on today's current events, I cannot follow them any more, they move too fast for my slackened perception. I thank my readers for their attention, especially the aging few who followed me from the start in 1924. And to the Foundation I wish survival into a future to which war will be known only as the recorded madness of a barbaric past.

LIST OF SUBSCRIBERS

Algemeen Nederlands Verbond (General Netherlands League), The Hague.
Mrs. Dr. J. Althaus-Günther, Germersheim (Germ.).
R. H. Amerman, New York.
Miss. Drs. E. H. Andriessen, The Hague.
Professor Dr. A. E. van Arkel, Leiden.
Mrs. J. J. A. Baartman-Runckel, Buenos Aires.
Dr. P. J. Barnouw, The Hague.
Mr. W. H. Barnouw, Rotterdam.
Drs. F. E. A. Batten, Amsterdam.
Professor Dr. D. Bax, Cape Town (S.-A.).
Jhr. Mr. G. Beelaerts van Blokland, The Hague.
Lic. F. Beersmans, Marburg (Germ.).
Miss Mr. C. R. Benthem Sypkens, The Hague.
Mrs. H. W. Berckenkamp-Rip, The Hague.
Mrs. A. W. G. van den Berg-van Lith de Jeude †, Amsterdam.
Bibliotheek v. d. Katholieke Leergangen (Library of the Catholic Courses of Study), Tilburg.
J. R. Blancqaert, Belgian Embassy, London.
Miss A. de Bloeme, The Hague.
Dr. W. Blok, Arnhem.
Peter Boer, Houston.
Dr. H. N. Boon, Brussels.
C. L. J. Bos, The Hague.
Professor Dr. F. C. L. Bosman, Pretoria (S.-A.).
S. van Braam, White Plains.
Professor Dr. P. Brachin, Paris.
Jhr. Mr. E. N. de Brauw, The Hague.
R. Bremmer, The Hague.
Professor Dr. R. Breugelmans, Calgary (Canada).
Mr. F. J. Brevet, Rotterdam.
E. J. Brill, Publishers, Leiden.
H. F. van den Broek, San Francisco.
Ds. A. L. Broer, Hilversum.
Prof. Dr. Henri L. Brugmans, New York.

Professor Dr. C. C. de Bruin, Leiden.
Mr. R. de Bruyn, Wassenaar.
Miss Drs. G. van der Burgt, Bonn (Germ.).
H. E. Buurman, Rotterdam.
Mr. W. F. L. Graaf van Bylandt, Impruneta (Italy).
Ir. R. Bijleveld, The Hague.
Calvin Knollcrest Library, Grand Rapids.
Mrs. A. J. Chutter-Kasteleyn, Washington.
Mr. F. J. F. Claessens, Eindhoven.
Richard C. Clark, St. Paul, Minn.
Mr. W. Cnoop Koopmans, Madrid.
Professor Dr. F. van Coetsem, Louvain.
Dr. O. Dambre, Gent.
J. Deleu, Rekkem (Belg.).
Mrs. A. E. Dommering-Koolemans Beijnen, Driebergen.
W. P. M. van Dongen, Rotterdam.
Mark J. Dresden, Media.
Dutch Immigrant Society, Grand Rapids, Michigan.
Hendrik Dijkstra, Houston.
John M. Echols, Ithaca.
William F. van Eck, M. D., East Haven.
Hendrik Edelman, Nashville.
Mrs. M. H. Eliassen-de Kat, Oslo.
Miss. C. A. Elink Schuurman, The Hague.
T. Elink Schuurman, Cascais (Portugal).
Lic. R. van Ertvelde, Bologna (Italy).
Professor Dr. G. A. van Es, Groningen.
Mr. B. van Eyk, Frankfurt/Main.
Professor Dr. Seymour L. Flaxman, New York.
Mrs. H. G. de la Fontaine Heinman, New York.
Frans van Walsemfonds, Eindhoven.
Elmer Garfield van Name, Haddonfield.
Professor Dr. J. G. van Gelder, Utrecht.
Gemeente Bibliotheek (Municipal Library), Rotterdam.
Germanisches Seminar, University, Hamburg.
J. J. Gerritse, New York.
Harry D. Gideonse, New York.
Professor Dr. J. A. Goris, Brussels.
Jan Greshoff, Cape Town (S.-A.).
Mr. C. F. Gülcher, The Hague.
Gymnasium Haganum, The Hague.
Mr. G. A. van Haeften, The Hague.
Mrs. R. B. Hartevelt-Schroeder van der Kolk, Bilthoven.

Robert Hausman, M. D., New York.
Professor Dr. E. van Heerden, Johannesburg (S.-A.).
Mr. P. Heering, The Hague.
T. Heines, Grand Rapids.
Mr. J. L. Heldring, Leidschendam.
Henry Heydenryk, New York.
H. S. Hogerzeil, Oosterbeek.
Mr. L. J. 't Hooft, Zwolle.
Mrs. H. H. van Hoorn-van Balen, Amsterdam.
Dr. H. R. van Houten, Vienna.
Jan van Houten, San Francisco.
Dr. U. Huber Noodt, Bern.
Dr. Annemarie Hübner, Hamburg.
Professor Dr. L. Indestege, Dilbeek (Belg.).
Institut de Néerlandais Université de Lille (Dutch Dept. Lille
University), Lille.
Mrs. L. Jacobson, New York.
H. Jacoby, The Hague.
Dr. J. M. Jalink, The Hague.
Dr. W. F. Jonckheere, Port Elisabeth (S.-A.).
Gerrit de Jong Jr., Provo, Utah.
G. J. Jongejans, Prague.
Mr. E. N. van Kleffens, Almoçagêma (Portugal).
Koninklijke Bibliotheek (Royal Library), Brussels.
Koninklijke Bibliotheek (Royal Library), The Hague.
Kon. Ned. Akademie van Wetenschappen (Royal Netherl. Academy
of Sciences), Amsterdam.
Pieter J. Kooiman, New York.
Mrs. G. Korthals van Schooten-Spinossa Cattella, The Hague.
Professor Dr. G. Kuiper, Amsterdam.
Mrs. Drs. Th. Kuiper-Weyhenke, Bergen (N.-H.).
Jacob Vander Laan, Grand Rapids.
Mrs. J. M. L. J. E. van der Laan-Claessens, Oegstgeest.
Professor Dr. Walter Lagerwey, Grand Rapids.
Professor Dr. B. Landheer, Wassenaar.
Ir. G. C. Lange, Wassenaar.
Professor. Mr. G. E. Langemeijer, The Hague.
M. D. E. de Leve, The Hague.
Mr. F. H. C. Losecaat Vermeer, Haarlem.
Professor Dr. J. E. Loubser, Port Elisabeth (S.-A.).
Fr. Lugt, Paris.
Bookhouse Henry De Lugt, Grand Rapids.
J. G. Luzac, The Hague.

Anthony E. Maas M. D., Camp Hill.
Mij. der Nederlandse Letterkunde (Society of Dutch Language and
    Literature) Leiden.
L. J. van der Maesen, Bennebroek.
Professor Dr. Joost A. M. Meerloo, New York.
Mr. G. L. J. Mens Fiers Smeding, Oberägeri (Switzerland).
Lie. J. L. de Meester, Freiburg i. Br. (Germ.).
W. Merkus, Paris.
Drs. J. H. Meter, Naples (Italy).
Mrs. E. Meyer-Kossmann, Wassenaar.
Ministry of Foreign Affairs, Brussels.
Ministry of Foreign Affairs, The Hague.
Modern and Medieval Languages Faculty, Cambridge (G.-B.).
Dr. J. de Mol van Otterloo, The Hague.
Mrs. H. Moolenburgh-Ekkel, The Hague.
Professor Dr. J. Moors, Liege.
Miss A. M. van der Most, Vlaardingen.
Dr. S. Micha Namenwirth, Cambridge, U.S.A.
Professor Dr. C. J. M. Nienaber, Pietermaritzburg (S.-A.).
F. Niessen, Raamsdonk.
R. Nieuwenhuys, Amsterdam.
Drs. J. B. van Nimwegen, Teteringen.
Drs. W. G. Noordegraaf, The Hague.
Drs. J. Notermans, Maestricht.
Mrs. M. Nijland-Verwey, Santpoort.
Mr. H. van Oordt, Velp.
John Paardenkooper, M. D., Moodus, Conn.
Mrs. A. van Panthaleon b.sse van Eck-Kampstra, Rotterdam.
Estate of J. C. van Panthaleon Baron van Eck, New York.
Charles A. Van Patten, New York.
Professor Dr. W. Pée, Brussels.
Mrs. J. C. Peltzer-van den Broeke, Laren (N.-H.).
Mr. L. J. Plemp van Duiveland, Amsterdam.
Miss Dr. A. J. Portengen, The Hague.
Professor Dr. S. Posthuma, Overveen.
Dr. E. van Raalte, The Hague.
Mr. J. J. de Reede, The Hague.
Mrs. A. A. Reerink-Pfeiffer, Bussum.
Professor Dr. I. Q. van Regteren Altena, Amsterdam.
Jhr. O. Repelaer van Driel, The Hague.
L. M. Reuvers, New York.
Dr. W. F. Roertgen, Los Angeles.
Miss. E. A. Roodhuyzen, Varsseveld.